MY WAR IN SOE

HARRY VERLANDER

TO, ALLAN TYRRELL,

WITH BEST WISHES,

H. Verlander

AUGUST 2012.

MY WAR IN SOE

by Harry Verlander

First edition published in 2010 by:

Independent Books
3 Leaves Green Crescent
Keston
Bromley
BR2 6DN
United Kingdom

Tel: 01959 573360 Fax: 01959 541129

e-mail: mail@indbooks.co.uk

web site: www.indbooks.co.uk

Jacket illustrations by Tony Watkins

Jacket design and page layout by Peter Osborne

Printed and bound in Great Britain by CPI Antony Rowe

ISBN (13): 978-1-872836-85-0

EAN: 9781872836850

CONTENTS

ILLUSTRATION

Maps

INTRODUCTION

Special Operations Executive (SOE) was formed on the direct orders of Winston Churchill in July 1940, to '...conduct warfare by means other than direct military engagement.' In reality this meant a commando type training regime and to be parachuted in behind enemy lines in teams of three men. They were known as Jedburghs (or Jeds) for reasons which, seventy years on, are not entirely clear. What is crystal clear is that they played an extremely important part in the liberation of France and, in particular, making a huge contribution to the success of the D-Day landings by attacking German reinforcements and slowing their progress to the front.

Having volunteered for military service at age 16, after lying about his date of birth, Harry Verlander became a member of the Kings Royal Rifle Corp (KRRC) and then went on to be transferred to the Royal Armoured Corps (RAC). Whilst at Caterrick Camp he took the opportunity to volunteer for a new unit which was shrouded in mystery. All that was known was that they required, 'Wireless Operators, for special duties which may include parachute training. Knowledge of foreign language would be an advantage but not essential'. Knowing a couple of French nursery rhymes, Harry and a colleague bluffed their way in and became Jedburghs, he had at least, in the interim, actually become old enough for military service but was still only just 18 when he was parachuted behind enemy lines as the wireless operator in the three man Jedburgh team HAROLD.

After the liberation of France Harry returned to the UK and again volunteered, this time for further Jedburgh service in the jungles of Burma, fighting the Japanese. France had been no picnic but the bitter hand-to-hand fighting in the mountains and steaming jungles of Burma was an experience which made a deep impression on all who fought there, and

Harry was no exception. He has recorded his experiences in this book and for this we must be grateful. Very few SOE personnel shared their experiences and as only eight Jeds, including Harry, remain alive in the UK, two in the US (OSS) and one in France, it is unlikely that any future works will be forthcoming from this tiny group of survivors. We are, therefore, indebted to Harry for this detailed contribution to modern history.

PJO - Independent Books - 2010

FOREWORD

By

Nigel West

Relatively little has ever been written about the Jeds, which is surprising when one considers the very substantial contribution they made to D-Day's success. The initiative had come originally from SOE's director, Colin Gubbins, in a note dated 6 July 1942 to SOE's Security Section which was responsible for the allocation of all operational cryptonyms:

> *A project is under consideration for the dropping behind of enemy lines, in cooperation with an Allied invasion of the Continent, of small parties of officers and men to raise and arm the civilian population to carry out guerrilla activities against the enemy's lines of communication. These men are to be recruited and trained by SOE. It is requested that* 'JUMPERS' *or some other appropriate code name be allotted to this personnel.*

There is no record of any further memoranda on this topic until the idea was given a practical test, codenamed SPARTAN, on 11 March 1943 when eleven SOE-trained Jedburghs were deployed as a mythical bridgehead was secured on Salisbury Plain and an Allied invasion force moved northwards towards Huntingdon. The exercise also included the infiltration of six SOE agents equipped with transmitters, all reporting to a receiving station in Scotland. The experience gained from SPARTAN formed the basis of a secret document circulated on 6 April 1943 by the head of SOE's Planning Section, Colonel M.W. Rowlandson. This in turn resulted in the basic Jedburgh directive which was issued on 20 December 1943 and formalised the arrangements that were to be implemented soon afterward with the intention of producing three hundred Jedburgh teams by 1 April 1944.

As it turned out this optimistic ambition was never to be achieved. Henry B. Coxe of the Office of Strategic Services (OSS), and a recently escaped PoW, Major Combe-Tennant, were placed in charge of the JEDBURGHS, and a training programme was devised by the Head of SOE's Training Section, Colonel James Young, and his OSS counterpart, Major John Tyson. Together they prepared a three-part course for all the volunteers who survived an extended interview with three psychiatrists: Preliminary training in Scotland, followed by technical courses at

Hatherop Castle in Gloucestershire (STS 45), Gumley Hall, Leicestershire (STS 41) and West Court, Wokingham (STS 6). This stopgap continued until 3 February 1944 when Milton Hall, (designated ME 65), became the main Jed training centre. This beautiful seventeenth century property was situated just seven miles from Peterborough and the surrounding estate provided ideal facilities for preparing the agents for their tasks. The radio operators went on to STS 54 for an intensive wireless instruction, and a parachute course was run at Altrincham, Manchester (STS 51a). Thereafter the graduates were given a five day field test under simulated conditions at Horsham in Sussex.

Milton Hall was to become the Jedburghs's principal home, and was staffed almost entirely by SOE. The first commandant was Frank Spooner, with Major O.H. Brown as Chief Instructor, and Major H.L. Trebilcock as adjutant and transport officer. Bill Sykes led a team of fifteen instructors who were supplemented by eight Americans. The organization was divided into three Companies, commanded by Majors H.A. Dorsey, M.C.M. Crosby and B.W. Gilmour. However, before the first Jedburgh team could be formed, in mid-March 1944, SOE experienced further difficulty in gathering sufficient personnel, but found a remedy in the recruitment of seventy Free French officers from the Middle East.

Once the training phase had been completed, and the Jeds were ready to be deployed operationally, the overall management was changed, with Colonel Smith and Major Coxe replacing Frank Spooner in command at Milton Hall. The composition of each team was chosen by Milton Hall's new Commandant, Colonel Musgrove, in consultation with his Chief Instructor, Major McLallen. On 27 April the first teams were sent abroad, all to North Africa accompanied by a U.S. Marine, Major Horace Fuller, in expectation of being dropped into southern France. Each team was allocated a cryptonym, usually an English first-name although the names of drugs were introduced latterly when the Security Section ran out of Christian names. The Algiers group were beaten into the field by HUGH, the first Jedburgh into France which was despatched from RAF Harrington on 5/6 June to the Chateauroux area where it linked up with the local *maquis* leader, *Philippe* of SHIPWRIGHT, and acted as liaison between his men, which numbered some two thousand spread across the French *Department* (District) of Indre, and a 1st Special Air Service mission codenamed BULBASKET. The latter was under the command of Major J.E. Tonkin and wreaked havoc among the enemy defenders until it was itself decimated by a battalion of SS infantry on 4 July. HUGH was not a typical Jedburgh because it consisted of two Frenchmen and one British officer, but this did reflect the relative shortage of OSS personnel available in mid-June. In fact, although more teams were to be dropped into enemy territory in the days following D-Day, the first American did not go into the field until Sergeant Robert Keyhoe of FREDERICK and Captain Paul Cyr of GEORGE landed in Brittany on 9/10 June. At the beginning of July a total of thirteen Jeds had been dispatched, of which seven had originated from Algiers. Altogether ninety-three Jedburghs were deployed, with losses amounting to twenty-one, the equivalent of seven full teams.

According to a secret SFHQ map of 5 July 1944, there were only four areas in France considered to be under total control of the resistance and cleared of enemy troops on that date. They were in the *departement* of the Ardeche, Drome, Savoie and Jura in the mountainous south-east of the country. That might be as expected, but the 'areas in which resistance has crystallized and intense activity is taking place' was limited to just five others, in the Morbihan, Indre, Vienne, Haute Loire, Hautes Pyrenees and Vosges.

Some of the circuits in contact with SFHQ on D-Day were huge, with more than a thousand *maquisards* under their command; others were tiny, consisting of just one individual operating alone. Some had no radio sets or method of communicating with SFHQ, although all could receive the BBC's prearranged coded messages. One, DIRECTOR, contained no-one trained in England.

SOE itself had been in a parlous state in January 1944, immediately prior to amalgamation of F and RF Sections. OSS had achieved little to speak of, and F Section was in serious trouble: Its only successful networks were in entirely the wrong places. The PROSPER and SCIENTIST disasters had left very few arms caches available in the north and north-western of the country, where they were needed most. Elsewhere, only a fraction of the supplies delivered to Yugoslavia had gone to France. Even worse, the two key circuits in the area of most strategic importance, ARCHDEACON and MUSICIAN, had come under enemy control. That, of course, was not immediately realised and led to further losses, including no less than seventeen SOE agents arriving by air, and Alphonse Defendini who landed by boat. By the Liberation, F Section had lost more than forty circuits in France, thirty-one of which had been eliminated by the *Abwehr* and the *Sicherheitsdienst.*

Thus, it fell to the Jeds to conduct the clandestine war against the Nazis, but it should be noted that not even the SFHQ planners fully understood at the time one aspect of its strategic role. As well as the general run of items singled out for sabotage, such as power cables, pylons and bridges, great emphasis had been placed on telephone lines as targets, and although SOE must have considered such operations useful, in that any interference with the enemy's communications grid is invariably helpful, it certainly never realised the vital nature of these particular targets. In fact the Chiefs of Staff were especially anxious to destroy all the German landlines so as to force the enemy to rely more on their enciphered radio transmissions which, as we now know, were the subject of an intensive and highly profitable programme of interception and decryption by cryptographers at Bletchley Park. The Wehrmacht had deployed five signals regiments in France, and all experienced unprecedented attention from the resistance during, and immediately after D-Day. This was especially true of the the unit stationed at Orleans which suffered unrelenting disruption from HERMIT, SHIPWRIGHT and WRESTLER, so much so that by the time it was evacuated to Germany it had failed to restore any of its major telephone circuits.

Perhaps of equal long-term strategic significance was the disruption inflicted on the French railways. The intention was to isolate the northern part of the country and prevent enemy reinforcements from reaching the beachhead during the first critical hours of the invasion. No less than 950 incidents of sabotage were undertaken during the night of 5/6 June, and confirmation was received that night of 486 specific cuts. The lines continued to be blown, trains derailed and locomotives immobilized throughout the campaign and in consequence the crack 2nd SS *Das Reich* Panzer Division took seventeen days to reach Normandy from Toulouse, a journey that ought not to have taken longer than seventy-two hours. Combined with the comprehensive deception campaign known as FORTITUDE which helped convince the German High Command that the landings were actually nothing more than a feint for a major Allied assault in the Pas-de-Calais, the bridge-blowing and rail cutting operations masterminded by SFHQ played a major part in ensuring D-Day's success.

One of those Jed survivors is the author of this remarkable account of his missions first in France, lasting more than four months from 15 July to 26 November 1944, and then in South-East Asia. It is a story told with his typical, self-deprecating humour, but make no mistake, Harry Verlander is a man to be reckoned with. Quiet and unassuming, he has a deadly, steely inner strength, and in the pages that follow we learn the unvarnished version of history, warts and all. He survived, but many did not, and we owe him a great debt for his compelling recollections. I am privileged to call him my friend.

Nigel West 2010

MY WAR IN SOE

By

Harry Verlander

DEDICATION

This book is dedicated primarily to my wife, Elizabeth, who, after listening to many of my stories, suggested that I write them down and, having done so, she noticed that the night sweats I had always suffered since the war, had ceased once the book was completed. My generation knew nothing of Post Traumatic Stress Counselling - the cure-all was a cigarette and a cup of tea, so maybe it has been a therapeutic exercise in laying painful memories to rest.

This book is also dedicated to the Jedburghs, past and present. May their memory live on in the minds and hearts of all those who knew them.

Harry Verlander March 2010

Chapter One - Evacuation

It was a reasonable summer, my last whilst still at school; I would be 14 on 27th December 1939 and thus able to go to work, but that seemed a long way off. I stripped down my bike yet again, taking it right back to its smallest piece, and scraped the framework free of its entire latest colour. It had already been blue, red, and green; the new colour would depend on what took my fancy on my next trip to Woolworth's. The bike had belonged to my father, passed on as my last birthday (and Christmas) present, replacing worn out roller skates which had served me well for the past few years. Our favourite game, hockey, at that time played in the local streets, had advanced from racing around on skates to bikes and was played with a puck which could be a ball, a stone, or blocks of wood; the hockey stick was any handy piece of timber, such as a loose paling from someone's fence!

The best local street to arrange a game was Essex Road, which was a no-through road. I lived in a small house on the High Road between Goodmayes and Chadwell Heath and next door to the Greyhound public house. A long paved passageway between the house and the inn led to the iron foot bridge over the L.N.E.R railway line. The bridge was ideal for standing above the express trains as they thundered underneath, smothering anyone there with thick smoke and steam. The drivers would sometimes give a blast from their whistle, which may have been a warning to children standing there, or perhaps it was a response to a friendly wave! The long footpath had served me well as a safe training ground for both roller skates and bike, but it was too narrow to be of much use for games or racing. Not being a resident of the Essex Road area meant of course the odd challenge from the local lads, which usually led to a minor punch up. These never lasted long as I'd had some boxing training when a lot younger so just words and threats, such as not letting them use 'my' passage way, were enough until someone would want to get on with another game.

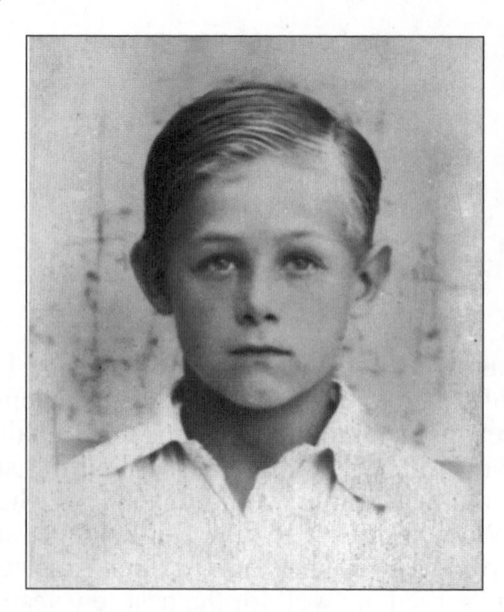

An early picture

In the evenings there was the Goodmayes Methodist church, which ran the GYP Club (Goodmayes Young Peoples Club). A first introduction to party games was not that successful as I didn't like the kissing games very much, and the girl I would have liked to be there was not allowed to join the club. May Creswell, the same age as myself, who lived in the house almost opposite, was a very pretty girl and in great demand by older boys, and I didn't stand a chance. However, what I enjoyed most of all was gymnastics and this was by courtesy of the Boys Brigade. It was Capt. 'K' (Kennelly of the B.B.) who was responsible for my re-naming of Henry to Harry (I rather fancied that it sounded a bit more masculine and took to it right away). Capt. K. also encouraged me to move on from ground exercises to using the more advanced apparatus such as the agility horse, parallel bars, rings, and high-bar. This was, of course, after being caught trying out some of the equipment for myself, after some of the younger members had been dismissed for the evening. 'K' probably thought it wiser that it took place under proper supervision. As it turned out later, I won a medal at the next Gymnastic Display evening, being the 'Boy Making the Most Progress' during the past year. This was perhaps, also, the beginning of a much fitter person which would prove to be of immense usefulness in times yet unknown.

Wednesday was market day in Romford, which I was able to visit during the holidays. In the mornings there was the full cattle market with its pigs, cows, bulls, sheep, ducks and chickens, with day old chicks always a good buy at one or two pence each, to be reared at home on scraps. Hens were kept to lay eggs and any cocks were fattened up for high days and holidays. A nice big Rhode Island Red cockerel was a must for a Christmas dinner. Later in the day the stalls remained, selling a variety of goods and food. I would take with me some freshly cut mint, and horseradish roots picked from the garden and sometimes, instead of selling direct to passers by, one of the butcher's stalls would take the lot. When this happened, if early enough in the day, it would entail a quick bike ride home for fresh supplies. This was my only means of obtaining any pocket money, which I proudly shared with my mother, and it would leave enough cash to pay for a visit to the cinema the following Saturday morning. After leaving the market I would often stop at a butcher's shop on the way home, where I had once seen some pigs being taken around to the back of the shop to be slaughtered. On following them, I stopped to watch by leaning on the barn door. The pigs were brought in one at a time and electrocuted with a large scissor-like apparatus with round discs on the end. This was clamped to the animal's head, the power switched on and the poor beast fell to the ground immediately without a sound. They were put into a large vat of very hot water and washed, scrubbed and scraped clean, then hung up head downwards, their throats cut and bled dry, the blood being collected into a vessel. After which they were swung round, head upward and the belly slit open, the innards removed and collected in various pans or buckets. The cleaned and prepared carcass was taken away and, after a quick wash down with a hose, the two men working there brought in the next victim. I was fascinated more than shocked; it was, after all, food to be eaten by someone soon, if not myself

A later picture with my first real glasses

At various times during the past decade there had been talk of war in other parts of Europe and young people, though hearing parts of these conversations, were usually left out of any discussions. This summer, though, the war talk was becoming more intense. I was being sent more often to the wireless shop to buy an accumulator for the radio as this had to be changed each week. It worked alongside the dry battery, and was not always in operation if money was tight. With no electricity connected to the house, being gas lit only, batteries were the only way we could receive any radio programmes. Only our parents would be allowed to touch the set, and children were told when, and what, they may listen to. My father had joined the ARP (Air Raid Precaution) and gas masks had been issued, and there was talk of air-raid shelters to come. There had also been some talk of children being sent to the countryside in case London was bombed.

It happened suddenly as far as I was concerned. Towards the end of August and, within a few days it seemed, arrangements were rushed through for me and my younger 6-year-old sister Lily to be sent away. My older sister Iris was over sixteen and working in London. Small cardboard suit-cases were purchased from Woolworth's and, from a list supplied by the schools, a change of under-clothes and toilet articles gathered together, not forgetting the gas mask in its own little box. Not knowing for how long children would be away, and most people thinking it would be for only a very short time, winter clothing wasn't even considered. It was more like going on holiday. I'd been on family day trips to Southend-on-Sea before and, the previous year, on a camping holiday with the Boys Brigade to Bridport in Dorset.

Mum and Lily in our back yard, about 1937

Departure day arrived and we were taken to the Chadwell Heath Junior School by our mother and handed over to teachers and other ladies who were unknown to us. I saw no boys from Mayfield Secondary School, my own school, only a few others like myself detailed to travel with younger siblings. We were then taken by bus to Goodmayes railway station and put onto a train, not knowing where we were going or when we would get there. Mother had given us a bread and cheese sandwich and some lemonade each for the journey and the train was soon on its way. At first it stopped at every station to pick up yet more children then, later, after leaving the London area, less often, until reaching the places where some children were taken off and the train went on again. After arriving in Beccles in Suffolk, we were taken with others onward by bus to the village of Worlingham. In the church hall there we were met by a group of adults and given refreshments but, although hungry, most of the children stood nervously at the far end of the room, with the adults congregated together by the door. The children were called forward, singly or in same sex pairs, to a table near the door where they were introduced to the people willing to accept them into their homes. With growing apprehension, we watched as all the children disappeared and we were the only ones left in this room, which began to loom larger by the minute. A few adults in the opposite corner kept glancing across to us, obviously discussing what should be done with the remaining two children. The problem was to find accommodation for a mixed sex pair and wishing not to split up families if at all possible. This was solved, reluctantly, by placing us in a pair of adjacent farm labourers' houses, about a mile down a lane south of the village.

Lily was placed with a rather odd trio, two brothers and a sister, probably still in their twenties. The older brother looked like a younger version of the 'Hunchback of Notre Dame' but nevertheless all were kindly, despite some strange and unusual habits. One story circulating was that a neighbour had been in the kitchen when the girl was about to cook a chicken, and was just in time to stop her putting it in the oven still complete with innards!

I was placed next door with Mr. and Mrs. Jude and their large family. There was not really any space but they made room for me by putting up a bed on the landing, part-way up the stairs. One of their two daughters was living there with her husband, the other, Peggy, who was the same age as myself, and the two younger boys, Jack, 11, and John, 8, also shared this very happy and busy household. There were two more sons, not living at the same house, who, when not working on the local farms, went out of Lowestoft on fishing boats. Another older married daughter lived in Beccles with her own children.

Evening meals were taken at 9 p.m. when the family sat down around a large round dining table. The centrepiece was an enormous oil lamp. The radio would be switched on and we would all sit quietly listening to the nine o'clock news before starting to eat. When the meal was finished and cleared away everyone went to bed. It was a few days after arriving, on a Sunday evening, that I first heard that war had been declared that day, the third of September 1939. Was that why the adults had been acting differently all day? I had sensed quietness in conversation whenever I approached any adults, as if I was being discussed or that something was going on that they did not want me to hear about.

Mrs Jude (right) and her sister

The following day things appeared to be back to normal as I joined the adults and children out in the fields to help with the harvest. Great fun was had chasing after the fleeing rabbits with sticks. The corn was cut by a large machine that threw out the cut and tied bundles ready for them to be stacked in small groups to dry. Working from the outside, going round and round the field, animals in the corn were driven towards the centre. As the area remaining uncut got smaller and smaller, more and more of them made a sudden dash for freedom, against cries of 'there's another one, another, another'; so many more got away than were caught! It did not take long to learn how to despatch a rabbit quickly with a sharp blow behind the ears just by watching the local lads, who were pleased to show off their skills. Lunch was brought out by mothers and older girls who had prepared it; large baskets of ham sandwiches, chunks of bread and cheese, with plenty of butter, with lemonade and tea to drink. Afternoon tea was even better, as far as the children were concerned. There was jelly and custard, cakes and buns, also apple and blackberry tarts as well as fresh fruit, with tea, lemonade or milk to drink and what looked suspiciously like jugs of beer, for the older men. Work continued as long as possible until it was either too dark or that particular field was finished. Like all who had helped that day, warmed through by the sun and fresh air, after an early supper I was soon happily fast asleep.

There were many days like this and I quickly took to the new way of life I found myself living. The dead rabbits, which had been laid out in rows in the field, had been shared between the workers at the end of the day. Back home the older boys showed me how to gut and skin them, and Mrs. Jude and her daughters dealt with the production of tasty rabbit pies and stews. There were, of course, other types of game that I had never seen or heard of before, in particular pheasants. And there were large numbers

Peggy, Mrs Jude's youngest daughter

Peggy's two younger brothers

of them. These had been left to fly away whilst everyone was working in the fields, but in the talk at supper time I soon gathered that these were also very good to eat. From the two older sons I learnt of the various ways in which these birds could be captured. Apparently they are very fond of peas, a line of which could lead them into a simple trap made out of a wooden box, placed open end downward with one end raised with a stick, high enough for the bird to pass under. The stick, attached by a long piece of string leading to a hiding place and pulled at the right time, allowed the box to fall, trapping the bird beneath it. Another, rather nasty method, was to use a strong fishing line, with a pea as bait. Or to arrange a line, with nooses hanging down from it, which would be suspended between the rows of kale. Apparently pheasants habitually fly between the rows and are snared in the same way as rabbits. Other ways suited me rather better, the fun way being to watch where the bird would land, or run to, when disturbed - usually not far away. If you stood still it would squat down and freeze, blending into its surroundings. Taking off your coat and walking gently closer, it was possible, though certainly not easy, to catch the bird before it fled. I found that the birds were more often quicker and craftier than I was! Their natural camouflage was so good that it was possible to almost tread on them before they took flight. The sudden, unexpected flutter of wings so close to one's feet, meant that the bird had flown and it was yards away before you could react.

One evening, when I was walking back to the house with the older boys, a pheasant flew into a tree at the side of the lane to roost for the night. We all stood still for a while to let the bird settle, made a note of the exact

Peggy by the house

place by marking it with a few stones then continued our walk home. After supper, plans were laid for a return visit. From the shed we collected a small tin box containing a sulphur candle and a sack. (Sulphur candles were used then to fumigate rooms after illness). When it was really dark, about an hour after supper, all three of us set off on our escapade. With just one small torch between us, we walked quietly back to the place we had previously marked out. I had noticed that whereas I often kicked the odd unseen stone, or trod on a piece of dead wood, which cracked loudly, and all sounds seemed even louder at night, my companions made little or no noise. After yet another 'crack' and 's-shush!' came a whispered, 'stay where you are! Don't move!' We went softly onward a yard or so more. We had arrived. The tin was placed on the ground under the tree, directly under the roosting bird, which could just be seen as a black oval ball against the lighter night sky. There was no breeze. The candle, lit by a single match, after just a few seconds, produced a wisp of smoke which drifted silently upwards towards its intended victim. A little later, perhaps only four or five minutes but which seemed much longer, there was a rustle of leaves and a light 'plop' as the bird fell unconscious into the sack that was being held out beneath it. As quickly and as quietly as we had come, leaving no trace of our presence, all three of us and our prize arrived safely back home.

Next day, as the pheasant was plucked and the feathers disposed of, I asked why I seemed to make more noise than my companions. 'We will show you' said my new friends and off we went across the field at the back of the house and into a small copse. The paths were strewn with debris, like dead wood, covered in rotting leaves. Ordinary walking, without care, made considerable noise as leaves are kicked and twigs are snapped. I was then shown how to walk without making a sound. This is done by placing the foot down gently, not heel or toe first, but level to the ground, with the ankle turned slightly so that the full length of the outside edge of the foot touches the ground first. The ankle is slowly straightened inward so that the foot flattened across its width and was flat on the ground before any real weight was put on it. By gradually increasing the body weight on the foot it is possible to feel any 'give' in the ground and move the foot before anything, like a twig, snaps. If all is well the whole body weight can then be passed on to the foot and the process repeated with the other one. Slow and tricky to maintain balance at first, it becomes easier and faster with practice.

There were many other country skills and traditions that I gradually picked up over the following few weeks. One of which was how and where to set rabbit snares. Another was how to make a really strong and accurate catapult. Mr Jude had shown me his own, one Sunday, which was so strong I could hardly pull it back to its full length! 'I will show you how to make your own,' he said, taking me to the copse at the rear of the house, and helping me to select the best type of wood and shape required. The piece chosen was of a 'Y' shape, about a half an inch thick, the two upper prongs being only a little slimmer. The wood, firm but springy, probably hazel, was roughly cut and taken home for finishing. After trimming to the correct size, slots were cut into the two prongs, from front to back. Then, on to a long piece of elasticised rubber, which was flat on all four sides and a quarter of an inch thick, a piece of slotted leather, approximately 1"x 2" was threaded and centralised. The ends of the elastic were then placed through the slots on the handle and each turned back outwards and tightly bound onto the prongs. From a carefully selected pile of round pebbles, stones were used to test its strength and accuracy on a row of empty tin cans.

Not all was fun and games. That dreaded word 'school' had been heard! Arrangements had been made for Lily to attend the local junior school in Worlingham, where she seemed to be reasonably happy, and I was sent to the senior school in Beccles. It sounded a lot better to me when I found out that I would be supplied with a bicycle for the journey. Unlike my old school back home where girls and boys were separated, this one had mixed gender classes. The lunch time meals were supplied at school, which I found interesting and easier to make friends. For this, tables were set in a large hall for six persons, for two children, a boy and a girl, from each age group, 11/12, 12/13, 13/14 yrs. The eldest pair would take on the role of parents and ensure that the others behaved well at the table. They had to teach the younger ones how to hold their cutlery correctly, and encourage them to finish and not waste their food. As the children were well mannered it was a pleasant duty. All the lessons seemed much more interesting and practical to me, and I found that I was being treated more like an adult. One of the lessons was French which I took to immediately. I have said many times since, 'I learnt more that last term in Beccles than at any other time in school!' Although I did not know it then, of course, French would be of far more use to me later, as you can imagine.

It wasn't long before the local girls became braver and approached these new boys from other towns. None that I knew from London, but there were a few from other areas. Their different accents seemed to be attractive, and I was also taking more interest in them. Small groups went swimming together at the weekends and to the cinema on Saturday mornings. Beccles swimming pool was an area sectioned off from the river Waveney. Swimming under the barrier between the pool and the river was one sport, and another, apart from chasing each other in and out of the water, was when both boys and girls would in turn climb up to peek over the partitions in the changing rooms. Of course the boys were told off by the life guards, even though the girls were usually the instigators! It was on these excursions, as well as at school, that I got to know Joan Rose.

My bicycle had been taken back after only a few weeks. This was because someone had worked out that by cutting across the fields it was less than the required distance to merit one. Disappointed at first I later enjoyed the walk and seeing the plentiful variety of game on my way home from school with, of course, my catapult in my pocket for constant practice. One memorable evening I could hear the loud quacking of ducks. The sound of their calls led me to a low fence at the edge of some trees. Climbing over the fence, a winding path passing through a few trees led me to a pond, where I spotted some fat juicy-looking ducks. Creeping quietly closer, catapult at the ready, I took aim. Then a loud voice shouted, 'Oi! You there! Stop or I'll fire!' Looking up I could see a very large man, with a very big gun! Without a second glance I turned and ran. There was a loud 'BANG' as I rounded a tree, bits flying off the bark, but I kept running, reached the fence, and leapt over it, tearing my trousers on barbed wire in the process, and not stopping until I felt safe. On arriving back at the cottage, I at first said 'I tore my trousers climbing over a gate, on the way home.' Later, when I recounted what had really happened, they all laughed, adding that I had better not go that way home again!

Just like some of the other couples, Joan and I spent more and more time alone together. Joan would often walk most of the way home with me before returning to Beccles, where she lived. We walked hand in hand whilst chatting about our day and planning what next to do at the weekends. Our first chaste kiss happened one evening when saying good night, and we must have enjoyed it because we tried it out several times before parting! From then on we were inseparable.

As Christmas and my 14th birthday approached, when I would be due to start work, and this being my final term at school, letters were passing between my mother and my adoptive hosts. There were concerns, too, about Lily remaining with the people she was living with, especially as the young woman was heavily pregnant. Arrangements were made for us to be collected by our father with his motorcycle and sidecar. After long goodbyes to my new school friends, adoptive family, especially Joan, and many tears, we departed with promises to return one day. By no means did all evacuated children have bad experiences in their sudden switch from town to country living. For myself, it proved to be part of a learning curve that was, in time, to become very useful. Both of us had had a wonderful, almost a holiday time, in Beccles; alas, for my younger sister Lily, returning home was not to be her last spell away from the family. She was evacuated again later in the war to Devon, into a very religious family, not returning home until 1945. Her strong West Country accent, acquired while away, made her into a figure of fun on her return which must have been very unpleasant and upsetting for her. The excess of religious dogma had also had an adverse affect on her. I did keep my promise and revisited the Jude family again in 1940. I cycled to Beccles from Chadwell Heath in the first week of my summer holidays, quite a feat, but sadly there was no happy reunion for me with my first love Joan Rose.

Chapter Two - Home Front

Finding Mayfield School closed when I got back home, and without taking any exams or receiving any school certificates, I started working with my father, a builder and decorator, who was now a full time ARP warden. Anderson air raid shelters had now been delivered to all houses with gardens and it was recommended that these be placed about three feet deep and covered with the extracted soil. When my father was off duty, we would do this for anyone willing to pay for it to be done. It was hard work digging the deep pits, erecting and bolting together the galvanised sheets, fixing wooden bunk beds inside, replacing the extracted earth over the top and sides, and making a sandbagged anti-blast wall at the front of the air raid shelter, which had wooden or cemented steps down to the buried shelter entrance. Some people even had three or four inches of cement poured down the sides and over the top of their shelter, all of which would be hand and shovel mixed (there were no mechanised mixers those days). There was also the arrival of Valerie, a new baby sister, on 14th February 1940. I adored her and carried little polyphotos of her nearly everywhere I went.

Soon after my birthday, in the New Year, I was placed in my first full time job. This was with Swans, a light engineering firm almost opposite Chadwell Heath Junior School. I was introduced to hand-operated metal presses which were used to cut and shape sheets of metal. By changing the tools the workers could gradually alter the metal blanks to the required shapes. The long handle from the weighted top of the press had to be pushed to start it turning and, coming down, caught as it spun round and rammed home, squashing the metal that had been placed between the top and bottom tools. There were no guards on these or many other machines in this small factory. I couldn't help noticing that several of the men working there had fingers, or parts of, missing, and one of them was the owner's son. Good for building up muscles but after two or three months it was time to look for another job.

My next, which only lasted a month or so, was in a brush-making factory in Grove Road as a maintenance engineer. I was more like a grease monkey than anything else, sometimes having to crawl into or under great combing machines to oil the moving parts. This work was mainly done whilst the factory workers, mostly women, were at lunch. Coming back early, the women would tease the boys by standing, legs apart, over them if they were still working under the machines, or pretend they had not seen them by feigning to start the motors. A cheeky lot, these ladies; they could be seen at times disappearing behind the stacked bales of fibre with the men. The other engineers warned me off with stories of what would happen to me if they got hold of me. I really didn't fancy being de-bagged and having my private parts greased, so I kept well away from them!

Essex Water Softeners, again almost opposite the Chadwell Heath School, was where I next found work and was by now almost fully employed in 'War Work'. It was here that I was introduced to 'universal grinding', exacting work with very fine limits on any of the pieces made. One of the tasks, that I was mostly set to do, entailed putting four flat sides on steel ball bearings! These would be softened, drilled through the centre and hardened again. They then became the centrepiece of a universal joint. I was to stay working at this factory until March 1942. Diversions at the weekends, with a co-worker friend, Tony Johnson, who lived at Noak Hill, included scrumping when apples were ripe enough. One evening, a farmer came out to check if his fruit was ready for picking while I was still up the tree, in my dark blue boiler suit, which was stuffed with freshly plucked apples. Hearing voices approaching, Tony warned me and promptly ran off. Too late to climb down, I curled up, hiding my face and remaining motionless. I could hear the apples being discussed. 'I think I'll leave them for another week' said the unknown voice. Waiting a while until the coast was clear, I came down with my booty and rejoined my friend on the road where we had left our bikes. Incidentally, the farmer had got it wrong, the apples were delicious!

Another of our escapades was rabbiting, after I had bought a ferret in Romford market. Equipped with nets and small metal pegs, (made at work), we were, of course, not always successful, once being chased away by a farmer. The usual bag we managed to take home was two or three rabbits each, most weekends. Food rationing had made these little extras very welcome. Chickens were also by now being raised at home. These helped out with eggs and table birds, augmenting the meagre rations.

Apart from news coming in about the war at sea and about the Germans' progress in Europe, most of the people in Britain were not directly affected by the war until May (this period later became known as the Phoney War) when Winston Churchill became the new Prime Minister. The retreat from Dunkirk had left the country and the Empire alone to carry on against Axis attacks in Europe and North Africa.

Preparations for defence against air raids intensified. Stirrup pumps, sand and water buckets appeared everywhere, especially on the roofs of factories and other large buildings. Emergency water supplies for the fire services, by way of large tanks, were erected in many side streets. These resembled small swimming pools and it wasn't long before they had to be covered to prevent children using them. More and more public air raid shelters were built, some surface ones of bricks, others in strong or reinforced buildings. Volunteers formed night-time fire watching teams for their own factories and offices. They would also go on to the roof if air-raid sirens went whilst they were at work, enabling colleagues to carry on working and not go into the shelters until it became too dangerous not to do so. Factories were working day and night to boost production, mostly in two ten-hour shifts and, with only an hour break between shifts and for mealtimes, they kept going twenty-four hours a day. The under-eighteen year olds were not allowed to do night work nor work more than forty-eight hours a week.

A 'Local Defence Volunteers' force was formed in May which, on the 23rd July 1940, was renamed 'The Home Guard'. The minimum age for joining was 17yrs. My favourite uncle Henry, a bus driver, had been killed during a raid standing at his back door. His wife and two children had just reached their air raid shelter but were still injured by the blast of one of the first bombs to be dropped on Dagenham. It had struck their garden, between the house and the shelter. Frustrated and angry at not being able to 'do' anything about this and the night-time bombing I first went up to town to the P&O shipping offices and tried to join the Merchant Navy. I was given a medical and accepted as a cabin boy, told to get myself vaccinated, and they would write to me when I was required. Having had the vaccination done by my own family doctor and not knowing that it had to be paid for, I was very surprised when my mother asked to see my arm when she received the bill, forcing me to confess. Incidentally, I never did hear from the shipping line! It was many years later that my mother told me that they had asked me to report for duty and that she had written back refusing permission because I was too young.

At the end of July the Battle of Britain had become more intense and moved closer to London. The spectacle of fighter planes chasing each other around the skies changed as bombers began attacking factories, power stations and shipping in the Port of London. The rat-tat-tat of machine gun fire from the fighters was taken over by the louder sound of fire from the anti-aircraft guns. At times the shrapnel from their shells fell like rain, throwing up sparks when striking the ground. By the end of August a few bombers were reaching London and the suburbs. Early in September, standing at my front garden gate, I watched as hundreds of large German bombers flew in formation overhead westward towards the centre of London. This was not the first wave; they had been bombing since early morning. The docks from Barking to London were already ablaze and now the planes could clearly be seen heading for the centre of town, anti aircraft shells bursting around them. As I watched, one of the shells burst between the leading plane and the two following behind it in the 'V' shaped formation. A stream of black smoke came from all three but they carried on until I lost sight of them. This was the start of continuous bombing by day, and later on, by day and night.

One evening myself, my mother and sisters, went into our shelter to sleep as we had been doing nightly since the bombing began in earnest. It was set deep in our front garden, between the house and the main road. Father, who was on duty as an Air Raid Warden, came and announced that although they were evacuating everyone from the adjacent houses, we would be safe there and we should remain in our shelter and not to leave until he came back for us. A bomb had dropped on the soft earth between the pavement and some advertising boards at the end of our short row of four houses (Iron Yard Cottages) and the next row of six (Railway Cottages) but failed to explode on impact. There was a small field the other side of the road around Chappells, the sweet factory.

In the early hours of the following morning the delayed action bomb exploded The ground shook and there was a muffled 'whomph', which woke everyone up. Dirt and dust fell inside the shelter and down the entrance steps. Not long after, Father, after clearing rubble from the door, asked if everyone was all right, and after assuring us that the house was undamaged, we all went back to sleep. Next morning I saw that a few roofing slates had been damaged and only one pane of glass had shattered as he had opened all the doors and windows in order to reduce the blast effect. There was a gaping hole stretching across the footpath to the other side of the main road. It looked about ten feet deep, with the rubble piled high around the edges even though a great deal of debris had fallen back into the hole. All the water mains, sewers, electricity, gas and telephone lines were broken and some old tramway lines, which had preceded the trolley buses, were twisted upwards towards the sky

There was a Home Guard unit based at Goodmayes railway station, at the back of which was an enormous shunting yard. Visiting there frequently, with my bike of course, I enjoyed talking to the men who were mostly ex-soldiers from the Great War. At first they said I could be their runner, which mainly meant getting their cigarettes and refreshments from the little café across the road. By constantly pestering to join and insisting that I was seventeen (instead of fifteen) on my last birthday, they finally gave in and let me become a Volunteer on the 15th January 1941, in B Company, 12th Battalion, K Zone, Home Guard.

February 1941 - Home Guard

I was equipped with a full army uniform, armed with a Lee Enfield rifle and bayonet, and began standard infantry training. Officers and NCOs were mainly ex-servicemen who were keen to serve and teach those too young or too old to be called up; there were also others from reserved occupations. Rifle training was particularly good with trips to a full-sized firing range as well as frequent use of an indoor small bore range, using an adapted Lee Enfield. In less than a year, I became an expert shot and was selected as one of eight, the only one from my Company, for the Battalion team in an Inter-Battalion small bore competition. We came first of the seven Battalions taking part and were presented with a silver cup at a cinema in Ilford, after watching training films, in January 1942. Back at the base at Goodmayes, the old soldiers said I had better be trained as a sniper! Other training included use of hand grenades, anti tank grenades, and Bren guns, with full-scale exercises out in the surrounding area. It was on one of these outings that I was introduced to a ploughman's lunch; a large chunk of cheese, a hunk of bread and an onion, accompanied by my first taste of beer. Felt a bit queasy after the beer though - didn't like it very much either!

The role taken on by the Home Guard was, at first, guarding damaged property. I was working in the factory by day and on a night duty two or three evenings a week. One evening when on guard in a badly damaged street, I spotted a dog sniffing and scratching around a large box with a tarpaulin over it. I chased the animal away and curiously lifted the cover to look inside, then wished I hadn't! It contained bits of bodies which were fortunately removed shortly after. Another day, when I was not working, it must have been a weekend, I turned out to lend a hand just after a bomb had dropped. Running down the street I spotted a small child. She looked like a broken doll lying in the road. I bent down to pick her up but to my shock and dismay I saw that her head had been almost completely cut off. Rescue teams then arrived and took over. I felt a sudden urge to go back home, to see if my baby sister was safe.

Later on in 1941, land mines were being dropped by parachute. Usually in pairs, these would explode on touching the ground causing wide spread damage by blast. Just one dropped in a street would demolish the nearest houses on both sides of the road, leaving a large saucer shaped crater. Those houses to the sides and to the backs of them would be badly damaged, though to a lesser degree. One got caught up in a tree close to Chadwell Heath railway station, hanging dangerously by its parachute until an army bomb disposal unit managed to defuse it.

Life still had to go on between the bombings. Work by day, turns of duty at night, certainly did not prevent visits to the cinema or the dance halls, especially on a Saturday. In the afternoon, my choice was a trip to the Ilford swimming baths for a vapour bath to get rid of the factory grime, followed by tea served with beans or egg on toast after a short nap, wrapped in a very large white towel. Then it was back home for a quick change of clothes to be ready for an evening out at one of the many dance halls.

It was an outing to a dance with Jack, a young friend in the Home Guard, one weekday evening, dressed of course in our uniforms to impress the ladies and wearing shoes instead of army boots for the dancing, which ended in a way we had not anticipated.

Jack had suggested that we go to a dance being held in a smaller hall, down by Whalebone Lane. The ones we usually went to were huge, like the Ilford Palais de Dance. Being a couple of years older, Jack said he knew some of the girls who would be there. Alas, the evening was not to end as expected. On arrival everything looked promising, plenty of pretty girls, not too much competition, and we soon found partners. The air-raid siren had sounded, but as usual, most people ignored it until the Fire Watchers warned of imminent danger. Only a short while after the dance had started, anti-aircraft guns could be heard overhead, with the sound of bombs dropping not too far away. It was obvious it was to be yet another bad night, and local! We decided to leave the dance and, as we were already in uniform, got on our bikes and went directly back to our Home Guard base in Goodmayes. Gas masks and helmets had to be carried at all times and I was heartily glad I was wearing my helmet as shrapnel was falling like rain. It could be heard as it whistled down, sending up a shower of sparks as it struck the roadway. As we rode, head down over the handle bars, approaching Chadwell Heath, one small, dice sized piece, hit the rim of my helmet, knocking it forward from the back of my head down towards my face. Stopping only to pick up the missile, we hurried on to our base.

On arrival at Goodmayes most of the men were already out attending incidents and there was a big one just up the High Road towards Seven Kings, in one of the residential roads. We were told to go and see if we were needed there. It was easy enough to find. It was thought to be a parachuted mine that had gone off, half way down a now almost unrecognisable street. The damage done was enormous. All the emergency services were already in attendance, Rescue Squad, Fire and Ambulance services as well as Wardens, Police and Home Guard. There was nothing more that we could do, in fact it was getting overcrowded! A Warden told us that he had heard of another incident the other side of Goodmayes Railway Station, so Jack and I turned back towards the station to seek out this other site.

Walking past the station towards Green Lane we saw some damage in Ashgrove Road, then going on to Kildowan Road, we found a large number of damaged houses. There was no one else to be seen, so it could not have been long after the bomb or whatever had gone off. There was still dust settling as we entered the road. Just a short way down on the left hand side we clambered over the rubble of a partly demolished house. It was only half its normal height and impossible to see into the house from the front. I remembered that my father had been in the toilet at the back of our house when our close bomb had gone off, so we decided to clamber over the top to reach the back garden, where I thought, there might also be a shelter. On reaching the back of the property there was nothing in the garden but rubble from the roof and upper storey, but the top half of the back door could just be seen, the bottom covered by a pile of bricks. Crawling over this mountain of loose bricks, glass and timber, I banged on the door and shouted 'Anybody there?' I thought I could hear a dog barking, and called out again 'Can anyone hear me?' This time I heard a man's voice answering 'We are under the stairs.' Assuring him that help was on the way, I went back to the front of the house, found Jack who was searching elsewhere and asked him to nip back to the Home Guard base to get help and inform the rescue squads.

Jack came back after reporting what we had found and joined me in starting to clear some of the bricks away from the back door. There were by now a few more people further up the street but still none of the emergency services had arrived. With only bare hands to work with, we cleared a space around the top half of the rear door then broke down and pulled out the top panels. We could then see that what had once been the kitchen was now full of broken timber, plaster and bricks that had collapsed down from the upper floors. The hole we had made was only about two foot square. Through this gap we reached in and started to pull out the bricks, one at a time. When the hole was big enough and we could no longer reach the bricks from the outside, as I was the slightly smaller of the two, I squeezed into the space we had made and, by squatting down inside, it was now possible to carry on passing the bricks out one by one. This went on for a long time. Whereas at first it was easy to pick up two or three bricks at a time, the bricks gradually felt hotter and heavier, until it was necessary to use both hands to pick up a single brick. With still no other help arriving the two of us took a short break, had a cigarette and listened to the sounds of the ongoing air raid, with exploding bombs and guns, some near and some in the distance. As I tunnelled on, I made use of gaps under the collapsed ceiling and floor. Twice the loose debris above was shaken down behind me, once completely blocking my exit. Jack worked inward, I outward until it was cleared, propping up the best we could with whatever timber came to hand. It was slow work, crawling in and out of the tunnel with every small piece that had to be removed. We had nearly reached the door under the stairs and could talk to the people, who appeared to be down in a cellar, when finally a Heavy Rescue team arrived and relieved us. Impossible to tell how long we had both been there, neither of us had a watch. We sat watching the rescue team finish the job. First out was a dog, then a lady, but it took a little longer to get the man out as he was injured. Covered in dirt and dust, our dancing shoes ruined, we were told to report to a rest centre at a church in Barley Lane. After a very welcome cup of tea, a brush down and a quick wash, we were given a large breakfast of eggs, bacon and sausages. By the time I got back home it was six o'clock, just enough time to wash, change and get ready for work at eight.

Incidents like this, some less, some more dramatic, gradually eased off as time passed and the ordinary mundane tasks of daily living took over. Germany was more occupied with Russia and our troops were holding out well in North Africa. Strange isn't it, I noticed, that earlier, when Russia was attacking Poland and Finland, the Russkies were the baddies, even in our pre-war comics. Now they were the goodies with patriotic songs being sung about them, 'My lovely Russian rose' to name but one! Just goes to show, I thought, you can't always believe all that you're told. Home Guard training, drill and duties went on as before, but there was more spare time and with it a young man's thoughts, as in spring, turned to other things.

There was a small café a little further up the road, across, and to the right, from the Home Guard base at Goodmayes railway station. This was where I often went on 'important' errands for the officers and NCOs, when they required refreshments and cigarettes. I soon got to know the young lady who owned the establishment, who happened to be disabled, and I enjoyed helping her in my spare time by collecting dirty dishes, sweeping, or helping her lock up and walking with her to the station where she caught a train to Romford, where she lived. We got on well together and whilst chatting one day she found out the sad fact that I didn't have a girl friend, and went on to say, 'My younger sister will be here with me tomorrow, would you like to meet her?' This was to be the start of a wonderful friendship. Joyce, about the same age as me, was a very pretty girl with lovely dark auburn hair. She had obviously heard quite a lot about me from her sister, and admitted later that she had asked her sister to introduce us. It goes without saying that we immediately got on very well together and it was not long before we were kissing goodnight when parting. Many a time, while waiting for the train to take her home, we sat on the station platform in the convenient black-out, in a long embrace that went on and on, breaking off only briefly to take a gulp of air. More than once a train would arrive and leave without our taking any notice of it, and we would have to wait for the next!

Chapter Three - The Volunteer

In early December 1941 the war extended to the Far East when America and Britain declared war on Japan, following the raid on the American Fleet based in Pearl Harbour. At last the Yanks would be helping us. It would be my sixteenth birthday on the 27th. Angry young men such as me were getting worried. We felt that we were not doing enough; we wanted to get back at the Germans before it was too late and dish out some of our own medicine. The war could not go on like this, we mused, it can't last another six, or perhaps nine months at the most. By then we would still be too young to be called up. Anyway, who wants to be stuck in a factory when there were more important things to be doing. Vengeance was on our minds.

I was maturing rapidly and chasing girls rather than rabbits. Dances, the cinema, and the variety theatre at the Ilford Hippodrome were becoming all the more attractive to me and, what was worse, who were getting all the girls? The boys in uniform of course. Something had to change!

A visit to the Army Recruiting Office in Romford was my answer. One day in March, dressed in my Home Guard uniform, I volunteered to join the Army. I had no qualms about adding two years to my age as I probably looked older than sixteen, and thought the uniform would help anyway. The kindly recruiting sergeant (!!?) helped me to complete the application forms, remembering as I did so to extend the periods I had worked in the different factories to match my new age. When asked about which regiment I would like to join, I remembered that Grandfather Ward, my mother's father, had spoken about The Kings Royal Rifles when telling me of his time in the Great War. Seeing this on the list of possible choices it sounded just right. So on the 19th March 1942 the deed was done. I had been signed up for '*The duration of the War*', was now a Rifleman and had to report to the 70th Battalion of the Kings Royal Rifle Corps in Winchester on the 26th March.

The first thing I had to do now was inform my mother, who at this very moment was still in Old Church Hospital, having given birth on the 15th March to David, a new little brother, giving rise to David's oft-repeated phrase, in later years 'He took one look at me and joined the army, couldn't stand the competition!' Our mother appeared to take my news without surprise and with perhaps some resignation. What she really thought is anybody's guess. The next time she would see us together was six weeks later when I came home on leave after finishing my initial training.

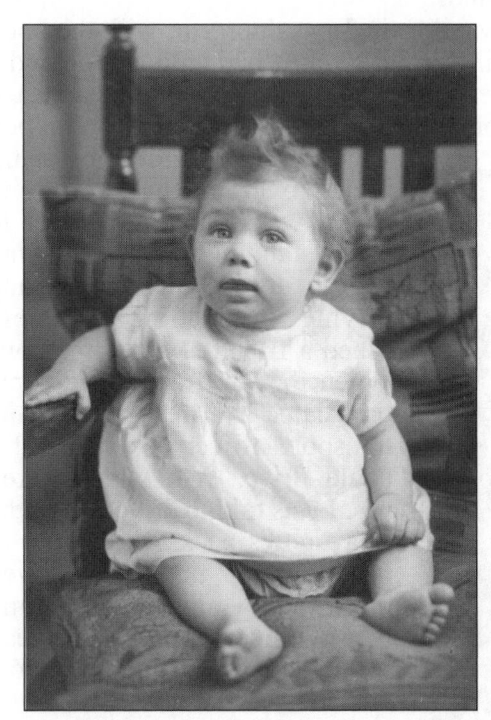

Younger brother David. He maintains that when I saw him I joined the Army

With just one week to say fond farewells to family, friends at work and the Home Guard, time passed very quickly and I arrived in Winchester well before my latest reporting time of 4 p.m. I had been told to take with me my uniform and all other equipment except my rifle. This proved to be a great asset. Whereas the others had new battle dress impregnated with a smelly preservative, mine had been cleaned and was well broken in. Now Rifleman No. 6856995, I was certain I had made a good choice of unit in the KRRC Their buttons were black, and boots were cleaned with dubbing, which meant neither had to be polished! Being a light infantry regiment, other surprises were the very quick, short paces of the regimental marches and that they carried only a small back pack. The rifle drills differed also from that of heavy infantry; no shouldering of arms, rifles were carried at the trail, that is, balanced in the right hand, parallel to the ground, at arm's length, and could on command be changed over to the left hand. This presented them as being ready for action at all times and looking very business like. The six weeks' basic training passed quickly and successfully. On my one and only 24 hour guard duty whilst in Winchester, I was made 'Stick Orderly' for being the smartest on parade. This meant I could sleep all night and was the duty officer's runner the next day, a nice cushy job. A lot better than two hours on and four off like the rest of the guard! From Winchester I was sent to Debden in Essex, to join the Young Soldiers Battalion of the 60th Rifles, as the KRRC was known. Here we were under canvas, eight men to a bell tent, sleeping on a ground sheet with a palliasse (a mattress stuffed with straw) to lie on. Our task here was to be the defence of a nearby aerodrome. For this we had only Bren guns and rifles, some in sand-bagged fox holes around the perimeter, and a few Beaverettes in which to drive around.

The Beaverette was a pre-war Austin Ten saloon car, with the body replaced by one made of quarter inch mild steel. It had an open top and a small slot at the front for the driver to see out of, which could be adjusted to a slightly bigger opening for non-action driving. It looked like a tin box with no lid. You got in by clambering over the back or front, and it was sometimes easier to drive standing up and looking over the top. Not having had any driving instruction, I simply asked a friend to show me how. When they were replaced some time later by Bren carriers, the transport officer asked me if I could drive. When I answered yes, I was told to drive one of the Beaverettes back to a factory in north London, not having driven more than a mile before in my life. With someone to map read we made it, only bumping into a bus once on the way.

October 1942 - King's Royal Rifle Corps (KRRC)

The Carriers were a great improvement. These small, tracked vehicles were fairly fast for their weight and very manoeuvrable, although a too fast and sudden change of direction could cause the tracks to come off. Putting them back on was constantly practised until it could be done at a reasonable speed.

As autumn approached the regiment was moved out of tents into Nissen huts, which had bunk beds and a central coke-burning stove, in preparation for winter; certainly a lot more comfortable. While on the subject of comfort, apart from trips to the local pubs, there were dances at Saffron Walden and even Cambridge, the latter useless in my opinion, too many Yanks! Clothes were collected and sent to a laundry weekly. The ladies dealing with the washing would often put messages in with our cleaned clothes when returning them, such as 'Are you single?' or 'Would you like someone to write?' Some even gave a name and address to write to. By this method I contacted May who lived in Forest Gate, not too far from my own home and easy to visit when on leave. Thus began an enduring love affair, well, for many months anyway.

The news that the Regiment was to be disbanded came as a shock to everyone. Lectures and interviews were carried out to find new posts, with tests to assess suitability. It had been explained to us that the desert war in North Africa had shown a need for more men to be trained in tank warfare. Because of my previous engineering work in the factories and after some of what I found to be very simple tests, such as dismantling a bicycle pump and reassembling it, I was told of the formation of a new unit composed of men capable of repairing or maintaining vehicles etc. in mobile workshops. This was later to become the new Royal Electrical and Mechanical Engineers (REME). A great deal of persuasive argument and a promise of a quick promotion to sergeant was applied, but I resisted, adding that I had joined the army to get out of that type of work. Anyway the bombing was still going on at home, and I was still angry enough to want a more direct kind of action. The outcome was to transfer me and a few others to the Royal Armoured Corps.

No longer a Rifleman, now a Trooper! Catterick Camp was not the only culture shock I came across after the 12th November 1942. After the beauty of the Essex countryside, here I was in a cold, damp, ugly area of nothing but army camps. From a regiment of mainly young volunteers, led by officers who were always there to help and guide men who would follow them anywhere, to officers you saw only if you were marched in front of them, which usually meant trouble. These men were mostly either prewar ex-cavalry too old for anything else, or young subalterns straight from their college cadet corps, who knew nothing about real life and commanded respect from no-one. The NCOs who were detailed to take all new arrivals through their basic training were also mainly regular soldiers and also from cavalry regiments. Those from other Light Infantry regiments, like myself, had to adjust to slower, longer paces and new arms drills. We also had to change all our black buttons to brass ones and our boots now had to be very highly polished. The others in my intake were mainly conscripts, many of them not too keen to be there. This was not the kind of army I had grown used to; all this shouting, bullying, and bullshit

After the basic training came the tradesmen training. At least the NCOs taking these courses were more civilised. We were taken through all the required skills for Tank work, Maintenance, Gunnery, Wireless and Driving. So at last I received proper driving lessons. Not easy ones at that!

We had first to pass the army driving test which consisted of driving a fifteen hundredweight truck, which had crash gears (no synchromesh on these). Driving in winter, up and down steep mountains, was not funny either. Being one of eight passengers in the open-backed lorry, with no seats, was pretty hair-raising too, with a big drop on one side of very narrow roads and getting ready to jump out if someone missed the gears and went over the top.

August 1943 - Royal Armoured Corps (RAC)

All men training for tank duties have to pass on two skills out of the three required. After their first tests in all three they are given their designated aims of being a combination of either, Driver, Gunner, or Wireless Operator. I was detailed to be a Driver/Operator as I wore glasses, which excluded me from being a Gunner.

The long hard winter and a just as miserable spring in 1943, had me swotting on wireless procedures, repairs and Morse Code. The driving was relatively easy and I switched to tanks and armoured cars. At least with these you got out of camp on to the Moors, or visited some of the more picturesque villages and towns. There were of course some diversions; a camp cinema, Salvation Army and NAAFI canteens, and the nearest town, Richmond, was pleasant in itself but, of course, the public houses were full of troops and fights between them frequent. Dances were almost a waste of time because of the shortage of partners. A trip to Darlington could be made at weekends, where, being a larger town, the cinemas and dances were a lot better. The Nuffield Centre was also a popular place to visit for refreshments and entertainment. During this training time at Catterick Camp one of my two closest friends was Anthony Stansfield, better known as 'Stan'. He was also ex KRRC whose number 6857000 was only five more than my own army number and never to be forgotten. We lost touch with each other after our training together when Stan was allocated to a Tank unit and I had to wait for a later posting. The other was Fred White. Fred and I were so often asked if we were brothers that in the end we gave up denying it to save the usual discussion that would follow if we said we were not

The relationship between May and me had become very intense since our first meetings in '42. All my leaves had been spent with her and letters constantly passed between us. On my last leave before being transferred to the RAC we had decided to marry and I had purchased an engagement ring (May was 19 and completely unaware that my real age was 16, not 18!). Needless to say we kept our betrothal a secret from our families. It was at my elder sister Iris's wedding on the 12th June '43 some seven or eight months later, that someone spotted May's ring and our secret was a secret no longer

Perhaps that was the real reason I received a 'Dear John' letter not long after returning to Catterick. Someone must have mentioned my real age. Devastated that the love of my life had changed her mind, I swore then that I would not marry until the war was over I remembered the times I had risked taking unauthorised leave just to see her for a day or two, travelling without a train ticket or a leave pass. Short of money, I had done this several times, especially when really bored with life at the camp. I would purchase a train ticket from Catterick to Darlington only, where I would change platforms and catch a night train to Kings Cross, dodging the ticket collectors and, on arrival at Kings Cross, go to the rear of the train, cross over to another empty platform and leave the railway station through an unmanned barrier. I remembered also the frequent times I had returned to camp late, reluctant to part until the last moment and missing a connection. Finally, having been caught several times, I received 14 days detention, which meant being confined to barracks (C.B) and doing extra duties. For the first week I was locked up in large room with about a dozen others, most of whom were awaiting Courts Martial. Among these men were conscripts who had no intention of staying in the services. Deserters who had been caught and brought back, and others who had received over 14 days detention, would be transferred to the 'Glass House'. They had nothing to do most of the day except exchange ideas and plans for escape and exist on whatever was available and, if not immediately to hand, how to get it or improvise. It's surprising what can be done with half a razor blade and a small piece of flint! A single match can for example be carefully split into four pieces. No match? A spark from a flint, struck with the blade onto a small piece of fluff scraped from inside a pocket or even the lining of clothes and gently blown into a small smouldering fire, can be enlarged if required, simply by adding paper or anything dry and combustible and gently fanned. Someone must have realised that I might be mixing with the wrong kind of people as my second week 'inside' was spent in a single cell It gave me time to reflect that, this time, I had been late back from a legitimate leave, with a correct pass and a good excuse for being late. The train had been delayed because of air raids in London and, consequently, missed the connection at Darlington. Of course you could not expect a CO who had probably never been in an air raid to understand. 'Should have made allowances,' he had said. What did he expect? Come back from leave a day earlier? Or perhaps ask the bombers not to come that evening? You can gather from that, that I was not too pleased, which added to my distaste of Catterick and the RAC. 'Ah well,' I mused, 'you get punished in this world, not for what you do, but for being caught. In future I'll make sure I'm not.' To think I even entered a boxing tournament because the entrants were to be given an extra 24hr leave pass to visit her! I was matched against an ex-pro boxer and took such a beating that I vowed that was the last time I'd box in the army.

Both Fred and I had qualified in the RAC as Driver/Operators, earning ourselves an extra two shillings a day. 'About the only good thing that's happened at Catterick,' I remarked. Now we were waiting to be posted to a unit, but with the North African campaign progressing well through the spring, by mid May the Germans and Italians had been defeated. Some of the men who had been in action there came back to the camp in Catterick. They were kept apart from others in the barracks and it was very noticeable that they were 'different'. Apart from their obvious sun tan, they seemed rather hyperactive, unkind rumours running around the camp were that they had a touch of the sun. The reason was more likely to have been to keep these battle hardened Troopers away from the 'rookies' in case they frightened the life out of them, telling them what they would in turn have to face!

The rookies (young new arrivals) had enough to put up with, having 'old' soldiers like myself, who had more than a year's service behind us, who knew all the tricks and dodges essential for an easier life in this forgotten corner of England. At 'lights out', when they were tucked up in their still unfamiliar beds, I would sing them to sleep with the saddest songs I could think of, such as 'Little man stop crying, I know why you're blue, someone took your kiddie car away. Time to go to sleep now, little man you've had a busy day. You've been playing soldiers, so put away your gun, the war is over for tonight. Time to go to sleep now, little man you've had a busy day.' What's a few sobs between friends?

When the duty NCO was due and on the lookout for idle hands to put on fatigues, I would disappear, usually to the gym, where I could at least be doing something that I enjoyed. Sunday afternoons, if not on duty, meant 'in bed or out of barracks'. For a small sum or cigarette ration, I could introduce some lonely soul to one of the better places to be in town. My own choice was one of the church halls serving free afternoon teas and cakes. It was also possible to meet a friendly mother, whose own son was away, who may invite a lonely soldier home for a meal, or even offer to do his washing. By now it was late summer, and what a summer! I can only remember one afternoon when we could strip off our shirts and bathe in the sun. An exaggeration perhaps, being bored out of our minds with the area, and keen to be away doing what we had joined up for in the first place. Fred and I scanned the notice boards daily in the hope of seeing something worth applying for. At frequent intervals there had been requests for volunteers for either Commando or Parachute regiments, airborne regiments and Glider Pilots, and even for the Palestine Police. Having applied for most, if not all of these and not had any response (as we both wore spectacles, we were probably not considered, even though both of us were classed as A1 fit). Then we spotted a small brief notice asking for; 'Wireless Operators, for special duties which may include parachute training. Knowledge of foreign language would be an advantage but not essential'. We read it, turned towards each other and both said as one 'This looks interesting' and we both immediately applied. After all, I knew at least two French nursery rhymes!

Chapter Four - Escape from Catterick

Within a couple of weeks we were both off to Oxford for 'interview' at one of the university colleges. On arrival, having first been required to sign 'Top Secret' security forms and swear on oath not to repeat anything seen or heard there this day, we were told just a little, in a series of lectures, about resistance groups in occupied Europe and the need for Wireless Operators to keep or make contact with the UK, emphasising that there would not be any monetary advantage or even promise of promotion. At the close of each session we were all informed that, as the work was entirely voluntary, if we did not wish to hear more or continue with these sessions we were free to leave. We would receive a 24 hour pass, to use before returning to our units, and were reminded that everything we had seen or heard was absolutely secret and not to be disclosed to anyone. Throughout the day the talks continued. At each session more details were given and more knowledge of their requirements made known. 'We don't want people who are offering their services just for promotion, you will be receiving just the normal tradesmen's rates' was quoted several times, and when questioned, answered with, 'Well, anyone who does this kind of work for monetary gain only could not be completely trusted, and possibly even change sides for the same reason!'. After a very good lunch, those of us remaining, about half of the 400 or so that had started the day, watched training films and were told that people with various skills, or at least more than one, were needed and that was why most had been invited from the Tank regiments. Less than a hundred remained at the end of the day which terminated with tests, private interviews and questions on previous experiences, also motives for applying; even asking about any, if unmarried, romantic attachments. I thought I had a good chance of being selected; my Infantry training as well as Wireless and driving experience with the RAC should help, and romance (at the moment) was definitely off the menu.

Several long weeks later, back at Catterick, I was on 'spud bashing' for reasons now forgotten (probably told a lance corporal where to go!). My right hand was bandaged from a scalding with hot water, but I was ordered to carry on working in the cookhouse regardless. Fred came running over to tell me that he had been told to pack up and be ready to leave the camp early next day. It looked as though he had been selected. 'What about me?' I said. 'Any one else going? 'None as far as I know,' replied Fred. So that was that, only time for a quick drink in the NAAFI that evening and Fred was away early next morning. Now I was really 'browned off' and contemplating some kind of revenge. Would an unauthorised absence be worth more detention? Certainly worth considering, I thought.

Panic is the only word for it. Early in the morning two days later, an out-of-breath duty officer, who had been sent on the double, to find Trooper H. Verlander 6856995, burst into the cookhouse where I was still spud bashing. Or more correctly dodging it; you can't peel potatoes with a bandaged hand! 'You should not be here,' he said. 'Get to the CO's Office immediately!' Bloody Hell! This sounded serious, now what had I done? It's difficult to think of excuses when you don't know what you're going to be charged with. 'Should I change out of my fatigues, sir?' 'No, come as you are, this is urgent.' On arrival at the Orderly Room I was greeted by a flood of words from all directions, 'You must know someone in very high places!' 'Someone's dropped a big clanger!' 'The Old Man's received a rocket from the War Office!' Very puzzled, I was marched in to see the CO who dismissed the duty officer, leaving us alone. 'At last you're here, Verlander, please sit down.' (This sounds very unusual, I thought.) 'I am afraid there has been an error on our part for which I must apologise,' he continued. (Very, very, unusual, went through my mind again!) 'We should have sent you off with Trooper White two days ago. Arrangements have been made for you to depart from here immediately and I would like you to take my letter exonerating you from all blame to your new CO' He went on to say, 'I don't know exactly what you will be doing when you get to your new posting, but I am given to understand you have already been informed of the utmost secrecy needed. Good luck, I wish you well, and success in whatever you do. Now you must hurry, young man, pack and be ready to leave here in one hour. Tell no one where you are going, come back here to collect your railway pass, a day's rations, and papers that you must take with you,' adding, 'My driver will take you direct to Darlington to make sure you get the next train to Kings Cross. Report to the Military Police, they will be expecting you and will see you safely on to your destination.' What a pompous twit! 'I bet he got a right old rollicking,' went through my mind as we shook hands before departing. Henley-on-Thames in Berkshire was my final destination after travelling all night and arriving just after breakfast. Almost the first person I met there was Fred White but it was just a case of 'Hello' and 'Goodbye' as Fred was one of a small group, packed and ready to depart for another unknown destination for his further training. That was the last we would see or hear of each other for the next three years.

Chapter Five - Introduction to SOE

The billet allocated to those staying in Henley-on-Thames was in a Victorian building in Countess Gardens, a private house adapted for their eating and sleeping needs. There were approximately fifty young men remaining, from various regiments, all with at least some basic knowledge of wireless operating, apart from other skills. The food was first class, accommodation adequate, comfortable, and there were even sheets on the beds. This was luxury indeed! Henley itself was warm and friendly, with more pubs than you could find in many a town. Certainly more than one could soberly visit on the same night and manage to walk home. A wonderful dance hall, where there were plenty of very willing and charming partners to be found! What better place to stroll with or without a companion than along the banks of old Father Thames? After Catterick, this was heaven. This was to be our 'rest home' for the next few busy months. The sting in the tail being, of course, work to be done and things to learn, all of which took place some few miles away at Fawley Court, a beautiful country house requisitioned, like many others, by the military. 'Even if it is now October, at last I'm among like-minded people who want to get on and 'do' something about this bloody war,' I thought. After a good breakfast, it was at first a pleasant steady walk from Henley to Fawley, which, over a very short time, changed into alternate running and walking and, as we got fitter, it became a steady trot all the way. The necessity of exercise became obvious when we found out that our Morse code sending and receiving speeds had to be increased, from the normal army speeds of 10 to 12 wpm, to 25 wpm so that our actual working speeds in the field could be maintained at approximately 20 wpm. Doing this meant many hours of just sitting, hour after hour, practising, sending and receiving blocks of five random letters in mock messages. Specialist Royal Signal Corps instructors, who themselves could reach an amazing 35 wpm, gently eased the new arrivals into the requirements needed for the work intended for them. Continuous da-da's and dit-dit's through a head set clamped onto the ears for hours on end could soon send a person mad To avoid this work proceeded with approximately 1 hour of Morse followed by 15 minutes outside on a rugby playing field. Usually this developed into a game of 'All In', which consisted of two teams, a rugby ball, no referee or rules. The object may have been to get the ball to one end or the other, but mainly it was to get the circulation going and some fresh air in the lungs. Once the required speeds in Morse code were achieved, next came the learning of international radio working procedures, and the use of 'Q' codes. These are a series of three letters i.e. 'QRT,' 'QPR,' which are used to replace longer sentences such as 'Are you receiving me?' or 'I am changing frequency,' 'Please repeat all after.' Following this there was the introduction to the Coding and Decoding of messages.

Fawley Court as it is now

Ciphering systems were complex and believed to be unbreakable, developed by a young Londoner named Leo Marks who came to Fawley Court, to tell us himself about the workings of the systems and of his numerous skilled and mainly female staff. He was very outspoken and admired by all, especially by the Cockney lads like me! Leo, who could swear like an old sweat, promised us that his aim was never to have to ask a radio operator to repeat a message, which could of course endanger the sender.

Then there was the presentation of the communication equipment which we were to use in the field. A combined mains or battery operated radio transmitter and receiver (B2 Wireless set, later to be known as the 'Jed' set), small dry battery operated receiver (MCR1), and a hand operated power generator (Type 45/111), for transmissions when no other power was available. The B2 was fitted into a small suitcase, or two smaller waterproof metal boxes. The MCR1 fitted into the magazine pouches of standard army webbing. The generator had its own carrying case. When required, a complete set of radio equipment could be fitted as back packs, which would weigh about 45lbs.

Training continued with indoor and outdoor transmissions and mock exercises. First was elementary parachute training followed by unarmed combat. Then came the introduction to hand guns, starting with a .22 Webley and on to .32 semi automatics. This was done in an indoor range constructed in the cellars of the main house. Our final personal weapon, a .45 Colt semi-automatic, was to be issued later.

Between times there were talks and lectures on the type of work we would be doing, which made a pleasant break from the continuous Morse exercises. There were also visits from rather strange men! They were usually elderly, small, foreign-looking gentlemen, often wearing half-framed spectacles, who were kindly and well spoken, frequently with an accent that was unrecognisable. Speaking individually, or to just a few of the men at a time, they would ask strange and often personal questions on a variety of subjects. Or present sheets of paper with drawings or pictures on them and ask for comments on what was seen or what they represented. (Rorschach tests). There were word association games, when an answer had to be given quickly to words like Mother, Brother, Cook, Lead, etc. Another test showed sheets of paper with what looked like blots of wet ink that had been folded in two to make a mirror image and you were asked what the image brought to mind. Answers that were given were at times hilarious or as ridiculous as the recipient felt at the time. Whatever they made out of the results no one knows. Perhaps we were all at least a bit mad. No wonder these psychologists were nick-named 'Trick Cyclists'!

Off duty at Henley, mainly weekends, if there were no talks, films or lectures, meant agreeable visits to the town. One unforgettable Sunday morning, 'Blondie' (Alfred Holdham), a Londoner, one of my new companions and I went for a walk along the river Thames. After walking a fair distance we came upon a lock and a Lock-keeper's house. We were just standing and admiring it when a lady came out and chatted to us whilst showing us how the lock worked. We, of course, were willing helpers when a boat went through the lock and afterwards she brought us out a cup of tea and some homemade cake. After chatting to us for a little longer, as we were getting ready to leave, she invited us back for Sunday Tea, when she said her family would also be there. Blondie, who had a date that afternoon, said he couldn't make it, but I said I would be delighted and promised to be back later that day. On returning to the lock keeper's house I was welcomed in and introduced to the rest of the family, the husband, who had been helping elsewhere and a son and daughter. They had also an older son, who was in the services, and said they were pleased they could help in a way they hoped others would for their own son. After a very good meal, much of which was homemade, and not forgetting many things were rationed, we all sat round the table talking and playing card games. Such kind and very thoughtful people, I thanked them for a wonderful day that I have never forgotten.

Although there were very many interesting hostelries to drink in, they were frequently short of supplies, which meant ,if there was no beer, drinking whatever was available! For me, this meant trying other strange beverages until then unknown. Brandy became a favourite. I did discover, however, that rum could send me to sleep whilst still standing! This happened when I visited the local ballroom and after just one glass of rum found I could do no more than stand propped up by a wall with half closed eyes. A lesson learnt; I had to go back to the billet for an early night. Not that any of the trainees were heavy drinkers, but it was normal to have at least one drink before going to a dance. It somehow relaxed one enough to approach a young lady and ask her for a dance; our pay did not stretch too far anyway! All the local people were very friendly and there was little competition from other armed forces and, as yet, few Yanks in the area.

Once or twice a week I enjoyed going dancing and my most frequent partner was a charming married lady whose husband was away in the forces. She had told me right from the start, at our first meeting, that she did so because she hoped that her husband, who also liked dancing, was also being helped through these troubled times and not feeling too lonely. Knowing that I had no girl friend at the time, she would also introduce me to single girls and encourage us to dance together. Satisfied with my present older female companion, who was also improving my dancing, it was quite some time later before I became attracted to Joan, a shy young lady who then became my companion until leaving Henley.

We had completed our intensive signals course by the end of December '43, with a few outdoor exercises, operating back to the base station. A very small number of those who had started three months earlier had failed, for various reasons, to finish the course. These would be offered posts as base operators, as the knowledge already obtained could have made them a security risk elsewhere. There was one, however, who 'disappeared' after he had been caught 'flogging' wine in town that he had apparently 'found' behind a bricked up wall in one of the cellars of Fawley Court!

Christmas Day in our billet at Henley was a delight for us all. The army cooks there certainly made it a very special day, serving up a festive meal that would have been exceptional in peace time. Yet despite shortages and rationing, they produced a full traditional Christmas Dinner with all the trimmings. Fully (well almost) recovered on Boxing Day morning, we awoke to a bright sunny day with a snow covered town. Someone thought it would be a good idea to go for a swim in the Thames. A small group of brave but barmy idiots agreed and joined me for a gentle stroll down to the town centre. We crossed over the bridge to a field beyond, climbed over the gate and ran through the snow to reach the river, which was about 30 yards away. Having put our swimming trunks on under our uniforms (none of us had thought about bringing a towel), we undressed and dived in. The river was flowing too fast to freeze but there was plenty of ice around the edges and it was bloody cold. I found this out as soon as I struck the water! Before I surfaced, I felt my whole body go stiff with the pain and shock of the coldness. It was difficult to move a limb and it was impossible to breathe. I managed to reach the bank, which was, fortunately, only a couple of strokes away, more by luck than judgement. Only two others ('Blondie' and 'Boxer') had actually gone in and all were hauled out, safe, but sorry! Without being able to dry off, all we could do was take off the wet costumes and put on our uniforms without underwear. We did not stroll back either, we ran, shivering all the way.

As a Christmas present, we were informed that we had all been promoted to Lance Sergeants. This was a pleasant surprise, even more so for me, my true age being 18 this 27th December 1943. Up until now we had been led to believe there would be no extra pay other than the normal tradesman payment as wireless operators, and when we had finished our parachute training we might get additional parachutists pay. Also that, after a short leave, we would be moving to another training centre where we would meet the people we would be working with. We now knew a great deal more about the work we would be doing, that we were members of SOE (Special Operations Executive) and would each be teamed up with two others, and that our main responsibility was for the communications of the group, also the training of members of underground resistance movements in the use and care of arms and explosives. Absolute secrecy about all that had been already learnt, and that which was to come, was of course essential for the safety of everyone. Therefore it was forbidden to tell anyone anything at all, about the training or the nature of the missions we were going to be entrusted with. Home on leave for the New Year, having been promoted, looking fitter than ever, apart from 'A streaming cold in the head, must have got wet somewhere!' the first question asked on your return home is, of course, 'What have you been up to?' I managed to get around that one by simply saying that I had been on, and passed, an advanced course of wireless training. The next question, strangely enough was usually, 'And when are you going back?'

The New Year found those of us remaining, back from leave and eager to find out what was in store at our new quarters in Peterborough. By the end of January, we had just enough time to kiss the local girls goodbye, promising to be faithful and to write forever. Well, for at least a few weeks! And we were on our way at last, for our final training.

This was to a magnificent mansion, called Milton Hall, set in a very large park on the outskirts of Peterborough. Here was where the teams of 'JEDBURGHS', as we were to be named, would be formed as we trained and worked together. The original aim was for approximately 100 teams of three persons to be made up, consisting of a British or American Officer, with a French Officer or other National Officer, plus a Wireless Operator, using an equal mix of American, British, and French or others such as Belgian or Dutch personnel, depending on the country the team were to be operating in. Some teams did manage this, but most ended up being with two of one nationality plus one of another. The team leaders seemed to prefer the W/T operator to be of the same nationality as them. The mixture of nationalities made it difficult enough for some to get their tongues around 'JEDBURGH', the Yanks pronouncing it 'Jed-BURG' as in Ham-BURGer, the French as 'Geed-BORE' and the Brits, who couldn't spell it twice the same way, coming out as 'Jed-BORO'.

The large grounds of the park had been arranged and fitted out for the final training, complete with the fuselage of a plane, out of which, jumping through the 'hole' into a sand-pit could be practised. There were indoor and outdoor firing ranges, areas for the throwing of hand grenades and the use of explosives together with assault courses, fitness, armed and unarmed combat areas. The main house and dairy were used as offices, lecture rooms, a rest room and 'Bar'. Separate sleeping quarters were in huts close to the main house between a few trees. When the W/T operators arrived, the British and French were mostly already installed. All of the American OSS men (Office of Strategic Services) arrived a short while later. (The OSS post war became known as the CIA, Central Intelligence Agency). They had erected a first aid post along the drive leading up to and close to the house. Recreation and dining facilities were shared by all. American rations were a great bonus. The P.X. supplies were most generous and certainly a lot cheaper than the NAAFI. Most if not all of the training staff were British, and what the British army cooks could do with these American supplies was really amazing. We certainly dined like kings. Cordon bleu? More like red, white, and bleu! It wasn't long before many of us were converted to smoking 'Camels', 'Chesterfields' etc. including the odd cigar or two. One thing did puzzle me, however. When talking to the American Wireless Operators, a few of them said they had volunteered only because they wanted to get sent to England and not out to the Far East. Now that they had arrived they were hoping to become base operators. I could not understand this at the time but, looking back and after first hand

Milton Hall

experience in the Far East later on in the war, I do now.

Jedburgh - September 1944 - SOE

Someone had the bright idea of getting everyone out on parade at the same time, in military fashion, in front of the mansion. This alone took some time; the British stood in reasonable lines of Officers and NCOs, the French, some Army, a few Navy, stood in a group, just looking on, wondering what was happening, and the Americans strolled up, hands in pockets, smoking and in a variety of dress and undress, chatting amongst themselves. Another small group consisted of a mixture of Belgian and Dutch personnel. The senior British NCO tried to call everyone to order as the CO approached. The Brits did make a reasonable effort to stand as required and on the command of 'Attention' did snap into a smart if sluggish pose. The French looked puzzled, shrugged their shoulders saying *'Quoi?', 'Qu'est-ce qu'il dit?'* The Yanks could also be heard muttering, among other unprintable comments, about only taking orders from their own officers. Result? Complete chaos! From then on, all Military and Regimental practices were abandoned. The mixture of ranks, some of which were quite high, nationalities, and different uniforms, had to be seen to be believed. All normal military customs had to be dropped because they would be ignored by some and not understood by others. So, saluting anywhere in the base was dropped. Even the 'Brits' were from many different units and wearing their own regimental uniforms. All trainees became, and were treated, as equals. This served to bond us well together and aided the formation of our teams of three. It was about this time that the Jeds rallying cry was first heard. Introduced by the Yanks at any moment that became boring or repetitious, it went: - '48, 49, 50, S..o..m..e, Shit'! Oh yes, there was also a slight change in the 'upper management' at Milton Hall after this fiasco. The CO and a few other Regular Army types quietly departed and a new CO, Lt Col Musgrave arrived. This man had been a Big Game Hunter in Africa. He gave some very interesting lectures and proved to be an excellent instructor himself when giving the practical demonstrations of survival techniques.

At one of his keenly followed demonstrations, available to anyone interested as was the custom of things now, he arrived with a sheep, selected from one of those that roamed the grounds as living lawn mowers. 'To stay fit enough to keep any operation going, you and those with you, must be fed! This is how you dispatch any suitable beast, skin it, clean it, and prepare some parts for storage as you cannot always be sure that more will be immediately available'. Cutting and rolling back some of the turf, he scooped out some earth, about the size of a washing- up bowl. The fore and back legs of the impending victim were tied together and a noose placed around the muzzle. The animal was then placed on its side, with the neck over the edge of the hole in the ground. He knelt down by its back, with the right knee on its shoulder, the left on the ground. Pulling back the head with his left hand, the right held a sharp pointed knife which quickly pierced through the neck between the windpipe and the neck bone, the sharp edge of the blade facing outwards, then cut through the windpipe and outward, the head pulled back, and the neck bone severed. The cutting was all completed in one fast movement without a single sound from the beast. As the blood flowed into the hole in the ground the feet were freed to allow involuntary kicking to pump out the remaining blood. The head was then severed and the carcass hoisted up on a nearby tree to be skinned. I noted that this was very similar to the way I had learnt how to skin rabbits, when evacuated to Beccles, but on a larger scale. Next came the gutting and cleaning of the carcass, followed by dividing the meat and offal up into manageable portions and being shown which parts should be consumed first, and those parts that could be conserved for use later. For example, slices of meat smoke-dried over a fire would last perhaps the longest, could be re-cooked, or eaten as it was while on the march. The main theme was nothing should be wasted.

As the session broke up and seeing the complete sheep skin still hanging upon the tree, I approached the CO saying, 'What are you going to do with that, sir?' 'Good thinking, young man,' he replied. 'It depends on your needs at the time, as bedding, or clothing. As I don't need this one, it's yours if you can find a good use for it.' ' I was thinking it would make a nice bedroom mat for my mother,' I said. 'Right, but you must get it cured first. If you haven't done that before, take it to the man in the cottage near the front gate. I'm certain he will help you. That's what I like, waste not, want not,' he added, on leaving.

Mother got her mat on my next leave, having taken my prize and inquired at the cottage, where a kindly gent had said 'Just put it in the water butt, lad, and if you come back next week it will be ready for you.' He had refused any payment but did accept a carton of American cigarettes, in exchange for information as to how it had been done. Incidentally, this item was passed back to me some years later. It had done good service in my bedroom in the years before fitted carpets and, after a professional dry clean, it was stored away in a cupboard until my archivist Clive Bassett became interested in adding it to his display of Jedburgh artefacts at

Small arms training at Milton Hall, initially using the .32 pistols before we moved on to the personal issue Colt .45 Auto

Harrington Carpetbagger Aviation Museum near Northampton and to whom it is now on loan.

We were all introduced to the various equipment that was available for us to use and allowed to choose whatever we thought would best suit our own needs. Some of the main personal arms and equipment, accepted by most, were the .45 colt automatic hand gun, a .30 American carbine with or without a folding butt, and the British fighting knife. The British army compass and binoculars were also favoured. As for dress, whatever you were comfortable with seemed to be the order of the day! All of us adopted the American parachutists brown leather three quarter length boots, and soft woollen pullovers, also the fur lined Parka jackets were popular. The British army camouflage smocks and woollen comforters (scarves that could be turned into a hat), were also thought to be the best for our type of operations. Many used a mixture of American and British leather or webbing belts, holsters and other equipment. All were issued with a Bergen rucksack. I had, by now, removed all signs of the Royal Armoured Corps from my uniform and reverted to wearing those of my preferred regiment, The Kings Royal Rifle Corps. Nothing was said; it was of no consequence now, only the 'job' mattered.

Until training was completed, all were confined to camp with one or two

In the walled small arms range (formally the walled garden), demonstrating conclusively that the two handed grip is not a modern American invention

exceptions, as not all personnel were novices at similar types of operation. The day began at six with physical training until six thirty. Breakfast was at seven, then a mixture of indoor and outdoor training with normal meal breaks until the evening meal. Evenings were spent in lectures or talks by those with previous experience of being in occupied countries, and survival techniques. There were also language courses in French and German. Finishing around nine left just a short time to socialise before lights out at ten p.m.

Of the several ways one could be transported into occupied terri-

Milton Hall

tory, either by a small light aeroplane, or by sea, boat or submarine, the method most expected to be used by the 'Jeds' as we had now become known, was at night by parachute. Training for this became the first priority and was completed before the end of March at Ringway with jumps by day and by night from aeroplanes and balloon.

Early days into the parachute training, showing off really, I was performing one of my gymnastic skills, learnt in my Boys Brigade days, leaping over the wooden horse during a physical training session, outdoors on grass, where there were no refinements like soft rubberised mats. The result was a bad landing, with full weight on my left leg, instead of both feet, when I touched uneven ground. There was a loud 'crack' heard by all as my left knee gave way and I was thrown sideways. Hearing various comments, the politest being, 'He's had it, won't be able to jump now,' really had me worried. Worse was to come after being carted off to the new American field first-aid post and examined by the Medical Orderlies... 'Look at this,' said one. 'I am sure he's got a broken patella!' whilst wobbling it about with both hands and calling others to come and look. They must have been hard up for entertainment! It took three or four men to strap up the complete leg and, with a great deal of kindness and sympathy,

Milton Hall turned into the training camp

got their first wounded soldier off to hospital.

Another surprise for me. The hospital was an American Field Hospital and I was in a ward full of Yankee soldiers and airmen, and surrounded by beautiful American nurses. The men were obviously older than I was and full of sympathy and curious because they had been told only that I was a British parachutist working alongside some Americans. On learning that I was a Londoner helped because they wanted to know about the bombing and how the people were coping with the rationing. The head nurse, Virginee, (it was obvious where *she* hailed from) was the darling of the ward. She had that lovely deep southern drawl that went with her very pretty looks and blonde hair, a typical southern belle. Although all the men were after her she parried them off with a smile and good humour. But she spent quite a lot of time with me, even visiting me when off duty. What she wanted really was to be shown around London and I promised to let her know when I was next given leave. Not that it was ever going to be possible, 'there is a war on, you know' and romances were made and broken in a very short time. This one started and finished, but was not forgotten, with a few kisses and a cuddle in the rest room.

The knee was not as bad as first thought. X-rays showed that no bones had been broken, just torn ligaments and damaged cartilage. Strapped up and after a few days' bed rest and a few more dashing around the corridors on crutches, it was time to go back to work. Saying goodbye to the folks at the hospital was hard. The Americans had been so generous already, often leaving things on the bed for me to use, keep or send home. I was now showered with many more gifts and given addresses to write to after the war. I sincerely hoped they would all make it back home safely.

Back at Milton Hall I was offered, if I felt I needed it, some leave to fully recover. Not wanting to fall behind the others or risk rejection, I accepted just a 24hr pass, 'To reassure my parents that I was OK', but thinking it would give me the opportunity to unload most of the presents, which included such things as ham and other foodstuffs as well as cigarettes and cigars. Then it was back to work.

The knee was still painful and swollen with water under the kneecap, so I kept it bound up as tightly as possible with a crepe bandage and was careful not to let it be known that it was still hurting. A sudden turn or twist to the left without lifting the foot, meant that the knee would

Milton Hall - Lectures with Lt Col Musgrave

Lecture on demolition. Subject headings are listed on the blackboard: 1/ What is demolition? 2/ Explosive, detonation, initiation 3/ Linking 4/Calculation 5/ Standard charges 6/ Incendiaries 7/ Conclusions

lock with a sharp pain that made the leg give way, and I would stumble or fall. Determined not to let anything stop me carrying on, I learnt how to live with it. When the knee locked it would stay painful. By trial and error, I worked out that by lying down and placing the instep of my right foot on top of the instep of the left foot, pushing down hard with the right leg and pulling up with the left leg, there would be a short sharp pain, a click in the knee, and it was all over and working normally. With practice I found I could do this in a few seconds and usually before anyone noticed. Outdoor field exercises and the final parachute training continued and by the time it was the W/T operators' turn to go to Ringway for their first jumps, the knee was fine provided it was supported by the crepe bandage.

There was a strange rumour going around on the journey to Ringway. Apparently we were followed. We were being watched anyway. By security officers. Nothing came of it as far as anyone knew, perhaps 'they' were watching each other whoever 'they' were. After travelling overnight, arriving at Ringway early next morning we were shown around, watched parachutes being packed, and given last minute instructions. Then we were led to a horrendous looking apparatus thirty foot up a flight of stairs. At the top, beside a hole in the floor, through which we were expected to hurl ourselves, was a small fan-like structure with a drum that had a very thin steel cable attached to it, making it resemble some kind of bottomless well. This cable, which didn't look strong enough to take a man's weight, was then attached to a parachute harness. One by one, we were all fitted into the harness, told to take up position as practised, and to jump through the hole as it would be done on the planes, having assured everyone that the 'fan' would slow up the drop to the ground enough to resemble a normal landing. What they didn't say was that as it was straight down, there was no forward motion as in a real drop, where you could roll over to break the fall, as had been practised off the backs of lorries. At last my turn came. Taking up the correct position, when the order came, I swung my legs over the side, concerned as to whether or not my knee could stand the strain. I made sure my legs were clamped together as they should be, then - 'GO' and down I went. When my feet touched the ground my body seemed to keep descending until my knees were up round my ears. With all the air squeezed out of my lungs by the upward pressure on the diaphragm, taking a deep breath, then getting up and walking away as best I could without limping, was difficult. The knee had not let me down, as it had been tightly bound. However, it was a big shock having it bent so much, but not too painful. The real thing was yet to come.

After lunch we were fitted out with our parachutes, driven over to an aircraft with its engine running, quickly boarded, and we took off! We had no time to protest or change our minds. 'Not only my first flight, I'm expected to jump out of this infernal machine!' I moaned. Scared? Of course I was scared, in fact I was convinced I was committing suicide. On reaching the point of no return, all fear of jumping and shooting out through the hole changed to the undesired feeling of not jumping out, of refusing to go in front of my comrades. So out I went, no feeling of falling, just a rush of air going upward, a sudden slight jerk on the harness, a glance up at the opened parachute, a feeling of elation in the unexpected quietness as I gently floated earthwards. Looking down I could see little ant-like bodies and collapsed chutes, then... Ambulances! 'Oh no, what are they waiting for?' I thought.

The ground seemed to come faster towards me as I got myself ready in the landing position. Then voices, the instructors on the ground could be clearly heard shouting orders, 'Keep your legs together, knees bent, face the front, use your guide ropes,' etc. to those not following their training. Travelling forward and half right, all too soon, I was down. Perfect, just a slight bump, feet turned a little to the left, a neat roll, up the right leg to my right side, over on the back, swivel round to face the chute as the wind in it pulled me to my feet. Then running round the side of the canopy, gathering it in by its cords, until now facing the wind, it collapsed. Beaming with delight and relief, like all the others around me, we waited to be collected and driven back to camp, watching plane after plane, full of troops also jumping and landing near us. These were the real Parachute Regiment men. One on landing, came towards us and asked, 'How many have you done up till now?' When informed it had been our first, he found it hard to believe and said they had to do three from a balloon before their first jump from a plane. Then, when informed that a balloon jump was to be our second and that night, he said a rather rude word and walked off unconvinced. Two other things happened as I watched men descending that day. I saw one parachute that did not open, its cords wrapped around the canopy. Ambulances were immediately moving towards where the poor chap would hit the ground, and when he landed he bounced back up almost twice his own height. Another parachute which had not deployed fully because the lines were twisted was falling too fast. The ground instructors called out to the man telling him to kick out forward with one leg, backward with the other until the spiral became undone and the chute opened in time. How important this was to be to me in the future I was yet to learn.

Elated, singing and chattering in the lorry all the way back to our evening meal, we tried to avoid too much reference towards the coming evening's trip, and our next jump. Most of us thought it wasn't so bad after all. When the time came, it was a little different. It was a lot quieter, and very dark, on the journey out to the tethered barrage balloon. Slung beneath it was a large basket and I was included in the first six who were told to climb in with the dispatcher and the instructor. An order was heard from the outside, 'Seven Up-Six Down.' A puzzled voice said (mine!) 'Someone here can't count, what's happening to the other one?' The sharp reply from the dispatcher was 'That's not for us! It's for the ground crew! It means seven hundred feet up and six jumping!' With 'seven hundred feet' going over and over in our minds, the balloon started to rise, and the only sound came from the machinery unwinding the cable attached to the balloon.

All were very quiet in the darkness, only the instructor had a small lamp. When the balloon had come to a halt, the centre panel was removed, revealing a hole to jump through, as on the planes. Everybody was checked to make sure our static lines were attached properly to the supports in the balloon, numbered off one to six and, when called forward, we sat ready on the edge with our legs into the hole. As on the plane, on the word 'GO!', with hands over the face and elbows tucked into our sides, we straightened our legs and shot down through the hole. On the planes, the static lines are left attached and dangling outside the plane, the slip stream keeping them out of the way of those following. This time, on the balloon, they were pulled back inside out of the way, as they would just hang loosely down, and could impede the next person jumping. When it was my turn, all was going well. 'GO!' and I went smoothly off the edge of the hole, out into the night sky. As before there was no sense of falling, just the rush of air going upwards past me. It went on and on, and on. 'I should have felt the jerk of the parachute by now,' I thought. But it just seemed to go on and on. I glanced up just as the chute opened and gave a sigh of relief, looked down and could see enough of the ground and landing lights to enjoy the rest of the ride down. The instructor I met on landing, said 'Well done, sir! Get back to the lorry and wait for the others.' To which I replied 'It took a bloody long time to open!' 'It always seems a long time after a jump from a plane, sir, It's only a second or two longer actually, without the speed of the plane and lack of slip stream to help you on your way.' Thanks very much,' I said, thinking, it's a pity no one mentioned it beforehand. I thought I was a goner. And what's all this 'Sir' business about? Does he know something I don't? I found out later that as the men on the ground could not identify the rank of anyone in their jump suits, and even more so in the dark, they were just playing it safe, and addressing everybody the same way. Ah well, it was a nice thought, but a bit ambitious.

The excitement of the evening's activity was dulled by tiredness. It is said that each jump is the equivalent of eight hours' hard work. What with travelling the night before and the practice jump with the 'fan' apparatus in the morning, we had done two that day, and were booked to do a repeat of the first one by aeroplane the next morning. Most of us just collapsed on our beds and slept through what was left of the night, without bothering to get undressed.

It was now Friday morning. After breakfast we were told that we would be free after our next jump to do whatever we wished. Passes and whatever travel tickets we required would be issued, but we must report back to Milton Hall by Monday morning. If anyone would like a longer rest, there was a choice of a morning or afternoon flight. No prizes for guessing! We all chose the morning one. Eager to get this last jump over, everyone was ready and willing to go as soon as possible. The Officers with us played their part well by easing us past others who were waiting, with tales of the need to get their men back to base urgently, perhaps even hinting that an operation was imminent. Working with people who wanted to get on with the job in hand was proving to be well worthwhile. The last of our practice jumps at Ringway went according to plan. In fact most of us were getting blasé, almost jump happy, wanting to go back and do it again. After lunch I was homeward bound.

Although this was an unexpected leave, Mother was not surprised at seeing me, as my youngest sister Valerie had developed the knack of saying to her, 'Harry's coming home soon,' whenever and just prior to my arrival. My parents wanted to know what I had been doing as usual, having spotted another small badge on my left sleeve as well the radio operators' badge. 'Just earned myself another two shillings a day, by doing a few parachute jumps.' 'You're not in a parachute regiment are you?' they asked. 'Oh no, it's just a safety exercise,' I answered, pointing to the badge which just showed a parachute supporting a square box. 'See, it's for dropping packages to others already on the ground.' 'Where are you getting all these American goodies from?' they also wanted to know. 'We are just sharing the same camp and supplies,' was all they needed to know, as I handed out presents from the PX. Feeling rather tired from the last few days' exertions, after lunch I told Mother that I would just lie down on the settee for a while to rest as I wanted to go dancing at the Ilford Palais. Some time later, Mother asked if I wanted a cup of tea and if I was hungry. 'Yes, please, Mum, what time is it?' 'Do you know what day it is?' she answered. 'Come and have some breakfast, it's Sunday and nearly lunch time! I tried to wake you last night, but you just turned over and went back to sleep. So I just put a blanket over you and left you there.' Having slept around the clock, I was not very pleased about missing the dancing, and it would not be long before I would have to be on my way back to Peterborough. 'Those three jumps in under twenty-four hours must have been more tiring than I thought!' I mused.

Back at Milton Hall, now that the parachute training had been completed, more time was allowed for other intensive training and outdoor exercises. Firing ranges, in what was once a walled garden, were in constant use. It was fitted out with several kinds of pop-up targets which were excellent, especially for the .45 automatics, when accuracy as well as speed was essential. The rumour had it that the American instructors for this were the renowned ex G-men They taught us not only how to take a steady longer distance aim, but also how to draw quickly, and from a crouching, boxing like stance, with the gun at waist height. To get this right we were told to continuously practise this action whilst walking around the camp. This made the camp look like a scene from a cowboy film with guns pointing at you from all directions and people shouting 'Bang'. In fact,

Norman Smith, one of the British Wireless Operators, could be frequently seen practising a fast draw with his .45, from a leather holster that hung low down from his American issue belt, and was strapped to his right thigh, cowboy style!

Not knowing if the weapons were loaded or not, it became rather dangerous, and pointing directly at someone had to be stopped after a few near misses. There were thirty rounds of ammunition available for practice every day if required, and as the ranges were often busy it was not unusual for pot shots to be taken at any promising target. Fortunately the grounds at Milton Hall were extremely large, allowing at least some of the local livestock to escape. The clock and the weather vane were not so lucky! The once sandbagged walls behind the targets in the small arms firing range still bear some testimony to the amount and power of ammunition used. The scars can still be seen today.

Some of the many and varied things to be learnt included the use of the *'Eureka'* and *'Rebecca'* systems, which aided aircraft to pinpoint the dropping zones (DZ's); guerrilla warfare; the use of captured arms and left hand drive vehicles. Training was given in setting various explosive devices including 808 plastic explosive, which could be shaped as required to suit the job in hand; the use of detonators and timing devices; armed and unarmed combat. Between these keenly followed serious sessions there were, of course, the more relaxed times. For example; we heard that instantaneous fuse wire acts in a similar fashion to an explosive and, when wrapped around a telegraph pole and set off with a detonator, it could cut the post right through. No names, no pack drill, but a disbelieving ad hoc group of international W/T operators decided to try it out on a tree that just happened to be of the right size. That it happened also to be between two of the huts was purely coincidental; that it fell neatly between the huts and not on us was pure luck!

There was also the time that I, who could drive any four-wheeled or tracked vehicle, but had never sat on a motor cycle, was offered the chance to learn. Sitting astride the machine I was shown the gears, brake, clutch and accelerator and told, 'There you are, you already know how to ride a bicycle and to drive, so put the two together and that's all there is to it!' This happened on a bend in the path near to and opposite the walled small arms firing range. Letting the clutch out gently, but not slowly enough, the bike with me on it, shot off out of control, scattering a group of Frenchmen marching towards me, and heading at speed for the brick wall. With unkind words ringing in my ears as well as, 'BRAKES!' I managed to stop inches from the wall, got off, left the infernal machine flat on the ground and swore never to get on anything like that again!

Exercises off camp, as well as being a welcome opportunity to get out of the grounds for a while, were treated with serious respect. We wireless operators travelled as far as Scotland to set up our stations and exchange messages, and many other places, sometimes out with our intended teams getting acquainted with each other. As time went on the Jeds, as we were becoming surer of ourselves, were finding some of the exercises of doubtful utility and were inclined to use our own initiative. Dumped miles from base, given a time limit and an emergency telephone number only, and without papers, money or food, we were told to find our own way back without being picked up by the Home Guard, the local or military police. This became a little too easy so, naturally, we pushed our luck a little at times.

The team I was training with once climbed aboard a goods train which was standing at a station to hitch a ride, not being too sure of it's destination or where it would stop. Grateful for a shortened journey, after a few hours' ride, we reasoned it was better to get off at the next opportunity than go too far and have to retrace our steps. Not like another unnamed team who threw caution to the winds and used their carbines to hold up a train going back to Peterborough demanding a free ride home. They must have been Yanks, or perhaps Red Indians!

Early one morning, after a two-day and night survival exercise and emergency rations only to live on, Blondie, another operator, and I were walking down a country lane on the lookout for something to eat. We must have looked rather scruffy in our woolly caps, camouflaged jump jackets, American parachutist boots and fully armed. Even frightening, to anyone who saw us. Anyway, we came upon a wayside refreshment cabin. The aroma of a freshly cooked breakfast tickled our noses and reminded us that we were two very hungry young men. All thoughts of finding raw vegetables, even a chicken or rabbit disappeared. The rules of having no papers, or money were going to be bent. We had both tucked away at least a one pound note for emergencies and this was definitely one! A very delightful and friendly lady, who had seen us approaching, invited us in, saying, 'You look as though you need a nice cup of tea.' Making us comfortable at a table, she continued to chat to us while offering a breakfast of bacon and eggs. She did ask a few questions between cooking and serving us, such as, in which part of the country had we lived before joining the army. On hearing that we both came from London she wanted to know which part and, when we told her, she said she knew the area well and kept us talking for sometime. In fact, we were on the point of leaving, and offered to pay for the meal. She had refused to accept payment several times, but as we stood up to go, I happened to look out of the window behind us. Just a short distance away, pedalling along in a wobbly fashion on a bike, I could see a rather large and elderly, out of breath, policeman. This brave lone woman, thinking that she was detaining German parachutists, had sent her husband out of the back door to get help! Luckily we were able to convince everyone that we were just British soldiers on exercises, without having been asked for papers, and the poor old unarmed bobby looked the most relieved of all of us!

We were lucky again that evening, after rejoining the main group of operators. It was raining and we were looking for somewhere to pass the night when our group spotted some small holiday huts or cabins in a field. They were unoccupied but beds could be seen through the windows. Well! This certainly looked better than sleeping outdoors in the wet! The result was that, although there were not enough beds for two to a bed, there were four or five sleeping bags across a bed in those huts we managed to get into (without causing any damage), which served as a reasonable alternative, at least for the smaller men; the taller ones preferred the harder but roomier floor.

I remember two other large night exercises, involving third parties. The first, in teams, was when we were ordered to infiltrate an American aerodrome and place dummy explosives on the grounded planes, to test the Base's air defences. On approaching our target, guard dogs could be heard barking, but as none could be seen, it was assumed that they had been locked up during the exercise. Getting into the airfield, some of us over, some under the perimeter fences, was not too difficult as there was some illumination on buildings and pathways in the distance. This meant crawling or keeping very low to approach the aeroplanes. Suddenly there was an announcement over the loud speaker system, 'Attention all crews, enemy agents on the base. Release the dogs!' Then, after a short pause, 'Shoot to kill!' Although no live ammunition should be taken on these exercises, many of the teams could be heard cocking their guns and loud whispers muttering about what would happen if they tried to come too close. Luckily after a few tense minutes, the orders were cancelled. On reaching the planes we found the air-crews had been sitting aboard, with interior lights on, all night, complaining that they had been waiting a long time and wanted to go to bed! A complete waste of time really as they had prior knowledge of the supposed attack; except that dummy explosives had successfully been taped to various parts of their planes. Someone would be in for a surprise in the morning! What the American team members said about it is unprintable!!

Another large all-night exercise involved a test for the Home Guard. They were to be on the look out for 'parachutists', protect a railway line and the waterworks pumping station. I can assure you they were very keen and took their training very seriously. The railway tracks had frequent guards and manned blockhouses. Only by going cross-country could our team get near to the railway line. We could see there was a heavy guard blocking the entrance to a low bridge that passed over a large lake or reservoir. Following the lakeside, thinking of checking the other end, we saw that where the trains passed over the lake there were supports for the bridge on small islands, not too far out. We looked for a boat or anything that would float, to ferry us to the island supports, but found nothing. Only one thing to do if we were to succeed. I stripped off and swam out with the dummy explosives, which are normally wrapped in a waterproof covering. Long before I got there, I was wishing I hadn't started. Climbing up to the tracks wasn't funny either, without boots, and in my underwear! The worst moment came when I could hear a train approaching as I fixed the dummy charges to the rails, and it was coming fast! At first I stood against the bridge but the track looked too close, so I placed myself flat on the ground as far as possible from the rails. As the train roared past, I could feel the slipstream pulling me towards the track and the train. Only by clawing into the gravel, which seemed to be moving with me on it, and pressing myself hard downward did I avoid being sucked under the train. Certainly not something I would like to try again!

After swimming back and running around to get dry, we were feeling cold and hungry so we decided that we would give ourselves up to the next group of Home Guard we met, but not before we had told some referees that the track had been 'blown', and where to find the evidence. The night ended with our being taken to the power station that the H.G. used as a Head Quarters, where most of the others were being held, and the bad news was that there was no tea left to drink!

The one thing missing in all this training was something that could bind all the different nationalities together as one unit. This was solved by holding a competition, open to everyone involved, to design a badge that would identify us as 'Jedburgh' members of SOE/OSS. The winning 'SF Wings' design was that of Capt. Victor A. Gough of the Somerset Light Infantry. This was officially accepted and issued to all the Jeds. This design and title 'Special Force' has since been used by many other units and indeed countries. The American OSS, later renamed the CIA, to this day, still consider the Jeds as being the founding fathers of their own Special Forces. Capt. Gough was dropped in the Vosges area on 12/13th August 1944. His French team member was killed in action on 4th September and his British Segeant, Ken Seymour, taken prisoner on 17th August and released in 1945. Capt. Gough's last message to London was on 18th

September. He was murdered by the Gestapo on or about 25th November 1944.

By mid April, after more than three months' training, and without being allowed to relax off duty in Peterborough, we were now considered fully trained, and at last we Jeds were off duty after the evening meal. The only rule was that we be back by 6.30 a.m. and ready for breakfast at 7 a.m. At Milton it had been a fun time as well as having its serious side. We had worked and played together in large and small groups. Now this would end and we would, from now on, be loners most of the time, relying on our own self discipline and the skills we had learned. We were now a complete international unit and all proudly wearing the SF Wings badge.

Approximately a quarter of the Jed teams were sent off to North Africa. In April 15 teams left and another 10 teams followed in mid May. These teams would be operating in the southern areas of France and Italy. The rest were left, very fit, ready for action and raring to go, at Milton Hall. I can remember hearing that only one person did not complete the course, believed to be an American who had, apparently, got injured in a knife fight down town. He was kicked out because if he couldn't look after himself at home, he would be of little use abroad and a possible liability.

Female company was, unfortunately for the boys, sadly lacking, apart from the ladies in the First Aid Nursing Yeomanry (FANYs) who were adored by all the Jeds and could be counted on to assist and advise on matters relating to the training, or the mood of the Staff Officers if you wanted leave, or help to get you out of trouble if you had been lax enough to get caught. They were always willing to listen and pleasant to talk to but, alas, not available!

Only allowed short leaves and not knowing when we would be required for final briefing before being sent into Europe, Peterborough was the choice for many Jeds for evening entertainment. The only problem was that there were many other troops, mainly American airmen, with the same idea. The French Jeds were popular, as were the Americans, and many of these would disappear, especially at weekends, further afield, perhaps to Cambridge or even London. The British Officers must have kept quiet about what they were up to and, like some of the radio operators, were either married or had regular girl friends. But the unattached, such as myself, sorted out our own preferences, be it pubs, dances or girls. For example, one renowned character, a large member of the American Jeds, an author who had also worked in the film industry as a stunt man, drove around in an open-topped car, usually accompanied by at least two gorgeous looking blondes. He addressed everyone as 'darling', even the more senior officers, completely ignoring their rank. If there was room, he would offer a seat in the car. At the other end of the scale there was a British Sgt radio operator, who was an experienced Commando before becoming a Jed. He was not only the smallest man in the outfit but he had the loudest voice you could ever wish to hear. Only afterwards did we learn that he had learnt French in Belgium and Algiers before the war, while considering a vocation as a White Father. His nickname of 'Kneehigh' belied his humour and height in the minds of all Jeds.

I met Valerie, a charming young lady, on one of my Saturday afternoon trips to Peterborough. She lived near the station in one of the railway cottages and having the same name as my youngest sister had helped us get acquainted. We often spent our free weekend daytimes together, walking in the countryside, parks and around the town. She was younger than I was and a little shy, and she was not allowed out in the evenings. She was a very pretty girl and, once, on seeing a notice about a coming Beauty Contest in a local park fete, was very reluctantly persuaded to enter. No, she did not get placed in the finals, but that did not matter as we were becoming more emotionally involved. But because of my previous experience, which had ended with a broken engagement, and my promise to myself that I would not consider marriage until after the war, I decided it would be better to cool off and gradually see less of her. After all I would soon be leaving and the future was unknown.

Evenings in town I had spent mostly in the dance halls and this was where I had met another young lady called Joan on a couple of occasions. Having previously enjoyed the privileges of being engaged, there were needs that a young and very fit person had to satisfy. Joan, being a little older and obviously much more experienced, had been very understanding when I had told her about not wanting to get too involved whilst the war was still going on. Walking her home after a dance one evening, we stopped for a while for a goodnight kiss and a cuddle in the park. This led to more passionate moments and she suggested that I go home with her, where we would be more comfortable. A bit taken aback by the offer at first, and wondering what her parents would have to say in the morning, any doubts soon disappeared once we were both tucked up in bed in a downstairs room. It was five o'clock by the time I left the next morning. It was about seven miles away from the camp and the drive on reaching the grounds of Milton Hall was nearly a mile long and I had to be back before breakfast! It was a Sunday morning and not much chance of a lift by a passing vehicle. Ah well, what better way was there of keeping fit!

It was now June, D Day had come and gone, and some of the teams had already left on their missions. Any day could be the last before departure and into Europe. Those of us still remaining were getting impatient.

My trips to Peterborough continued in a similar pattern until it was my turn to go.

Now spending nearly all of my spare time with Joan, although less of it dancing, I did learn more about her and her family. There were just three women living at the house. The two bedrooms upstairs were occupied, one by her younger sister who was courting an American; it was she who informed me that Joan was pregnant before I met her, and to make sure I was not blamed for it! The other was occupied by their mother, whose husband had been away in the army for a long time. The mother was also pregnant, by the British soldier she was now living with. All three appeared to be unconcerned, which may sound strange to some but this was part of the uncertainty of war time. It had been going on now for over four years and long separations had left many women as well as men very lonely. Some were bound to seek comfort wherever they could find it.

Our team usually met after breakfast, mainly to discuss what was going on in France and to hear about the progress of other teams already operational. It was now July and the invasion forces were still being held back by German defences in Cherbourg. Supply lines were very busy there and transport for the teams difficult to obtain. There was also the danger of rousing the underground organisations too soon thereby inviting retaliation by the occupying forces.

Our turn for final briefing came a week before our departure. Quickly and quietly on a Sunday morning we were told to get packed and be ready to leave immediately. No time for goodbyes, apart from to those sharing the same accommodation, although I did manage to contact one of the American Jeds, who often travelled to and from Peterborough with me, and asked him to let my recent 'companion' know that I had been 'transferred elsewhere'. Before lunch time we were ready, with all our operational kit packed and personal effects handed in for storage. After lunch we were driven by car to London, taken to a small hotel that was exclusive to SOE, told not to leave the premises and then introduced to the American security officer who would be responsible for us. He would go with us, and be with us at all times, until our departure. As we did not take too kindly to our 'nursemaid', the team was led out that evening by our leader to the Dorchester Hotel for a quick drink before going to bed.

Next morning we were collected and delivered in turn to both Dean Street and Baker Street for final briefings. We were given our team name of HAROLD and our own respective code names: Maj. V.E. Whitty as *'Ross'*, Lt. P. Jolliet *(nom de guerre - Rimbaut)* as *'Tyrone'* and Sgt. H.A. Verlander as *'Sligo'*. The area selected for Team HAROLD was a large one covering the Vendee and Deux Sevres *departements* of France. It was known that there were several small groups of underground movements in the area but because of recent 'cleaning up' operations by the Germans, there was no radio contact with the UK. For this reason we were to be dropped in 'blind'; that is to say, without a 'reception committee'. We scoured maps together to select a possible dropping zone and settled for the north-east side of a wooded area just north of the village of L'Absie about 30km north of Niort and 25km west of the town of Parthenay. The wooded area was divided by a roadway running north/south, the largest section to the west and a smaller part to the east. There were no buildings marked on the maps, so this should mean just a short run to get under cover before dawn. Our main task was to contact the groups, combine them into a larger active force, if possible under one leader, to cut the lines of communication, that is, telephone lines, roads and railways, and to try to prevent or delay the large numbers of German reserve troops in the area from being able to travel northwards towards the advancing Allies. It was known that from east to west there were a large number of enemy forces between Poitiers, Niort, and La Rochelle which also had large numbers of naval personnel. Between the north and south area, between Tours, Saint and Angouleme, there were also many troops and troop movements. It was not known if any of the 'safe houses' in the area were still operative and we were advised to treat them with caution. The one thing that surprised me the most at the time was not to expect that everyone in France would be willing or able to assist us, that about only 25% of the population could be expected to be pro-British, 25% would be pro-German and the other 50% would not want to be involved. Only many years later, older and wiser, did I realise that in order to exist when forced to live under a hostile regime, the first priority is the survival and safety of one's own family.

The good news was that we would be getting an extra payment of ten shillings a day 'danger money' paid into a Post Office savings bank account whilst active, and this would not be shown in our pay books! That evening the Major took the team out to a Spanish restaurant in an arcade off Regent Street. He was not too pleased that our 'nursemaid' insisted he stayed with us. The poor chap rarely spoke, never smiled, and looked thoroughly unhappy with his job as escort and guardian to the team.

During the following two days the briefings continued in much the same manner and included receiving radio and cipher plans, escape kits and emergency rations, deciding also on the extra arms, explosives and other equipment we would be taking with us. Additional information was passed on to us about the large number of enemy DF stations (direction finding) in our area, 19 in all, including mobile units. It would therefore be advisable to change position and radio frequencies as often as possible and not transmit messages for longer than five minutes on the same frequency. We were reminded also of a danger period approximately one month after arrival, when after carefully following the training and not being discovered, we would be liable to relax our guard and think it easier than it really was. Four to six weeks was the operational life of a radio operator; get past this point and you will be working automatically and more likely to go on for a long time. Finally, on Thursday we were given a large sum of money for our own personal use, in French Francs and American Dollars. An even larger amount would be also taken with us, for the team's use and to pay for any local assistance. We were now ready to go and were invited to meet General Koenig, the man who headed all the security forces in France. He proved to be a very pleasant and genial host and, after our meeting, invited the team to stay for the evening meal with him, leaving 'Nanny' to be looked after by the General's staff.

With Friday came the news that we should be prepared to leave London after lunch the next day. The Major told me that he was going to spend his last day with his wife. He had apparently not been married for very long, and, as I lived in London, I could also go home. Pierre had made arrangements to visit friends and we all agreed to meet back at the hotel between ten and eleven the next day. 'What about the Yank?' I asked. 'Leave him to me, I'll see to him,' said Whitty. I never did find out how he got rid of our nurse but he did turn up on Saturday morning smiling for the first time that week!

It took just over an hour to get home by bus. I told Mother only that I would be too busy to write myself (not that I did so very often and still don't!) for a while, but my HQ would be sending her regular notes about my well-being, until I could do so myself. My mail would of course be passed on to me, but may be delayed at times. All this had been arranged during the final briefing. I went for a rare drink in the Greyhound pub next door with my father that evening but of course could not tell him what I was really about to do.

Chapter Six - Out of the Frying Pan (or Moonlighting!)

Saturday 15th July 1944; at last all the waiting, all the frustration of not actually doing anything positive about this war, and the damage it had been doing both at home and abroad, was over and perhaps now all that training was going to be worthwhile and be turned in to something real rather than practice.

The team met as arranged and after lunch we had last minute briefings in which we were informed that two SAS Officers would be sharing the aeroplane with us. As they were also jumping 'blind', they would give armed assistance if needed and in return they would require their messages to be relayed for them until they became established.

Late afternoon our equipment was collected for packing at the aerodrome, the team following in a staff car after the evening meal. At the time I only knew that we were travelling to an airfield somewhere in Gloucestershire, only discovering that it was Fairford many years later. The plan was to leave at 22:30hrs the ETA (Estimated Time of Arrival) 01:30hrs.

It was already dark when we arrived. Impossible to see much of the aerodrome, just a small hut in a dim light, where we were introduced to the two SAS officers. No names were exchanged at this time, but we learnt later that they were Capt. Burt (British) and Lt. Poisson (French). It was decided they would jump first as they carried all their equipment with them in leg bags and would be ready to assist if necessary as we followed. The team had already agreed that Pierre should have the honour of being the first to land on home ground, I was to follow, then Valentine, the Major (later he preferred to be known as HAROLD, the team's name). We were introduced to the pilot and the navigator, who told us they had managed to get a 'scratch' crew together, that they were a mixture of nationalities, British, Polish, and Canadian, but were certain they could drop us within a half mile of the DZ (dropping zone) we had chosen. After a last hot drink of tea, we put on our overalls, protective sponge hats and parachutes, and walked out to the plane which was as black as the night. I could only just make out the shape. I was expecting a smaller plane and I had heard that it was a 'Short' Stirling Bomber but this looked enormous. So much for 'Short'! I found out later that this was the name of the manufacturers, not the length of the machine. In addition there was no sign of the moonlight we were expecting.

The engines were idling as we climbed up a ladder and entered the plane through a small doorway. Once on board, in the dim interior, we could see enough to notice not only the size, but the emptiness of this great hulk of a machine. All this for just our small group of five bodies and three tea chest sized panniers containing our kit. No seating, so we just squatted down leaning back on our parachutes against the unpadded insides of the plane. I could see no sign of the hole through which we had been taught to jump, so asked the dispatcher how we were going to get out. 'Through the bomb doors!' he shouted back, above the increasing noise of the engines. Later he explained how we were to exit from this infernal, giant, coffin-like box with wings. We were to line up behind him when called forward, he would attach our static lines (which we would carefully check), and he would then lead us to the edge of the interior bomb doors. The lights would go out before the outer bomb doors were opened. He would go down on one knee and we were to move forward until we reached him. He would tap us on the backside and shout 'Go!' when he got the signal from the pilot, then all we had to do was jump off the edge of the bomb bay. We couldn't talk as the engines roared even louder as the plane took off. Nothing else to do so I just leaned back on my 'chute and tried to relax. It was expected to be a three hour flight, going well out over the Atlantic, to avoid the fighting still going on in the north of France. It wasn't long before I was asleep.

The dispatcher woke us with a mug of hot coffee that he poured out from a flask. 'It won't be long now,' he said, so we added a few drops of brandy from our hip flasks as it was quite chilly in the unheated aircraft. We watched from the rear of the plane as he then pressed some buttons that opened the interior doors of the bomb bay. The doors opened upward from the centre, almost the full length of the fuselage, to the sides. The lights were still on and we could see down into the empty belly of the bomber where its deadly cargo would normally be held. It looked long enough to hold a couple of buses and almost as deep. We took up our positions, hooked up the static lines and waited by the edge of this swimming pool-sized gap. 'The lights will have to go out now,' the dispatcher shouted, 'or they will see us from below.' When the interior lights were switched off, the lower bomb doors were rolled sideways and upwards leaving a great big hole in the bottom of the aeroplane. There had been no windows in the plane for us to see what it was like outside. Now we could see quite clearly, after being in the dark for so long. There was bright moonlight lighting up the ground that we could see passing beneath us. We could distinguish roads, fields, even buildings, some of which had lights showing, totally unexpected as the blackout at home was strictly kept. The red signal light came on and we were all ready for the jump when the green light lit up. Then in quick succession it flicked on and off. Green, GO, Red. Green, GO, Red. Green, GO, Red. The next Green would be mine! I shuffled forward, reached the dispatcher, his hand was on my backside and he pushed as he shouted 'GO!' I was diving almost head first out of the plane, no danger of touching the sides. It was like jumping off a cliff into a great void of silence.

To be more certain of landing close together we had elected to be dropped fairly low to the ground. The minimum height for a safe landing by parachute when using a static line, which is attached to the plane and assists in pulling open the parachute, is about 300 feet. We must have been just over this minimum because we were not very long floating down.

When my 'chute opened, my first surprise was looking down and seeing that I was approaching a roadway with houses each side of it, some with lights on, and street lighting. This was not on the map I thought, this does not seem right, it looks like a village! I landed very quickly in a field on the edge of the village, only just missing what I thought were telephone wires which, I discovered later, were power lines. Had I hit them I would at least have put the lights out before frying! Pierre had come running up to warn me, I'm pleased to say. He had landed further up a slope in the same field, but the Major was not so lucky; he had a hard landing on the road in the village. The plane was now circling above us, waiting for our signal, showing that we were ready to receive our kit and supplies.

We raced up the slope away from the village to get as far away as we could before the plane returned. The plane came over the village again as we shone our torches upward and gave our agreed recognition signal and down came two parachutes instead of three. The first landed neatly a few yards from us, then almost at the same time, the second hit the ground at speed and bounced, with its only partly opened parachute streaming out above it. The third one we had not heard pass overhead, it must have been the first out, and dropped somewhere in the village, but we had no idea where it had landed. We had one trenching tool with us so Pierre and I set about burying our overalls, caps and 'chutes, in a ditch at the edge of the field. There were also the two panniers to collapse and dispose of. One was intact and contained Pierre's rucksack and additional supplies to make up the weight. The second one was badly damaged and, as luck would have it, contained my rucksack and the spare radio receiver. When we had tidied up we joined the Major, who was still searching for the third pannier in the village. We had spent far too much time looking, for our own safety, and I had to remind the Major that, although we had arrived on time, it was now nearly two thirty. He was not best pleased, especially as he knew it was his kit that was missing, but much worse, from my point of view, was the fact that this meant all our wireless equipment was missing. We returned to the field where we had landed. The two SAS men were ready to leave, so we shook hands and they went up the field heading northwards. I asked Pierre where they were going and why they were not staying with us until we reached the woods we were aiming for, after all we were still very vulnerable. He said they had their own mission to get on with and, as it was getting late, couldn't wait with us any longer.

We moved off ourselves, north-west at first, and when clear of the village, south-west, the direction in which we had expected to see the woods. The metal frame of my rucksack, which had been badly damaged in the drop, was bent and the straps holding the bag and frame together were broken on the right side. Not only was it uncomfortable, every time I leant or turned, the 90 pounds of equipment in it swung round to the left almost throwing me to the ground. I had to repair it the best I could with some string but even this kept breaking. I ended up walking and climbing over fences half turned at the waist to the left, with my right shoulder forward just to keep it balanced. We kept to the fields and walked across country, in the general direction in which we expected to find the woods, but had no idea where we were, or how far away. We kept to the hedgerows as much as possible, even seeking higher ground at times, searching for some sign of a wooded area. At first light, I shinned up a tree and used my binoculars to scan the surrounding region. Nothing, not even a small copse where we could hide. It was after five o'clock before we spotted a field of grain, still green, standing up to about our midriff, which might conceal us. Walking around the edge of the field, each of us entering one at a time from a different direction, we lay down near the centre of the field, not together but within talking distance. Exhausted, I lay flat on my back and fell asleep. On waking, I could feel my face burning in the bright sunshine. Shielding my eyes I could see, in the distance, on some higher ground, buildings and people walking about. 'Anyone awake?' I said softly. Pierre answered with, 'Don't move, we will have to stay like this until dark. It's also Sunday and there will be plenty of people out and about all day.' It was very hot, the sun shone down on us all day. We dare not move as a pathway between us and a village ran down one side of the field and we could hear voices as people walked by. Remember, we were in full army uniform, wearing our camouflage smocks and woollen caps, unable to move without drawing attention to ourselves. Hungry, hot and thirsty, not able to eat, drink, smoke or even pee. At least, not until nightfall. The 16th July was a bloody long day! I sucked a pebble to quench my thirst (a tip that I had picked up somewhere). It gets the saliva working, but doesn't stop your belly from rumbling.

When at last it was dark and quiet enough, Pierre, the only one who had brought some civilian clothes with him, managed to change and went off to try and find out exactly where we were. Meanwhile the Major and I checked over the equipment we had between us. The spare radio receiver with my kit was useless. It rattled, all the valves were smashed, and much to my chagrin, Whitty threw it in disgust into a drainage pond in the corner of the field. I had proposed keeping it for possible spare parts. He was in a bad mood, having lost all his kit. He had drunk all his whisky from his hip flask and asked if he could have some of mine. I had not touched my flask which contained brandy (for emergencies), and offered him a drink from my water bottle, and shared an American K ration with him. He claimed my binoculars, saying his need was greater than mine and that, when I think about it, was the last I saw of them. We waited until Pierre returned with the news that we were about 17 kilometres away from where we had hoped to be! Two local men, whom he had contacted, were willing to assist us on our way, and brought with them some bread, cheese and wine.

After a very welcome but quick snack we were at last on the move again. This time Pierre and I did not have to carry our rucksacks as our guides put them on their bicycles, which they pushed along while we followed behind. We walked all night, stopping only occasionally to rest and sip some red wine. Just before daybreak, we reached a farm and were met by two more men, who were to take over for the next stage of our journey. The exchange took place in a large barn, at one end of which was a stack of straw bales from floor to ceiling. Behind these there was a room-sized space in which we were to spend the day and prepare for the next night's march. On arrival, we had been greeted by the farmer with enthusiasm and refreshments. With the three of us, our two guides, plus the next day's two guides, this made quite a party. There was a great deal of hand shaking and men embracing men, in a manner that I was yet to get used to! My French

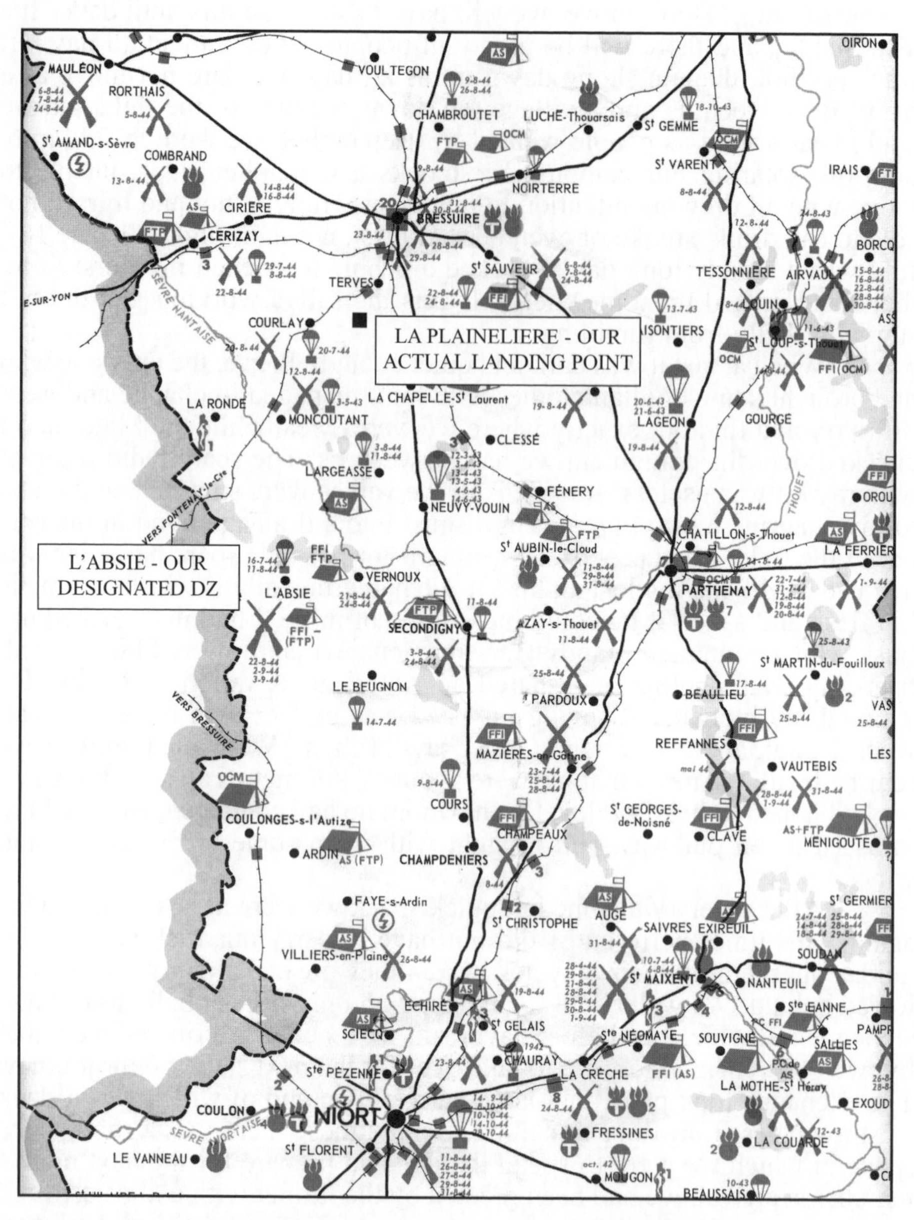

Part of a French map of the Deux-Sevres area showing the actions of the various Resistance groups. Some dates and positions are inaccurate.

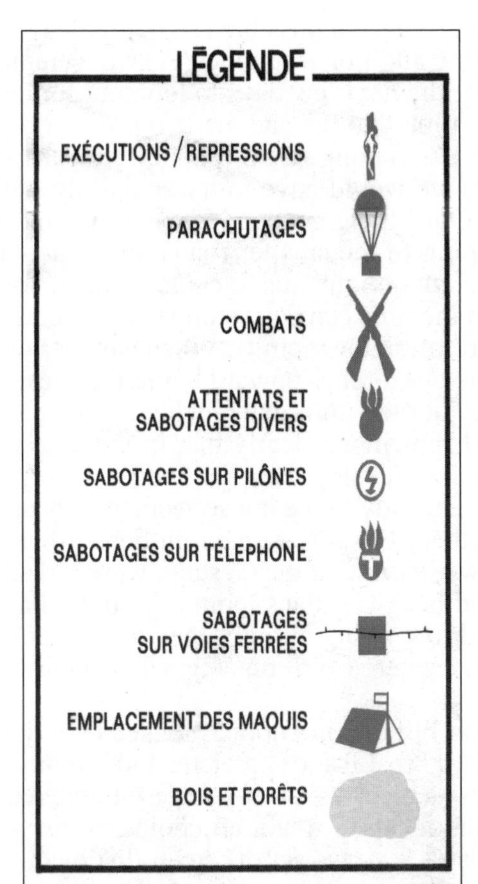

was not good enough to follow much of the conversation, but I accepted gratefully any food that was offered, hard boiled eggs, strange looking and tasting cheeses and hard thin slices of a kind of sausage I had never seen before. All very welcome but I was very thirsty, and not yet used to drinking wine. It certainly did not quench my thirst like a good cup of tea! Standing apart from the others, as I couldn't follow what was being said, I noticed a bottle of clear liquid that was being passed around. Asking Pierre if I could have a drink of the water, he took the bottle away from the others, saying something and indicating towards me. They stopped talking and turned to watch me drink. I guessed something was odd but thought it was a white wine. Being very thirsty I sniffed the contents and, not smelling anything unusual, opened my mouth and filled it with the liquid. As soon as it touched the back of my throat and I tried to gulp it down it felt as though my mouth was on fire. The whole lot came spraying out over the onlookers who were already laughing in anticipation, having been told that I thought it was water. As my French education improved, I learnt that it was a local brew of eau de vie, a raw spirit, and although pleasant when sipped, is not recommended to be drunk in gulped down mouthfuls!

We spent all day Monday 17th hidden in the barn (with a bucket for a toilet) resting, disturbed only when some cattle were brought in that evening. With the arrival of our guides, we learnt that the missing pannier had crash-landed through the roof of a lean-to at the rear of the baker's shop. This explained why we had not been able to see it and we now knew that all the main wireless equipment was beyond repair. Isolated and not able to contact base, we had at least arranged a possible DZ before leaving England, which was supposed to bring additional supplies. As we were not too far from the area, we decided for the next few days to look out for any planes for an hour or so around the time that we had made our own drop, hoping they may come looking for us. Having no 'S' phone (a means of speaking direct to a pilot overhead) we would have to try signalling with torches, two of which we still had. Our little convoy of five and two bikes set off again around 23:00hrs, keeping to the smaller roads, in silence as much as possible. Fortunately the moonlight and clear sky made our enforced march agreeable and when the time came we stopped at a suitable site and waited, listening for any aircraft in the vicinity. Whenever any one heard the sound of a plane, we shone our torches upward but nothing came of our efforts. We continued on our journey until dawn, when we reached a lone house down a narrow lane. I remember clearly that in the lane we passed down were some fruit trees and, leaning over the hedge, managed to pick a few apples that we shared. The lady of the house seemed very agitated and anxious about our being there but was calmed by her husband. The reason became obvious when we learnt that the Gestapo were already looking for us. Apparently there had been Germans lodging in the village where we had landed. Having heard low flying aircraft, they had reported it, and later picked up gossip from elsewhere from someone who had drunk too much wine.

We moved on and were soon billeted in another house. This time we even had a bed as well as a cooked breakfast of omelette and tomatoes. The bread though, as elsewhere, was as black as tar. It was very thick, hard and difficult to swallow but, like the locals, we had no choice but to get used to it. Refreshed after a good day's rest, we set off again that evening for another night's march. Stopping once more in the early hours of the morning, we listened for any sounds of aircraft, hoping that someone may be out looking for us, or indeed the SAS men, who had also expected further contact. As we had not been able to send any signal back to base our hopes were not high, and we heard nothing. At daybreak (19th) we came to a copse which, though not large, was dense enough to give us cover for the day. We slept on and off most of the morning, taking turns to keep watch. In the afternoon we had just finished some of our emergency rations and buried our rubbish when voices were heard. Pierre worked his way towards the sounds and returned with the unwelcome news that a German patrol was on its way towards us. Choosing to split up and hide separately, we went in different directions deeper into the thicker bushes. Not having had much time, we were still very close to one of the pathways through the trees when we heard them talking but, fortunately for us, they were making quite a lot of noise. With my .45 automatic cocked and ready, I found myself in a drainage ditch with some bushes between myself and the path they were walking along. Remembering from my scrumping days that if I kept very still and covered my face I escaped detection, I fervently hoped this tactic would work again. Not daring to move or look up to see what was happening, I could hear, but not understand, what was being said. The footsteps stopped, the talking ceased, then, after what seemed like an age but was probably only minutes, there was talking and laughter again as they moved on. The spot they had chosen to relieve themselves was only a yard or so from where I lay, fortunately well camouflaged! We did not sleep any more that day and were glad to be on the move again that night. Our guides arrived with two men from L'Absie in the late afternoon, one of whom was to stay with us for the last leg of our journey. So far no names had been exchanged between us or our guides, everyone being careful, both sides fully aware that this may be a potential trap being laid by the Germans. After all, there had been an intensive roundup of resistance workers in a large area of the south-west of France since the spring. In addition to our army ID papers we had passes, in French as well as English, signed by Gen. Eisenhower, and Gen. Koenig. We informed our guides of prearranged messages that would be broadcast after the BBC's French news each evening. After much questioning and checking of papers it was agreed that 'Fernand' would take us on, the other, an older gentleman who was referred to as 'Captain', leaving us. As previously, we set off late that evening and reached the forest of L'Absie in the early hours of Thursday the 20th. This was where we should have been, about the same time, the previous Sunday morning!

Chapter Seven - L'Absie - 'Le Bois Des Anglais'

Here we were to learn that the two men we had met the day before were the elderly retired French Captain Michonneau, and a M. Fernand Gougeard, who was an electrician and owner of the local electrical supplies and radio repair shop. Having heard one of 'personal messages' given out by the BBC, *(1. Il a les cheveux longs et frises; 2. Il a le nez droit; 3. Il a une sale gueule),* both were now more relaxed in our company, very pro-British and soon became our firm friends, staying with us and giving every possible assistance the whole time we were in their area. They were an unlikely matched pair, the Captain being very military and of the extreme right politically, excitable, over enthusiastic and perhaps a little eccentric. He worshipped the Major, referring to him as *'Mon Commandant'* or *'Le Major Harold'*. The team's young French Lieutenant was addressed only as 'Pierre' and, as for me, I was *'Le Petit Radio Anglais'*. Fernand, on the other hand, who was inclined towards the opposite end of the political spectrum, treated everybody as an equal, and was very calm and helpfully efficient. The two men treated each other with respect, but were rarely to be seen together and appeared to speak to each other only in the course of mutual business. Their relationship was purely that of France and the resistance movements, coupled with their willingness to assist the team. It was mainly due to the efforts of these two men that the team was able, over the coming weeks, to make contact with the many different leaders of the various underground resistance groups.

On arrival at the Foret de L'Absie, the Captain rejoined us and, having now heard the BBC's identification message, told us that he had a place for us in the smaller woods, just a little to the east, in les Bois de Vernoux which he owned, and he would be honoured to receive the team there. He and Fernand led the way to a clearing in the woods where there was a lorry, in the cab of which was a civilian domestic-type radio which ran off the vehicle's battery. Fernand had been using this to receive the BBC news, which would then be circulated in the adjacent area, taking the battery home for recharging whenever necessary, and aided by a small local group of maquis. It was suggested that we used this clearing as a camp, sheltering in the cab of the open truck in bad weather. This was a little too exposed an area and we chose a place deeper in the brushwood which gave us greater cover from prying eyes. The woods were being used to produce charcoal and along the paths were frequent piles of thin branches and the occasional tall wigwam - shaped stack of wood, with a wisp of smoke curling out of the apex. These were tended by a few workers and the resultant charcoal was not only used for heating and cooking; it was an important product which, when heated in a contraption fixed to cars and lorries, produced a gas which was used as a fuel instead of petrol. To outsiders, the work carried on there gave not only a cover to any visitors, but made it possible to have a small camp fire without the fear of any smoke looking suspicious.

With the help of the owner, a shelter was constructed of branches about seven foot high and roughly eight foot square. The Major and Pierre slept in their sleeping bags under this canopy, and it was used during the day for meals and later for meetings. I chose to go a little further into the brush making my own 'nest' beside a large boulder under low bushes, using my camouflage gas cape as a waterproof cover at night and when raining. For our ablutions and drinking water, there was a spring just a few yards away which kept a small basin-sized hole in the ground full of clear fresh water. Although assured that the water was good for drinking, it was mutually decided that it should be boiled before doing so, particularly after we discovered that we were sharing it with a resident toad! Mr. Toad, who was quite well built, appeared to be reluctant to leave and objected to others helping themselves from his supplies, croaking his disapproval as he watched from a short distance away! The same day as our arrival in the Bois de Vernoux, Fernand presented the Major with his kit that had been salvaged from La Plaineliere, the village where we had landed. Only unbreakable items such as clothing had survived the drop. The radio, however, which was still in its suitcase, was completely smashed and useless.

Still without any contact with base, our immediate task was to get a message back to the UK. The local group leaders wanted confirmation that the team was genuine before approaching, so we asked them to write their own 'personal message' so they could hear it repeated by the BBC, and read out at the end of French news broadcasts. Unable to send the message ourselves, this, and our own request for a new radio, along with the details of a DZ for supplies, had to be conveyed to an area where SAS groups were known to be operating. Two areas were tried, Pierre to the Vendee and Fernand to La Vienne, using bicycles for transport. The message, *'Le roi est au parc bleu'* was selected and not until this was transmitted back by the BBC, giving proof that we were from the UK, did the other resistance group leaders deem it safe to contact us. One more problem arose when we found that the pages of our code books had stuck together!

The code books, about the size of a paperback novel, contained pages of randomly selected letters, in blocks of five letters. Only two identical copies of each set of books are printed; one set for the team, the other held at the home base in the UK. Beneath these blocks of letters the message is written, the two letters one above the other, then transposed by the aid of another chart to produce a third letter, which in turn would be the letter actually transmitted. Other security measures were also contained within the message which could indicate if a message was genuine or sent under pressure by adding or leaving out other special items.

Usually the code books were printed on thin, easily disposed of paper as all the blocks of letters are only used once then destroyed. These are known as 'one time pads'. Most unexpectedly, we found that our books had been produced on photographic paper! When we wanted to use them we found that the dampness of our camp in the woods had caused the sheets of paper to stick together. When we tried to separate the pages, many sections were ruined and useless. None of us knew anything about photography, so I suggested having a word with a local photographer and showed him a couple of ordinary personal polyphotos that I always carried with me in my AB 64, of my sister Valerie and brother David, that were also stuck together. Using these as an example we found out that soaking the prints in water was all that was needed to separate them. This led to the amazing sight, back at the camp site, of pages of code books being dunked in water until they came apart and then laid out in the sun to dry.

It took three days for Pierre and Fernand to return, Fernand being the most successful, having made contact with 'Samuel' (Maj. Maingard SAS) further west of L'Absie. Pierre had more of a problem trying to persuade the *FTP (Francs Tireurs Partisans),* a communist led group of the resistance. They had a radio contact with someone but refused the team permission to use its own quartz and radio frequencies to contact our base, or transmit a message for us on theirs. The *FTP* groups were more numerous and perhaps the most organised of the resistance groups. As time went on they proved to be the most difficult and awkward to deal with. Another large organisation was the *AS (L'Armee Secrete)* which was commanded by ex-military men. Other smaller groups were bound together by their trades or professions, such as railway or post office workers, both of which were important and useful because of their specialist knowledge. The team's task of getting all these under the banner of the *FFI (Forces Francaises de L'Interieur)*, and getting them to accept an overall leader, could not get started until we could prove ourselves trustworthy and having the authority from the UK to do so.

Not that this first week in France had been all action. The team had been kept isolated in the woods, apart from short daily visits from 'Mon Capitaine' as he was addressed by the Major, and less frequently by Fernand. We had used up all of the K rations we had brought with us and were forced to break into escape kit supplies, which contained concentrated compressed cubes of oatmeal and caramel etc, and hard-packed dark chocolate. Being too hard to bite into, it had to be scraped with a knife to make a hot chocolate drink. The K rations contained a packet of five cigarettes and all were reduced to saving our 'dog ends,' our own supplies having rapidly run out. Sachets of dried lemonade powder and coffee were also included, but no tea! Apart from cigarettes, tea was missed the most, especially by us Brits, who were finding it difficult to really quench our thirsts with anything else. Dried spent tea leaves were mixed with 'dog-ends' and ended up being smoked in a pipe.

Remembering tips I had picked up when evacuated, and with nothing much else to do, I cast a hungry eye about for any game. It seemed to be scarce, not even many birds were to be seen. It had been a long war for the locals and they must have been kept very short of food. Even so, I cut and shaped a Y-shaped handle to make a catapult, then showed it to Fernand, explaining with the help of Pierre, that I needed some good strong elastic to complete the weapon. While this was being done (it took a day or two to finish), I got to work on making some snares out of wire and string that I had found in the woods and off the fences. Finally, I had a complete miniature fishing kit which I had brought with me. This contained everything required; hooks, lines, weights and dried bait. All that was needed now was a rod. This was easily cut and made from the plentiful supplies of wood around me. Creeping about, and only possible to hunt in the early morning or late evening, success was limited. Two small fish from the lake in the wood after several attempts and one rabbit a week later!

Pierre, being the one with civilian clothes, was the only team member who could circulate by day. German patrols were far too frequent for the other two of us to risk being seen and we could only venture out at night. This meant long hours during daylight with nothing to do except rest quietly or chat softly about anything we could think of, and this was becoming tedious. During one of these little chats, Whitty confessed to reducing his age to volunteer for this type of mission. He was over forty and thought he would not have been allowed to jump so had knocked a couple of years off his age. He also admitted that he had chosen to team up with two younger members to help reset the balance. Up until this time, Pierre, who was nineteen, thought that he was the youngest. There was nothing left for me to do but to admit that I was still only eighteen, not twenty as they believed, and that I would not even be nineteen until the end of December. All thought it bizarre that SOE had not found out about the deception, (or had they?) and not mentioned it.

A listening watch was set up to monitor all the 'personal messages' at the end of the BBC's French news service, now that our first messages had been sent. It was important the locals received confirmation that the team were who we said we were and had the authority from the Allies to instruct and lead them. We ourselves badly needed supplies of food and equipment as well as a replacement radio. Nothing had been heard by Saturday 21st but, even so, it was decided to organise a reception committee at the DZ given in the message that evening. Very few of the local resistance were eager to assist, still most unwilling to risk betrayal or a German trap. Fernand, Michonneau and two of his forestry workers, however, joined us. They had arrived with a 15 cwt lorry that was powered by gas, produced by the charcoal burning cylinder attached to the vehicle. Parking in a narrow lane, we ran through the procedures with the helpers so that if they heard a plane, they could take up their positions quickly. We then waited, hidden in the trees at the edge of the selected field. Between roughly midnight and 3am, planes were heard but nothing near enough for them to see any signal from the ground. This was repeated on Sunday evening, again without success. Now into our second week, we were feeling frustrated at not being able to make any real progress.

Pierre's English accent was fairly good, and we got on well with each other, spending any idle moments practising my schoolboy French. Obviously with nothing else spoken but French around me, I listened intently and found that I could understand more and more, but was not as yet confident enough to join in any conversation. While Whitty spoke good French, it was obvious he was British from his very strong public school accent. Some people remarked on it or made fun of this and this became more noticeable as more visitors arrived and I listened to their conversations. This made me more determined than ever to learn to speak the language properly and, if possible, without such a strong accent. Making note of any frequently used words or phrases that I didn't understand, I would later ask Pierre for clarification and with the aid of a small dictionary very quickly built up a larger vocabulary. It was still some two or three weeks before I dared join in any conversation. At first, by the time I had, in my mind, translated what was said, and translated my thoughts back into French, the conversation had moved on so far that my replies were out of context! Only after about my third week in France did I start thinking in French. From then on, by listening, repeating and thinking it over and over again in my mind, I not only made rapid progress but was often complimented on my pronunciation. I had, in fact, been learning and improving that which I already knew, in the same way as a young child would learn how to speak. After my first month in France, I found that I could speak the language reasonably well and with the local accent. Writing and reading was a different matter entirely, having not practised this at all!

The biggest improvement the second week brought was an arrangement by which we received an additional supply of food. Michonneau had organised this with a farmer's wife, whose fields were adjacent to the woods. Each day she would place a basket of food at the edge of a field as though it were meant for the farm workers. After they had gone home at the end of the day, I was given the job of slipping out of our hiding place to collect the food and return the empty basket each evening. There was perhaps sufficient food in the basket to make one good meal for one person, but of course this had to be shared by all three. Even at the farms, which could manage a little better than the townsfolk, food was in short supply, particularly bread, which although black, was better than nothing at all. Pierre obtained what he could when out on a bicycle during the day in his civilian clothes, mostly having to pay black market prices for food and cigarettes. Even so, at times he returned empty handed.

Some of the more important people we needed to contact were still reluctant to approach us. There were also numerous small groups from surrounding towns and villages, but having those all visit the woods could attract undue attention to the area. There was a great deal of German movement going on and we could not risk moving about by day in uniform, so it was decided to obtain civilian clothes and identity papers. Having a local Gendarme on our side helped! A photographer was brought into the wood, who hung a cloth on some trees, did his job and produced some passport-type photos. In less than a week the ID cards were produced, complete with new names and a history of being farm workers fleeing from the battles taking place on the north coast. These cost one thousand francs (about five pounds) each, most of which went to the poor soul who risked placing and retrieving them, among others, on the German Commandant's desk. Pierre purchased 'blues', working clothes as worn by the locals, for us two, and also passed on to me a pair of brown cord trousers and a light blue and white shirt, which he had brought with him from England. Whitty, being rather large and wishing to look smarter and create a good impression, chose to have a suit made; being a farm labourer perhaps did not appeal to him! The tailor was a neighbour of Michonneau. At about the same time, Whitty also obtained a corset, to ease the pains in his lower back which he had been complaining of since landing heavily on the roadway in the La Plaineliere. Bicycles, too, had been obtained through the efforts of 'Mon Capitaine', making it at least possible to get about during the day. The German patrols were frequent and they were nervous because of increasing attacks on them by various small resistance groups and the French section of the SAS, who were very active in the surrounding areas. It would have been impossible and extremely foolhardy for us to circulate in daylight wearing a uniform without being spotted.

We were beginning to feel isolated and desperate, the lack of response to our messages requesting replacement radio, food and equipment from base was worrying, and there were no means of knowing if the messages were being received in the UK. This showed mostly in the changing moods of Whitty at times. When only the three of us were together, he would stomp around like a caged animal, cursing all and sundry, blaming everyone else for all our problems. This could swiftly alter to being all sweetness and charm on the appearance of a visitor, and even more so, if a bottle of something stronger than water was presented. Having drunk his fill meant a peaceful end to a day, but he'd be more 'liverish' than ever the next morning. The long periods of having absolutely nothing to do, the need to be constantly quiet yet alert were having, at times, a serious effect on our leader. He was a large man and when frustrated he became more like a school bully, the complete opposite of the team spirit that he had shown during training. This did not go down well with Pierre and myself and often led to serious rows.

One such early argument that I remember well, was when he had said, 'As you have no wireless, you can take over my washing and cleaning my equipment for me.' To which the reply was, 'I'll clean and take care of your firearms if you can't. You might need them, to defend me, but I'm not your bloody batman, Sir! If I wanted to be one, I wouldn't be here now!' Whitty blew up, saying, 'If I give you an order, you will obey, or I'll have you court martialled when we get back home!' Pierre got between us as I was replying, with 'You've got to get there first! The way you're carrying on, you're not likely to make it!' Pierre managed to calm things down by changing the subject. Later that same day, Whitty put his arm around my shoulders and said to me, during a discussion on the merits of getting married early or later in life, 'If you wait until you're at least twenty-eight, my son, before marrying, I'll come to your wedding!' He had of course, had a few glasses of wine by then!

By the end of the team's second week in France, the Allied forces in Cherbourg were still being held back by fierce defensive fighting by the Germans, with both sides reinforcing their troops. This was probably one good reason for the lack of response to our calls for assistance. At least three more messages had been dispatched, carried by brave young students on racing bicycles, who attracted little attention from the occupying forces, cycling being a well known hobby of young French boys. They also enjoyed practising their English with me and I, in turn, improved my French. Alas, no replies were received, although Michonneau claimed that he had heard a BBC announcement among the 'personal messages' after the French news, 'Message for HAROLD, have patience, we have not forgotten you.' As no one else had heard it, we were not certain if he had said this just to cheer us up. Cheer us up? He did indeed, by organising a magnificent Sunday lunch with his and Fernand's family. We all sat down to eat in a cabin by the lake in the woods, wearing of course, our civilian clothes in case of curious passers by. Another first, so many different courses, some unknown till then, and dishes of unusual flavours to taste. After the meagre diet over the past two weeks, it seemed my stomach had shrunk; I regretfully had to leave some food untouched.

Entering into our third week, the hours of inactive frustration were eased a little by more frequent visits from both large and small active resistance groups, and also some potential political leaders preparing to take over as soon as the occupying troops were driven out. Having learned of our presence, some were obviously vying for recognition or favours, the need for urgent supplies of arms and ammunition being the priority of the active members. Important information was being gathered by the team, mainly by listening to the complaints of our visitors about other groups. The *AS* for example had had no arms passed on to them from the *FTP* who were known to have received parachuted supplies via *'Samuel'* group and from the well supplied *FTP* sources of la Vienne. It was suspected that they were storing items instead of using them, possibly for their own use at a time that they thought fit to do so. It was also suggested that they were aiming to take over the moment the Germans departed and before a new French government replaced them. We listened but were careful not to be drawn into taking sides in these political matters, although we did decide to check that any future supplies were fairly distributed. The SAS officers, Burt and Poisson, also made short stops in passing but brought little or no information or supplies with them apart from saying that their group was expanding to the north of the team. Burt was unwell and had to be taken care of by Fernand's wife in L'Absie for a few days until he could rejoin his group in the Bois d'Anjou. Two other fairly frequent visitors to our camp were the local jovial Gendarme, who could be relied upon to pacify any curious Germans, and who would arrive with at least one good thing to eat, usually obtained via the black market. The other was the local vicar, who always announced himself by saying 'I've brought you a bottle of red wine.' He also carried with him his own glass, and after measuring out a small glassfull into our mugs, he sat chatting to us until he had finished the rest of the wine in the bottle by himself!

With the increase in mobility, by courtesy of the bicycles and sometimes a car powered by a gas-producing cylinder attached to the rear luggage rack, we were now also able to meet some other interested parties who were still wary of being seen with us. Still unable to give definite proof of being genuine and in contact with the UK, it was, nevertheless, a time to educate ourselves about the strengths of both political and military possibilities. Trips out of the woods, though risky, were at least a welcome change of scenery and a chance of a decent meal.

One such trip out to a nearby village, an invitation to lunch and an opportunity to meet one of the area's potential political leaders, along with a couple of active resistance men, sounded like a very good idea. A good meal for a change, uppermost in all our minds! We still existed on the meagre rations of the one basket of food left for us by the farmer's wife each evening, supplemented by occasional gifts from our two stalwart friends, Le Capitaine and Fernand. We set off in two cars, dressed in civilian clothes, our American carbines out of sight in the boot and .45 semi automatics under our clothes. The journey was uneventful and pleasant. On arriving at our destination the cars were driven into a garage and the doors closed behind us. It was decided to leave the carbines in the cars and keep only our .45s with us. Whitty had his tucked into his belt behind his back, Pierre and I had ours under our jackets. After walking a short distance, there, around a corner, was a small but rather pleasant café restaurant. On entering we were introduced to the others and the group, now consisting of eight persons, was seated, four each side of a long table. I was beginning to understand French meal times better now. They seemed to go on for ages, with many small dishes of food interspaced by long pauses for talking and drinking. Warned beforehand that I was not to say anything, as my French was not yet good enough, I kept quiet and tried to follow the conversation, which rapidly became faster and louder, and increasingly incomprehensible. Seated at the end of the table, next to the entrance with my back to a wall, I had a good view of the whole establishment and mentally worked out quick exits, just in case it became a necessity.

The aperitifs and first course over, a long pause followed for more loud chatter, interrupted only by the entrance of four German soldiers. They walked past with just a glance and a nodded acknowledgement towards the group and sat down at the other side of the café. The French, who must have been used to this after their four years of occupation, kept the conversation going with hardly a break, and it wasn't long before the German presence was being ignored. Partway through, the next courses, a meat dish with plenty of sauce which required mopping up with bread, was served and with eyes only for the food and my need for more bread, I watched as it disappeared around the table and ended up at the far end. Pierre and Whitty were sitting further along in the centre of the table opposite me and, having failed several times to attract their attention amid the loud laughter and chatter, when at last I caught Pierre's eye, I said out loud, in English, 'Can you pass the bread please?' It was as though the whole world had stopped talking at the same time. I suddenly realised where I was and what I had called out! The silence was deafening and seemed to go on forever. Whitty's hand moved round to the back of his trousers towards his .45, Pierre glared at me but quickly replied in French, and the conversation carried on. My hand was also moving towards my .45 as I looked towards the Germans, but I was relieved to see that they had not noticed my *faux pas* and were still eating and talking amongst themselves. Thus I lived to dine another day!

Other daytime excursions in civilian clothes during this third week, where we were made to choose and select several possible DZ's, with the assistance of a mobilised unit. This was not without the risk of running into German patrols en route. On two occasions we had to open fire and shoot our way out of trouble to avoid capture, one near Parthenay, the other close to Bressuire. These had to be quick hit-and-run defensive actions before the enemy had time to react because of the shortage of ammunition.

As further proof of the authenticity of the team it was decided that we should demonstrate our capabilities by using some of the 808 plastic explosive we had brought with us. The target chosen, by an arrangement with one of the active groups, was to be the water tower and pump near St.Maixent railway station. Pierre and I prepared the charges in the presence of the group, who had produced a rough sketch of the target, and instructed them at the same time. They wanted Pierre to set the explosives and pencil timers and Pierre asked me to go with him to watch his back, whilst Whitty remained with the rest of the group keeping watch outside the station. On the night of the 2nd/3rd August the approach was made across some fields. There did not appear to be any guards and the access to the target was fairly easy. Entry, too, was not difficult via a partly open window. We took our time, making sure that all was absolutely perfect, knowing all too well that we were being tested ourselves. Everyone was well clear of the site before the first charge blew 30 minutes later. There were no casualties and damage was reported to be considerable.

Two days later, with another group, we cut the railway line running between Niort and Poitiers and derailed a train carrying German troops. The selected target area was where the railway line curved and crossed a roadway. There was high ground to one side of the track, with trees and bushes, giving good cover and sighting for the attack party. The other side of the track was flatter with more open country and little cover. Using 'fog signals' as detonators, the charges were set to blow about 100 yards before the curve, on the inside rail, so that the train would tip over on the bend. It went even better than planned with the train tipping over on its side ripping up a long stretch of rail and ending up spread across both track and roadway. As the engine and some of the coaches that had toppled slowly over settled, some of the Germans clambered out and were greeted by short bursts of automatic fire from sten guns and a few well-aimed rifle shots. Before the enemy could retaliate, and again because of our shortage of ammunition, we dispersed rapidly, hampered briefly by having to cross a stream, part of the Sevre Niortaise River, and getting very wet. We learned later that German casualties were 11 dead and 35 wounded and that the line was unusable for several days.

Without any radio contact and little to do, we rested for the rest of the day and night back in our camp, only to be awakened early in the morning by the barking of dogs. At first we thought it was just the dogs of a nearby farm, but it persisted and seemed to get louder. Pierre and I worked our way through the brushwood to the edge of the woods and could plainly see in the surrounding fields German soldiers, some with dogs, spread out but in sight of each other, all around the forest. Not surprising really as there had been other attacks by various groups, including the SAS in the area, and the occupying troops were getting more agitated with their own movements endangered. Slipping quickly and silently back, we broke camp and cleared all traces of occupation, burying and hiding anything we could not carry, and split up to hide in our own pre-selected places. My choice was to climb up into one of the few tall trees, having first urinated around the base, hoping to confuse any curious dogs. With any luck they would pick up the scent and leave their own to cover mine. This was a trick I had heard of somewhere, probably Beccles, in my poaching days. We were unable to get out of the wood and had to lie low all day. We found out later that the German troops had surrounded the whole of the forest of L'Absie and the [1]Bois de Vernoux, entering from the western side and combing the woods, searching for any signs of the maquis. By night fall they had covered the largest of the two forest areas, up to the road dividing L'Absie from Vernoux. Finding nothing suspect they abandoned their search. Luckily our hideout in the smaller Bois de Vernoux was left untouched, but we would have to find a new place quickly as a return to continue the search could happen at any time. Having to lie quiet all day with no chance of escape was not funny. Whitty found it difficult to handle and spent most of the next 24 hours pacing up and down like a caged tiger, blaming all and sundry for everything and anything he could think of. Pierre and I kept out of his way as much as possible until his mood, and at times, quite vicious temper subsided.

A temporary shelter was offered away from the woods and closer to the nearby farm that had been supplying our evening meals. The accommodation, though, consisted of sharing one section of two brick built huts. Linking them was a roof covering some rabbit hutches, the other hut housing chickens. Just about large enough for the three of us to live in, complete with animated alarm clocks! The concrete floor was a lot harder to sleep on but at least it was drier. The charming elderly lady owner had been forced to accommodate Germans at the farm in the past, where they had even built a small rifle range. She had treated them with civility and they, in turn, had been respectful to her so it was considered to be reasonably safe from suspicion, at least for a short time. There was also a distinct improvement in the rations now that the lady realised how short of supplies we were and how many there were of us to feed.

Chapter Eight - Hot Times in the Hen House

On Monday the 7th August, just over three weeks since our arrival, a complete new set of wireless equipment was received. It had been dropped with supplies to the SAS, who brought it from some forty miles away. Regretfully nothing else we had been requesting, such as rucksacks, food, ammunition and explosives were delivered. Nevertheless a day to remember after such a long wait. All three of us, accompanied by Fernand, were grinning from ear to ear as we walked along an upward sloping path, which led from our 'chicken-run homestead', passing some trees on the left to a place at the top of small hillock. A well placed 30ft tree stood on the brow begging to be selected for the honour of supporting the aerial. A length of string, tied to a piece of wood as a weight, was thrown up and over one of the branches. The other end, attached to the aerial wire, was then pulled up and backward from the tree, into a position where it pointed towards the UK. This was done by the aid of a compass. A second wire was placed along the ground beneath the aerial as needed, to act as a counterpoise for the transmitter. The wires were connected to the radio and we were ready for our first signals to be sent and messages to be received. The power for the receiver was obtained from a small dry battery. For the transmitter, a hand generator mounted on a small tripod was used. This had to be turned at a steady speed and, by watching the meter, kept an even as possible 200 volts flowing to the set. This job was to be shared between Pierre and Fernand

This was a testing time for me as we sat on the grass under the tree looking like picnickers out for the day. I was praying that this was going to work. The possibility of it failing was not worth considering; there were no spare parts anyway! I checked my schedule for the umpteenth time, running the call signs again and again through my mind, then, looking at my wristwatch, wondered if it had stopped. Base should come up on air at 16:00hrs GMT. Already tuned in, the last few minutes went on for ever. Then suddenly I heard 'da dit dit, da da, da dit da dit' - D, M, and C continuously repeated. Base's call sign coming in so loud I had to quickly reduce the volume before cutting in with my reply, CKT - 'da dit da dit, da dit da, da'. After the opening procedures, my first message was sent and I started to receive their reply. It started well, with Whitty, Pierre and Fernand crowding round to listen and watch as I wrote down the random blocks of five letters as they were sent. Part way through, I was forced to cut in and halt the process, asking base to wait until I called them back. What had happened was this. The three onlookers had kept interrupting, with 'That was a D', or 'He wrote down P. I'm sure it was an A, he's getting it wrong!' and so on. I tried at first to ignore their comments, but it finally broke my concentration and I had to stop. To say I blew my top would be putting it mildly! 'Will you all please be quiet! Until I'm finished. If you think you can do better, it's yours. You can take over! Or you can let me get on with my job and I'll explain something you know nothing about later!'

Taken aback by my outburst, they urged me to carry on. Nothing more was said until after the set was packed away and we had returned to the shelter. I then explained my actions to them, saying, 'When receiving Morse code at speed, you are listening to one letter being signalled while still writing one or two of the previous ones that you're holding in mind. If watching closely, you will notice that the person receiving will still be writing even two, three or more letters after the signals have stopped. In a similar way, as when taking down dictation, you can only write down the words after you have heard them, while still listening to what is being said. Knowing some Morse, it was easy for you to recognise the odd letter being sent while I was still writing down previous ones but what you did was dangerous for us all. I was on the air much longer than necessary. Don't forget that one of the 19 DF stations in this region could pick us up within five minutes, ten and they could be on their way knowing our exact position!' Apologies were expressed, accepted, and from then on the radio sessions were conducted in complete silence, although not always without at least some cheeky banter beforehand.

At last I was in business, with two-way schedules to keep twice a day and a broadcast to listen to each night for incoming messages only. All the messages had to be coded or decoded of course, keeping me very busy. Quite a relief after the long hours of boredom and inaction during the past few weeks! For the rest of the week there was a burst of activity on all fronts. The news coming in from Normandy had improved, with Allied breakthroughs out of Cherbourg reported in several places. It would not be long before a general uprising of all underground forces would be called for. The political infighting locally had not yet been settled and urgent meetings between the maquis and the team were called. Messages were sent requesting arms and equipment for them and supplies for us. It was also obvious that the area of both Deux Sevres and the Vendee counties was too large for us alone, with the many local resistance groups getting larger all the time. Deux Sevres was keeping us fully occupied and we requested the assistance of another team for the Vendee region.

At one particular meeting between the *AS* and *FTP* leaders with Major Whitty in the chair, aiming to get them and other smaller groups all under the banner of the *FFI* and to elect a common leader, long and vicious arguments developed over the unwillingness to share arms and equipment by the *FTP*. They had received plenty from various sources but the *AS* had none, or very little, passed on to them. The *FTP* was also adamant that they wanted to keep control of their own members. The leading players were Col Edmond Proust *(alias Chaumette)* of the more disciplined *AS*, and Maurice Robin *(alias Major Michel)* of the larger *FTP*. It ended with Major Whitty losing patience with them all and banging his fists on the table in a rage, declaring firstly, that all future supplies would be controlled by him and the Jed team, and only they would decide who received a share and secondly, that if the *FTP* did not accept Col Chaumette as the combined head under the banner of the *FFI* he would stop any further supplies reaching them full stop! It certainly brought the meeting to a close, the *FTP* reluctantly accepting, and their Major storming off like a mad bull! The team then sent a message to Gen. Koenig in London with its recommendations, the reply back from him agreed, saying that '*Chaumette* was our (French) friend.'

It was the 11th August before we received our first successful drop of supplies with arms, money and equipment. More military items, like gas capes, bandages and uniforms, than automatic weapons, such as Bren guns and ammo, were received, but the drop was overall very welcome. The operation went off fairly smoothly apart from an early incident when I recall spotting a group of four or five men around a container open on the ground where it had landed. I pointed them out to Whitty who was supervising the loading of equipment onto lorries. He told me to go over and stop them and make sure the contents remained intact. Running across the field I called out to them in my best French (which had by now improved a great deal) to put back the items they were sorting over, close the container and carry it over to where the vehicles were standing. At first they made out they didn't understand me, and after I had insisted, they complained that it was too heavy to carry. Not to be outdone, I tipped the container up on its end and managed to balance it on my left shoulder. No sooner was it up there that I realised I had grossly underestimated the weight of the confounded thing. Determined to show them that it was not too heavy for one person, let alone two or more of them, and not wanting to lose face, I walked off with the full container back across the field to the lorry, regretting every step. I don't know how much that container weighed but I do know that I could, at that time, easily run while carrying a 15-stone man on my back! All in all, a very pleasing and successful night in which we had, at last, been able to prove our worth, and the first of many more drops to come.

An attempt on the 15th August to receive more parachuted supplies and another team of Jeds ended in failure. When we were en route to the dropping zone with the reception committee, we unfortunately ran into a German convoy very close by. Not knowing if this was accidental or if the enemy were acting on information received, the exercise was cancelled, but not before a great deal of firing was exchanged on both sides. Luckily, there were no casualties among the group and, although we didn't wait to find out, we heard later that the Germans had suffered several killed and many more injured.

There was still a great deal of movement by enemy troops, usually in small convoys because of the frequency of attack from resistance groups. Great care had to be taken because they were still numerous enough to take very drastic retaliation measures against the local population. Between the 8th and 15th August there had been an increasing number of actions. The Germans made a large attack on one of the SAS groups in the Bois d'Anjou, where Lt Poisson was wounded. Underground groups ambushed a German convoy near Parthenay destroying 8 vehicles and killing thirty of the occupying troops. Another smaller convoy was stopped on its way to Poitiers by felled trees and shot at from the side of the roadway. We were also by now being recognised for who and what we were and wore uniforms most of the time, only donning civilian clothes if circulating during the daytime locally, or near the camp site.

The next parachute drop was expected on the night of the 17/18th August, bringing in Jed team TONY to assist in developing the Vendee area. This time the reception committee set off in smaller groups and joined up at the dropping zone between 23:00hrs and midnight. Lookouts were posted at the surrounding road junctions. The actual DZ site was conveniently screened by trees and a wood. The arrival had been confirmed by a BBC 'personal' message after the French news broadcast earlier that day, saying *'Message pour Harold. Trois amis pour vous ce soir, nous disons trois fois'*. This indicated that we should expect three persons and three planes that night. The first plane arrived at about 01:30hrs. I gave the pre-arranged recognition signal to the plane with a torch light while others placed around the field shone theirs steadily upwards to indicate the size and shape of the ground. The plane banked and came in on its first run and dropped the three parachutists who were rather slow in exiting, making their landing too well spread out. Two of them landed in the field, the third overshot and came down on the other side of some trees. They regrouped together and centred on me in the middle of the dropping zone. I passed them over to two of the young maquisards who escorted them to Whitty waiting by the lorries, ready for loading. Only two of their panniers, containing personal equipment, were found immediately, the other one turned up about half an hour later. Two other planes followed the first approximately 15 minutes later. They made one run each, dropping, in all, over two tons of supplies. Everything was over and cleared away by about 02:15hrs. The new team was introduced to a resistance group leader from Parthenay, who would be escorting them to contacts in the Vendee region. They then departed after making arrangements to meet up with Pierre the following day. As for us, we were now having to change camp more frequently because of constant pressure and searches made by the occupying forces and were not, at that time, even sure of where we would be staying the next day or two.

The order for a general uprising of all resistance groups had begun between the 13th and 15th August in France. The Allies had at last broken out of their beachhead in Normandy and a second successful landing of Allied troops was made in Provence on the 15th August. The occupying troops were regrouping, with some moving away north and east, others pulling back to the west coast. They were not at ease and as dangerous as cornered rats.

I had my two schedules each day for sending and/or receiving messages, and the broadcast messages at night for receiving only. Between times, there was the coding and decoding to be done, all of which was, at times, keeping me well occupied. Any spare time I had was spent instructing in the use and maintenance of arms and explosives, whenever new, usually younger, people arrived to join the maquis groups.

Our stalwart companion Fernand, from L'Absie, being an electrician, had produced a transformer he had adapted for use with the wireless set. This made it possible for me to work alone whenever I used the set in premises with an electricity supply thus eliminating the need to have someone crank the hand generator and act as lookout. It allowed me to get on my bicycle or go off by car away from the campsite and transmit from different areas each day. This had the added advantage of making it more difficult for direction finding vehicles to pinpoint my position, keeping them on the move and therefore more visible. Being on the air for five minutes was enough to get a fix on the sender and in ten minutes they could be well on their way to reaching the transmitting point. This also freed the two other team members to travel about the region visiting the various smaller resistance groups, who by now were being absorbed gradually into the *AS* or *FTP*, both of which were now operating under the command of Col Proust as members of the *FFI*. Col Proust was, at about this time, eager to reform the 114th Regiment that had been based at St Maixent L'Ecole prior to the occupation, and was anxious to reclaim the barracks as soon as possible.

Facilitated by the increase of available transport, due to the ever frequent actions in the *Departement* de Deux-Sevres by armed groups, and the capture of fuel as well as arms and ammunition from the enemy, we were often now working separately, Whitty at meetings with senior military men and politicians, Pierre visiting active groups and me dealing with all communications and some arms training. All-in-all things were going fairly well. We were not getting under each other's feet and were kept busy. Even Whitty's moods had improved, except when he failed to get his own way over something or was feeling liverish after a heavy night away. Pierre and I had by now worked out that he was better left alone and ignored when these occasions arose, and that all would be forgotten later when he would be his old friendly self again.

On one of my excursions away from the camp to transmit my radio messages in a room in small hotel, I was sitting in the bar having a quiet drink while waiting for transmission time. I was approached by a young man, who introduced himself by saying 'Do you remember me?' It was only when I noticed that the man had one leg shorter than the other, and wore a thicker-soled boot on one foot to enable him to walk properly, that I recalled where I had seen him before. It was in London, when we were both staying in the SOE hotel during my final briefing! Although we had not spoken to each other at that time, only having a brief nodding acquaintance, we were soon chatting away like old friends. André (probably not his real name) was a Belgian who worked alone for the French section of SOE and had been in and out of France several times before. He was staying at this hotel at the moment, only recently arrived back in France. Transported sometimes by aeroplane, this last time he had parachuted in. He said it hadn't gone too well and he had landed in a river. We had some lunch together and as we went up to our rooms, André invited me into his, saying 'Here is something you must see!' All round and across his room, hanging up to dry and looking like Christmas decorations, were brightly coloured French bank notes!

Messages were often carried between the team by young students on bicycles and it was often several days before all three of us were together for mutual exchange of news and discussions about the progress being made. It was as yet impossible to organise a large group of maquis and arm and train them together in the same area. There were no forests large enough in the *departement* for this type of operation. Therefore small attacks were made throughout the region causing a great deal of disruption to the occupying forces and a serious interruption of their free passage, except by large convoy, and even these were always in danger of a surprise hit and run attack, or a delay by road block and controlled explosive devices. The occupying troops were by no means impotent, quick to return fire and to attack towns and villages in retribution. Fortunately casualties were a great deal fewer in number for the local people than for the enemy. This was to be the pattern until after the end of August and the retreat of all the German forces in the *departement* by the 6th September '44.

Through an agent of the French section of SOE we had received information about ten train movements of goods and troops. These were due to move out of La Rochelle for Poitiers soon after the 20th August. This news was rapidly passed on to groups further south of the *departement* who cut the line in five places and destroyed a large crane, the only one big enough in the area to raise a locomotive. One train was derailed and it took three days to clear the line. London was also informed for possible air attack. Though we were not directly involved in this instance, on the 24th /25th another train was derailed by our action at Parthenay. This time it was done by jamming the points instead of using explosives. The Germans were in the process of moving troops and material from one of their supply dumps southward, possibly to La Rochelle which still had a large garrison. Some lorries were still laden and these were driven away by a group from Parthenay. This was combined with a raid on a supply dump and the resultant very welcome appropriation of approximately 40 tons of food!

During the sixth week after our arrival in France, from the 19th - 25th August, there were over thirty incidents in the Deux Sevres *Departement* of various sizes, where small groups of the *FFI* attacked, destroyed or captured vehicles from the occupying troops. Many prisoners were taken and far more casualties suffered by the Germans than by the maquisards. The following week there were another twenty-five casualties for the enemy. Among the occupying troops there were many other nationalities - Italian, Russian, African and Indian, all with German, usually 'SS' officers in command. Some of these had travelled northward from the south-west coastal towns, such as Bordeaux and were making their way without supplies, north-eastward, staying south of the Loire valley hoping, no doubt, to reach the retreating German army south of Paris before the Allies from Normandy arrived together with those heading northward up the Rhone valley from the south of France. The whole of the Massif Central and southwest of France had been left to the underground Free French Forces to clear by themselves aided by, of course, SOE/OSS/Jedburgh teams and the French section of SAS.

Several actions took place between the 21st and 24th August, very close to our main base at L'Absie. There were several skirmishes, notably at Vernoux, where the team had an HQ in the woods, and the nearby 'homestead' with the chickens and at Secondigny, where there was a long established mobilised group that even had at one time, a camp for German prisoners. In Vernoux, 3 Germans were killed when a vehicle was destroyed and, on another occasion, 80 Germans in 8 vehicles were attacked, with 7 killed, and 1 *FFI* wounded. At L'Absie a vehicle carrying ammunition was destroyed and 4 enemy killed. This vehicle happened to be an ambulance displaying a red cross! The perpetrators were an unknown renegade group from another area. Not surprisingly, this attracted a reprisal. A large convoy of mixed-race occupation troops arrived the following day to collect the dead and hunt for those responsible. They started to round up anyone who happened to be out on the streets and knocked on doors of houses around the town square, making plenty of noise and firing bursts from machine guns. They separated the men from the women and children, and roughly questioned them, demanding to know who was responsible for the outrage. Some were clubbed with rifle butts or kicked if they were not moving or answering quickly enough, and they threatened to shoot all the inhabitants and burn the town if answers were not forthcoming.

Fortunately for L'Absie, when the German commander arrived, he was met by the chief of the Gendarmes. They knew each other, and he was able to persuade the German that, as he well knew, there are no resistance workers here and the Germans had never had any worries when stationed here. He had just about managed to convince the commander that it was not any of the local inhabitants, when shots were heard. A car containing two *FFI* had driven into the town. The driver was killed and the other young man managed to evade capture by running away and jumping over fences. In answer to the question 'What's this then?' and waving the *FFI* armband taken off the dead man, the Gendarme pointed out that it was stamped on the underside 'Vienne,' evidence that the dead man was not a local but from a group in Vienne, another county, outside of this department. Presenting him with the name of a non-existent, as it happened, group at last convinced the German and they withdrew, taking their dead with them. On hearing explosions and shots from our hideout at the farm, we entered the town by a side road to find out what was going on and arrived just in time to see the troops withdraw. Not that we could do very much against such a large force of around a hundred men, other than inform the mobile group at nearby Secondigny. When we met up with the dear old Captain Michonneau he was not too pleased that we had exposed ourselves to danger on the town's behalf. Relief and smiles, however, soon returned after a few glasses of wine!

Not knowing if this was the last we would hear of this episode, it was decided to move our HQ. If a more thorough search of the area was made we could have been discovered. We were transferred by car to another farm which was a fairly large place, reasonably remote with more than one entrance to provide an easy exit if required. The farmhouse itself was a large rambling, yet comfortable, one-storey building. We were greeted with open arms by the farmer and his wife and treated to a feast of farmhouse food before being shown around the property and grounds to get our bearings. The evening ended with our being conducted to our own bedrooms. Luxury indeed! And this was not all; the beds had to be seen to be believed! The comfort and style of a French farmhouse bed has to be experienced to realise its full potential. Getting into and sleeping in it is an art in itself. I took one look at the bed and thought, at last, a real comfortable bed to sleep in. A positive treat after the last six weeks of damp ground or hard floor in a sleeping bag!

The double sized bed had a well-made hardwood frame curved at the head and foot and decorated with carved scrolls. The base rested just an inch or two off the ground, and on it there were three mattresses surmounted with an eiderdown. It looked so inviting and irresistible, but actually getting into it proved to be a different story! The bottom mattress was packed with straw, quite firm and about one foot deep. On top of this there were two more very soft mattresses, both filled with feathers and both at least twelve inches thick. Not counting the eiderdown cover, which was also quite substantial, this meant that the side of the bed was over three feet off the ground. Being filled with feathers meant that when one sat on the edge of the bed, it just flattened down almost to the straw mattress at the bed's edge, while behind and on each side of the sitter, the feathers puffed up to wrap round the body like a cocoon. After several attempts I decided the best way to get into the bed was to take a flying leap into the centre, throwing myself flat on my back. I pulled the eiderdown over me and there

I lay, with the heavier parts of my body sinking deeper than the rest. My head was lower than my feet, which had sunk just a little into the feathered mass, and my backside was the deepest, almost down to the straw mattress. The rest of my body curved upwards, with my outstretched arms resting lightly on the top to maintain some sort of balance. I had to stay in this boat-shaped position otherwise, when trying to turn on to one side or the other, the soft feather bedding just came up and wrapped itself around my face. Talk about sleeping on a cloud! Nevertheless, it was very warm and comfortable and I did have very good night's sleep.

Breakfast the next morning, sitting outside in the sun, was a delight. A large bowl of drinkable coffee, even though it was a substitute, freshly baked (almost white) bread; none of that black stuff here! Home made butter, cheese and pate. The farmer joined us, but having been up and working earlier, he chose to drink a glass of red wine instead of coffee. It seemed like the start of a good stay. All good things come to an end though, sometimes a lot faster than we expect or hope!

As we stood up from the table and started to stretch our legs, a car was heard, fortunately before it was seen, driving up from the main entrance. The pathway curved round passing the front of the house, then carried on to another exit in the opposite direction. We scrambled quickly to get our firearms and took up defensive positions. When the vehicle got closer we could see that it was a black French Renault car with guns pointing out of the front and side windows. As it pulled up in front of the house we kept it covered, not knowing or expecting visitors. It could have been Vichy police, or deserters from the mixed-race troops among the occupying forces who had been badly treated by their German officers, or as was now happening, isolated German troops trying to escape capture. Raiding lone farms was their only hope of getting supplies.

Four noisy youths leaned out of the windowless car saying they had come to join us. Pierre, who was nearest to them, ran up to the car and pointed his .45 at the driver's head and read him the riot act. I know he swore and re-baptised them. Those were not only some of the first words in French that I had learnt but a few new ones as well! These over-enthusiastic idiots had driven like this for some distance and passed more than one village in doing so. By now, someone could be following them. Pierre made them turn round and leave in a hurry, while all we could do was pack up and leave ASAP. The farmer was trying to console his poor wife, who was in tears as we departed hoping that we were wrong and the youths had not been followed. Whitty was, of course, puce, though not exactly speechless, and remained in a filthy temper for the rest of the day. In less than thirty minutes we had repacked and driven away en route to our camp with the chickens. As we glanced back, only a short while after leaving, I could see smoke rising from a building a mile or two behind us. We got out of the car to look, as it seemed to be in the direction of the farm. 'We had better keep going,' said Whitty. Nothing more was said until we reached our destination.

There was not much space for the three of us to lie down back at the chicken run, and no time to think about this last episode. Messages had been received that a large drop of supplies was due that night 26/27th August, so we would not need our beds very much anyway. Passing on the information and arranging for sufficient transport to be available kept us well occupied. We were expecting 8 plane loads, approximately 8 tons of ammunition and other military equipment, all of which had to be quickly dispersed. The *AS* and *FTP* were working closer together and wearing FFI insignia more frequently and, with their numbers increasing daily, the overall plan of creating a new military unit under the command of Col. Proust, to be based at St. Maixent as soon as it was cleared of Germans, was now foreseeable in the very near future. Most units were desperate for supplies of arms and ammunition and this drop was awaited with great anticipation. Political and civilian affairs were also well in hand and covert plans had been in progress for some time, the main participants being a M. Pineau and M. Hudeley, both of whom had visited us in the Bois de Vernoux. They had authority granted to them by the Free French government in North Africa and were preparing to take over on the collapse of the Vichy regime. The drop was arranged to be spread over two DZs; one to the north and the other in the southern areas of the *departement*. This was very successful except that, yet again, the supplies sent contained a surfeit of equipment and bandages when it was arms, ammunition and motor fuel that was required. The recipients, as you can guess, were not too pleased. However it would not be long before the new military force could be formed with companies of ex-*AS* and *FTP* resistance men, with their own officers leading them.

The enemy were well aware of the many drops now taking place but were unable to stop them, being dominated by the Allied push eastward in the north and upward from the south of France. Their garrisons along the Atlantic coast were standing firm and there were signs of remnants in the region packing to join them, no doubt with orders to make a stand. Those still remaining were concentrated more in the larger towns for their own safety but were still very dangerous and mobile. Attacks on the enemy were now a daily occurrence and spread over the whole of the *departement* of Deux Sevres. These ranged from some quite large conflicts resulting in as many as fifty of the enemy killed and around a hundred wounded, to firing on isolated vehicles. Fortunately casualties among the FFI remained very light with hit and run tactics. Many of the towns left with only a skeleton force in occupation were targeted and the enemy driven out, captured or killed. Niort, the county town, after daily attacks on men and vehicles, was taken by the *FFI* on the 28th for a short time before it was retaken by a German force coming from the Poitiers area. The *FFI*, having too few arms or ammunition, had to withdraw.

At the end of August, Captain Burt of the SAS rejoined us at the farm in Vernoux. This time he appeared to be very ill. We were already short of space in our chicken-run accommodation and had some difficulty making room for him. On top of this, he was moaning and groaning all the time, frequently perspiring, and with his whole body trembling. He insisted that he was all right and did not want to see a doctor.

Whitty became more agitated by the day as he could not sleep properly with everyone so close together, and he was not enjoying the hard floor either. During the day he stomped around cursing everyone and everything. His ever changing moods were a constant annoyance to both Pierre and me, and trying to avoid conflict with him was at times impossible. Heated verbal exchanges became a common occurrence when either one or the other was dragged into an argument with him. He could switch from being a charming, even fawning, person in the presence of people he wanted to influence, to being thoroughly obnoxious to others at the drop of a hat.

I remember the date well because of what happened on the 1st September. Whitty had written and transposed a message on his own, which was something he sometimes did, probably because he wanted to keep its contents secret or not discuss it with either of us. Pierre and I would just ignore this with a shrug of the shoulders, putting it down to his eccentricity. Normally he would gladly let anyone else do the work rather than have to do it himself. When it became time to transmit the message an argument ensued over the correct time of the next transmission. I told him that the last one was at 08:00hrs and the next at 16:00hrs. 'Rubbish!' he exclaimed. 'Those were the times yesterday, how can that be correct? The times change daily!' I endeavoured to explain to him that the times of transmission were according to whether or not it was an odd or even date and that the day before being the 31st August and this being the 1st meant both were 'odd days' but he angrily interrupted with a stream of abuse, adding as he had done so on other occasions that he would have me Court Martialled if I refused to obey him. He stormed off up the slope to an area that I had used on previous occasions, ordering me and Pierre to follow him. Pierre indicated to me by putting a finger to his lips and shrugging his shoulders, to say no more and we followed with the wireless equipment. I was seething with anger as we fell in behind him. I'd had enough of his abuse and was convinced he was acting in a manner dangerous to the whole team. In a rage I pulled out my .45 colt, cocking it automatically and was about to point it at the centre of his back, when Pierre placed his arm on my wrist and whispered in my ear, 'No, not now, this is not the time or the place. You will not get away with it!' I don't know if I could or would have done so. At least, not in the back, I thought, as we followed him. Of course we could not make radio contact until the correct time, and Whitty went off grumbling to himself, leaving us two to wait until it was time for our connection to be made. Neither of us mentioned this episode ever again.

The following day we were woken by the sound of a few isolated shots being fired. They appeared to be coming from the direction of L'Absie. Pierre went off to scout out the cause of the firing, while the rest of us started to break camp and cache the wireless and other equipment in the nearby woods. Pierre returned with the news that an unknown number of Germans had entered L'Absie. They had erected road blocks on all roads leading into the town and were arresting anyone entering or leaving.

Being well aware of what had happened in Oradour-sur-Glane, we were concerned that L'Absie might suffer a similar fate as this not too distant town to the south-east, in Haute-Vienne. A similar blockage of all roads had culminated in the complete destruction of the town and the death of almost all of the inhabitants. With this in mind, the camp was cleared of all signs of our presence and any heavy gear was hidden in pre-prepared places in the woods, leaving us light and ready to flee with only our personal weapons to hand. There was though, one problem. What to do about the sick SAS Capt. Burt?

Whitty was very agitated by now and showing signs of panic, and apart from throwing orders about to anyone within reach, did very little more than pace up and down getting more and more red in the face. He sent Pierre off towards Secondigny to contact the mobile unit of the maquis. Fernand, who was in the process of making arrangements for Burt to be looked after in his own home by his wife, had planned to move him that very evening. He could only be moved at night for obvious reasons. Meanwhile, Whitty gave me the unenviable task of having 'to take care of him'.

Although fully dressed, Burt was wrapped in a blanket, hardly able to stand and was shaking so much that he stumbled as he tried to walk. By then we expected the arrival of the enemy at anytime, with one of their road blocks only a short distance from the lane leading to our hideaway. I had no previous experience of witnessing anyone with such an illness or fever and was beginning to think the poor man was losing his nerve or suffering from a form of shell shock. Capt. Burt was frequently making quite a lot of noise with his gasps and groans, as I escorted him to a hiding place I had chosen. This was amongst a fairly large pile of timber, cut from the woods and stacked to dry, with space enough in the centre for the two of us. Major Whitty, by now in a near panic, ordered me to keep him quiet, saying, 'I don't want you captured because of him. Leave him if you have to. If the Boche get him, you know what they will do to him, so shut him up!' When I queried as to how this should be done, he answered, saying, 'You've got a knife, haven't you, so shut him up for good!'

He was referring to an incident that had happened in the same *departement*, just a few miles north of our position where a large group of about three dozen SAS, on an operation against a German garrison, were finally forced to surrender when out of ammunition and surrounded by over 400 men. After interrogation by the SS and the Gestapo at Poitiers, thirty bodies had later been found buried in a forest. Although the Germans had reported them as 'killed in action,' all had been shot in the head. The team were already aware of a standing order, supposedly issued by Hitler, that all parachutists in or out of uniform were terrorists and should be shot.

From where we were hidden, by a path at the edge of the woods, I had a clear view each way with a possible exit at the rear. I knew that I was a good shot and had every intention and was fully prepared to keep anyone at bay for as long as possible. A little anxious but strangely calm and having no intention of carrying out Whitty's orders, I found myself thinking that if anyone deserved to be removed, it was Whitty himself. I had lost all respect for him and his bombastic moods. With nothing left to do but keep alert and a close eye on Capt. Burt, I wondered what had changed Major Whitty. He seemed at times to be a totally different person to the one he had been back in Peterborough. The pressures over the past seven weeks seemed to have been too much of a burden for him to bear. No longer calm, friendly and helpful, he'd changed into a domineering bully-boy. We had been hiding there for a long time and Capt. Burt was now asleep and perspiring profusely, but at least he was quiet, most of the time.

A week ago it had been Cerizay just 25 kms north of L'Absie that had been attacked and bombed with mortar fire in retaliation to resistance activity a few days previously. They had burnt down and destroyed a large part of the town after shooting several hostages. The nearby village of Montravers also suffered at the same time. During some random shooting of anything that moved, a woman and her daughter were killed in the morning. That same afternoon a German convoy ran into a small SAS led group of *FFI,* which resulted in the death of a German and an SAS man being wounded. He was found the next day, his head crushed, either by boot or rifle butt. Several hostages were taken, four of whom were shot. There were clear signs now of the Germans moving across the region in several directions, and they were being harassed whenever possible. Their retaliation was usually swift and brutal.

No Allied troops had ventured south of the Loire. After breaking out of the Cherbourg peninsula they had pushed on eastward to Paris and with the advance up the Rhone valley from the south of France racing to join them, large numbers of any remaining enemy troops in the centre and west of France were being cut off. Their movements seemed to indicate that they had received orders to hold out in large pockets along the Atlantic coast. Short of supplies, they were angry and dangerous on being attacked by the *FFI* who were now intent on liberating their own country. Supplies to the resistance had been coming in by infrequent air drops and arms and ammunition were still in short supply.

Nevertheless, conditions had improved for the team recently. Over the past few weeks we had been existing on irregular meals, grace of whoever's company we had been in. The small amount of food supplied by the local farmhouse in the evenings was barely enough for the three of us and, at times, it had to be shared with others. Whitty had said that he did not want the locals to know that we could not survive without their help, and he was reluctant, thinking it too risky, to deal with the black market. We had been reduced at times to nibbling survival food from the emergency and escape packs we had brought with us, and these were as good as finished. My hunting and fishing skills were useless as there was certainly a lack of any game to catch in France. Nothing like those days in Suffolk where poaching could sustain an army! However, food was becoming more readily available and of better variety and, for over a week now, American cigarettes had been obtainable from the black market. Even tea, which had been greatly missed, had appeared once or twice. Tea that had been stored away, we had been told, for the day the English returned. It was easy to believe, too, as it had a musty smell and tasted of mildew!

All these thoughts of food made me feel hungry and realising it was well past midday, and hearing what I thought were voices, decided to investigate. I ventured out of my hiding place, quietly edging towards the sounds I had heard. On reaching our hideout at the 'chicken run' I discovered Whitty holding court with Pierre and two or three others. Chest puffed out, belly pulled in, a stance that he used when trying to impress an audience, there he was, enjoying some bread and cheese, with a bottle of red wine in his hand. 'Oh, there you are,' said he. 'I wondered when you would turn up!' I helped myself to some of the bread and cheese, and broke up a small piece of bread into my mess can and then soaked it in milk. 'What are you doing with that?' asked Whitty. 'Capt. Burt must eat something, even if he is only partly conscious,' I replied. Whitty came back with, 'Oh, he's still with us, then?' Pierre butted in and said to me, 'I'll come back with you to see him.' It did cross my mind to wonder whether Whitty would have thought to send some sustenance to me and my charge if I hadn't turned up at that moment.

On our way back into the woods, Pierre brought me up to date about what had been going on in L'Absie. Apparently the group of Germans had again started to block the roads in and out of the town and rounding up anyone they came across in the streets, firing at intervals more for effect than anything else. Our friendly Gendarme once again talked them out of taking any action, and also warned them that there were rumours of large groups of armed and well organised men from surrounding areas not far off. Not being well armed or numerous themselves, the Germans packed up and departed just before Pierre had arrived with the mobile group of maquis from Secondigny! It was thought likely that the larger garrisons of Germans were now withdrawing towards La Rochelle, and that the danger was now only with smaller groups trying to join them to make a stand there. They were short of supplies but still very dangerous. We intended to move again that night to avoid any further threat to L'Absie, which had proved to be so helpful to us. Fernand had agreed to take care of Capt. Burt, and his wife would look after him until his fever had passed. Between us we managed to persuade Burt to eat a little of the bread and milk, then carried him back to the camp and made him a little more comfortable, although he was only semi- conscious and probably knew very little of what had happened to him that day. That was not all, because soon after dark Fernand arrived with a hand cart. Poor old Capt. Burt was laid on rugs, covered with more rugs and topped off with a layer of twigs and firewood. He was at least quieter now and sleeping, as Fernand, Pierre and I pushed and pulled the cart all the way into the town. We carried him into Fernand's house and his wife took over the job of helping him to recover. A very brave woman, as discovery would have meant certain death. I heard later that he did recover and had carried on operating in the area, but I have never met him since that day.

Whitty was asleep, but at least packed and ready to leave when Pierre and I got back from town. By the early hours of the morning we were on our way, this time in the direction of the garrison town of St. Maixent-L'Ecole. I was driving, Pierre navigating, and Whitty fast asleep in the back of the car. Arriving at dawn outside a small school in the outskirts of the town, we were installed on the first floor above the class rooms. The school was closed, as it was still the summer holidays. The effect of the lack of sleep over the past week or so and the intensified activity had occasioned us to use certain tablets from our escape kits. One set of these was Benzedrine capable of keeping a person awake for an additional 8 hours if required, but when the effects wore off it was almost impossible to stay awake. We had both taken some the evening before and were the first into our sleeping bags. It was well into the afternoon before we were awoken by Whitty demanding if we intended to stay there all day!

After setting up the wireless set, using the mains electricity supply for power, and tuning in to my afternoon schedule, I was finished for the rest of the day. The following day I met a young student who was to be our runner at this new location. As he used a racing bicycle to travel around when delivering messages, he usually wore full racing cyclist clothes, creating the impression that he was just out for a practice run. He spoke a little English, so we spent spare moments practising and improving our bilingual skills, and strolling in the grounds of the school. Meanwhile Whitty, who had somehow come into possession of what looked like a 'Sunbeam Talbot' open-topped touring car, went out visiting with Pierre. When I enquired how he had come by the car he sidestepped the question by just saying, 'Rather nice, don't you think? You're not driving it, but I'll take you for a spin if you wish!' He was at least in a better mood than he had been of late. That same evening all three of us did go off in the car. It was to visit a retired high ranking naval gentleman who had invited us to a meal. We arrived at a double-gated house, drove up the drive and parked the car inside one of a pair of garages.

After being introduced to our host and the other guests we were entertained with a sumptuous meal that lasted for several hours. The talk was mostly about the retreating German occupation troops and planning for the takeover of the principal towns of Deux Sevres by the already well organised civil authorities. The main German garrison troops had apparently pulled out, all indications being that they were heading towards La Rochelle, with only a few administrative troops remaining to operate essential services. Not knowing whether the troops would be returning or be replaced, the local *FFI*, still very short of arms and ammunition, were uncertain when it would be safest for the resistance to move in and officially take over the towns. The more important news that reached us was that Team TONY, which had been brought in to assist Team HAROLD in the La Vendee area, had received supplies by sea near Les Sables-d'Olonne, a much needed share of which was destined for us. Pierre and I would have the honour of going off to collect it. Transport had been organised by a M. Brivin, who had already assisted on other occasions when supplies had been dropped in by parachute. This excursion to the coast, although not a holiday trip, went off without any problems, travelling there one night, and returning the next. The stores had already been unloaded and stored in a warehouse.

Chapter Nine - The Sixth of September 1944

This was the day chosen for the liberation of Niort, the county town of the Deux Sevres after nearly 4 years of enemy occupation; an occasion that was to be imprinted forever in the minds of everyone there on that long awaited day. It was decided that we would present ourselves in uniform, dressed as smartly as possible, without wearing our parachutist's camouflaged smocks, and unarmed. We did not want to impose our presence or appear as a replacement of the recently departed Germans. This was to be a day for the many resistance workers, a long awaited opportunity to allow them to show themselves and receive acknowledgement for their years of defiance and sacrifice for their country. It would give back respect, both to them and their country. Nevertheless, I felt naked without any firearms at all, so decided to keep my .45 semi automatic tucked in the inside pocket of my battledress blouse.

We were driven into the town, along with some others, in a couple of closed cars. There were already many people lining the streets when we arrived at the town's reclaimed barracks, to take up a position in a convoy of vehicles and marching men. We moved off around midday ready to parade around the town, first stopping at the Town Hall for the introduction and installation of the new civil authorities. Then off we went again to where all were to congregate in the centre of the town, on the Place de la Breche and around its very large square. Colonel Chaumette, chief of the newly formed *FFI* and the new civilian authorities, was to take the salute. A mobile group of the *FFI*, some of whom I had worked with, spotted me at the Town Hall and approached Pierre and Whitty. They pleaded with them to allow me to travel with them on their vehicle. Whitty turned to me and suggested that I would be better off with them than standing around with him and the other officers. He looked pleased at the opportunity to get rid of me, I thought. He was already standing among other officers with his chest puffed out and belly held in, full of his own importance and, naturally, me being 'only a sergeant', I had to be kept in my place! He stepped between me and anyone who approached to speak directly to me. I think he was jealous of the attention I was getting. My French pronunciation was by now better than his, even though my vocabulary and grammar were still limited. I know this may sound big headed, but I had lost all the respect that I had previously held for him prior to our arrival in France.

Joining the men on their vehicle was an honour and a pleasant surprise. Marc Bignoneau and his wife Lily, who was a Scot, were the first to welcome me aboard. Marc, who sold cheese and other dairy produce in the town's market, had earlier lost the top of one of his fingers. Climbing into a truck, his Sten gun had fired off a round accidentally; his finger was over the end of the barrel when he put the gun down a little too heavily! Lily hailed from Motherwell, had two teenage children, and had been living in the area since before the war. She promptly promoted herself to the non-existent post of official interpreter. I was placed on the top of the driver's cab, between him and an English speaking Lieutenant, who was the local pharmacist, together with a captured heavy machine gun. Very convenient for holding on to! The rear of the truck was packed tight with the rest of this group of *FFI*, not all of whom were French. Some were other nationals driven into this area by the war, several of them being Polish. The vehicle was one of several captured from the enemy, others from the groups of *FFI* from the surrounding areas. The leading vehicle, with me on board, moved off and was positioned towards the front of the parade behind some of the marching men. One of the of the following vehicles contained six German prisoners who had been rounded up that very morning at Mauze, 25 kms south-east of Niort. Three of the *FFI* group involved had been injured in the skirmish which was quickly terminated.

Bands playing, we proceeded out along the roadway, steadily at first, singing 'The March of the Partisans'. There was a roar of approval from the crowds lining both sides of the street. Cheers, laughter and tears. Flags of all the Allies accompanied the French Tricolour, many sporting La Croix de Lorraine. Some had survived the war, waiting for such a day; others had been hastily made from any available material, as was the bunting, hung from anything that could be reached. Progress along the route was slowed by the eager crowds and the parade was frequently brought to a halt. Whenever they could the joyous people pressed forward even more, wanting to shake hands and embrace as many of the men they could reach. This became even more enthusiastic whenever the *FFI* officer sitting beside me introduced me by shouting back to the crowds, 'This is the first

English parachutist!' They reached up to touch me, many trying to get me to come down and join them. Others sent up scraps of paper to be autographed, bottles or glasses of wine were passed around and anything else they could lay their hands on as gifts. Some of the young ladies pressed their visiting cards into my hand after I had signed one and passed it back, begging me to write or contact them. Many managed to find a way to get up close enough to embrace me and I was in constant danger of being dragged down amongst groups of over enthusiastic females! They had to be discouraged by a great deal of good natured humour. Others wanted me to address the crowd and were asking questions, which I managed to answer with the help of my companions. The whole experience was overwhelming and highly emotional. I had never experienced such an enthusiastic occasion or been made so welcome before in my life.

German soldiers in Niort 6th September - keeping very close together. They were keenly aware that it wouldn't take much for them to be carted away and summarily shot.

By 2 o'clock we had finally reached the town square and we formed up in front of the invited V.I.P's., representing both the military and civilian authorities. The space between us was left for a march past of the *FFI* groups and what was to become the companies of newly-formed 114th

Regiment of the French army. To a roar of approval, the band started to play 'La Marseillaise', followed by the British and American National Anthems, which were also treated with due respect and applause. After the presentation of the new administration to the public, the march past, in honour of the resistance, commenced. To the strains of 'The March of the Partisans' and the loud acclaim of the populace, these men who, by necessity, had been operating for many years under cover and unknown to most of the population, were at last being acknowledged. There were, of course, sceptics, who would remark that many had only appeared now that the enemy had departed, conveniently forgetting that those who had survived were those who had managed to keep their activities secret. Aiding and abetting any covert action had been punishable by death, usually after torture, and would also bring widespread reprisals to their families. The risks that these 'Soldiers without Uniform' took, through their own choice, were enormous, greater than that of any other military man.

(Left) Lily, who was married to Marc Bignoneau, standing between Tom Henney (right - see page 140) and Harry

(Below) Liberation parade - La Place de la Brèche, Niort - September 1944.
Harry is on top of the vehicle to the left of the flag

After the grand parade on the Place de la Breche, the convoy of vehicles and men dispersed throughout the town, gradually splitting up into separate smaller sections. By now I had more than a few problems on my mind. I had to get back to the rest of the team and had no idea where they were; there would be code work waiting to be done, no doubt reporting on the day's activities. I'd missed the 13:00hrs schedule and the next at 15:30hrs was rapidly approaching. Most urgent of all was the fact that if I did not soon answer a call of nature, I would be in a rather embarrassing situation! Getting down from my position on the vehicle would still be risky, surrounded as it was by over eager females still trying to grab hold of me. Making my most urgent problem known to my companions, we at last pulled up outside a bar and they cleared a path for me to run in. Reaching the toilet was like running the gauntlet, but I just made it in time, but not without being smothered by well meaning kisses from ladies of all ages! Looking in the mirror, I saw that my face was covered in lipstick and had to give it a good wash before returning. I must have been kissed by every girl in town I thought. All but one, though. Who was that girl with a bicycle, who had kept appearing in front of the truck every time it was brought to a halt? Mme Bignoneau had kept calling her forward, wanting her to climb up to greet me, but she had always declined.

There were a few nasty incidents on the return journey when the vehicle stopped to prevent some hotheads as they attempted to attack small shopkeepers, using it as an excuse to damage or loot property. I was forced to draw my .45 and show it to them before they backed down. They had been accusing the shopkeepers of collaboration with the occupying forces, without knowing the whole truth. Often they had been given no choice, and were frequently a very good source of information to the underground units.

(Left) Cigarettes and flowers, riding in the liberation parade

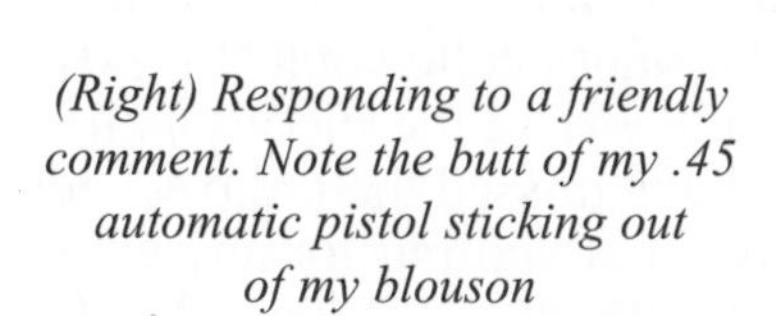

(Right) Responding to a friendly comment. Note the butt of my .45 automatic pistol sticking out of my blouson

Colonel Chaumette (nom de guerre) - real name Proust - accepted leader of the FFI, talking to Major VE Whitty

When at last the vehicle got back to the Town Hall, it was greeted by a very red-faced and angry Major Whitty. He was standing, hands on hips, among a group of military officers and civilian officials who were all quite pleasant, except Whitty, of course. The Major called out, 'Come here, you!' pointing at me, and then he bellowed, 'Where the bloody hell have you been? I've been waiting for you! You have missed the radio schedule! You should have got back here earlier!' Without waiting for any explanation, he carried on with one of his favourite threats. 'I'll have you Court Martialled when we get back home!' I tried several times to point out that it was he who had sent me off with the mobile unit and that I had no other earlier opportunity in which to return. Pierre and Col Chaumette tried to calm him down but he was in no mood to listen to anyone. He had obviously drunk far too much. Pierre came to the rescue once again, saying, 'You know what he is like by now, forget it. Tomorrow he will have forgotten all about it!' There is a lot of truth in the old saying, '...after the Lord Mayor's show, there always follows a dust cart!'

We returned to our accommodation in separate cars, and there were no messages for us when I tuned in to the nightly broadcasts that evening. The next day, the 7th September, there were to be further celebrations and parades in St. Maixent l'Ecole, the home town of Col Chaumette. It was also the home of the ex-training school for the Gendarmerie. It had been taken over by the *FFI* although not yet in use as barracks. For reasons only known by him at that time, Whitty had kept this information to himself. It was to the empty barracks that Pierre and I were sent to work, early in the morning by Major Whitty. There were messages to be coded and transmitted and any which we received were to be decoded and ready for him when he returned. The first schedule was between 08:00 and 09:00hrs, the next in the afternoon from 16:00 until 16:30hrs. There was no electricity at these empty barracks; we were the only persons there. No food either, although there was at least some water available. Fortunately Fernand had chosen to go with us and it was he and Pierre who took it in turns to crank the handle on the generator. This supplied the necessary power for the wireless set and Fernand also went out shopping for some refreshments. It was only when he returned with something to eat and a bottle of wine, did we realise what was really going on in the town. So this was Whitty's revenge! Or was he disappointed at not being the centre of attention the previous day? He'd certainly made sure that we were occupied elsewhere, completely unaware of this second liberation parade.

Informed that we would be changing our address yet again, we spent the next morning clearing up and packing. We had lodged in so many different places since our arrival in France and experienced so many varying and degrees of comfort and discomfort. The next billet, however, was to be a surprise that we could never have dreamed of in a million years. We drove away in our two cars, guided by another vehicle. Within a half an hour we had reached Niort and drove through the centre of the town, passing La Place de la Breche, down the road by the Post Office to La Place du Roulage. In front of us stood a mansion with double wrought iron gates, and a porter's lodge with garages at the side of the entrance. Most amazing and unexpected of all was the very large colourful banner, over the full width of the gates, complete with the French Tricolour and the British Union Jacks flying at each end. The wording on the banner in very large letters, read, 'ETAT MAJOR BRITANNIQUE.' This was to be our residence and General Headquarters, from this day on.

Chapter Ten - Place de Roulage

Approaching the main entrance we were greeted by a butler who welcomed us warmly, then introduced us to the lady housekeeper/cook. These two very efficient and charming people were charged with looking after us and taking care of the running of the house during our 'sojourn' in Niort. Entering by the double doors at the front of the house, just off the entrance hall on the right was the kitchen, and on the left, a stairway led to a bathroom which was on the mezzanine floor. The bedrooms, with their own washing facilities and toilets, covered the floor above. Doors at the end of the entrance hall led into a very large reception room and lounge. The dining room was on the right with a door connecting it to the kitchen. Each member of the team had their own bedroom with a double bed. The long windows opened out onto a balcony overlooking the garden, which had a striking collection of statues between it and the house. Certainly first class and very comfortable accommodation.

It did not take very long for us to install ourselves, travelling light as we were now in the habit of doing. My room was on the far right corner, looking out over the rear garden, and just a few yards away and a little taller than my window, was a tree. Just the right height for the antenna, I decided. With my wireless installed and connected to the mains, thanks to Fernand, who had supplied me with a transformer, I was now completely independent. No need to pack everything away each time it was used. With a chair and a table too - what comfort at last! This would certainly help to speed up the ciphering as well as the ease of transmitting and receiving. It would also be possible to listen in to the night time broadcasts without getting out of bed; if there were no messages for me, I could just switch off the lights and go back to sleep!

Seeking out the butler, my first request was about the bath. Did it work, and if so, when could I use it? Having received confirmation that it did, and that I could make use of it whenever I wished, it was not long before I was lying back in the tub, having a good long soak in hot water for the first time since leaving London! It was wonderful; time to relax, time to day-dream, after two long months of washing and shaving in cold water, more often as not, in the woods using water from the small spring that had served not only us, but also the local wildlife. There was soap too. This had been in short supply lately. This was heavenly, and even more so when I was asked if I had any clothes that needed washing! Or was that a gentle hint?

Team HAROLD - Lt Pierre Jolliet (nom de guerre - Rimbaut - code name Tyrone) Maj. Valentine Whitty (Ross) and Sgt Harry Verlander (Sligo)

Dinner that evening set the pattern for meals whenever the Major was in attendance. He was now playing the part of Lord of the Manor, as he strutted around, chest puffed out, stomach held in, a stance we had so often seen before whenever he was out to impress anyone. A role that suited him down to the ground. Now there were servants he could talk down to who would obey him without question. He ordered that those dining with him should not be seated until he had taken his place at the head of the table. Set times were given for all meals; any late arrivals after him would also not be tolerated! 'The Germans could not have done it better,' remarked Pierre, when he and I were alone after dinner, and we agreed that playing along with him and his funny little ways was the only way to make living with him bearable. True to type, he was indeed, often pleasant and friendly again. There was now of course, less immediate pressure or threat from the enemy locally. Breakfast was at 8a.m and it just had to happen! I woke late, dashed downstairs, to find the others already there. 'Sergeant, you are two minutes late, make sure it doesn't happen again!' 'Sorry Sir,' was the reply. 'I just didn't wake up early enough.' 'Well make sure you do in future!' And that was all! I had a word with the butler after breakfast and arranged for an early morning call. 'Certainly, sir,' had been the reply. 'I will bring Monsieur a cup of coffee also if you wish, it will be our secret.' I'd made a new friend! Can't fool butlers for long; they don't say much, but observe all that's going on.

L'Absie on Liberation Day - Harry standing far right

Over the next few days we were kept busy with the planning of two more drops of arms and equipment, in different areas, on the night of 10/11th September. There were also several visits to a small aerodrome close to Niort, which had to be cleared and made ready to receive all further supplies. Getting aeroplanes to land would certainly increase the supply of equipment needed to contain the large numbers of enemy troops now ensconced in pockets along the Atlantic coast. There was also still a great deal of training to be done in reshaping the former various resistance groups. More normal military activities now required them to contain the German remnants that had been observed building defences and laying mines in the region of La Rochelle. Running the new HQ soon settled into a reasonable routine. There was a variety of meetings, some just social, others to discuss more serious matters, with civilian officials as well as military personnel. Occasional visits were also paid by rather well dressed and elegant ladies. These were treated with tact and, later, with amusement by the Major. He would enlighten me after they had departed by explaining that it had been another invitation for us to visit their homes and dine with them. The reason being, having been obliged to accommodate German officers, by having them billeted in their homes, they were eager to demonstrate to the local populace that they had not been collaborators and, to prove it, were now accepted by the British. It was impossible to sort the truth from the fiction, so excuses had to be made to avoid any further scandal. One such, rather large, lady, sporting many rings and much jewellery as well as a fur coat, was very insistent with the Major. After several polite rebuffs, she suggested that he allow his sergeant to take his place, adding that she had a daughter who was about the same age and she was sure that they would be compatible. Fortunately she did not speak English, so he was able to warn me before he replied, giving his regrets that I was far too busy at the moment and would contact her when work permitted me to do so. Satisfied at last, she handed me her card after writing the young girl's name on it and added that perhaps I would be able to help her daughter with her English!

Among the first visitors who called on us were some of the people who lived in Niort and had frequently assisted us. Marc Bignoneau, the cheese merchant, and his wife Lily, whom I had met at the Liberation parade, arrived with gifts of cheeses and butter and an invitation to a celebration on the 11th September, of Paul Huvelin, a pastry maker, and his wife Andrées' 10th wedding anniversary. These people, and other commercial tradesmen such as M. Brivin of 'Transports Brivin' and Raymond Thimer, a wine merchant, had eased much of the resistance problems of supply and mobility. Having to continue working and trading under the occupation, their passive resistance produced much of the intelligence required to combat them. Only I went to the anniversary party, which took place at a village hall in the outskirts of Niort, starting in the afternoon and carrying on until the late evening. It commenced with an aperitif then a sit down meal. The drinking and eating of various dishes went on throughout the rest of the day, interspersed by music and dancing and even at one time, a stroll around the village with the first female company I'd had for a long time. A very enjoyable outing for me indeed!

Now that there was no need to constantly seek out a different safe transmission site, I obviously had more spare time. The bicycle I had used back in the L'Absie area had been left there, but here at Niort I was presented with a real parachutist's bicycle! It had been dropped with supplies some time ago, but was useless because it was so unlike a civilian bicycle. The main frame was almost oval in shape, it could be folded in two, and as no brakes showed on the handlebars, it was necessary to back pedal the machine in order to control it. With no mudguards and painted khaki, its origins were to say the least, glaringly obvious, but now it was going to be put to good use around town. Before long, however, I was found other jobs to do. My infantry training was put to good use and this consisted of instructing some of the men in the care and use of the arms and equipment being supplied. They were then going on to teach others in the companies that were now being formed into the new 114th Regiment. Part of the training consisted of showing them how to quickly strip down, clean and reassemble the arms. Pierre, meanwhile, had been allowed to go off to visit his family, who lived further south near Cognac. He had managed to pass messages to them earlier, but this was the first time he could be spared. That area had been cleared of Germans who had been pushed back into another pocket around Royon.

Harry, Tom Henney and Wally Adams - Niort September 1944

There were several pockets holding large groups of Germans stretched out along the west coast of the Bay of Biscay, between St. Nazaire and Royon, and they appeared to be centring on the two main areas of Royon and La Rochelle. Apparently they had been ordered not to surrender, but they still had to be contained and prevented from breaking out or raiding the nearby farms for stores. The lightly armed *FFI*, increasingly mobile, could do little more than keep a close watch on them. From their thinly spread lines messages would be passed back to the mobile units, which enabled them to converge on any nearby area and rapidly attack any sortie made by the enemy. Plans were put forward for additional help to be sent. Men and materials were needed to assist with the clearance of mines and to help mop up these groups. Air drops had dried up and very few Dakotas were now arriving at the airport at Niort. They were probably busy elsewhere, after all the Allies were still fully occupied in the north and east of France and Belgium. Information was received through Team TONY, who were operating in Les Sables-D'Olonne area and were in touch with the American forces in Brittany. Further aid was requested from them and also from the UK via the sea routes successfully used earlier. Heavier arms such as artillery and anti tank guns as well as machine guns were also needed for the new 114th French regiment, now enlarged and developed.

Socially, things were rapidly improving. Free periods enabled me to wander off into the town. At first I made little progress as I was frequently stopped when recognised by the locals who, wishing to personally welcome me, showed their appreciation by shaking hands, offering drinks and cigarettes and issuing invitations to visit them. Young girls pressed visiting cards into my hands, giggling as they ran off, hoping no doubt that I would get in touch sometime later. Older ladies, often wanting to embrace me in the middle of the street, I found rather embarrassing, but even worse was the men wanting to do the same! Gradually as I became a more frequent sight in the town it became easier to circulate with only a wave of recognition as I passed by.

To visit Marc and his wife Lily meant walking right through the town past the market square and down along the river bank, through riverside gardens to reach the home they shared with their two teenaged children. I spent a great deal of time with them, not least for the reasons that it was a relief to hear and speak English again, and to be sure of a decent cup of tea. I helped Marc make new wine from the grapes grown in his own garden, and taste the freshly pressed grape juice. On another occasion we went fishing in a small rowing boat further down the river. After trying but not having much luck with our fishing lines, and not wishing to return home empty-handed, Marc suddenly produced a hand grenade. Pulling over to the bank, we climbed out and after resting for a while with a glass of wine, we threw what was left of the bait and the bread and cheese sandwiches towards the middle of the river, followed a few minutes later, by the hand grenade! This certainly brought a quick result; over a dozen stunned fish came floating to the surface. We leapt back into the boat, quickly collected our ill-gotten gains, and set off homewards before curious eyes approached. I told Marc that I considered it a waste of a good grenade and that I wasn't too fond of them anyway. My own way would have been to use only the detonator stuck into a large potato! This was the method I had learnt from some of the old soldiers in the Home Guard. On seeing the results of the catch, Lily was surprised that we had done so well, and suggested that we should have thrown some of the smaller ones back. But we never let on about our rather unorthodox fishing methods!

As both Whitty and Pierre were frequently out and about elsewhere, I was often left behind to look after our HQ. There were of course, the radio schedules to attend to and the coding and decoding of most of the messages, not all of them though, as Whitty now often did the encoding himself. This did not please me very much, as it meant that I was isolated from what was going on, and in some cases, not even sure of where the others were or what they were doing. I was left for long periods, several days and nights at times, alone at the HQ to deal with anything that happened there, including the meeting and greeting of any visitors and making notes to pass on to either of the two officers on their return.

When taking a short break, I had two favourite places where I could be found, if the other two team members were not present. First place to look was the kitchen. If I was not there, you could find me in the bar of the Hotel de la Breche. The kitchen was where I chose to eat with the butler and the cook, rather than dine in solitary state and be waited on. They were at first reluctant but soon became more relaxed as we chatted and got to know each other better. Cook was a kind, friendly, motherly type, and for me, who had always enjoyed helping my mother in the kitchen as a young lad, this was almost as good as being back home. She asked me what kind of meals I preferred, French or English, and did her best to please me. My favourite French dessert that she made for me whenever there were enough eggs available was a large bowl of egg custard. The separated whites of the eggs whisked and puffed up when cooked in the milk, and floating on the surface of the finished yellow custard *(Les Oeufs a la Neige),* looked and tasted delicious! Although not too fond of garlic, which seems to be a staple ingredient of French cuisine, getting used to French cooking and flavours was an education in itself.

The bar in the Hotel de la Breche was presided over by a lovely lady, Celestine. She could always be found there and ruled her little kingdom in a firm but friendly way. Everyone in town seemed to know her, a mature and very pleasant person. I would sit there either drinking coffee or having a glass of something stronger. Although not a particularly busy place, there was usually someone with whom to pass the time of day, play a game of cards, or poker dice. On a morning coffee break one day, a surprise visitor staying at the Hotel came over to join me. It was André, the SOE agent with the banners of bank notes, whom I had met before in the area of L'Absie when out seeking different sites to set up my radio equipment. While discussing the changes in the situation locally, the topic of more exact numbers of enemy troops now boxed up in the La Rochelle area came up. André mentioned that it might be possible to get behind their lines with a guide, by using a farm that was very close to the area. We agreed to say nothing to anyone until André had had time to find a safe route through his own contacts.

All the towns in the Deux-Sevres region had been celebrating their liberation and these fete days were spread out over several weeks. Whitty may have attended some, if not all of them. This is not known for certain, but he did frequently disappear for a day or three, or more, and not say where or what he had been doing. Pierre did not go to the one organised at L'Absie for the 17th September as he was left to take care of matters at the HQ, but Major Whitty and I attended. The whole town turned out, many of them unaware that they had been hosting the Anglo/French team. Now, only recently informed of what had been going on in their midst, they gave us a tremendous welcome. There was a short parade around the town (with me being mobbed again by several young ladies at every pause), which finished with a visit to the cemetery. After paying our respects to the local martyrs of the resistance, a reception and a *'Vin d'honneur'* were held at the Town Hall. The day was rounded off after the appropriate photographs had been taken, with a feast of a meal with those who had assisted us in our earliest and most difficult days. Incidentally, on meeting Capt. Michonneau after the war in 1947, I was shown and listened to a gramophone recording of a radio broadcast that Major Whitty had made 'To the French people.' When and where this was done is unknown.

News of the possible arrival of another shipment of arms and equipment for the newly formed French regiment, and an additional five Jed teams to assist in the west coast areas, was received and expected towards the end of September. This was a very welcome relief from the inactivity in the La Rochelle area. The enemy were fairly quiet, only sending out foraging parties to obtain additional rations. These were chased back as soon as they were spotted by the *FFI*, but shortage of arms and ammunition curtailed any immediate retaliation on their part. Training in the newly formed companies of the 114th Regiment was progressing slowly, with some assistance from the Free French Army Officers arriving from North Africa. Heavier armaments and machine guns were needed if the enemy troops were to be contained or forced to surrender. Estimates of their strength varied greatly, ranging from 10,000 to 100,000.

Chapter Eleven - A Couple of Trips to the Seaside

After discussions about the possibility of getting into the La Rochelle area with SOE agent André, I brought up the subject again when we next met in the bar of the Hotel de la Breche. André informed me that he had already done a trial run and I said I would talk to Pierre first to get his reaction. Pierre thought it was a good idea and well worth the risk, but thought that Whitty might think differently. As neither of us had seen or heard of Whitty for several days or knew what he was doing (he had become even more secretive recently), it was decided to go ahead without him. He could be told after the event if necessary. The three of us met the next day and decided that the next weekend would be ideal. If we could be in La Rochelle for Sunday the 24th September, when it would be perfectly reasonable to see people walking freely about the town, enjoying the sea breezes, we would have more of a chance to pass unnoticed amongst the local population.

In civilian clothes, the three of us set off in a car early on Saturday morning and arrived about three hours later at a remote farm, which was divided by a stream, the other side of which was the 'occupied' area, and could easily be reached by simply crossing a wooden bridge. After a meal with the farmer, we crossed the bridge and walked to a barn with him, where we found a horse and a small cart, which we loaded with some sacks of recently-dug potatoes. Getting dirty enough by doing so, we soon appeared more convincingly like farm labourers. That evening we ate a snack of bread and French sausage and pate, washed down with red wine, and then slept there ready to move off the next morning. We set off on the next stage of our journey with Pierre leading the horse and André, who had papers and passes obtained from the farm, riding on the front of the cart next to me, holding the reins. We felt rather exposed as we had to leave all our arms behind at the farm. When we reached a narrow dirt track out of the farm, two German soldiers stood up as we approached. This was to be expected as we had been briefed by the farmer, who had prepared a small package containing some bread and pate for them. They looked untidy, tired and depressed, but perked up and smiled when they saw the package and started to eat. Only after their first bite did they nod and say 'Danke, danke,' taking only a cursory glance at the cargo of potatoes. At the end of the lane we turned into a country road and journeyed on, Pierre now sitting on a sack in the back of the cart. We saw one patrol in the distance walking south away from us, so we continued in the general direction of La Rochelle. Not until we were on the outskirts of the town did we see another patrol. This group looked more efficient with someone in charge. One of the soldiers stepped into the road holding his rifle in one hand and signalling with the other for us to stop. I reined in the horse and held it steady while Pierre jumped down and went forward to hold the horse's head. The German, who appeared to be in charge, walked around the wagon, poked at the sacks and demanded to see our papers in German, not French. Andre pulled out the papers he had been given and answered in German that he had orders to take these goods to the address on the forms that he was showing him.

After checking the three sets of papers, he waved us on. Could have been a tricky moment, that! Our journey continued towards the town centre for quite some distance. After passing through a residential area, we turned off the main road, down a side road and into a quiet lane. On reaching a barn-like building, we drove straight in and the doors were closed behind us. One dubious looking character took over the horse and the cart and its contents, and we were ushered through an office to a back room by another. It was by now around mid-day and food and wine were provided while we talked and were advised about when would be the best time to make the return journey. The false papers authorising this delivery had given instructions for the cargo to be delivered to a German barracks, but these goods were intended for the locals. This operation had obviously been used before to bring merchandise in from the countryside areas to the poorly supplied townsfolk. They were being assisted by a well-organised gang of black marketeers!

Changing out of our 'blues', overalls that we had worn over our other civilian clothes, and now presented with bicycles, we continued on our journey towards the centre of town. André led the way a few yards ahead of Pierre and me in order to split up our group a little. More people were out and about now on this sunny Sunday afternoon as we approached the coastal areas. We avoided any guarded areas that could be seen but made mental notes of places, material and any visible staff and defences. We stopped occasionally, usually at a small bar, to get a drink and visit the toilet. We sat together and compared notes, each concentrating on one or more items to aid our memories. It would have been too risky to have been seen writing things down, or have anything found on us if questioned.

It was getting late in the afternoon when we were sitting outside a seafront café. This was going to be our last stop before heading back. We were getting tired and relaxing our guard, as it had so far been too easy. We sat there watching people strolling by, enjoying the afternoon sun. Local couples, young and old, some with children, made it difficult to remember where we were. Only seeing unfamiliar naval and army uniforms passing by brought us back to reality. We sat there at a table with four chairs, occupying three of them, drinking coffee, while next to us there was another table still vacant. A group of five men in naval uniform arrived and walked up to the empty table, the tallest of whom appeared to be of a higher rank. He turned towards us and addressed us in German. Neither I nor Pierre understood much of their language and Andre answered for us all, with only a few words, adding that, regretfully, the others did not understand. The officer had quite politely asked if he could have the use of the spare chair at our table. As he sat down, he turned to us again and apologising for his bad French, asked if the coffee was worth drinking. Then he laughingly added, in reasonable English, 'I can speak English better than French!' The trio joined him in laughing at his joke, while we three were almost choking on our coffee! Not knowing how close he had been with his chance remarks, he turned back to converse with his companions. That had been too close for comfort and we were desperate to leave, but were unable to go too soon in case it looked suspicious.

Some of the Germans wanted beer, but there was none, so they settled down with some wine and the others had coffee. Once they had been served and were engaged in conversation, we called for our bill and even after we had paid, we sat there a little longer, not wishing to be seen as in a hurry to leave. As we stood up to go, the German who had spoken to us also stood up. He reached into his pocket and pulled out a packet of cigarettes. He turned towards us and muttered something like, 'Spanish rubbish,' shrugged his shoulders and added, 'But that is all I can offer, have a nice evening!' In exchange, I offered him a packet of 'Weekend' French Virginia type cigarettes that were sometimes available if you were lucky. Fortunately we had not taken any American cigarettes, which we now often smoked, with us. With the exchange of cigarettes and thanks, in a mixture of broken French and German, we departed with smiles all round, and hidden sighs of relief once safely out of sight. This was not the last time that the German Naval officer and I would meet, but that is another part of this story!

We collected our bicycles and made our way back to the building where we had left our other, more ancient, form of transport, with André leading, as he was the only one who knew the route. Pierre and I followed, again with a reasonable distance between us so that we would not appear, at a casual glance, to be travelling together. We saw only one patrol on the way back, which took no notice of us this time. On reaching the building where we had left the horse and cart we went down a passageway into an entrance, where we left the bicycles. A man then conducted us through the building into the yard, where the horse and cart stood ready. The man who appeared to be the one in charge of the enterprise, and whom we had met on the way in, spoke only to Andre. After changing back into our 'Blues' and now looking more like farm workers, we set off the way we had come, back to the farm. When we reached the barn where we had originally picked up the horse and cart, a man was waiting to take over from us. By now it was getting dark as we walked back to the farmhouse on the other side of the bridge. Again we had been lucky and not run into any patrols, only seeing one in the distance, moving away. We stopped long enough to have a quick meal with the farmer and his wife, and then set off again in the car on the last leg of the journey.

We felt exhausted now the adrenaline that had been keeping us on our toes was fading fast. The journey was mostly in silence and we had to change drivers twice to keep awake. On arrival back at La Place de Roulage, the butler greeted us and offered to make a ham omelette for supper, which, to his surprise, we declined, choosing instead to retire and meet again at breakfast, saying that we would have the ham and eggs then as an English breakfast. This we did, then spent most of that Monday going over, collating and recording the details of what we had observed. Estimates of 100,000 troops were well out. We put it nearer 10 or 20,000. But there were a good few armoured vehicles that we had seen and some heavy weaponry, the positions of which we marked on maps. Although food was in short supply, there seemed to be enough to exist on, at least by the troops. Some of the soldiers looked tired and weary, but the naval personnel, like the ones we had met at the café, seemed to be in better health and spirits. The shops looked rather bare with nothing worth having on display, many of them closed and boarded up. Overall we agreed that the exercise had been informative and worthwhile. It had been worth the risk, but getting involved with the black market was not something we would care to repeat too often. We all agreed to keep quiet about that part.

André had gone off on business of his own and I was not to see him again until safely back in the UK. Pierre and I had to catch up on the radio messages and ciphering, having been away and without the Jed set.

Fortunately there was very little to do with Whitty still absent. When he did return a couple of days later, we were able to inform him that two more ships were expected by Team TONY in the Vendee region on the 27th September. There would be some supplies for us as well, and our area. Five more Jed teams were also being sent in, to assist in the coastal areas. Pierre had already been in contact with M. Brivin, the major transport firm and the local *FFI*. Allowing enough time for unloading, we arranged to be in Les Sables-D'Olonne on Friday the 29th. Whitty's response was that he was far too busy to go, so ordered Pierre to take me with him. An arrangement that we both preferred anyway! I thought I would take the radio with us, but Whitty thought that it would not be necessary; he could listen in and take any message if need be. That really surprised me; all Jeds had been trained to cover for each other, but this was a first from him! Unlike last weekend, this time we could wear our uniforms. The areas we would be travelling through were by now cleared of the enemy. The *FFI* were also now proudly wearing their armbands all the time, and not only when they were on an operation. This had been normal practice since the liberation of Niort.

The small convoy set off in the early hours from Niort heading for Les Sables-D'Olonne, a journey of at least 100kms, which took us about three hours. On arrival we found that the ships' cargoes had been unloaded and stored in a warehouse. Our share of the approximate fifty tons was twelve and a half tons, which was ready for loading. Team TONY had the same amount. The remaining twenty-five tons was intended for *Mission Shinoile.* Of the five Jed teams, one, Team RAYMOND, was allocated to our area and would operate out of St. Maixent. Another, Team SIMON, was to stay with Team TONY, operating in and around Les Sables D'Olonne. The other three teams were to be attached to *Mission Shinoile* further north and north-east, and south of St. Nazaire and the river Loire. One of these teams, Team FRANK did join Team HAROLD later in the Niort/St. Maixent region. By the time all the equipment had been loaded, the new arrivals had already moved on. With the return journey to think of, there had been no spare time to socialise. With only a short break for a meal, we were soon on our way back to Niort, arriving back at the Place de Roulage in time for a well-earned supper.

Chapter Twelve - A Few Social Occasions

That left Saturday to catch up on the wireless messages, which I did quite quickly because I wanted to be free on Sunday. A long standing invitation out to dine by my wine merchant friend Raymond Thimer and his wife had been accepted, to which I was greatly looking forward and, although I had already been introduced to several very good meals and the French way of serving up a continuous variety of foods, this was going to be rather special. Not the least in that it would be accompanied by a selection of choice wines, a different one with every dish! Major Whitty, being in a more affable mood these days, agreed to my returning late that night and, as he was unwilling to rouse the butler and his wife who slept in the small gate-house cottage, or to be disturbed himself, even gave me a key to the front door.

Greeted warmly by Raymond and a small group of family and friends, I was offered a choice from a large variety of aperitifs. These were accompanied by an even larger selection of canapés. These were easy enough to tackle, even when unsure what they contained or would taste like. All different shapes, colours and flavours, a pleasure to eat, but what exactly to drink with them was the burning question. In fact, when Raymond asked if I had a particular favourite, I was forced to admit that I didn't know one from the other, only that I had tried one that tasted of aniseed with water added, but the smell of it made me feel sick! 'That was Pernod, not to be confused with this one, which is a local speciality called *'Pineau Des Charentes,'* I was informed. I duly tried it, liked it right from the start, and from that day to this it has been my favourite choice. It is a blend of white wine and brandy originating from the Cognac area in the Charente. The dinner continued throughout the evening, each delightful dish accompanied by a different wine to taste, a veritable banquet, with pauses between each course for smoking, talking, joking and laughter, with deep discussions about the merits of the last dish. Mme Thimer, like many

French ladies, was an excellent cook and hostess. Not that this was an orgy of eating and drinking, oh no! The dishes were served with just the right amount to savour the flavour. The drinks were poured or changed only to complement the food. The evening finished with coffee and cognac. A 'mellow glow' would perhaps best describe my demeanour as I returned home that night.

Happy and contented, if a little unsteady, I reached the closed gates of La Place du Roulage. I fumbled for the key I had been given and then realised that it was for the front door of the house and not the gates! Nothing daunted, I started to climb over the gates and discovered they were not locked. I walked up the drive past the garage to the large double doors, trying not to make any noise. The key fitted the lock all right, but whenever I turned it to the left, or to the right, nothing happened. After several attempts I gave up and decided to walk around to the back of the house to see if I could get in through my bedroom window, which was at the back of the house on the first floor of the right wing. It had a small balcony and full length shuttered French windows; all I had to do was get up there! The right-angled corner between the main part of the house and the wing, in which my room was located, looked a likely climbing spot. However, in the gardens there were some life-sized statues sited a few metres apart, close to and following the contours of the house. Slipping or falling on to any one of these would not be recommended.

Notwithstanding, I climbed up in the corner using the angle and small ridges between the blocks of stone for foot and hand holds. Once I reached my floor level I then had to inch my way along a very narrow ledge, around the corner and along the ledge again to reach the balcony. After climbing over and reaching the shuttered windows I found that they were bolted on the inside and I could not get them to open. Feeling very frustrated by this time, I then had to return to the ground the same way as I had climbed up, clinging by my finger tips, and pressing my body close to the walls. Defeated by the house I returned to the garages near the gates, found the doors unlocked and settled down in the back of the car for a well earned sleep. I was woken early in the morning by the butler who explained to me that the front door key did work, but only if it was turned not once, but twice! At breakfast, after I had smartened myself up, the Major asked if I had heard anything unusual during the night. Apparently he had heard noises and thinking someone was breaking in, went downstairs with his .45 to check the windows and the doors. I of course, admitted nothing, other than I had slept very soundly, but not saying where.

With the arrival of October came a more relaxed time, with even Major Whitty in a more relaxed mood. He had introduced me to a charming lady who spoke good English with an antipodean accent. They had known each other from a time before the war, when both had property in the south of France, he explained. The only other information I gleaned was that she had apparently been in France during the occupation. I already knew that the Major's wife was a New Zealander, but this was not her, and thought that this was perhaps the connection. Many years later it transpired that the Major's friend had been the SOE agent Nancy Wake, codename White Mouse. The lady stayed only a couple of days and did not stay overnight at the HQ; at least as far as I know, because I was myself now spending more time out and about socialising.

Heavy demands on aircraft which were busy supplying the Allied troops advancing on Germany meant supplies would no longer be arriving by parachute. The formation of Companies for the new Regiment was advancing well, but they still needed large supplies of equipment. They were taking up positions, as soon as they were fully trained, in the line facing the encircled enemy around La Rochelle. Subsequent larger deliveries had been organised and these would be by aircraft landing at Niort airport. The next was to be on the 8th October.

Meanwhile, often alone at our HQ, I was in need of a good haircut. I had mentioned this on my last visit to Lily Bignoneau, who had organised a meeting with her hairdresser. Picking me up from the HQ one morning, we walked for about 10 minutes to the rue de Brioux, a road to the left, just after the railway station and stopped at number 55, a large terraced house. We were welcomed in by two charming young ladies. The front room of the house had been converted into a hairdressing salon and they were the only people living in the rest of the house. It was owned by Marcelle, the elder of the two girls; the other girl, Lucette, was her assistant. After being introduced and during the customary aperitifs before lunch, I realised that I had seen Lucette somewhere before, and remarked on this to Mme Bignoneau. 'You certainly have,' she had replied, 'on the 6th of September at the liberation parade. This is the girl on the bicycle. You were waving to each other, but she was too shy to climb up onto the lorry, the only girl in the town not to kiss you that day!' Lily knew the girls quite well and they had been pressing her for some time to arrange a meeting. Both were ardent anglophiles and had learnt a great deal from Mme. Bignoneau about the UK. The girls' own worst encounter with the occupation troops had been very early in the war, when only part of France was occupied. Lucette's mother lived in the unoccupied zone at Vienne, south of Lyon. They had decided to try and reach her and get themselves away from the occupied area. Their plan was to pass through a farming area that straddled the demarcation line. Unfortunately the two girls were caught and put in prison and forced to spend a week in one room that was so packed tight with other women that they couldn't all lie down at the same time. They had no proper toilet or washing facilities, so of course, the smell was appalling. They only succeeded in getting out by paying a large fine. Others were not so lucky, and were sent to labour camps. The Jews amongst them knew that they had no hope of release. Some had already been there for several weeks.

Aeroplanes landed with large amounts of material at Niort Airport and were a great relief. Following the delivery on the 8th October, there were others on the 10th, 14th and 28th. These supplies were added to those received by ship and passed on to us via Team TONY. They had been in contact with the American Forces since early in September, north of their area at Nantes and St. Nazaire, and had also received some supplies from them. All these, combined with German captured arms and ammunition, improved the Regiment's capabilities no end.

The trips to and from the airport gave me the opportunity to meet two other Jed wireless operators. One was 'Wally' (Walter) Adams of Team RAYMOND, which was attached to the garrison of the 114th Regiment at St Maixent. As he had not been given any radio or schedule, any messages were being dealt with by Team HAROLD. Although he did visit me at Niort several times, and was admitted to Niort Hospital for a short time when unwell, he was billeted too far away to help out with the radio transmissions. Whereas, Tom Henney, of Team FRANK, who joined me at the end of the month, had a room at the Hotel De la Breche. He had arrived without his own wireless equipment and was only too pleased to be able to help out with my work at the Niort HQ.

Major Whitty was rarely in residence and, as ever, not very forthcoming in what he was doing, or when he would be returning. Although I was used to this by now, it made life difficult whenever visitors to the HQ called. All I could do was to take down messages, if any, and promise to pass them on as soon as possible. Pierre was also away for long periods because of his work alongside Colonel Edmond Proust (*Chaumette* had by now reverted to his real name) and senior French officers of the Free French Army arriving from North Africa and the UK. These new arrivals were to assist the newly formed 'ex-resistance' regiments from over a wider area, covering both La Rochelle and Royon, where the large concentrations of German troops were encircled and held at bay. They were incorporated into the rapidly forming new French National Army, under General De Larminat, Commander of the French Forces in the West, now based in Cognac, and it was expected that all further supplies by the end of October would be delivered by road transport.

Tom Henney and Harry
Niort November 1944

Tom and I got on very well with each other and soon worked out ways in which we could get out and about together in our free time. For example, Celestine's bar at La Breche Hotel was nearby, very convenient for short morning or afternoon breaks. There we could sit as long as we liked drinking coffee, or something stronger, and playing cards or more often than not playing Poker-Dice, either together or with other French patrons. At other times, longer breaks meant that we could walk through the town, down to the riverside home of M. & Mme Bignoneau, where we knew we were always welcome, just in time for afternoon tea. The evenings, when not invited out for a meal, called for excursions into town to try out the local bars and possibly meet other young people, preferably female. If all else failed, there was always the blue baize billiard table in the lounge at the HQ. Being able to play with someone was an improvement, although as the table had been constructed without any pockets, the games were restricted to scoring 'Cannons'.

Some of the more memorable times worth recording include that, following introductions to my hairdressing friends, Marcelle and Lucette, we dined out with them on several occasions. Our favourite night spot was the 'Caveau'. This small restaurant, down in a cellar, was decorated to resemble a cave. On the walls were colourful paintings of French Cavaliers eating and drinking. Only about six to eight tables were placed around the walls, and the proprietor sat on a raised podium at one end. Aperitifs were taken while waiting for everyone to settle in their pre-set places. The meals were only served after all the diners were seated and ready to eat. You were all expected to arrive and be seated at a set time. The menu was limited to the Chef's choice, in other words you were his 'paying' guests! It was impossible to get a booking without the owner's agreement, who also informed the patrons of the day's menu, if you were accepted. Once everyone was served with the first course, mine host would rise from his seat to read a poem or short story from his script. This same procedure followed with each of the several courses, all of which were accompanied with the appropriate wine. When the cheese course arrived, he would sing a song or two and then encourage everyone to join in as the dessert and coffee followed with, of course, more wine as and if required. The usual pattern was that, by then, each table would take it in turn to entertain the others with a song, a recitation, or a dubious story. Having eaten well and drunk enough to break down any barriers still remaining, the evenings passed very agreeably indeed. We would join in with the French, singing *'Chevalier de la Table Ronde'* and we would give our rendition of, 'On Ilkley Moor ba' tat' in English!

On another occasion, when we had been invited out for an evening with my wine merchant friend Raymond Thimer, Tom, when asked what he would like to drink, had requested whisky. Raymond regretted that on this occasion he did not have any, but offered him a glass of what he was drinking which turned out to be Pernod. Now this is a drink that is always served in a glass with plenty of water. Tom had worked in Liverpool docks before joining the Army, and drank his whisky neat. No matter how many times he was advised not to drink Pernod without water, he insisted, and had two glasses, one after the other. He sank to his knees in less than half an hour, in a deep sleep. We had to carry him back to his room at the hotel and put him to bed. The next day I called in to see how he was and found him still asleep, on the floor. When he finally woke up, he told me that he had got up twice in the night, felt very thirsty and drank some water, then passed out again before he could get back into his bed!

Tom Henney

Whereas sorties out with Marcelle and Lucette were chaste and reasonably sober, there was one particular evening when out with other young ladies, which turned out to be completely different. When Tom arrived in Niort, he already had a regular girl friend, Michelle, a very pretty dark-haired girl whom he nicknamed 'Mickey' and who often shared his room in the hotel. On one particular day, it must have been a fete day or a Saturday, we two lads were joined by 'Mickey' and a blonde friend of hers called Giselle. We all adjourned to a Café in an arcade in the town centre which was frequented by mainly young people. There was some music and dancing and we enjoyed ourselves talking and mixing with other young couples. As we were the only 'Brits' in evidence, this was of course an added attraction. We were drinking only champagne and as fast as one bottle was emptied another took its place. Not that we drank it all ourselves, we did share the odd glass or two with the neighbouring table. Nevertheless, at the end of the evening's entertainment, when it was time to settle up, there were nine bottles of champagne on our table to pay for, including the extra one that we had decided to take with us.

Feeling very frisky and unwilling to end the night there, we walked back towards another street that had a few hotels and bars in it. Being rather late, most were closed for the night, but we did find one hotel still open except that the bar was closed. A request for a room was at first declined, after all we still had another bottle of champagne to drink! But, after much insistence, especially by the girls, the two couples were reluctantly shown to a room at the top of the building, the landlord and his wife saying regretfully, that this was all that they had available. It was a dingy but fairly large room with two double beds, a lamp with no shade, a single light bulb hanging from the ceiling, and bare boards on the floor. Not that we were too concerned, the wine had kept us merry enough to be able to laugh off any doubts. At least the beds looked inviting and there were a couple of glasses by the wash basin.

It wasn't long before we were all stripped off, light out and into bed, giggles and other noises off, the girls exchanging banter in French and the two lads in English. There were no other distractions, that is, apart from Tom asking me if I had a match, at a very inopportune moment! Silence reigned for a short while as the wine and exhaustion took effect and we fell asleep. Not for long though. Mickey was saying something to Tom that he did not understand and he asked me - 'What does *'Punaise'* mean, Harry? She keeps repeating it, *'punaise, punaise,'* and I don't know what she is on about.' 'Drawing pin, I think,' I replied. 'Something's up,' said Tom. 'Can you put the light on?' It was pitch black in the room and I fumbled around and found the switch by the bedroom door. When I turned round, the sight that greeted me was a naked body, Mickey's, wearing nothing but Tom's brown leather jump boots. She was quickly joined by Giselle, who put on my boots and joined her friend as they both marched up and down the floor, stamping on a swarm of bed bugs! Apparently *'Punaise'* was the same word in French for 'drawing pins' as for 'bed bugs'! Still with everyone stark naked we stripped the beds, and when Mickey lifted the mattress off her and Tom's bed, it was alive with these big round beasts. All the bedding was taken off the beds and shaken vigorously out of the window before being remade and we got back into them. Not for long though, the 'magic' of our night of romance had faded, we were unable to sleep, so gave up and went home. Certainly a night out that we would never forget!

Chapter Thirteen - An Unexpected Guest

By mid November, at the team's Niort HQ, the situation was that there was now less work for me to do. The French had taken over their own affairs. Both the Major and Pierre, as had been the pattern for some time, were rarely in residence, and I was kept in the dark as to when they would return. At this point, I received an unexpected visitor.

Col Carleton-Smith, who was from the Head Quarters of Special Force and responsible for the Jedburghs, arrived by boat at Les Sables-D'Olonne on the 12th November. He had been touring the Vendee area visiting the teams operating in and around the La Rochelle pocket before arriving in the Deux Sevres on or about the 15th November. He arrived unannounced in the morning at our HQ to be greeted by the only person in residence, myself! I explained that both of the Officers were away and that I was uncertain when they would be returning. After offering to arrange accommodation for him in the house or at the local Hotel, both options were declined by the Colonel. 'I have,' he said, 'still other visits to make before going on to Paris and I am sure that you can put me in the picture here and bring me up to date. There is the possibility of another operation elsewhere that I wish to discuss with you anyway.'

A conducted tour of our HQ at La Place du Roulage impressed the Colonel, who commented on the size and comfort of our accommodation. In particular my room, which was a combined sleeping and working area, where my wireless was set up like a permanent radio station, with desk space for rapid coding and decoding of messages. 'Congratulations,' he said. 'You have certainly finished up in rather better circumstances than when you first arrived in France!' Over morning coffee I gave the Colonel a run down on the current formation of the 114th Regiment, which now had one Battalion based at Niort and two Battalions at St. Maixent. The Regiment, along with others from surrounding areas, had several

Companies of men in positions around La Rochelle and were successfully containing the enemy. These Companies had been formed from the surrounding areas and had retained many of the original leaders and men from the resistance groups, some of the older men returning to their homes. Many young men were joining the Regiment, which was now rapidly approaching 3000 men, for the duration of the war. Training was being assisted by the arrival of Free French Officers as well as Jed teams HAROLD, FRANK and RAYMOND in this area. Minor injuries had been incurred by Lt. H. Chaulais of Team RAYMOND whilst dealing with land mines. Sgt. W. Adams of the same team had spent a short spell in hospital and Capt. I. Isaac of Team FRANK had recently been admitted to hospital in Niort, for an as yet unknown reason. The Colonel said that he would visit him before leaving Niort. The enemy forces now surrounded and contained in the La Rochelle pocket were reasonably quiet and apparently under orders not to surrender.

By mid-day Tom Henney of Team FRANK joined us for lunch. During and after the meal the Colonel told us that he was seeking W/T Operators for similar duties in the Far East. He complimented us and the other Jeds on the good work done in Europe, and he said that now the need for Jed teams and in particular, men trained in radio and communication procedures, was a priority requirement. It was expressed that terms and conditions were as before, that it was absolutely voluntary, and, unlike other service personnel, we would not be required to stay there for the statutory three year tour of overseas duty. We would, he said, be brought back to the UK on completion of our missions. If we did not desire to volunteer for the Far East we could return to our parent units. There would be no stigma at all in our choice and it was perfectly acceptable should we wish to decline. The missions, he warned us, could possibly be more dangerous against the Japanese, but further training and acclimatisation would be given before taking part in guerrilla warfare in the jungle. 'That is why there is no pressure whatsoever on you to accept,' he added. Both Tom and I decided on the spot. We both agreed that anything was better than returning to the tank regiments, and the chance of seeing other parts of the world was enticing. The Colonel shook hands on the deal, saying, 'I thought you would agree and certain that you would volunteer to go. I have brought a small present for you, which I didn't tell you about beforehand in case you took it as a bribe! I assure you that I would still have given it to you if you had turned it down, your work here has been excellent and much appreciated by the French authorities.' He left the table, returning with two excellent razors, each in its own red cloth case. 'These are from me personally,' he said, shaking our hands again and wishing us well and a safe return home when our work was completed. The Colonel departed that same day, without waiting to see the two remaining officers of Team HAROLD, leaving it up to me to speak to them and pass on a written message.

Another two days went by before Pierre returned and I was able to pass on information to him about my recent visitor. He neither knew where the Major was nor when he would be back, so he said he would take me to St Maixent the next day to see Col Proust *(Chaumette)*. The *FFI* chief could then arrange for the necessary passes for me and Tom to travel to Paris. This left us Sergeants just a few days to tour around saying goodbye to our new found friends. No, not only our lady friends! There were also families, such as Lily and Marc Bignoneau the dairy produce merchant, Raymond Thimer the wine merchant, Paul and Andree Huvelin, cakes and pastries, Alfred and Jeanine Miot of the Parisiana Bar, and not forgetting dear Celestine who ran the bar at the Hotel de la Breche. Then of course, there were our hairdressers, Lucette and Marcelle, and Lucette's aunt who was caring for and bringing up a baby girl named Annie, about the same age as my 2 year old brother David, who had stolen everyone's heart. All these and many others did not leave much time for extraneous liaisons, but we did manage to kiss a few other fair maidens goodbye! Our last evening in Niort, the 22nd November, we spent having dinner with Lucette and Marcelle at their place in the rue de Brioux. At the unearthly hour of 5 a.m the next morning, we were awoken by Pierre, who was knocking on the front door, endeavouring not to wake the neighbours, wanting to make an early start en route for Paris.

Souvenirs were in short supply so we had very little to take home with us but, by courtesy of Raymond, we did have four bottles of cognac each to carry. Tom still had most of his equipment and packed it all into his Bergen rucksack. I had been told by Pierre to leave the radio behind as he would be returning to Niort. My rucksack had been so badly damaged at the 'Drop' it had consequently been dumped, so I had been using my sleeping bag as a make shift 'Kit Bag'. The bottles were well protected and wrapped around with spare clothing. The trio were chauffeured to Paris in a large black Renault car by an ex-*FFI* man now in the 114th Regiment Leaving Niort before 7a.m, we were in Paris by eleven, with only one brief stop for refreshment at a Royal Army Service Depot. This was where we saw the first Allied soldiers since leaving the UK. Quite a surprise, especially hearing so much English spoken, and the amazing taste of real army TEA! At last some thing to 'really' quench the thirst. Without doubt the most missed item of all, a good old cup of tea!

Chapter Fourteen - Hello and Goodbye to Paris

We reported in at the Hotel Cecil in the rue St. Didier in Paris, which ran between the Avenue Victor Hugo and the Avenue Kleber, not very far from the Arc de Triomphe. After we had been allocated our rooms, Pierre took me along to an even grander Hotel on the Avenue des Champs Elysees where he said Major Whitty was waiting to see us. When we arrived we were greeted by the Major who was standing alone at the bar, glass in hand with a big smile, looking rather pleased with himself. He shook both of us by the hand saying, 'Ah, well done, my lads, we've all made it then! Come and enjoy a Champagne Cocktail with me!' He then carried on complimenting us on the work we had been doing, without mentioning where or with what he had been occupied. This reminded me of the drinks we had shared in the Dorchester Hotel before our briefing, the toasting of each other to a successful mission, and the pleasant friendly atmosphere at that time. Now it was all over, the Major was back to his old self, full of bonhomie, wishing me good luck on my next mission to the Far East.

Pierre was, for the moment, returning to Niort to be with Col Chaumette and the Free French officers; there was, of course, still a large garrison of German troops at La Rochelle contained by the *FFI*. Major Whitty said that he was uncertain about his next mission, but there had been talk of an operation which entailed jumping in close to prisoner of war camps to secure their safe release and this really interested him. 'Why don't you join me?' He suggested. I was very surprised by this offer, considering some of the past treatment dished out by Whitty, and my answer was to excuse myself by saying that I had already given my word to Col Carleton-Smith that I would go to the Far East for my next mission. I secretly told myself that I would never volunteer to work with someone like him ever again. The major's dual personality had been difficult to comprehend, let alone handle. Perhaps he was too old to stand the stress and strain, and he lacked the patience needed at times when there was nothing to do, to stay quiet, rest and wait, sometimes for hours on end. I also felt that the fact of the extreme youth of the other two members had been unfairly used to help balance the team. Declining a second glass of champagne, I made my excuses, saying that I had to get back to my hotel for a meeting with Col Carleton-Smith that afternoon. Pierre and I departed, having once more shaken hands, wished each other farewell and good luck. This was the last time that Major Whitty and I were ever to meet; he died the following year. I only learnt of this many years later, and the circumstances are still unclear, one source reporting that he died as result of old wounds and another as having committed suicide. Pierre and I said very friendly goodbyes to each other after returning to the hotel. We did not know it then but we would have to wait forty years before meeting again!

Later that afternoon Tom and I were invited to meet Col Carleton-Smith in his office. After some debriefing he gave us some 'fatherly' advice about the pleasures and dangers for young men alone in Paris, adding that the attractions were also far too expensive for British servicemen's pay. He gave us the addresses of affordable canteens and clubs set up especially for the British military, as only the Americans can afford the alternative places, he had added! The Colonel, a really charming and friendly man, spoilt things a little at the end of our chats together, by asking if we had any of our operational money left over. The crafty old devil, I thought, I bet he wants it for himself! Quick thinking and deft fingers produced a small portion of my French Francs, with the remark, 'This is all I have left of these, but I do still have all the American Dollars that I had been given in London.' Satisfied, the Colonel handed back a few French Francs to tide me over, plus another English one pound note for my journey back home. This was tucked into another pocket well away from the remainder of my French money. Tom, who had obviously closely followed the proceedings, did something similar by adding that he had handed over most of his spare money to his French Officer, who was with Captain Isaac and still hospitalised in Niort. Both of us left feeling just a little guilty at deceiving such a nice kind gentleman!

Later that evening of the 23rd we went for a walk round the hotel and the Arc de Triomphe, just taking in the sights and getting our bearings. Rather tired after a long day we were early to bed. The next day we went further afield and in the evening found ourselves near the Lido de Paris. There was dancing, a band in the centre of the dance floor on a raised stage, with the dancers circling round to the quickstep, the waltz and other popular dances. On another level in the same building, there was another band, this time playing to those who wished to jitterbug the night away. The whole place was full of Americans, who were the only ones able to get partners. We gave up after watching the others for a while, and wandered off back to our hotel, stopping once on the way to visit a dive that featured strippers and sold very expensive drinks. Bored after a short stay, we decided to call it a night and returned to our temporary home.

The 25th November '44 brought forth a vast improvement to our fortunes. During the afternoon while wandering up and down the avenues and boulevards, we noticed that the streets seemed busier than before, with a lot more local people out and about. There were many large groups of ladies, all wearing huge, colourful fancy hats, parading joyfully along the pavements. It was not very long before we found ourselves surrounded by one of these groups. They linked arms, encircled Tom and I and refused to let us go until we had embraced everyone of them! It did not take too long for the lads to do as requested, whereupon the girls broke their chain, said goodbye and skipped off to catch their next victims. It did not take the two boys long to realise that all we had to do was walk along the road looking innocent and allow ourselves to get caught. As the afternoon moved on to evening, the groups became merrier as whenever we passed a café, drinks were often passed out to us. When we asked some of the girls who were willing to dally long enough to talk to us to explain the meaning of this celebration, we were informed that it was the fete of St Catherine, the patron saint of milliners, hence the hats!

Later still that evening, one group of six or seven ladies who seemed pleased that we were British soldiers, took us to a small Café restaurant and treated us to a meal. They refused to let us pay for anything and after the meal took us, along with two of their men folk, on a tour of several small night clubs that the local Parisiens were using. When they learnt that we had been assisting the French resistance we were made very welcome everywhere we went. We were toasted by all and sundry and then, in the early hours, the girls put us in a taxi with one of their escorts to make sure that we got back safely to our hotel. What a wonderful time Paris had given us! We hadn't spent a single franc on this very pleasant evening out. Paris had been liberated for three months and they were still celebrating!

We spent most of the next day 'resting' only getting ready to go out after the evening meal. Fully refreshed and on our way out of the hotel, Tom bumped into a French man in civilian clothes whom he had known earlier. They stood talking together for a while before Tom turned to me and said that his French friend was going to take us both out somewhere that evening. I reminded Tom that we were due to leave Paris the next morning, so we had better not be too late back. Ignoring that possibility, at about nine o'clock we were taken by car to a night club. Tom's friend, after having spoken to the owner, whom he seemed to know quite well, introduced the gallant pair to him, who then took over and escorted us into the establishment. The interior, which looked rather chic, was dimly lit with tables placed around a small dance floor at the back of which there was a raised stage. We were given a table, well placed at the rear but a little higher up so that we had a clear view of the stage and the entire room which was neither too large nor too small. The other tables were filled by well dressed couples and small groups of people. Soft gentle music enhanced the ambience of it all.

Sitting alone, just the two of us, we must have looked somewhat out of place. Then the lights dimmed further and the curtains opened, showing a Spanish village scene, and the music changed to a Latin rumba rhythm. One beautiful girl entered from the right, another from the left, meeting centre stage in step with the rhythmic beat, and they commenced to dance around each other. Their long black hair and knee length dresses with ruffled skirts, rising and falling as they twirled, dancing and stamping to the music. They followed their first dance with two other different dances, finishing to a great burst of applause from the clientele. After a final encore the music changed back again to dance music, and couples rose to dance. As we had no partners we were unable to join them but this was soon rectified when the proprietor approached our table with yet another bottle of champagne, and bringing with him, and introducing, the two girls who had been dancing on the stage. Charming company they proved to be, about our own age too and we were all soon perfectly at ease with each other. Sometime later, we asked them if they would like to go on somewhere else, to be away from where they worked. This the girls were unable to do because they had to repeat their act at eleven o'clock, but they could leave afterwards before closing time at midnight. They begged us to stay until they were free and we agreed, impatient as we all were to leave, because the evening had developed distinct possibilities and whispered hints of other pleasures passing between all four of us held a certain promise of better things to come.

True to their word as soon as their last performance was over, all four departed together. On bidding goodnight to the owner and offering to pay, he simply said there was no need; it had all been taken care of! As the girls with their new companions walked down the road, we asked if they would like to go to a café for a drink or some coffee, but they said it was probably too late and anyway it would be better if we waited until we got home. An invitation that neither of us were in the mood to refuse! We came to a large apartment block, no lifts working, and climbed up the stairs to the top floor. By the time my amour and I got into the flat and closed the door, my companion, still high on the adrenaline built up by her last performance on stage, was busy heating up water in large pans on a stove, preparing for a bath. She explained that this was the only way as normal services were not yet working properly in Paris. When the bath was ready she helped me to undress and bathed me first, then, after wrapping me in one of her silky dressing gowns, put me to bed, telling me to rest while she bathed. I promptly fell asleep! I only woke when I felt the lithe young body sliding into the warmed bed and cuddling up very close. Soon we were entwined in our first amorous embrace, and then another, this very athletic young maiden was in no mood for sleep. Honour bound to keep pace, I was glad that I too was very fit! Thus passed the night in which I was to learn that there were many alternative positions and techniques in the art of lovemaking that I had never dreamed of. Sleep never came into the equation!

On leaving about seven o'clock in the morning, I was walking just a few yards down the road, unsure of which direction to take, when I bumped into Tom. He, by some strange coincidence, had also just left his partner and was doing the same thing! We eventually found the road leading to the Arc de Triomphe and from there found our way back to the hotel where, outside, stood a partially loaded lorry. A cry went up as we approached. 'Come on, you two, we've been waiting for you!' Dashing upstairs we grabbed our kit and within a very few minutes were on our way out of Paris en route for Dieppe. The journey in the back of a troop transporter, not the most comfortable mode of travel at the best of times, went mainly unnoticed as much needed sleep overtook the pair of us. Relief came only when the vehicle made brief stops for refreshments at roadside army supply depots. On our arrival in Dieppe, we were informed that there was a ship sailing shortly and it would avoid a long wait if we were to sail with it.

Chapter Fifteen - Anything to Declare?

We accepted the offer of a quick trip home and soon found ourselves on a small tramp steamer which was returning to the UK by going eastwards along the English Channel to the Thames Estuary, arriving at the London Docks. 'That's fine by us,' we said to the Skipper. 'When will we get there?', only to be informed that it depended on the rest of the convoy, which was forming up in the Channel where the ship would receive a message as to where its position would be. We would also have to wait for all the other ships to arrive and take up their positions. Fortunately the weather was kind and the sea fairly calm, so we sat at the stern of the ship where a large gun was mounted, talking to the only Royal Navy man on board. His job on this Merchant Navy boat, we were told, was to look out for and fire on any enemy aircraft or submarine that might appear. There seemed to be only two other merchant seamen on board. One of them, later on, came up with a message from the Skipper saying that he wanted to have a word with us. Joining him on the bridge he told us that he was waiting for a Navy patrol boat to give him his sailing position orders. They would be arriving soon and he was going to ask if they could take his two passengers off and land them in Newhaven. This would save us a day or two of travelling around the coast and up the River Thames.

This sounded like a good idea to us and was agreed upon. Once the captain had received his instructions, when we reached mid-channel, we exchanged our mode of transport for the Royal Navy's very fast and powerful patrol boat. Not too tricky a task, with the help of a couple of the Navy's finest, who at once took us below where, on a hot stove, stood a brew of very strong tea. It was in this galley that we learnt that the patrol boat could not take us into the English port until it had visited all the ships in the convoy and handed over their sailing orders. To cap it all, some of the ships had not yet arrived. 'Don't worry,' we were told. 'We are on the radio to Newhaven and they are going to send out a motor launch to collect you when we get a little closer to the harbour.' Sure enough, even before sighting the port, a small launch arrived, crewed by two Wrens. Another change of transport! First our baggage, then one after the other, we jumped aboard and sped away. No chance of chatting up the ladies although we did try, but the noise from the powerful motors made it impossible to hear what was being said. Three ships to cross the Channel! Definitely something to remember!

The only damage done by throwing our belongings from ship to ship was to two bottles of brandy in Tom's rucksack. As mine were still intact I gave one to Tom so that we both still had three bottles each. On landing, we were ushered into a hut at Newhaven harbour and were greeted by a hatless man in what looked like a naval uniform, who began asking what we considered to be far too many questions! 'Where have you been? What have you been doing? How long have you been away?' for example. We answered by telling him that we were sorry but it was secret and we were not permitted to say. Losing his patience and raising his voice, he uttered those immortal words - 'WELL, HAVE YOU ANYTHING TO DECLARE!' 'Yes!' I replied, remembering the address and telephone number I had been given before leaving Paris. 'This is a telephone number you can ring. It's a Whitehall number at the War Ministry, and they will confirm anything you need to know, after we have spoken to them!' Looking a bit disgruntled, he made the call and passed the phone over to me. Asking for the room number I had been given, I gave them our code names and told them where we were. Of our inquisitor, they said, 'We will speak to him. He is probably a customs officer.' Not knowing what that was because I had never been abroad before, I had to be told that it was part of the man's job. After the person at the War Office had spoken to the 'Customs Officer' he did become more helpful, and without asking any more questions, took us along to the Military Police office. Whitehall had also spoken to them and they were already preparing railway travel documents for our journey to London. We had very little English money so we asked the MPs if they could exchange some French Francs for us. They couldn't help, but advised us that most banks would exchange small amounts. If we hurried we may have time to get to a bank before they closed at 3 o'clock. While waiting for the time of the next train going up to town, we just made it to a bank and were able to change one 1000 Franc note for five English pounds each. After arriving and reporting in at the War Office, we were sent home after a further short debriefing, for one week's disembarkation leave before returning to Peterborough.

It was late in the evening of the 27th November before I arrived home, much to the surprise of my parents. My mother had received regular letters from HQ explaining only that I was doing important work, that they were in touch with me, that I was fit and well and would contact them myself at a later date as soon as I was able. Meanwhile, they would keep in touch with her and pass on any short message to me whenever possible. Because operations were still going on, I was able to tell even my parents very little about my work. They were surprised enough to learn that I had not only just returned from France but could now speak French! The fact that I had been assisting the French resistance was a bit too much to believe at the time, so it wasn't mentioned. I did tell them though that I would probably be going to the Far East soon. As they knew more about the war in Europe than in the Far East, they were less concerned about my well being.

The Allies were still having a hard time pushing the Germans out of Belgium back into Germany. London and cities elsewhere were still being attacked by the V2 rockets and as they arrived without any air-raid warning, some people were sleeping every night in air-raid shelters. It was, though, a great relief to know that my family was safe, and to be back home with them. It felt good to have a beer in the 'Greyhound' next door with the neighbours and even better, was May Creswell, who lived opposite, agreeing to go out on a date with me and kissing her goodnight on her doorstep!

That completed my mission to France. Soon I would be back in Peterborough preparing for the next. The SOE French section, Jedburgh teams and Special Air Service teams sent into the west and south-west of France, south of the Loire, had helped the French resistance liberate the whole area themselves without assistance from any other ground forces and gave them back the pride and self respect they deserved after suffering a brutal German occupation of over four years. The good work done by these and other undercover teams and resistance fighters in other areas, allowed the Allied forces to advance rapidly eastward, north of the Loire, and northward up the Rhone valley. General de Gaulle himself credited them with advancing the Liberation of France by at least six months as well as being worth several divisions of ground troops.

PART TWO

Chapter Sixteen - Change of Direction

On my return to Peterborough, after disembarkation leave, I found a completely different Milton Hall to the one from which I had departed. It now resembled a transit camp with teams also returning from missions, re-equipping, and setting off again to their various new and unknown destinations. Even the numerous training staff had been reduced to those occupied with the well-being and kitting out of their charges, most of whom were silent about what they had been doing, grateful for their safe return and pondering on what was to come, resting and thoughtful rather than making excursions into town.

Those going to the 'Far East' were shown and issued with light tropical gear and received their inoculations against a variety of tropical diseases. Joining these, the only changes I made to my personal arms were to obtain another fighting knife, because the tip of the original issue had been broken off whilst in France, and exchange my American semi-automatic rifle with a 'fixed' butt to one with a 'folding' butt, as I had found it difficult at times to conceal the weapon. Being a Light Infantry Rifleman at heart my first choice had been the fixed butt type, possibly because it resembled the type of rifle I had used in training and the butt could, if necessary, be used as a handy weapon. I later regretted the exchange as, when in Burma where concealment was less of a priority, I would have preferred the fixed butt version; in retrospect, this choice of weapons for these two operations would have suited me far better the other way round. However preparations for the forthcoming sea journey were suddenly brought to an abrupt halt after being in Peterborough only four or five days, when I was called to the CO's office.

No, not in trouble for once; it was to ask me if I would mind *not* going to the Far East just yet! They wanted a volunteer for another operation in Holland, where they urgently needed a Wireless Operator. Ah well! I mused, although the Germans are being difficult to shift out of northern Europe, there are already advances being made into parts of Germany further south, with the French now joining in and the Russians making good progress in the east. Despite the setbacks at Arnhem it should not be too long before they are defeated. Any operation in Europe now would most likely be a short one. Anyway, so what! It's been offered, who knows which option would be the best, Europe or Far East, Germans or Japanese, what's the difference. There won't be any peace until they are both stopped. Agreeing to go to the Netherlands meant handing back the tropical kit I had just received and getting ready for this next assignment.

A couple of days later I was back in London, to Dean Street and Baker Street, staying overnight once again at the same hotel I had used before the French trip. During this briefing I was informed that the team I was to join was already in the field. They had lost their man, they explained, when he was arrested after a gun was found in a car in which he was travelling. It had just been unlucky, having been stopped in a random search. The area I would be going to was in the north of Holland, where there would be a reception committee, and I would be jumping into a pre-arranged dropping zone. All seemed neat and tidy. Then I was allowed to go home and wait there for a few days whilst final flight plans were made. Contact would be made either by a message via the local police station, or if less urgent, by a Post Office telegram. In addition, I was given a direct contact telephone number to ring in a week's time. Having no telephone at home I was instructed to do this by going to the local police station in Chadwell Heath and they would put me through to the SOE's office in Whitehall. By then it would have been mid-December, probably about Monday 18th, when I first rang for further instructions. That was when I was told to stay where I was, at home, and ring them every morning. As they explained, there was difficulty with foggy weather at the time which made it uncertain when I would be called, but it could be at short notice. It would be quicker for me to get back to them in London from home, than if I went back to Milton Hall in Peterborough. This I did for a few days more until they said it was still uncertain when I would be needed, but to stay at home until I was contacted by them again. It was rapidly approaching Christmas, and my 19th birthday on 27th December, (or my 21st as shown on my Army records!). Day after day passed, every one of which could have been the last at home for some time. Christmas and birthday came and went without news, both being well celebrated with family and friends, all somewhat puzzled at my rather long stay at home but who had, of course, to be kept ignorant of the true reasons I was there.

During this long and uncertain period I was able to celebrate as though there were no tomorrow. Without having any pay-days, the money problem was solved by ringing the changes at any new bank to which I was close and exchanging a few more French Francs, using the same excuse as before, that I had just returned and this was all I had to get home with and that I would be much obliged if they could change a small amount. Whilst on leave, I was able to visit my old haunts, the Ilford Baths for a steam bath or a swim, and the Ilford Palais de Dance. Not, however, the Ilford Hippodrome, as this famous variety theatre had been destroyed by a V2 rocket! All the local cinemas were still functioning, Chadwell Heath, Seven Kings and Ilford all in full use.

The cinema was perhaps the best place to get news about the progress of the war. Taking advantage of the foggy weather, there had been a concerted effort by the Germans in a counter attack in the Ardennes, where they endeavoured to cut off and isolate the British forces, who were advancing along the northern coast into Holland through Belgium to Antwerp. This had been going on from about 16th December and it wasn't until the end of the year that they were beaten and pushed back again by the American forces. This battle, which came to be known as the Battle of the Bulge, probably held up the Allied advances for more than a month; it was almost certain to have been the cause of my delay in getting into northern Holland and completing the mission there. It was the New Year before I finally received a message telling me the mission had been cancelled and to report back to Milton Hall.

Only many years later did I learn that 'Bunny' Austin, the wireless operator I was to replace, had been captured on or about 4th December 1944. He had been held in prison until 4th April 1945 when he was murdered along with other prisoners by a German SS officer, who shot him in his cell, just before fleeing as the Canadians entered the area. Bunny's Jed team, DUDLEY, must have carried on for some time after his capture, as the Dutch member Major Brinkgreve was killed in action on 5th March. To date it is unknown what happened to the team leader, US Major Olmsted.

Once more back at Milton Hall after a protracted mission and extended stay at home, I found out that a large number of Jeds, including Tom Henney, who had shared some good times with me in France, had already been shipped off and were on their way to India. They had not been the first, others had gone before them. After being re-issued with tropical kit, I was once more ready for the journey to the other side of the world. There were two other Jed radio operators ready to go with me, Alfred Holdham, better known as 'Blondie', and Peter Colvin. We were given ten days embarkation leave and a sailing date out of Liverpool of 24th January. The only others travelling in the same small group were five or six British and French Canadian officers, the latter on their way to support the Free-French in French Indo-China. On arrival at Liverpool Docks, although the name of the ship had been removed for security reasons, it did not take too long to for the word to get around that it was the luxury P & O Liner 'Otranto'. Not a military transport ship but one that had been adapted for troop transport. This meant, in true Army style, Officers only on the upper decks with cabins and use of a dining room, NCOs, middle deck, and Other Ranks down below, in hammocks! The tables on which they had all their meals were underneath the hammocks which had to be taken down and rolled up before the meals were served. The tables also served as stepping stones when the lads wanted to make use of the hammocks. Originally the Jed party had all been allocated cabin accommodation, but on boarding, we three sergeants lost ours to an extra ENSA group of entertainers, who had joined the ship at short notice and were also bound for the Far East. Our officers complained loudly at this, giving the excuse that they needed their three NCOs for planning the special operations they were being sent out to do and it was essential for them to have constant and easy access to them. They did manage to at least get special permission for us to be on the upper deck at any time other than night for sleeping. This worked out quite well, apart from having to go down below to the hammocks at night to sleep and eat at the tables down there. There were also rest rooms on one of the lower decks with access to the open deck for recreation with, of course, separate NCOs' and Other Ranks' areas. We were, however, able to sit or roam about at will on the upper decks amongst the officers, where some of the best entertainment was in the upper deck cinema and theatre. This was also where all the ENSA entertainers were accommodated, although they did frequently go down below to entertain the other ranks. Over all the liner was well filled with Army personnel and, considering the wartime circumstances, all were made reasonably comfortable.

Chapter Seventeen - All at Sea

Slipping out at night, the ship made headway towards the Atlantic, in darkness of course, as there was still a complete blackout in the UK. It had to join other ships and take up its position in a convoy. The next morning other ships were spotted in the distance, fore and aft as well as on both port and starboard sides. The convoy took a wide sweep out into the Atlantic before turning south, keeping well away from the French coast, as German submarines were still active in that area. For these first few days the seas were very rough and many of the passengers were ill and unable to eat, or keep it down if they did. The waves were so large that an aircraft-carrier about mile away to starboard, could be seen when on the crest of a wave, but disappeared completely as it sank in the trough between the waves. Like a massive see-saw, the Otranto went up as the carrier fell, rising and falling at least thirty feet as the waves rolled beneath. A cheer would go up from the watching troops as the carrier reappeared. It seemed to be having a rougher time than the Otranto, as it pitched and tossed as well as rolling from side to side. It also appeared to be well laden, with stores and aircraft on the flight deck. Sometimes it would go very quiet when it seemed to take a little longer to reappear, as the watchers wondered if this time it had actually sunk. Whenever this happened, a few more watchers would make a dash for the toilets!

It took a full week to reach Gibraltar, the first of the five it would take to reach our destination, where we were all greeted by the amazing sight of the 'Rock' being lit up. The ship, too, had lights on and flags waving, and bands were playing on the shore as it dropped anchor in the harbour. After over five years of blackout in Britain, the sight of all these lights was reminiscent of Piccadilly, Blackpool and Southend's illuminations all rolled into one! The sight fascinated everyone on board. The troops were lining the decks, staring and singing: 'When the lights go on again, all over the world'. Many were reluctant to give up and go to bed and stayed up all night admiring the view. The liner spent the night and all the next day in the port before moving off again, this time in the direction of the Suez Canal. The Mediterranean Sea area being in complete control of the allies, the ship sailed on unescorted, although lights were dimmed at night in case of air attack. In February, as it now was, the temperature was rising and almost as warm as early summer in England. The sea was calm and the journey was becoming more like a luxury cruise daily.

At Gibraltar the troops had received their first week's pay of one pound; all other pay had been stopped. This was to avoid too much money being lost in gambling! We three sergeants had spent quite a lot of our spare time playing cards in the Sergeants' Mess and were broke long before we reached the port. Sitting spread out around the table playing a game we had never heard of before, called 'Shoot', a pot of money built up as each player in turn would 'shoot the pot' by trying to beat the pot's hand (or something like that). Losers had to add their bet to the pot, thus every time someone else tried to beat the pot, it had doubled. The idea was that if you could win when the pot was large and only lose when it was small, you may be successful. Having watched carefully whilst penniless, our gallant trio realised that we were frequently playing against each other. This had to change! We devised a plan with signs to signal when one of us had a really good hand. The other two would shoot the pot with losing hands, so that by the time it reached the player with the very good hand, the pot was a lot larger. As these occasions arose infrequently, no one noticed our ploy. It is enough to say here that all three of us arrived in Bombay with a lot more money than we had boarded with, and had not drawn any more of our pay whilst on board!

Port Said was the next stop, although not for too long. A few men were ferried off by lighter as the ship awaited its turn to enter the Suez Canal. The decks were now always crowded with men looking over the sides of the ship at the amazing changes of scenery. There were small boats with goods to sell, the Arabs throwing up a rope attached to a basket to collect the money. Small boys dived for coins thrown down to them, which they put into their mouths, having caught them before they sank too deep. Whenever the Arabs spotted a woman on board, they reached down to the hem of their garments, pulled it up over their heads, to show that they were not wearing anything underneath! As the ship moved into the canal, leaving the merchants behind, it narrowed more and more until it was necessary to look straight down the steep sides of the ship to see any water.

Sitting on deck gave the impression of the ship being drawn along on a bed of sand. It was even possible to talk to people on the high shore banks as the ship progressed slowly along. On reaching the 'sweet water' canal, a large inland lake, a wide expanse of sea and river water, we noticed there were many more ships. Some were tied up by the shore being 'coaled up'. This entailed a continuous line of men carrying a basket of coal on their heads. They filled their baskets from a barge tied to the ship's side, then climbed up steps at one side of the barge with their load carefully balanced. After tipping the contents of the basket down into the ship's hold, they carried on along the deck to descend down another set of steps, returning to the barge and exchanging their empty basket for another full one. This non-ending stream of ant-like bodies carried on by day and floodlit night. As the Otranto moored here for two days and one night, the troops on board were ferried ashore in batches for a route march. Try as we may, we failed to dodge this excursion; no-one was excused! Being allowed off the ship for a while was one thing, a 'Route March' another entirely. Even though, since arriving in Egypt, we had exchanged our uniforms for tropical kit, this place was hot, dirty and dusty. No people, no buildings, just sand and more sand. Glad to be back on board, hot and sweaty, there was an unusually long queue for the showers!

The ship continued on down the shorter second part of the canal, much the same as before with occasional sightings of people and buildings. Anything interesting caused a mass of bodies to dash from one side of the ship to the other. Right from the start of entering the Suez Canal, warnings of the danger of causing a sudden list by doing this were frequently broadcast, especially in some of the very narrow parts of the canal. It may have been better not to have mentioned this as it did encourage some to see if it really could delay their journey! The port of Suez was, however, safely reached and the ship was once more out into the open seas.

Once out of the Gulf of Suez and into the Red Sea, most noticeable were the clear waters and abundance of fish that could be seen. Porpoises swam alongside and raced ahead of the liner and flying fish skimmed a few feet above the bow waves as they fled out of the ship's pathway. Peering ahead of the ship through the clear water, other fish could be seen darting about, not wishing to be run down by the monster approaching them. Ahead was the next port of call, Aden. This time the ship docked on arrival in the harbour, just long enough for a few more passengers to disembark and to take on fuel and supplies. Another interesting place, different sights and aromas but, with no time to explore, the ship was soon on its way again. On its last lap the days and weeks passed all too rapidly, with two thousand miles still to go. Next stop Bombay!

Entertainment on board was well arranged and constantly changing to keep the passengers occupied. For example, daily sweepstakes on how far the ship had travelled in the last 24 hours, horse or dog racing parlour games, and a variety of entertaining shows and music put on by the ENSA groups. There was even some dancing on the officers' upper deck, the only place you could find any lady partners. On the outside lower deck though, something quite different. A boxing tournament had been organised!

This was a very popular event for the main body of troops of infantry and artillery men. Notices went up, seeking volunteers in all the different weights. Of the three JED sergeants, Blondie, Peter, and me, only Blondie was keen to take part. Remembering my own experience of army boxing back at Catterick I tried to dissuade him but was unable to discourage him. On the day of the contests, the ring was set up, and an enormous crowd of soldiers were packed tight all around it, perched on every possible vantage point. They had seen the programme of events which, as normal, started with the lightest weights and worked upwards to the heavy weights. The very first contest, a feather-weight, was between a sergeant and a private. Yes, it was Sgt Alfred Holdham (aka Blondie)! He was of a very slight build, only about 5ft 5in tall and weighed approximately eight and a half stone. Nevertheless he was very fit, strong and wiry. Both he and I had sparred with 'Boxer' Wilde, a real boxer (who had been gentle with both of us), when in training at Fawley Court and Milton Hall. It was every soldier's dream; the possibility of a Private getting his own back on a Sergeant legitimately. The excitement was intense, with loud cheers for the private and catcalls for the sergeant! Non-stop humorous banter, such as, 'Now's your chance!', 'Give him one for me!' was how the matched pair were greeted when introduced. As the bell rang for the start of their three round contest it went almost silent with anticipation as they touched gloves, until the first blows were struck and the roar went up again as both men gave a good account of themselves. Gradually, as the bout progressed, Blondie proved to be faster and more aggressive, although both were well matched and put on an excellent show. At the end, both men were given a rousing cheer and Blondie won on points. The spectators were at least satisfied it had been a very good bout. If remembered correctly, both winners and losers were awarded a bar of chocolate for competing!

Following perhaps one of the highlights of our voyage, things settled down again into a now familiar routine, with we three sergeants either watching the antics of the sea life or the human life on board, joining in with any competitions and enjoying the frequent entertainment put on by the ENSA groups, playing cards (and still winning), or just chatting amongst ourselves about anything that came to mind, such as family, friends back home, the 'fun' parts of our training, which although intense had been enjoyable, and not forgetting the girls we had left behind! We tended to avoid any talk about our last missions in France, or speculation on what lay in store on the next; in retrospect, strangely enough, except for Sgt Peter McLeod Colvin 7945551 ex-The Sherwood Foresters (RAC), who had dropped into a very hot spot in Brittany with Team FELIX. On more than one occasion he had mentioned that what we were doing 'was rather dangerous' and he expressed himself by saying 'We cannot always expect to get away with it!' Although such thoughts were shrugged off at the time, sadly, he was killed along with the rest of his team when their plane crashed on take off, en route for a mission into Burma. Certainly not the way he would have envisaged.

Chapter Eighteen - Overland Journey, with Hitchhikers

It had taken all of five weeks to reach Bombay, and when we awoke one morning we were already tied up in the harbour, having been aroused by the noise and unfamiliar smells of India. The troops were lined up and prepared for disembarkation, dressed in their khaki shorts, boots, long socks and puttees. We were also handed a pith helmet to wear, which soon marked everyone as new arrivals. Cries and shouts from old hands ashore greeted us with such comments as 'Get your knees brown!' Despite all the sunbathing on board, we still appeared to be quite pale compared to those already ashore, most of whom were wearing the latest issue of Australian bush hats. The small party of Special Force men were allowed to go ashore as soon as their escort arrived, whereas the others were allowed off the ship only when their transport was ready for them.

Hard luck for one of the more senior officers in the SOE party, however, as he was given all our travel permits and timetables and was lumbered with being in charge of our group of loners. Apparently the troop train taking us to our next stop in Madras would not be leaving until after lunch, leaving us with time to spare in Bombay. This rather clever man had a word or two with another who had been sent there to greet us. A tourist trip around the sights of Bombay was rapidly organised, and transport arrived in the form of a rather ancient but well decorated bus, complete with a turbaned driver-cum-guide! This would at least help to keep everyone together, it was thought, and up to a point it did. Amazing sights were seen whilst being driven around the town, colourfully dressed Indian ladies were admired (all the boys had been starved of such pleasures for five weeks) and given appreciative glances, shops full of clothes, jewellery, leather goods and possible presents galore for the folks back home. The three gambling sergeants, enriched by their successes at cards, now had plenty of extra cash to spare. At a market square we walked around the stalls and watched entertainers, some playing instruments as young girls and boys danced, others were jugglers and acrobats. Most fascinating of all were the snake charmers, who played a small flute as a cobra rose out of a basket and swayed from side to side seemingly in time with the tune. As lunch time approached we were taken to an army rest centre to freshen up and eat before making our way to the railway station. Overall, this was a very pleasant tour of the town. We had seen much of the good and a little of the parts that were pointed out as being not advisable to venture into, and where the available females were best left to their own devices. Thoughts of which came to mind after lunch when everyone was gathering together for the trip to the railway station; two of the French Canadians were missing. A worrying moment for the poor soul in charge until they turned up just in time to catch the bus for the station, explaining that they had just nipped out to buy some presents to send home. They looked hot and flustered and not everyone believed them!

Leaving Bombay we continued the long journey to our final destination at Colombo in Ceylon, (Sri Lanka), which was still over a thousand miles away, as the crow flies - but troop trains don't! The next destination was to be Madras. However the train accommodation was excellent and sleeping cars had been allocated for the entire group, the officers in two berth compartments, and the three NCOs had a four berth compartment for our sole use. Each sleeping berth compartment had its own separate room for ablutions and toilet facilities. There was no connecting corridor between the compartments or carriages therefore only when the train stopped was it possible to descend and converse with other travellers. The route taken to reach Madras is unknown but it took five days and four nights, stopping frequently to discharge troops in various parts of the country. For meals, the train would pull in at a railway station where tables were arranged along the full length of the platform. Ample supplies of a variety of foodstuffs and drinks were ready to be served into mess tins as fast as they were presented, which were then taken back onto the train for consumption. All very well organised and satisfactory, except for the wild life! Flies, small birds and the odd stray dog were to be expected in such a hot climate, but, for the uninitiated, the flocks of very large scavenging skyhawks, diving down on unsuspecting rookies to steal the food out of their mess tins as they walked back to the train, were really scary! These birds, all were to learn, were everywhere in India and were tolerated because they helped to keep the streets clean. Not surprisingly they were colloquially known as shitehawks! The soldiers had to run for it, hats covering their food, trying to reach the safety of their carriages before they lost the lot! Daytime passed reasonably well, with nothing much to do but look out of the open windows at the ever changing scenery, keeping an eye open for any wild life to take pot-shots at. Not that anyone in the sergeants' compartment would do such a thing. Would they? Whenever the train came to a halt and sometimes seemingly miles from anywhere, professional beggars, traders and small boys appeared apparently from nowhere. Some must have been surely travelling with the train. The young boys were the most insistent with their offers to do odd jobs, such as clean the compartment, shoes etc. On each refusal, they tried other ploys including offering themselves or their sisters! Oh yes, at one such pause in the journey an officer walked back down the track, and on passing the sergeants' compartment, asked if they had heard any shots being fired from the train. 'Oh no,' was the reply, 'for you to hear anything it must have been from the front of the train, nothing was heard back here!'

When we finally reached Madras, it was completely different in style and character to Bombay, cleaner and tidier, with neat small open-fronted shops and larger stores. Many well built blocks of offices and interesting buildings could be seen as we were conveyed in a troop carrier to a small army transit camp to pass the rest of the day and one night. The next stage of our journey would start early in the morning, leaving us enough time after a shower and a good clean up for a short trip into the town. This time, as not everyone wished to go out, the sergeants decided to hire three rickshaws for our tour. These were available from outside the transit camp and were well accustomed to being of service, and known by the camp to be reliable. We were given a very good tour of the town and were out for over two hours, long enough to see it light up as the evening drew in and we enjoyed a very pleasant break. It was good to get back to camp and sleep on a bed that didn't move. Come to think of it, this was the first real bed we had slept in since leaving the UK.

Colombo, still over 600 miles away, would be at the end of the next stage of our journey, with yet another overnight train ride, fortunately also with sleeping-car accommodation and, departing before lunch, we would arrive for the ferryboat early the next morning. This time, having had time in Madras to plan our journey, sufficient supplies of beer, whisky, snacks, sweets, chocolate and any other essentials we could think of, had been obtained well in advance; far more prudent, as this would eliminate bargaining from dubious traders at track-side stops on route. It was noticeable that the further south we travelled, the darker the skin tones of the population became. The villages passed also appeared to be poorer and more primitive, contrasting greatly with Madras where the lighter brown skin tones and smartly dressed people had made the area look neat and tidy, more pleasant to visit. The outdoor temperature had been rising steadily as we journeyed closer to the equator. Inland and away from the coastal areas the heat was particularly noticeable. No doubt travelling so much by night had assisted us to adjust better than having to voyage in the constant heat of the daytime. Lack of twilight, the rapid change from day to night was also surprising, and not as expected. The crossing on the ferryboat from India to Ceylon came as a refreshing change as we stood in the prow of the boat, in a position as far away from the crowd as possible. Although still warm, the morning sea breeze cooled us down so much that after an hour or so we had to seek out a more sheltered spot. Were we three merry men getting acclimatised already? Just another train journey, another couple of hundred miles to go through a much greener landscape, many more trees, some even jungle like, and we would be in Colombo.

Peter, Blondie and I, happily not weary of travelling, stood outside Colombo railway station to have our photographs taken, not too sure what day of the week it was as we had long ago lost count of days, or even adjusted our watches to the correct local time. It was in fact Saturday, 3rd March 1945; five weeks and four days since leaving Liverpool. After a quick look around the part of town adjacent to the railway station, an army transporter took us to the ME 25, base camp, 40 miles and just over an hour's ride away in Horana. Pleasantly situated amongst green coconut palms and rubber trees, the airy accommodation was built with local materials of wood, bamboo and palm leaves, with small huts for the men and larger ones for dining and recreation. Here we were to get acclimatised, receive jungle training, and team up again for our next missions. The first thing I did on arrival was to report to the M.O. For several days I had been scratching an irritating itch that the others thought was just 'prickly heat'. It wasn't, however. The doctor informed me that I was carrying some 'stowaways'. Foreign bodies roamed on my person! 'The cure is simple' said the medic. 'Just shave off all your bodily hair, except that on your head. Take extra showers, put on clean clothes twice a day and get the rest washed and re-washed until you're clear. Repeat if necessary a week later'. The unwelcome visitors, which had probably hitched a ride from the ship, were quickly disposed of, but it was not funny or easy to shave one's own body. Very tricky positions, a good balance and several mirrors were required to achieve the task without shedding too much blood!

Chapter Nineteen - Acclimatising

As new arrivals we were loudly greeted by many of the Jeds we had trained with back at Milton Hall. We were all now part of Special Force 136 which had been operating in the Far East for some time. We also learnt that others had already gone off on operations into Burma and Malaya, some even to Australia for operations in Borneo and the Dutch East Indies. I met up with Tom Henney again on arrival (we had spent the last stages of our French missions together). Tom had travelled out to Ceylon a month earlier and was already teamed up and ready to depart at any moment. We bunked down in the same hut and managed to celebrate frequently, until Tom departed some two to three weeks later. In fact, celebrations were a nightly ritual for everyone and quite a lot of alcohol was consumed every evening. The usual pattern after dinner was to be seated in the NCOs mess drinking anything that was available; the week's ration of beer could easily be consumed during one evening session! There was, however. a goodly supply of known and unknown wines and spirits. As there were only half-pint glasses available and water was scarce, it meant that whenever someone fancied a change and ordered a bottle of hock for example, instead of whisky, gin or rum, it was placed on the table for all to share, and used as a 'top up' to anything remaining in the glass. This produced some rather peculiar mixtures, adding to the hilarity of it all. Self imposed entertainment went from yarns to jokes until the sound of singing reverberated around the camp, with songs from home, old and new, switching to sentimental, and old army ballads. The words became ruder and cruder as the evening raced the booze to a conclusion, and casualties staggered back to their bunks. Tom and I had a pact that when one of us thought the other had drunk too much, he would stop drinking. This was to make sure both got back to bed safely by taking it in turns to carry the other back to their hut. A mug of cold water and/or a slapped face was the usual treatment meted out after being given a fireman's lift over a shoulder, making sure the person was still breathing, before putting him to bed.

Personal arms we had retained as issued back at Milton Hall were a .45 Colt semi-automatic, the short American parachutist's .300 carbine, fighting knife, etc. and in addition, here, we were given a machete. A new uniform was supplied in 'jungle green' and our brown leather US parachutist boots were exchanged for green canvas three quarter length, rubber soled ones. Training was practically non-existent, it being assumed we were all more or less experienced, having already been involved with the real thing, albeit in another theatre of war. There was to be some jungle training given, the nearest over 50 miles away. Even this was not thought to be very much like that which would be encountered. A small arms firing range adjoined the campsite. Inspecting it on one occasion when walking through a few trees and scrub, I found some neglected pop-up targets which looked as though they hadn't been used for some time. This probably explains why there was a sudden appearance of an enormous lizard like creature. It stood eighteen inches to two foot high, almost five foot long, from nose to the tip of its long tail. It turned its head to look at me in disdain, flicked its tail and wandered slowly back into the bushes, by which time I was returning to whence I came, walking a little faster!

The only training exercise I remember was being taken by lorry to the north of the island to a place with a name so long it was referred to as KKSA. After being dumped nearby and alone, I was to observe an RAF aerodrome and radio back to camp, without being caught, of course, the lorry returning a few days later. There were no hand generators for power so this had to be supplied from a 12 volt car battery. This, my radio, arms, kit, rations and rucksack all had to be carried. Setting up my wireless on arrival at the scheduled time for the first report, I discovered that the battery was almost flat. The strong signals from base could be heard, but my signals were so weak they could not hear *me*! Drastic action was called for! Facilities for recharging the battery were within sight, where better than on the aerodrome? Easy - by leaving most of my kit hidden at the site where I was camping and carrying the car battery, I walked unchallenged into the unguarded airport. I asked the first person I met where I could get it exchanged or recharged. I briefly explained that I was on a map reading 'exercise' and that the vehicle had broken down. A sympathetic flight sergeant took it and said it would need at least 24 hours to recharge, kindly adding that I would be welcome to stay and offered the use of an empty billet which they had available. The offer included the use of the sergeants' mess. Not wishing to push my luck too far and get involved in too much conversation, I declined saying that I had sufficient rations with me.

After being left to my own devices I just walked back to the camp in the nearby forest to collect the rest of my kit, including the wireless equipment. Undisturbed, I was able to set up the radio in this new accommodation, plug into the mains supply for power and maintain my transmission schedules at the appropriate times. Having been able to wander about the base unchallenged, I could send a comprehensive report of its contents. Staying for two days and nights before reluctantly deciding to leave, I did not wish to spoil it all by having my real intentions discovered. To protect my hosts from any unpleasant consequences as to the lack of security at the aerodrome, I did not tell anyone how I had obtained my information when back at Horana. They didn't ask and probably didn't care anyway!

Acclimatisation, that is to say, getting used to the constant heat, change of diet and generally accustomed to foreign parts, took the form of many visits to Town (Colombo) and Sea (Bentota). Frequent transport to and from the camp at Horana made it easy to visit Colombo. Although a port with a plentiful supply of Naval personnel, the available Wrens were all spoken for, as were most other European ladies. Not that the Jeds had much opportunity to entertain such thoughts! The local ladies, beautifully dressed in colourful clothes, were rarely out and about alone, though like most of the Ceylonese, they spoke very good English without the strong accent found on the Indian mainland. This was due, I discovered, to having British language teachers, whereas in India, English was more often taught by Indians. The Ceylonese were very sociable and well educated. I came by this information when talking to a friendly native lady and her husband, who was mad about cricket, at the Colombo Beach, Mount Lavinia Hotel, a beautiful spot that overlooked the sea, with a sheltered cove to one side which was ideal for swimming. The hotel was very popular for afternoon tea on the terrace, watching the world go by, before perhaps a tour of the well stocked numerous shops, selling spices, clothes and jewellery; almost anything you could wish for. All in all, Ceylon was a very green and pleasant place to be. Palms, coconut trees, rubber plantations in abundance, brightly coloured sights, be it saffron robes of monks, or elephants with brightly decorated heads and eyes, yoked oxen pulling painted carts along well made roads, or just happy children waving to passengers in vehicles passing through their villages. Beggars, plentiful in India, were rarely seen here, leaving visitors with the impression of a well maintained and prosperous country. It was even possible to send home by post a parcel of Ceylonese tea. As I was not a prolific letter writer, I knew that my mother would certainly appreciate an addition to her rations instead.

A trip to the sea and the beach at Bentota was the preferred destination on Sundays, for a swim in the warm waters of the Indian Ocean, a good excuse for shedding one's clothes and getting a deeper tan, which was important for the yellow stained pale skins that all now possessed, a condition brought about by grace of a daily dose of Mepacrine. These small saffron coloured pills were for the protection against malaria, but after a short while, saturation and a yellow hue took over the whole body. Constant perspiration produced yellowish stains on clothes, but fortunately any permanent trace was prevented by frequent and daily washing of these items. Not by us, I might add. All chores were taken care of by a plentiful supply of local helpers! The newly acquired colouring seemed less noticeable on well tanned bodies, or perhaps one got used to everyone showing the same symptoms.

A government rest house at Bentota was handy and available for refreshments, in and amongst the palm trees, running the length of the wide golden sands of the beach. The inviting sea was a mad dash of 30 to 40 ft away. New arrivals trying to reach it unshod were a sight to be seen. The very hot sand made them jump from one foot to the other in a primitive dance of surprise and pain. Those who tried to reach the sea rarely made it, having been obliged to return to their towels before getting half way. Any that did, not relishing the 'hot-foot' return called out for their sandals to be thrown out to them before they made the attempt. Jeds, being nice kind gentlemen (?!!) of course, delayed such requests with rude banter before relenting. Once in the warm sea of the Indian Ocean, the delight of swimming in its clear waters was a previously unknown pleasure, although swimming too far out looked risky, judging by the frequent appearance of rather large fish with big fins! This being before swimming masks had been invented, it could not be fully appreciated that there was an abundance of marine life just below the surface. The local fishermen had built wooden jetties out into the sea, and on the ends of these they had a crane-like structure which lowered a large square shaped net with dead fish offal as bait in its centre. This would be left for a while and when gently raised, bring up with it a goodly supply of small and medium sized fish and crustaceans. All these delights had to come to an end however, as from time to time small groups of men were called away as and when duty called.

Was it by design or sheer coincidence that the three sergeants, Pete (Peter McLeod Colvin), then Blondie (Alfred Edwin Holdham) followed by Harry (Henry Arthur Verlander) were called forward alphabetically? Peter was the first away on a mission at the end of March, a little more than three weeks after arriving in Horana. He and the two Captains in his team (G Marchant and P Vickery) were all killed when their aircraft crashed on take-off at Calcutta's Dum-Dum airport on or about 1st April '45. They had been on their way to strengthen a group already established in Burma. Blondie too was away and off to Malaya a few weeks later. Then it was my turn. I had been approached by Major (Sandy) Boal and Captain A Coomber, who asked me if I would like to join them. Capt. Coomber had been with Team SIMON in France working in La Vendee and I had briefly met him there. We got on well together and were keen to get going ASAP. After a short delay following the tragedy at Dum-Dum, briefing began the second week in April. We were told that we would be joining an established group, WALRUS, which was part of Operation 'Character'. Led by a Colonel Tulloch, the operation was in the Karenni hills, close to the Siamese/Burmese borders, and was not expected to be a long one. Monsoons were due, and they would probably have to be brought out in three or four weeks' time. This was because it would be practically impossible to supply the group by air once the rains started. Sounds reasonable enough, easily manage that, we all thought! Couldn't get there quick enough!

Left to right - 'Blondie', Harry and Peter Colvin at Columbo Station

Chapter Twenty - A Trip or Four by Dakota

The team's journey commenced with a flight to Calcutta from Colombo in a Dakota fitted out to convey civilian passengers, nice seats to sit in, windows in lined walls to look out of, very comfortable, I thought, and not as noisy as the bare, unfurnished military planes I had used up until now. This time I'll be landing in it. No jumping out, another new experience! We took with us only our Bergen rucksacks containing a change of clothes and emergency supplies and, of course, our personal arms needed for the mission. Included in the emergency supplies was a large amount of old Indian Rupees, old coins only, (Victorian) because they contained more silver, paper money being of no use whatsoever to the hill tribes where we were going, whereas the high silver content of the Rupees could be turned into jewellery for their wives. Inconvenient and heavy to carry around and liable to rattle at the wrong moment, at least they could be buried without loss or damage, as long as you remembered where you had hidden them. The rest of our possessions had been packed into kitbags and suitcases and placed into store at Horana whilst we were away. Valuables and items to be returned to next-of-kin, if the occasion should arise, were parcelled up separately and handed to the Staff Office. As in Europe, when unable to write home whilst in the field, regular messages were sent home to parents etc., to let the recipient know that all was well. As the plane descended to land, I was looking out of the window not knowing what to expect and, as it bumped a couple of times along the runway, thought that it was not much better than jumping out!

After a final briefing and a night's rest in Calcutta we were taken to Dum Dum airport. Our aeroplane, a military Dakota this time, stood already loaded with supplies to be dropped on the same early morning flight. In the hanger we were fitted out with our parachutes and the rucksacks and carbines packed into panniers. Hot drinks in flasks and sandwiches were taken aboard by the dispatcher to whom we had been introduced, along with the crew. It was going to be a long flight to and from the Dropping Zone and it could take over eight hours for the round trip. The crew said their orders were to let us jump only if the correct ground signals were seen, and on a previous flight they had occasion to abort the drop and return. Because of the length of the journey, there would be only enough time to make two or three circuits of the DZ. 'So be ready. We are hoping to get you in this time on the first run,' we were told.

Settling down in the plane for the long journey, making ourselves as comfortable as possible on the floor, trussed up in our parachutes, resting heads on any convenient softer packaging, all three team members were at last on our way. It was very cold and we were unable to talk without shouting above the noise of this thin bare-walled, unheated bone-shaker. True to form, I stuffed something into my ears and relaxed into a sometimes disturbed sleep. Remembering what my mother had often said, 'That's just like your father; you can sleep anytime, anywhere, even if your backside is in water!' We were woken by the dispatcher who handed us a hot drink of tea. When he shouted that we were nearly there, we got up and hooked up our parachute static lines to fixtures on the plane. The door was opened and we could at last see out; a mass of green trees on hillsides as far as one could see.

The aeroplane banked as it dropped lower over a valley, and a few huts and dark marks on the ground where fires had once been, could just be made out. The plane pulled up again and circled around the area. A few small bodies appeared and, after another circuit, fires were lit and the team got ready by the door, awaiting the signal to go. The plane went around again, this time higher and wider still, waiting for the identifying signal to be displayed on the ground. Coming in for a third time, a small group of people could be seen waving, but still no correct signal from the ground. The team were ready to chance it but the pilot said no. He could not allow it and if he waited any longer there would not be enough fuel to get back to base. The door was replaced and the plane pulled up and away. Disappointed, we were just going to take off our parachutes when the dispatcher remarked that we had better keep them on as they may come in handy if the plane runs out of juice. We all laughed at first, but not when we later learned that the plane would be landing at Cox's Bazaar and not returning to Calcutta, because the aircraft was very low on fuel. When we did land they told us they had only enough left to keep us all in the air for another twenty to thirty minutes!

Evening meal, a bed and, after breakfast, they were going to try again, was the latest news. The second attempt started well. Flying from

Cox's Bazaar, the shorter distance was expected to give them a little more time over our rendezvous. Settling down once more, any rest we expected to get was disturbed about two hours later by bad weather. It was giving us a bumpy ride, throwing everyone from side to side. Information from the cockpit was that it was only a localised rainstorm and we were flying through the rough weather and were, meanwhile, to hold on to straps attached to the sides of the plane! Feeling far from well, I lay on my back with eyes shut, wishing I was elsewhere, as the aeroplane was battered from side to side. Suddenly I found myself suspended floating in mid-air, as the plane dropped like a stone from beneath me, for what seemed like several seconds, although it was probably not more than a split second before I landed back on the floor with a bang. Not long after this the plane was lifted rapidly upward again. It was like being in a fast lift and my body was pressed down hard onto the floor. The pilot asked if everyone was all right, then said he was turning back as we were over high ground and turbulent air currents over the hills were causing the sudden rise and fall of the aircraft. This time the plane returned to Calcutta and we were all greatly relieved to be back on firm ground.

Still keen to get the journey over as soon as possible, the team agreed to a third try the next day, after confirmation had been received by radio that a reception committee on another ground was ready for us. Apparently, when we had flown over on the first attempt, the arrival of a small group or patrol of Japanese had unexpectedly appeared. The villagers had fled into the bush, and fires were lit by the Japanese hoping to get something for nothing. The reception committee had watched it all from a nearby hillside, unable to warn the plane. It was more than just fortunate that the pilot had refused to let us jump. Would it be third time lucky? We would see, and I am sure I was not the only one offering up a silent prayer!

The day started hot and dry as usual at Dum Dum airport as the team boarded once again on our third attempt. Same plane, same crew all determined to get the job done successfully at last. We shook hands confident that this day, 2nd May, was going to be THE day. The flight itself was smooth and we had no trouble at all reaching the DZ. As was my norm, I had rested, sleeping most of the way. Roused by the dispatcher when in sight of the dropping zone, I said 'We were only trained to jump out through 'the hole' like all paratroops are. In France I had to jump out through the bomb doors of a Stirling bomber, this time there's a door! How do I get out?' 'Easy, you can go first,' was the reply. 'Just stand ready, looking outward at the door, holding on to the handles at the sides. When it's time for you to go, I will tap you hard on the shoulder and you just step out. Just like going through any doorway.' When the door was opened, I took up my position as instructed, making sure I was hooked up, and from this vantage point I had a good clear view of the basin shaped valley into which we were dropping. After a dummy run, the pilot throttled back and dipped slowly down just clear of trees. From high on the surrounding hills, down towards the valley, I could see people, the signal fires, and the recognition sign on the ground. Then came a heavy thump on my left shoulder and I pushed off with my hands and putting my right foot forward at the same time, stepped out , only to find out later that this was wrong - I should have jumped out keeping both legs together! The slipstream caught my outstretched leg first and it spun me out and downward like a top. The parachute was pulled out and fully extended but only partly opened. I was falling too fast, and still spinning. Looking up to see what was wrong I could see that all the parachute cords were twisted like a rope and this was stopping the canopy from developing fully. Remembering seeing similar problems back at Ringway during training, I kicked out in the opposite direction to the turns on the lines running down to the webbing harness, at the same time pulling the webbing end of the guide lines above my head wide apart to hasten the unwinding of the cords. Slowly at first, then with a final jerk, the chute opened fully, checking the rate of fall. There was just enough time to look down to see how far I had to go before reaching the ground.

Instead of gliding towards the cleared level landing area in the valley, I had dropped straight downward and was part-way up the green bush and tree covered hillside. With legs now tightly together and elbows tucked in, hands up, (as taught when falling into trees) covering the face and not knowing what I was falling into, I crashed through bushes five to six foot high, which helped to brake the too rapid descent but not enough to prevent a very hard landing. The slope of the hillside caused my right leg to touch ground first. All my weight was taken on this leg and the right side of my body. A sharp pain was felt in my foot and right leg, then at my hip at the joint. As I crumpled up into a ball, my head was jerked backward to the sound of a 'crack' from the back of my neck. Then, as they say, the lights went out. But only for a second or two! Trying to stand I found that I could not put any weight onto the right leg. The bushes did not help either; there were thorns pricking into me, my clothes were torn and hooked onto broken twigs, and part of the parachute was caught up above my head. Pulling it down and cutting off some of the fabric and cords, I wrapped and tied strips around the instep of my right foot and ankle which was the most painful. It also helped to keep the sole of my green canvas jungle boot attached which was torn and almost ripped off. Then, as I was trying to stand again, I heard someone approaching. Not knowing if it was friend or foe, I pointed my .45 colt in the direction of the sound. A thin machete slashed its way towards me and a little brown barefoot figure in black shorts, wearing a small cap on his head, looking very much like pictures of Japanese army wear, appeared. On seeing the .45 pointing at him, he dropped the machete to his side, smiled and held out the other hand beckoning me to follow him. On seeing that I had difficulty in standing, let alone walking, he then acted as a crutch, taking most of my weight on his shoulders and together we worked our way down the hill along the path that had been freshly hacked. This first encounter with a Karen proved to me that, only averaging around five foot tall, they were well built, strong, stocky, also very friendly types. That is, at least to the Brits!

Chapter Twenty-One - Local TLC and a New Mode of Transport

The first European to greet me as I stumbled along the last slopes to more level ground was what at first I took to be an older man with a grey beard. He was only a little taller than the Karen, but he was wearing the standard jungle green uniform. 'Are you all right, laddie?' he asked and continued, 'I'm Tulloch, but you can call me 'Pop', everyone else does, we are all equal here.' It was the Force 136 Colonel, I/C of this group! Like everyone else in the field no insignia was worn on their uniforms. The Japanese, too, like them, would try to pick off the officers first. 'Have you broken anything?' Pop asked, offering me a swig of rum from his flask. After I had assured him that I didn't think anything was broken, but was obviously having trouble putting any weight on my right leg, the Colonel got me carried up to a small cave in the hillside where I was joined by the two officers I had jumped in with. They brought with them my Bergen rucksack, and confirmed that they had had a successful landing.

The new team and the Colonel sat together eating a light meal of rice and vegetables, discussing our next move. All the supplies had to be cached before nightfall and this area cleared, just in case the plane had been observed and the two officers were needed to assist in this. Pop had sent for the doctor, who was at another camp, to check my injuries and was expected to reach the cave in a couple of days' time. I, meanwhile, would have to wait where I was, alone, until Doc arrived. This was no surprise to me, if you can't walk here, there is very little alternative. The whole of my right side, from neck to toe, hurt so much I was past caring what happened next. Being alone suited me fine; I was not feeling very sociable anyway. My bed consisted of the remains of my parachute with spare clothes rolled up for a pillow. I had enough water and food to keep me going for several days, emergency rations in my rucksack, a supply of cigarettes, and a torch to boot! After taking a couple of pain killers, probably aspirins, and later, after dark, a sleeping tablet from my emergency escape pack, I managed to sleep reasonably well.

I had been awake for only a short while when a movement at the cave entrance had me reaching for my carbine that lay by my side. One figure, then another, was silhouetted, back lit by sunlight at the entrance. A barefoot man, with a woman carrying a basket held in position by a plaited band from her forehead to each side of the bag on her back, came in and squatted down. The man offered me a cheroot to smoke and the woman took from her basket a gourd, which had a thin hollow cane poking out of the top of it, and some cooked rice that she'd unwrapped from a large green leaf. They were obviously Black Karens from their mode of dress; the man wore only black shorts and had an embroidered 'Shan' bag hanging from one shoulder. The woman had a very short black skirt, made of a strip of cloth which only just reached around her and was tied at the waist, leaving the left thigh uncovered. Another piece of black cloth was draped to cover her left side from under the arm down to the same length as the skirt, across the body and then attached over the right shoulder. A black band around the waist held everything in place, although most of the right breast was visible, as was the left thigh when walking or squatting.

Lt Colonel 'Pop' Tulloch with Burmese sappers and miners

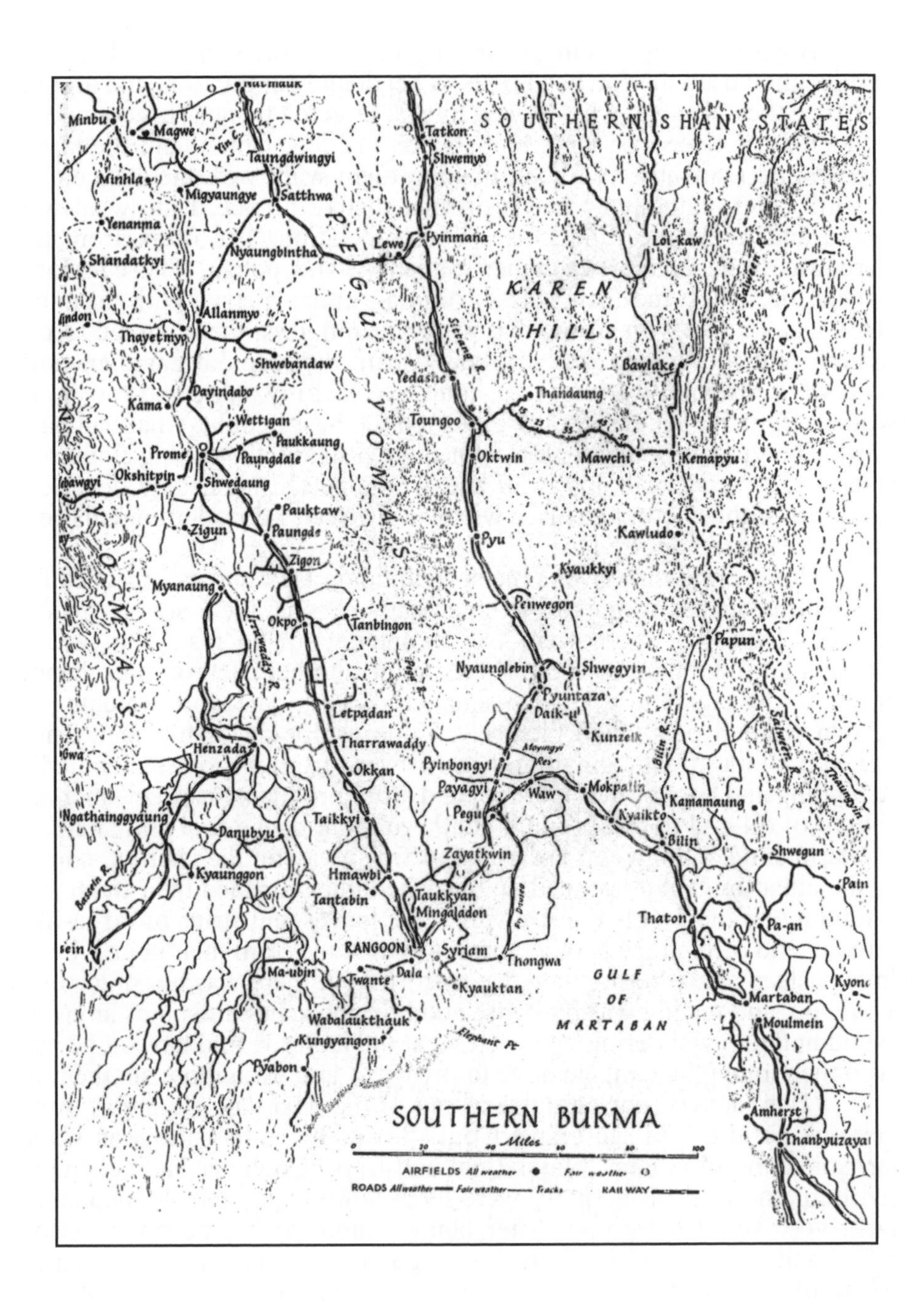
SOUTHERN SHAN STATES
Minbu
Magwe
Taungdwingyi
Minhla
Migyaungye
Satthwa
Yenanma
Shandatkyi
Nyaungbintha
Lewe
Pyinmana
Tatkon
Shwemyo
Loi-kaw
KAREN HILLS
PEGU YOMAS
Allanmyo
Thayetmyo
Shwebandaw
Sittang R.
Salween R.
Yedashe
Bawlake
Thandaung
Dayindabo
Kama
Wettigan
Toungoo
Paukkaung
Prome
Paungdale
Oktwin
Mawchi
Kemapyu
Okshitpin
Shwedaung
Pauktaw
Zigun
Paungde
Pyu
Kawludo
Zigon
Kyaukkyi
Myanaung
Penwegon
Okpo
Tanbingon
Irrawaddy R.
Papun
Nyaunglebin
Shwegyin
Pyuntaza
Daik-u
Letpadan
Kunzeik
Henzada
Tharrawaddy
Bilin R.
Salween R.
Pyinbongyi
Okkan
Payagyi
Waw
Mokpalin
Kamamaung
Ngathainggyaung
Pegu
Kyaikto
Danubyu
Taikkyi
Bilin
Zayatkwin
Shwegun
Kyaunggon
Bassein R.
Hmawbi
Taukkyan
Tantabin
Mingaladon
Thaton
Pa-an
RANGOON
Syriam
Thongwa
Ma-ubin
Twante
Dala
Kyauktan
GULF OF MARTABAN
Martaban
Moulmein
Wabalaukthauk
Elephant Pt.
Kungyangon
Pyabon
Amherst
SOUTHERN BURMA
Miles
0 20 40 60 80 100
AIRFIELDS All weather Fair weather
ROADS All weather Fair weather Tracks RAILWAY

Apparently, as an aid to carrying heavy baskets on their backs in the hills, they used the forehead with its headband contraption, and around each knee they also had what looked like tar covered twine. This completely covered the knee in a large ball-shaped fashion, which held the knees apart and permanently half bent, making them walk with the stance of a downhill skier. Although I had a distinct dislike of rice, I ate what was offered and made the right noises of appreciation. The drink from the gourd was home made rice wine, refreshing and potent. The cheroot I enjoyed too; it left me feeling less pain and rather merry! With no interpreter, using signs with words that were meaningless, they pointed to my leg and right foot which was still bound with the strips of parachute silk and cord. Loosening the boot they could see that my ankle and foot were swollen. By using hand signals I indicated the best I could, what had happened. The visitors spoke together for quite a while, then using fingers to indicate they were walking away and would return later, they departed. The effect of the cheroot and rice wine taking over, I dozed off again (possibly with a smile on my face!)

Hunger and thirst woke me several hours later and as I reached for my small haversack to get at the emergency rations, the Karenni visitors returned. This time there were two women with the man, the second woman a lot older than the first. Handing me another cheroot in exchange for one of my cigarettes, the man squatted down by the wall, watching as the two women positioned themselves one each side of my feet. They stroked both legs, massaging lightly downward from the knees then undid the binding and boot of the right foot and, after producing a sweet smelling mixture of oil and herbs, began a gentle rubbing of the foot and ankle. It felt warm and soothing as I lay back, puffing away on the cheroot, enjoying the attention being lavished on me. The ladies finished their treatment by binding up the foot and ankle with wide leaves and strips of raffia-like material, and offered me another drink of rice wine from their gourd. I was almost asleep again before they departed! In fact there was not much else I could do, and resting was probably good for the aches and pains anyway. I could not help wondering however, what the ladies would have done had I also mentioned the damage done to my neck, and even more so, the hip!

'Doc' arrived during the morning of the next day. He didn't mind everyone calling him Doc, and I only learnt his full name was Capt. Harrison some time later. Major Boal and Capt. Coomber had accompanied him, and also in the party were local guides, two female elephants, and a very small baby one. After being examined by the doctor (who sniffed and tasted with the tip of his tongue the curious mixture wrapped around the injured foot), he strapped it up again with more conventional material and pronounced that as nothing appeared to be broken, I was fit to travel provided I kept off the foot and rested it as much as possible. 'May take a week or two before you're walking on it again,' he had added. The doctor was a well-liked pleasant person who had been brought in to deal with other injuries to earlier members of this group (there had also been fatalities on the initial drop), and had travelled many miles between this and other groups in the greater area of operation Character. Surprised that he also carried arms, I mentioned to him that I had always thought that doctors were unarmed. To which he had answered, 'If anyone wants to fire on me, they won't know I'm a doctor, and I have the same rights as any one else to defend myself. I've no wish to be captured anymore than you do!'

Meanwhile the elephants had been loaded and were ready to leave. Willing hands assisted me down to join them on a journey to another camp. One of the beasts was made to go down on its knees, and I had to crawl up its trunk to reach a pannier strapped on its back, where I was to sit on sacks of rice. A mahout sat astride its neck, using a stick with what resembled a boat hook on the end of it, to steer the animal left or right by using the hook to pull its head in the desired direction. For its forward motion, he used his right foot, rubbing and digging in his toes behind the beast's ear continuously. Whenever he stopped doing this, the animal stopped walking. Using his foot, not unlike a horseman's spur, but with the toe instead of the heel, he increased or decreased speed, by the frequency of the jabbing of the toes.

The elephant was encouraged to rise. One leg at a time, front feet first, left then right, tipping me backwards and sideways with each movement, so I quickly grabbed hold of the sides of the cradle in which I was sitting. Then the back legs straightened up, right, then left, throwing me forward again in a circular motion. When the animal moved off this circular movement continued, caused by the elephant's gait. Being such heavy animals, they like to keep three feet on the ground all the time when walking and they achieve this by moving one leg after the other. Riding on their back is akin to being in a rowing boat in a not too calm sea, and after a short while I was beginning to feel a little sea-sick. Only the unusual mode of transport kept me occupied. So much to see, so much to learn, everything a new experience, and this was just the beginning.

The convoy moved off at a slow but steady pace led by local armed guides, followed by the elephants and about a dozen porters. It went up and out of the valley and into denser forest, the pathway narrowing until it was only the width of the animal's feet. These footpaths, which were to become familiar to me, were known as elephant paths, very narrow at the base, wider a little higher up to accommodate the width of their bodies where the paths were well used, densely overgrown in others. Even so I was frequently brushed by overhanging boughs and wet leaves. Any foliage hanging too low, or fallen branches or trees, were dragged down and off the path by the elephant's trunk. Some larger items were trodden on to break them before being thrown out of the way and if too big to lift, were pushed aside by a lowered head and a rolled up trunk. Previously trained and used by the Forestry Commission, these amazing animals were a pleasure to observe doing work that they seemed to enjoy. Nothing was so delightful to watch than the baby elephant, its tiny legs obliging it to run alongside, in and out, back and forth between the two adult beasts, holding its trunk high, at times making little noises with it, or being gently pushed out of the way by one or the other, who never let it out of sight. Their antics and excitement were reminiscent of a puppy-dog out to play. It could only have been a few months old!

From the brow of the hill surrounding the valley, as far as one could see, were yet more and even higher hills. Although our destination was not many miles away, to reach it we were obliged to climb and descend many of them, some so steep the paths zigzagged to and fro, lengthening the journey considerably. To negotiate parts of very steep hills the elephants had their own special method. Going upward they dropped down onto the knees of their front legs and kept their back legs fully stretched, reversing this to front legs, normal walking position and going down on their rear knees when descending. This was to adjust their body weight's high centre of gravity. If they tried to do otherwise and keep all four legs extended, they would be in danger of being top heavy and topple over. On one particularly steep descent, for a short distance, the elephant I was riding on slid down on its belly, its rear legs fully extended backwards, using its trunk as an extra leg and brake! On another occasion my mount stopped dead and refused to go forward despite energetic efforts of the mahout. We were at the time on a level narrow path running along the side of a hill. I had to get down while the mahout persuaded the animal to go down to a lower level and bypass the area it would not step on, then climb back up onto the main path further along the track. The reason for the animal's refusal, I learned later, was that they test the ground first when putting a foot down and sensing that it was not firm enough for its weight, pulled back. The second elephant, smaller and lighter, did cross this patch of soft wet earth, but slowly and carefully.

Breaks in the journey were made every hour or so, when we reached a convenient spot for the walkers to rest. At these times the baby elephant went directly to its mother for a feed; trunk up, mouth open it suckled away until it was satisfied, then sat down beside one or the other females to rest, both of whom seemed to be taking care of it. By the end of the day's journey, the poor little soul was very weary, still having to run to keep up and staying close to an adult. On arrival at a village where the group were to spend the night, as soon as we came to a halt in the centre of the village, the youngster stopped dead, just flopped over on its side, legs outstretched, in the middle of the road, and was asleep before it hit the ground. With all of its gambolling back and forth, it must have covered twice the distance! The two females took up positions one each side of the infant as soon as they had been relieved of their loads, guarding their protégé. Some of the village men came out to assist with the unloading, others, mainly women, kept the children out of the way, under control and watched from a discreet distance. Another interesting thing learnt during the pauses on the journey was that the elephants could carry loads of about 400lb, a lot less than imagined, on their backs, their main strength being in using their body weight to pull or push by simply leaning on objects. Porters on long distances, being short but sturdy, would only carry loads of up to 40lb, less than half the weight of a Jed's full kit!

In larger villages, such as this one, in the centre of a cluster of randomly placed bamboo and dried leaf type huts on stilts, a more permanent structure was often found made of harder wood, more European in style and resembling a school house. These were Mission huts, erected and used by various religious groups, usually different sects in each village, which caused the local population a great deal of confusion over which was the correct version of Christianity. Fortunately, they were united by their loyalty to the British and their hatred of the Japanese. My two officers and I were offered accommodation for the night in this more sturdy building, which was also well off the ground but did have a safer looking stairway than the rickety bamboo constructions used by the locals to reach their huts. Inside it was bare, had a solid wooden floor and was reasonably clean. No other decoration on the walls except here and there, Japanese paper money notes, for which they had no other use. We ate the 'K' rations we had brought with us, and drank some of the rice wine rather than the water that had been left for us in bamboo tubes, which was rather muddy looking, and its purity was more than doubtful! We made our beds on straw mats on the floor. The hut was unlit and, as it was now rapidly getting dark, we were soon asleep. As I closed my eyes, I could still feel the movement of the elephant ride, rocking, and rolling in the circular motion that I had felt ever since I got down off the beast that had carried me there.

We were awakened in the morning by cockerels crowing and pigs grunting as they scratched for food under the huts where all unwanted food was usually disposed of. The water in the bamboo tubes was used to wash with, as like all the other Europeans in the group we had not shaved since arriving in the field, and we were soon ready to move off again. As for other toilet necessities the least said the better; taking a clue from the others, I had wandered off to a quiet spot in the nearby bush with a shovel. On continuing our journey after a brief breakfast, I decided to test my right foot and leg a little whilst on flatter ground and attempt to walk part of the way. Having been advised to walk behind the elephant I held on to its tail for support, whenever in need of assistance. With nothing to carry, this worked quite well and I was able to hobble along reasonably well. The swelling had reduced and it was getting less painful to stand. The pace of the elephants is steady but not fast, easy to keep up with. Progress was being made, and the short elephant's tail was of great help, especially when going up an incline. However there was one thing I had not been warned of! Being so close to an enormous backside obstructed the view somewhat and being herbivores they were constantly eating, taking advantage of anything within reach, resulting in a serious and pungent wind problem. Having been caught by hot blasts more than once, it was prudent to keep a close watch on the danger area at all times, and of course, there were bigger things to come if you did not get out of the way quick enough. Nevertheless, the exercise was doing me good and sharpening up my agility at times!

The second day's journey was much the same as before, hills to meander up and down, other ranges to negotiate in the distance. These 'hills' as they were referred to, were of various heights ranging from about 3,000 to 6,000ft, mainly covered in a dense jungle of trees and shrubs. Here and there, on more level areas or cut into the hillside, could be seen cultivated patches where the 'bush' had been cleared or burnt back. Rice was grown in paddy fields wherever there was any available water, in steps or terraces, the water gently flowing down from one level to the next, tended by the women, of course, who carried everything needed in their 'head' baskets. Finding that walking too far was painful, I spent most of the journey on my 'highchair' with a wonderful view, getting down to walk only a short distance at a time when the continuous circular motion on the elephant's back became too uncomfortable to bear. It was a difficult choice to make, hobbling along on a painful foot with unwelcome odours, or feeling sea sick.

That evening's halt was a welcome relief. The baby elephant must have thought so too, as after a quick feed it was certainly the first to be asleep. It had been running alongside. like the previous day, and when I was walking it would walk by my side, occasionally turning its head towards me and looking at me straight in the eye before running on ahead, trunk held high, as though trying to encourage me to do the same. This village was a very small one, only half a dozen or so bamboo huts. No large building this time. Our beds for the night were to be on the balcony at the entrance of someone's home. There were no windows in these huts, just a little daylight peeping through the thatched walls, with a cooking fire in the centre of the one room. After a meal made up of a mixture of American 'K' and Australian one day rations, of which we had a good supply, we boiled water given to us in bamboo tubes from a nearby stream, which looked reasonably clear, to make some tea. We also had some eggs, purchased from the villagers, to hard boil and add to our next day's snacks. Finally we were given a straw mat each to lie on and wrapped ourselves up in our 'chutes on the open balcony. It was cooler this way in the almost never ending heat. Expecting to arrive on the third day, we started off earlier but had still not arrived before dark. With still a good way to go, we stopped in a clearing in the jungle which was being prepared for farming, to camp overnight. The elephants had to have their panniers taken off, of course, and, as on the previous night stops, a long chain was attached to one of their legs to stop them roaming too far.

This was when we all discovered that sleeping on the ground was not a good idea. Being frequently bitten by flying insects by day was one thing, by night insects that had not been noticed so much during the day took over. Or should I say crawled over! Ants larger than any ever seen before got everywhere, and if they found flesh they bit hard. And they brought their pals with them! Beetles, spiders and other unknown species, all creeping and crawling into unwanted places! By completely covering the body under the folds of our 'chutes that we used for bedding was the only way to get any sleep. Hammocks with mosquito netting had been promised back at Horana, but were not available when we left. I don't remember seeing anyone else with one whilst on the Burma mission either. The whole team were very glad to leave the next morning, having passed an uncomfortable night in the open. We were even happier when we arrived around midday at a fairly large and reasonably well established camp, and were greeted with a cooked meal.

Chapter Twenty-Two - Captain Campbell's Camp

After eating nothing much more than emergency rations since our arrival in Burma four days previously, a properly prepared meal, however simple, was very welcome. This also gave us the opportunity to meet the camp's occupants. In fact I had at first been introduced to a very hairy and black bearded Captain Campbell who was I/c, and was amazed to see a Japanese soldier squatting behind him, holding an American carbine. 'What the hell is he doing with that?' I had exclaimed. 'Oh, don't worry about him,' the captain replied, 'He's my 'boy', he's cleaning it.' Later I got a more detailed explanation and was told the man had been wounded when captured. The locals, who were all for finishing him off immediately, were dissuaded from killing a wounded man by Campbell, who at the time had said that if he did not die from his wounds they should at least let him get better first. Shoot him later after a trial if necessary! Strange reasoning but these were even stranger times. Campbell, in answering further questions, had said the Nip now considered that his life, having been saved by Campbell, now belonged to him. He was going to try to get him out of the country after the war, and not hand him over to the authorities. Campbell, was a bit of a 'Lone Ranger', spoke several languages; had been involved in the Spanish Civil War (fighting on both sides at different times); and was now aiming to get the 'Jap' back to England by way of South America, where he had also been before and had some connections. He frequently entertained the visiting team with his tales of travel around the world; how much was real or fictitious we shall never know. 'Doc' was also in this camp and it was here we learnt that his real title and name was Captain Harrison, although not from him; he was quite happy to be known only as 'Doc', or Doc Harrison, if you must! After checking me over again he assured me I would soon be well enough to walk, provided I took it slowly and rested as much as possible for at least another week or so. Capt.

Campbell had been put in charge of a platoon of Burmese sappers and miners to replace their own officer, Major (Tiny) Lewis, who was injured when jumping in.

Captain Campbell's Japanese 'Batman' at work

When Pop arrived the following day he put the 'New' team in the picture. WALRUS HQ consisted of himself, Lt-Col Tulloch, a signals section officer Capt. Troward, and Sgt Neville Wood. In the section of Burmese sappers and miners led by Major Lewis, were also Maj. Charlesworth, Lt Rennie, Sgt Carroll, Sgt Cliff, a platoon of sappers (one of whom had been killed when jumping in), and Khan Chauk, presumably an interpreter. Capt. Campbell's original duty was most likely Intelligence. Maj. Warren had arrived with the MO, Capt. Harrison, probably to replace the injured Maj. Lewis. Two teams were already established out in the surrounding area; Major Denning, Capt. Cockle, Sgt N Smith, and Capt. Wilson, Capt. Steele, and Sgt D Gibbs. The new third team, being of course, Maj. Boal, Capt. Coomber, and Sgt Harry Verlander, were to be given an area of their own further east, close to the Siamese border. On this operation most of the personnel were original Special Force 136 men. There were six ex Jeds in WALRUS who had volunteered for Force 136, and they were the officers Denning and Coomber, and sergeants Wood, Smith, Gibbs and Verlander. A few of the officers had been, pre-war, working in Burma with the forestry commission but most, like the Jeds, knew nothing about the country or the language. The total area of the WALRUS operation extended approximately 75 miles southward from Loi-Kaw and 50 miles westward from the Siamese border. On some of the maps they had been given there were many blank areas marked as 'un-surveyed jungle'.

Sergeant Neville Wood on the radio

The Colonel, Pop Tulloch, had a long friendly chat with me, checking on my health and fitness and on what I had done previously. After learning about my Infantry, RAC, wireless and other training with the Jeds, also about my operational mission in France, he seemed well pleased and said he was glad to have me with them. Meanwhile Pop ordered that I was to rest my leg for at least a week and then the team could settle a new area; first the two officers were to visit Capt. Wilson's team taking supplies with them. He then added that he didn't have a spare radio transmitter for the team, and that they were not very successful in the hills anyway; runners would be used for carrying messages to and fro most of the time, also adding, 'Harry, you can make yourself useful by keeping an eye on and protecting your two officers, as well as training some Levies' (Levies were local tribesmen).

In Campbell's camp, which had a radio, we received news that Germany had surrendered; it must have been the eighth or ninth of May. This called for a celebration! A large black pig was purchased from the village, on the hoof, or on the trotter, to be more precise and of course had to be despatched and prepared. This brought back childhood memories of Romford market days and watching the butcher do likewise, the method and circumstance being rather different however. The reluctant beast was dragged squealing into the camp with one rope around its neck, another tied to a back leg by the local village men. A ladder-shaped framework of bamboo was made and strapped along the back of the pig. This contraption was then stood almost upright with the pig's head to the top, its rear legs tied down at the bottom. The squealing stopped suddenly. It's unknown how they stunned the animal. It was surrounded by bodies that were performing some kind of ceremony, but when they drew back, the pig was slit the full length of its belly and its throat was cut. Blood was collected in pots and then it and the sacrificed pig were carted off to be divided up and shared out.

Captain Campbell's Camp - Campbell is sitting cross legged in the front row

Headquarters group - (seated left to right) Capt. Steel, Capt. Wilson, unknown Levie, Don Gibbs (wireless operator)

A great deal of rice wine was consumed and the main meal that day in the camp was certainly an improvement on what we had been living off up until then. It had been mostly only rice, with occasionally a little chicken or egg to augment the American or Australian pre-packed one-day rations which, although excellent, did become monotonous, and were not meant to be in constant daily use. I was yet to discover over the months ahead that rice would become the main staple diet. To quench the never-ending thirst, sometimes there would be tea but it had to be drunk with or without milk or sugar, in what ever combination happened to be available, out of a bamboo cup. The tea leaves of course were never thrown away. They served as an addition to any dog-ends, if you had any left, to be smoked in a hand-made bamboo pipe. The attraction of the American ration packs, if and when there were any available, was that all contained a packet of five cigarettes. The Australian packs had powdered lemonade which made an excellent thirst quencher, very useful on journeys when added to the water-bottle, but alas no smokes.

The celebrations ended that day with a cloud burst. There had been a few other days when it had rained for a short while, the hot sun drying out steaming clothes whilst you journeyed on. This time it was the heaviest rain the team had encountered. Warm water poured down so dense that it obscured surrounding trees and huts. First we dived into the huts and watched from the entrances. Then, as the rain eased a little, first one person then another ran to the sides of the huts, where the water was cascading down off of the thatched roofs, and stood under the waterfall that nature had provided. Someone produced some soap, off came all our soaking clothes and we began to wash, not only our bodies but also our garments. It was not long before all the Europeans in the camp were stark naked, enjoying a communal warm fresh water shower! It was certainly the first time since leaving India that we had an opportunity to have a good scrub up. All being naked out in the open air seemed so perfectly natural that no-one appeared to be in the least bit embarrassed; although someone shouted it would have made a wonderful photograph to show our grandchildren!

Optimists all, as ever; we had to be or we would not survive in such deprived circumstances. The rain stopped as suddenly as it had started, the flooded high ground in the camp was quickly drained by rivulets of surface water racing in all directions down slopes, forming new streams in the lower parts of the hills. Refreshing the atmosphere, the temperature still high, the rising steamy mist enhanced the odours of vegetation in the surrounding bush, making it a pleasure to stand in the porch and take deep breaths of invigorating air. If this was 'monsoon' weather our first experience of it was not so bad after all, even had its good points. Good clean, fresh rain water to drink and fill the water bottles with, a wash and brush up and a bit of laundering as well! Now fitted out with a new pair of jungle boots, replacing the ones ripped on landing, and having sewn up my torn trousers, I was feeling a lot happier and ready for anything that may or not may happen.

Officers Boal and Coomber went off the next day with porters and supplies for the Wilson-Steele-Gibbs camp, leaving me behind to recuperate. Our team had been given an Anglo-Burmese as an interpreter, a very large fat chap. He never looked too happy at being involved with the operation, easily scared and, the team were to find out later, prone to disappearing whenever danger was remotely apparent. When passing through or stopping overnight in a village with him, the poor chap would be a figure of fun to all the children and women who surrounded him, pointing at his rather large belly. Apparently they had never seen a fat man before. He was pretty useless to the team and had probably been passed on by others down the line. As new arrivals, our team was the last resort.

By the time Major Boal had returned I was walking reasonably well again, having exercised as well as rested, and keen to rejoin the team. In addition I had made myself useful around Campbell's camp by assisting the camp's Burmese radio operator, Ba That. An easily remembered name, shades of 'Ilkley Moor' ba tat! Not having the advanced wireless training the Jeds had, he had been experiencing difficulties in making contact with the other operators in the WALRUS group. After realigning the aerials and re-tuning in the set, I took over the sending and receiving of messages. Don Gibbs was the first to notice a difference in touch and speed of the operator's Morse at the other end and, puzzled, he sent a code message back asking, 'WHORU?' By using operator 'chat', our first meeting in the field was established with such as UBETR & OKBTR. Capt. Coomber had stayed on at Capt. Wilson's camp to reconnoitre the area around Dawtama, where our newly arrived team were hoping to set up another camp, and seek out a new site and possible Levies to train and arm for the team.

Note: *Sappers and miners – Sappers and miners were part of the Burmese Army with an officer in charge. They were engineers who built bridges, dug earthworks and laid mines (miners).*

Chapter Twenty-Three - A Trial of Fitness

There had been several actions taken against the Japanese convoys along the main road running north and south through the WALRUS area. When preparing for another raid about 10 days after my arrival, Capt. Campbell asked me if I would like to come along. 'Give you a chance to get out of this place and try out your legs,' he had said. Getting up and about all day by then, bored with doing odd jobs, I was only too pleased to join him. 'This is what we are going to do,' he explained. 'First mine the road in two places, aiming to knock out the first and last vehicles, then open fire with all we've got on whatever is left standing between the two explosions.' This type of ambush works well and I had been involved in similar actions before in France. It must have been the 16th or 17th May when we set off, just a small group of sappers with two officers and one sergeant. We were to meet up with another group from Pop's HQ near the intended site. It was a good hike of over 12 miles to the roadway, which took most of the day. Reaching there before dark, the sappers were able to place their mines and have the fuse wires hidden and running back into the bush to where one of the officers would fire the detonator. The place chosen was a fairly straight stretch of road which was used as a supply route and had deep storm drains each side of it. It was overlooked on one side by a fairly steep bush covered slope, with denser jungle behind; that was to be the withdrawal route. This group was positioned at the southern end, HQ group attending to the northern. The rifles and Bren guns were positioned high up on the hillside, where I was hidden at the edge of the jungle, with a good clear view over and down onto the road. By nightfall we were all ready and settled down for the night. It could be a long wait. The road was frequently used to convey troops and supplies to and fro towards the region of the Mawchi mines, but there was no way of knowing when they would pass this spot.

Rangoon had been taken on the 4th May by the British, who were now beginning to drive the Japanese northward. The army was advancing southward down the western coastal areas of Burma, along the Arakan Yomas mountain range and the Irrawaddi River. The only escape route, or supply routes, remaining for the Japanese forces now were through Siam, over the Pegu Yomas and the Sittang and Salween rivers, through the southern Shan states and the Karenni hills. All of these escape routes were now covered by groups of Special Force 136 (and Jeds) who together with trained local tribesmen (Levies) had the job of harassing if not stopping them.

Sleep came only in short periods this long dark night. I was constantly disturbed by biting insects that managed to wriggle their way into and under my clothes, even wrapped up as I was, not unlike a mummy, with parachute remnants draped around any piece of flesh not covered by uniform or boots. Bloody things get everywhere, up your nose, in your ears and, if you fall asleep with your mouth open, whatever you may swallow doesn't bear thinking about! Then, at first light, I crept back amongst the trees for a refreshing drink, a snack from a K ration and a pee. Back to keep watch on the road. Nothing! Not even a stray dog! Hour after hour it seemed; the mind wandering. Who are these people, the Japanese? Germans, I had good reason for disliking them. They had killed my uncle Henry, injured his family, bombed and killed many of my neighbours and friends. But they were Europeans like us. The Japanese I had only heard about or seen in news reels at the cinema. Shooting at Germans caused me no ill feeling, only justifiable revenge. But that partly destroyed village we had passed through on the way here was different. I was told that the Japs had, in passing through, killed those unable to run away into the bush, the sick and the elderly. The remains of a skinned dog had been left hanging from a tree. Any other animals or food were destroyed before leaving and huts damaged or burnt. Why would that have been necessary? They had used the village to rest overnight and this was their repayment. Did they not even consider that others like themselves would have been grateful for food and rest, had they treated the occupants with kindness or respect. The local people had welcomed us, given us food and shelter. I wondered why? They must have been living contented lives before all this started.

The long wait was broken by a distant rumble. Yes, vehicles were approaching. Suddenly everyone settled into a position where they could observe the road, to see clearly and yet careful not to be seen. Cigarettes were stubbed out, no movement, as the convoy crawled slowly into view, first one covered lorry, and then another vehicle passed. A third drew level and was in my sights when a loud explosion to my right brought it to a sudden halt, as it nearly ran into the one in front of it. Then a second explosion to my left, as figures emerged, slowly at first, from the backs of the lorries. The rifles opened fire on them, more jumped down faster and dived for cover, some under the vehicles, most into the ditches each side of the road, several not making it. Bursts of fire from a Bren gun and several Stens followed by some louder explosions to my left. The HQ group must have had a two inch mortar aimed at the vehicles, some of which were on fire. Anyone who moved on the roadway was fired on immediately as, having the advantage of height, even those seeking cover in the ditches were in danger.

The slightest movement could be seen as even if only a small part of a body was not protected it became a target. Shots were being returned from the partial cover given by the ditches, each one drawing attention to itself, then as suddenly as it started, the order to cease fire and retire was given by a blast on a whistle. I had emptied one magazine and was counting my shots in this one, fifteen in each, only five remaining. Must keep some in hand, I was thinking, as I wriggled back out of the firing positions towards the cover of the trees behind us. As I stood behind a tree and looked back down onto the road I could see burning vehicles and bodies lying on and beside the road. One injured man was dragging himself along the ground crawling towards the ditch, another standing over him with a pistol pointing down on him. This man had come out from behind one of the vehicles and it looked like a Japanese officer. He shot the injured man in the head, turned and appeared to be ordering others to get out of the ditches and to cross the road, pointing towards where the attack had been coming from. Stunned by the sight of the Jap killing one of his own men, I wanted to take just one more shot, but I was grabbed by one of the sappers and urged to leave quickly whilst it was still possible. 'So this is the kind of people we are fighting against,' was the thought that remained in my mind for a long, long, time as I left the scene.

The return to our camp was uneventful. For the first few miles we were split up into groups of twos and threes, avoiding paths through unused areas of fairly dense jungle. Until well away from the action area, and gradually catching up with each other for the last stretch, hardly a word was spoken until we reached the shelter of our huts. Even then we just ate and drank a little, not to celebrate however. It was getting dark, peace, quiet and sleep was what we needed most, but that did not come easily, too much to recall, running over and over again in the mind. How long had the action taken? One day there, one day back, from the first explosion until the last shot? It seemed like hours, everything happening in slow motion, yet it could only have been a matter of minutes; five, ten, fifteen? No, couldn't have taken that long, to use only twenty five rounds.

It was probably the couple more swigs of rice wine rather than exhaustion that finally got me off to sleep...

Chapter Twenty-four - Onward Eastward to Visit Wilson's camp

Major Boal had joined Capt. Coomber, now at Capt. Wilson's camp. Satisfied that I was now fit enough I was ready to rejoin them and, having had no real problems on the excursion to and from the road, prepared to follow them on about 20th May. Another supply or exchange of goods had been prepared and was due to leave, some for Major Denning, some for Wilson, some for Boal and company. That destined for Major Denning was diverted northward before crossing the road eastward to reach Wilson's camp. A caravan of three elephants and four or five mules set off loaded with food, arms and ammunition, escorted by some of the Burmese sappers and local Levies. This was the first time I had seen mules and, up until then, was unaware of there being any in the field with us, and never found out if they were dropped in by parachute or obtained locally. In fact it was the only time that I was to see them whilst in Burma. It is possible that the mules had travelled up to WALRUS from one of the other groups in the field. I did find them interesting to watch though as each mule, with its own driver, was led at a steady pace, seemingly un-perturbed by the load they were carrying.

The caravan was well spread out in single file because of the narrow elephant paths used in all these journeys, as were the men accompanying it. Leaving at first light, which was the normal procedure and making full use of available daylight, there were several hills and valleys to negotiate and streams to cross. Many of the streams were now running fast and deep because of more frequent rains. The mules climbed the uphill slopes, even when steep, without too much persuasion, seemingly picking out the best footholds; going down was slower but still looking for the best and safest ways down. On reaching water, now running down most of the valleys, they stopped to drink. They were very reluctant however to enter the running water, hesitating, trying to turn back, and having to be coaxed or led across. At one particular spot where the river was running very fast and deep in the centre, the poor beasts had to be unloaded and made to swim part of the way across and clearly did not appear to enjoy the experience! The porters had to carry the supplies across a very fragile looking bamboo bridge with only a rope handrail secured at intervals along the bridge. With some of the other men I chose to get wetter than we were already, and cool off by wading and swimming across. This was not that easy either, the current was very powerful, and we could not have done so carrying our own equipment. The water was a lot colder than we expected too.

Elephants in use similar to those we used

It had taken a long time to negotiate the river and reload the mules. The elephants had taken it in their stride, showering themselves (and their loads) as they crossed, apparently enjoying themselves. Once all were across, I joined the other men resting and eating lunch on the bank before splitting up. From then on the main party headed north for Major Denning's camp; Bill Beatson, the fat Anglo-Burmese interpreter was with me, taking one elephant and a few porters on to Capt. Wilson's camp with us. Over the next two hills we wound our way up, then down again, until reaching the valley where we had to cross the main road. We then needed to go on yet again to another hill until we reached Kyebogyi, a large village two or three miles east of the roadway. All went well, apparently, until we approached the road. The narrow elephant path widened a little as the ground levelled out and the porters halted whilst I and a couple of Levies went forward to check that the road was clear. It was noticed that Beatson was sweating profusely but then so was everyone else, wet with perspiration, it being of course very hot and humid. However, he was not very happy about crossing the road in daylight. Protesting strongly against it and refusing to accompany the others, he complained about the risk of being seen should anyone pass by. Ignoring his protests the road was reconnoitred first, then in small groups and with brief gaps we all crossed over the road safely. That is, all except Bill Beatson, who had disappeared! Even after a couple of Levies had returned to find him, he could not be traced and I decided to press on without him, arriving at the end of our journey in Kyebogyi just before dark.

Capt. Wilson's camp was actually in the village, which being one of the larger and more important ones, came as a surprise, as in other smaller settlements most of the huts were built on stilts, made of bamboo with a dried leaf thatched roof. Here, however, there were other more solid buildings, such as a school house, a rest house and another that was most likely that of the chief or head man of the area, the Sawbwa of Kantarawadi, whose name was Saw Shwe. Being only a few miles from the roadway and well marked on the maps, it did seem rather imprudent to me for it to be used as a base camp. The Wilson team had been established there for about three weeks though, and had cached supplies away from the village, in case a quick enforced departure was called for. The new arrivals were greeted by Major Boal, who introduced me to Captains Wilson and Steele. The other member of the team, Sgt Don Gibbs, needed no introduction as we had trained together at Fawley Court and Milton Hall. Over a very welcome evening meal, which consisted mainly of boiled rice with very little chicken and some bamboo shoots, I also met a Capt. Lockett and another sergeant, Sam Gallear who for some unknown reason I got to know as 'George'. These two, plus a Burmese, Paul Chi Swe, known as 'Chiswick' and a Karen, Maung Tin, were 'E' Force operatives whose task had been that of locating POWs. They had so far been unsuccessful and had been taken under the wing of Capt. Wilson's group.

The schoolmaster's house, which was probably also the school, was used to house the group. In one large room our bedding was arranged, as normal, on mats around the walls. With all the exchange of news and information being passed around, the arrival of supplies, and also letters from home that had been recently been dropped in to read, it was quite late before all were asleep. It had been yet another long and tiring day and I had no difficulty in sleeping until late the next morning. Most of the others were up and about before I awoke. Don had brought me a mess tin of tea to drink which was most welcome, even though it was almost cold before I drank it. My injured right leg was causing some discomfort after the long walk getting to Kyebogyi and I was glad of the extra rest, having said nothing about it on arrival, not wishing to be sent back or left behind again. Poor Don was having a bad day. He had messages to attend to and the steam generator which recharged his batteries was playing up. Then Major Boal, as the highest ranking officer there, was given the task of judging Sgt Gallear ,who had been put on a charge by his own officer Capt. Lockett, and Don was required to 'march him in'. On top of this, Don had received some sad news from home in one of the letters that had just been brought in, about the death of his father.

It had been noticeable that Lockett and Gallear were not exactly friendly towards each other, even being quite rude when either was addressing the other. Lockett had accused his sergeant of disobeying his orders by going after and shooting up some Japs and deserting his duties as a radio operator by doing so. He wanted Gallear Court Martialled. To placate Lockett and put a stop to this phoney charge and the arguments between the two antagonists, Major Boal reduced the sergeant's rank to Signalman pending a decision from Pop Tulloch who, in due course, refused to let the charges go through or allow the reduction in rank. This was after Pop had received another report from the Wilson camp about Capt. Lockett.

At that evening's meal, after Major Boal had gone off with the Captains Lockett and Wilson to report to Pop Tulloch, Capt. Steele had gone with two elephants to assist Capt. Coomber at Dawta-ma, where they were preparing a drop and possible landing zone in the new team's operational area, leaving we three sergeants, Gallear, Gibbs, and Verlander, to dine with the Sawbwa Sam Zai. Bill Beatson was also there, having at last turned up just in time to eat! The conversation turned around recent events and the hostilities between Lockett and Gallear, during which Gallear mentioned that he had seen Lockett inject morphine into his arm when they were in Siam. When Gallear had queried this he had been told to mind his own business and that he needed it for a bad toothache. At this point I spoke up, saying, 'That may explain something that has been puzzling me ever since I arrived here. Getting dressed my first morning after arriving, I noticed that my emergency first-aid kit had been opened. I tied it up again after checking it, but at first didn't notice anything amiss. Later I discovered that my morphine tube and needle were missing. I've been waiting and watching before saying anything because I was unsure when or where it had happened!' These first aid kits were a standard issue that all troops carried and they all reached for theirs and found that they had also been robbed of their morphine capsules. All three sergeants stood up as one and made for Lockett's bed, which had been left unmade. Beneath his bed mat we discovered several used empty morphine tubes! We decided to leave them where they were and show them to Major Boal on his return.

By the time Major Boal had returned, Gallear had departed for Pop's HQ camp and, after a brief investigation, the Major, finding that the sergeants were not the only ones without their emergency supplies of morphine, gave a message to Don Gibbs to radio back to Pop, explaining the 'Lockett affair'. Lockett himself stayed on at the Wilson camp. Don had organised an excellent radio room for his own use and had regular contact with Pop's HQ, as well as a direct contact with the army that he could use if required. His only problem was with the steam generator he had for recharging batteries, which kept breaking down. After a great deal of effort and ingenuity, at least whilst I was at the Wilson camp, it was working reasonably well and also supplying the camp, or at least one room, with electric light.

Frequent rain storms and heavy clouds were making life more difficult, and air supply drops were rare. Major Boal, who was apparently an architect pre-war, spent some of his spare time designing and erecting accommodation for the Wilson team. Having enjoyed a pleasant week's interlude with them it was now time for the team to move on and head for Dawta-ma.

Porters were recruited to carry the few supplies that could be spared, and Major Boal and Capt. Coomber were to take the lead with a couple of armed Levies, followed by one loaded elephant and the porters. I was at the rear, as rearguard of the column. My task was to keep watch over the porters, although there was rarely any problem of their going astray or loss of goods en route. The journey would take a full day's march, only eight or nine miles south east of Kyebogyi, but the steep hills between the two places and available pathways would double or even treble the distance we would have to travel before reaching our destination.

Chapter Twenty-Five - Home Sweet Home in the Bush

Setting off early in the morning it was raining again, as it had been on and off for some time, now more and more frequently. At times, when the paths were through dense bush and almost completely covered overhead by taller trees, it was impossible to tell if it was still raining or if it was just the residue dripping from the branches. Most of our journeys along the hills and in the valleys were through this type of terrain, only in occasional clearings, made by the Karens for cultivation, was it possible to see some of the sky and, on higher ground, to get a rare distant panoramic view of the jungle-covered landscape ahead and surrounding us. It was, as always, very hot and with the wetter atmospheric conditions it was becoming steamier. We were constantly wet through, either by the rain or with perspiration.

Boal and Coomber strode off ahead, checking the route and making sure it was clear, intending to make an hourly halt for the porters to catch up and rest. Their long legs, (Major Boal, being a Yorkshireman, was well accustomed to hiking in the hills and dales back home,) were covering more ground than the rest of the convoy each hour. This meant that by the time the porters, ushered along by me, reached them, they were rested and ready to take off again! By the time it took the porters to put down their loads and water had been passed around, the two officers were ready to journey on again. The intended ten minutes break had already lasted for over twenty for them, and they pressed on, leaving the others only a short time to load up again and be off within their ten minute respite. Not wishing to fall too far behind the leaders I had to urge the porters on, keeping them close together, frequently overtaking them and walking back and forward again and again, making sure that all was well and encouraging any stragglers to catch up. This meant, of course, that I was covering more than double the distance each hour. Similarly at each hour's halt this pattern remained.

Towards the end of the fourth hour's march, when we were due to halt for a longer period for a lunch break, I was feeling exhausted and finding it difficult to keep up with the porters, unsure if I could go on much longer and unable to hitch a ride on the elephant as it was already well loaded. The injuries received on my heavy landing were still causing a great deal of discomfort, added to which was the effect we were all now suffering from, that being the drastic change of diet. Food was limited to mainly rice, on which the locals appeared to thrive, but they were used to eating large quantities of it. Although it was supplemented by American K or Australian emergency rations, and occasionally a small piece of a scrawny chicken scrounged at great expense from the villagers, I was not too fond of rice anyway. This was due to an enforced diet of 'boiled rice only' for three months when I contracted yellow jaundice as an 11 year old. Water was also a problem even though boiled or treated with chemicals (when available) before drinking. Constant thirst was difficult to quench. Even drinking water from a spring was a risk and the rains had turned streams into a light brown soup. Sucking a pebble kept the saliva going and the mouth from being dry but was no substitute for a good cup of tea! The resultant culminating attack on the bodily system was, apart from reserves of fat being used to nourish one's own body, the rather frequent and urgent need to empty the bowels. The 'squits'or 'runs' as it was known to us, or medically, acute diarrhoea. One of the joys of being in the tropics!

There was no use seeking a drink from my water bottle, which had been empty for some time now, and it was not yet time for another break and a rest; I was beginning to fall behind. All the porters were out of sight as, yet again, the path climbed up and around the steep hill ahead of me. Too weary and weakened to go on, I stumbled and fell onto my knees. There had been times when I had offered up a prayer; after all, I had been brought up as a Christian from an early age, attending Sunday School at the Avenue Mission in Chadwell Heath and church parades with the Boys' Brigade at the Goodmayes Methodist Church even if not a regular visitor. There had also been times in France when I had prayed and sensed that someone must have been watching over me who was due for a vote of thanks. This time it was different. I prayed as never before. It had real meaning, not solely a few words of thankfulness. I made promises, asked for help and the strength to continue. A few minutes later I was up and, taking a deep breath, pressed on up the hill. Slowly at first, then using the short paces of the infantry, and with the faster pace music of the Kings Royal Rifle Corps' Regimental March ringing in my ears, my steps quickened until I reached the top of the hill, where I could see the others who had apparently just arrived. The faster, shorter marching paces of light infantry regiments, which were developed for the quick deployment of troops from one area to another, were also ideal for this hilly terrain.

The porters were setting down their loads and preparations were being made for the lunch break. In the clearing just over the brow of the hill there was a magnificent view over and along the next part of our route. Relieved at being able to catch up, I squatted down with the two officers and a small group of Levies who were lighting a fire. Whilst the Brits tucked into their K rations, the Karens produced a small animal they had caught and were preparing to cook. Strangely enough, although the jungle was rich in wildlife, it was rare to see anything other than domesticated animals near the villages. Pigs, chickens, dogs and, near any water, the odd water buffalo, yes, but the wilder beasts had learnt to keep well away from humans. If only the creepy crawly insects and, in particular, leeches did likewise, this place could be a paradise. The poor condemned creature that had been caught by the Karens was no larger than a male ferret, with a fox-shaped head and ears and, stretched between its fore and back legs, a flap of skin that it could use when gliding from one tree to another. Someone said it was a flying squirrel; if so, it was at least twice the size of any European squirrel. They did not say how they had captured or killed it, and as soon as their wood fire was burning well, with plenty of red hot cinders, it was tossed onto the hot coals. It had not been gutted or skinned, its fur was burnt off and its skin, when cooked, resembled that of a thin crackling of pork. As it had not been gutted or cleaned before the cooking of it, an offer of a small portion to taste was tactfully declined, with the excuse of it being too small to share!

Refreshed from the longer break the team and porters moved off again, this time with me in the advance guard along with Major Boal. During the break I had asked to swap with Capt. Coomber just for a change of scenery, company etc., rather than admit I had discovered that I had been walking further than the others by going backward and forward, time and again, keeping everyone together. This last stage was expected to take another two hours or so. Along the hillside, at first gradually descending into the valley, we wound our way up and over yet another hill, keeping a sharp eye open for any stray Jap patrol, and occasionally sighting Karens working their small fields cut into the hillside or in their paddy fields wherever there was water. Water and fields also meant that a village would not be far away; water that was usually as brown as the surrounding earth, bathed in by wallowing buffalo as well as people and carried back to the villages in bamboo tubes for cooking and drinking! How they purified it, or not no-one asked, but it was certainly necessary to at least boil it well before use. Amazingly the villagers looked strong, fit and cheerful, perhaps their rice wine helped to purify their systems. Not long after our second hourly break we found ourselves walking up a gentler slope. Now the path was widening as it turned first left then right, then left and right again, as it climbed upwards until we reached an area that had less and less jungle, fewer trees, before it opened out to an almost clear and flat summit. This was it, an ideal dropping zone and, with a little work, an area large enough to build a landing strip!

The two officers had chosen well and put in a lot of work on a camp site amongst some trees at the edge of the forest, close to the area that we were to develop as a reception area, good for training new recruits and receiving supplies. A shelter had been constructed - Major Boal using his civilian skills judging by its construction and design - nothing like the local buildings. It consisted of a long platform about 24 ft long, 8 ft wide and 18 inches off the ground, sectioned off into three separate compartments, screened on the platform by a 3 ft high wall on three sides, leaving the fronts open. Corner and central posts were arranged to hold a sloping roof from front to back, approx. 7-8 ft high at the front to 5-6 at the rear. The completed covered area, including extra space on the ground in the front, was about 25 ft long by 15 ft wide. The frame was made entirely with green bamboo, including the flooring of the sleeping area platform, where the large thick bamboo poles had been split and opened out length wise. These made excellent, well-sprung floorboards. The walls and roof were covered by plaited leaves, but most of the front remained open for quick and easy access. The team could sit on the edge of their approximately 8 ft square sleeping area and still be under cover in a dry space, their kit and bedding of matting and old parachutes off the ground. Home sweet home; well, it seemed like it at the time!

Only after a good night's rest did we really start to unpack and settle in at our new camp. It had been a hell of a long and arduous march. The previous evening we had only enough energy remaining to eat emergency rations, arrange our bedding and gratefully collapse into them. The porters, after having received their pay, disappeared, most likely going on to the nearby village. The new encampment had been placed well away from the village to allow it some protection if discovered by the Japanese. The first few Karen volunteers wanting to join us and become Levies turned up that first morning, but were told to wait until further supplies arrived, probably by air. This is what the team was planning for, as we had only a few supplies for ourselves at that time and could not yet feed any extra men. The rains and heavy clouds of the monsoon season had been making it difficult to receive regular drops of supplies and equipment.

Without additional arms and ammunition we could not start training the Levies. We retained just a few men to assist in the preparation of the dropping zone and potential landing strip. The elephant, or rather the mahout who was in charge of it, was dismissed because it had been noticed that he had been treating the elephant cruelly. Instead of the normal stick used to guide the animal he used a long very sharply pointed weapon that resembled a sword or long dagger. He jabbed the poor beast with it to steer and cuts could be seen on its head. When unloading he was seen jabbing at its legs to make it go down on its knees, and the elephant had bellowed in protest. Later, when standing, as the mahout turned his back to walk away, the elephant lowered its head and was moving towards him, getting ready to charge. The mahout turned and stabbed the animal several times in the upper part of its trunk, drawing blood, until it backed away. This was unusual behaviour for a mahout. Others we had noted were very attached and firm but gentle towards their charges.

Food was a constant worry, always on the mind. With the team we had brought two tins of composite rations, eight-day/man packs, supposedly enough for one man for eight days or eight men for one day! The only addition to these was a few 'K' and Australian one-man/day emergency packets. To supplement these, a small amount of rice was purchased from the village, but the villagers did not have a chicken or eggs they could sell to us, although they did say that perhaps later they could get something from another village. There would be enough for the three of us for a week or ten days, if we were very sparing. Messages had been sent requesting supplies before leaving the Wilson camp, but no reply had been received yet, if or when food, arms and ammunition could be expected.

Two extra weapons the team had acquired on our journey, probably because no one else could find a use for them, were a .22 rifle and a Sten gun, both fitted with silencers. The rifle could be useful for shooting game without making too much noise, but the Sten gun??? Just cocking a Sten made an unmistakable loud metallic sound; firing a single shot would be like striking two pieces of iron together, as the bolt flew forward and back to reload; on automatic it doesn't bear thinking about; akin to banging an empty oil drum with a metal drum stick - sounds that would carry at least as far as an un-silenced shot! I did take an interest in the .22 rifle though. The thoughts of bagging something edible were tempting. I had remarked on the sound of barking the evening before and the Major had said that it was probably barking deer, down the hill at the watering hole. Figuring that it would be too difficult to return in the dark, I planned to pay a visit when next there was a moonlit night. A little poaching was required if we were not to starve.

Meanwhile, using whatever was available from the 'compo' tins, I attempted to bake some bread using porridge oats, flour and anything else I thought might be useful. The tin itself became the oven when stood on stones around a fire. The lid, having been cut on three sides only, was pressed back to form the door. The result was not a complete failure but I had to eat most of it myself! My next effort was a considerable improvement. Making use of some chopped-up tinned fruit with the flour etc, I managed to produce a fair, if rather flat, fruit cake. I then attempted to make some rice more palatable by using dried milk powder and chopped-up tinned fruit to make a rice pudding dessert. A mixture of tinned meat and meat products with tinned and local vegetables developed into a reasonable stew-up, in which the remaining bread was dunked. This got me nominated as 'provisional' camp Chef. On the other hand, quenching thirsts was really difficult without the complete requirements for a good cup of tea! For long periods it had to be drunk with or without milk, sugar, or both. Even reasonably clean water would have been an advantage. Other drinks depended on what could be found in the American K or Australian one day packs, such as coffee or lemonade. Emergency escape packs were only raided in desperate times. These contained, amongst other things, compressed cubes of oatmeal, caramel and chocolate. The dark hard chocolate made a good cocoa drink when scraped into a cup of boiling water. In a similar way porridge could be made with the oatmeal and dried milk powder. The enriched caramels, as with the other compressed cubes, were also very hard. These had to be kept in the mouth for a long time for them to dissolve and were very good at suppressing hunger pangs.

As we had no radio, messages were sent by runners to Wilson's and Pop's camps giving our map reference position and requirements. Nothing else could be attempted until replies and supplies arrived, except to get on with preparing the landing strip and dropping zone; between, that is, thinking of nourishment and trips to the toilet, the dreaded 'runs' being a constant problem. It was impossible to dig a pit for a toilet -no tools, apart from anything else - so, as for the natives, a scrape in the bush had to suffice. This was not as simple as it sounds. No sooner had a scrape had been prepared (if one had sufficient time) and position taken, a buzzing could be heard, getting louder as it approached. Then a thump on the nearest tree announced the arrival of an enormous black beetle that fell to the ground and started to waddle towards the squatting target, which speeded up the process no end! Larger and fatter than a man's thumb, these dung beetles never failed to turn up, seemingly to be able to read one's mind and almost to arrive first and be waiting! Fortunately there were nicer sights to see in the bush, such as the beautiful butterflies with wings as large as the palms of two hands held together. That is, whenever the sun came out, for at this time there were more frequent cloudy wet days than clear skies and no rain storms. It wasn't until the end of the month that a plane was heard but, unfortunately, because of low cloud it did not reach the team's DZ. We discovered only some time later that Wilson's team had received an unexpected drop at nearby Kyebogyi, which they had assumed had been intended for Pop's HQ!

Chapter Twenty-Six - A Short Excursion

June started with the Japanese getting curious about the frequent attacks on their convoys along the Loi-Kaw/Bawlake road. A small village just a few miles south of Kyebogyi was destroyed and Kyebogyi was itself shelled by mortars or a field gun. There had been reports of Jap patrols near Boal's camp, too, at Dawta-ma, but nothing developed into anything serious and the enemy troops did not search as far as the village. Major Boal meanwhile, unable to develop a fighting group of Levies without supplies, chose to reconnoitre the areas around the north, south, and east of the camp.

A small group headed off northward towards Loi-Kaw, Major Boal, me, and the Sawbwa of Kantarwadi, who had arrived with three elephants and their mahouts with a handful of Levies as guides. We took a route away from any main roads and along the valleys and wherever possible we used the narrow elephant paths. It turned out to be a very pleasant and peaceful safari-like journey, stopping overnight in villages on the way, being fed by the 'happy to see us' Karens, who also insisted (without too much persuasion) we share with them some of their home made brews! The elephants too seemed to be enjoying the trip through the jungle paths, helping themselves to anything they fancied on the way and clearing overhead branches for the mahouts and their passengers, using trunks or their weight to push away or stand on and break fallen larger boughs. Once, on a path through the bush, the leading animal spotted a large fruit hanging from a tree. It stopped, reached up with its trunk to pull down something that I had not seen before, a large green oval shaped fruit, the thick outside skin resembling that of a pineapple. The elephant placed it on the ground between its two front feet and using the left foot and trunk as a prop proceeded to scrape the right foot down the side of the fruit to break it open. The mahout got down and relieved the animal from its chore, cut the fruit open lengthways with his machete, kept half and gave the remainder back to the elephant. Inside there were layers of bright yellow sticky morsels of very sweet date shaped fruit, spreading outward from a central stem. These he picked out using two small pieces of bamboo as chopsticks and passed them round for all to taste. To my surprise, after seeing a date-shaped stone in the centre of each of the pieces of fruit, the taste was that of a very sweet banana. Delicious!

When closer to Loi-Kaw, the Major and the Sawbwa went on alone, prudently leaving the rest of the party in a village, whilst they checked on what was going on nearer the town. This proved to be a wise decision when, on their return, they reported that it was evident the enemy were preparing to make a stand and were building a defence line in the area with a fairly large force, but they were unable to ascertain the exact number of troops. Unable to pinpoint a particular target away from local inhabitants, it was decided, at least for the present, not to call for an air strike. The group then returned by a different route, travelling south-east towards a small river which joined the larger Nam Pawn River. This would lead them back in the direction of their camp, and about five miles east of Dawta ma.

Once down in the valleys, close to the river and on more level ground, it should have been a pleasant change to walk more instead of riding on the elephants most of the time, except that, with the heavy rainfalls of late, the ground was very muddy. The rivers and streams were running deeper and faster and the overhanging trees and bushes were constantly dripping, making it all a not too agreeable journey. Whether to walk or ride became a matter of frequent changes of mind and mood. Either way had its discomforts. Ride and be dripped on, brushed by wet branches, and rocked to and fro from side to side until feeling seasick, or walk. Walking still meant getting wet from dripping trees, clothes snagging on thorny bushes, and slipping and sliding on muddy patches or wading through puddles and streams. Not forgetting the constant unavoidable heat and steamy atmosphere. Added to all this, apart from flying insects, were other more prevalent pests. Leeches! These were, of course, no strangers to the travellers, having encountered them on previous journeys, especially after going through any water when they were usually only seen after they had taken their fill of an unsuspecting victim's blood, dropping off when clothes were removed, or when a warm trickle of blood was felt somewhere on the body, often still attached there they would be, quenching their thirst.

Here they could be seen on the wet ground lying in wait for a likely meal ticket to pass by. Whole armies of them, stretching up off the wet path, just the tip of their tails on the ground, swaying from side to side, thin black worm-like bodies just two inches long, 'S' shape, not unlike miniature snakes preparing to strike. No good stamping on them, their rubbery skin was too tough to damage and they would simply climb up onto the boot! No matter how difficult the task of reaching flesh, the little blighters could wriggle between the tightest of clothing and always win. Advice given for removal once attached was never to pull them off as this would break off the head and the remains could cause an infected sore. Better to wait, let them drop off when they had taken their fill, or apply the lighted end of a cigarette to the offending object which would make it pull out its head and drop off. All very well, if you have plenty of cigarettes which, of course, were in shorter supply than food and, arguably, even more precious. A hot pipe was no help either; more likely to burn the patient! Fortunately, a tip learnt from the local populace was a lot easier and simpler. They (and their visitors) carried a small green sweet lime, and a squeeze of the citric juice applied to the offender's body not only made it retire, it passed away!

From enquiries made in villages and observations en route, the river was being used to transport supplies to enemy troops, at least between Loi-Kaw and Bawlake, possibly further down river to their army on the southern front. But this was infrequent. If this was because the river at the moment was in flood, or shortage of material, we could not be certain. The traffic also appeared to be in both directions, therefore a good possible target for us in the near future. Ideal places were looked for and noted for use later, bends in the river, away from villages, good escape cover. If and when supplies got through there was plenty of potential to keep us occupied for some time. Praying for a decent, long enough break in the weather and a plane or two getting through, we headed back to the camp at Dawta ma. En route we passed through a small village that had been burnt down and completely destroyed. There was no trace of any people or animals remaining, but there was a very unpleasant odour. So we pressed on and this unpleasant smell seemed to get stronger and more unpleasant as we progressed. The stench was unmistakably that of rotting flesh although no-one wanted to say so or believe it. On entering a small clearing only a mile or two away from the vandalised village, we had to cover our mouths and noses because of the foulness of the putrefying flesh. Lying on its side there was a very large dead elephant. It had been shot in the head with several bullets and its soft under belly had been hacked open and it looked as though some of its internal parts such as heart and liver had been removed to be eaten. According to the local guides and Levies this was the work of the Japanese, who would always take what they wanted and destroy anything that was of no immediate use to them.

Back at the camp, we nursed the sores on our legs. The smallest scratch seemed to become quickly infected. It would then develop into a festering sore that got deeper and larger without treatment. Sulphur tablets had to be crushed and the powder brushed into the wounds to assist the healing. Poor, inadequate diet was also beginning to have an effect on our general health. Uncovered flesh to allow sores to dry was also an invitation to insects and flies to lay their eggs, though the resulting tiny maggots, albeit disgusting to see, actually helped the healing by eating away rotting flesh and cleaning the wound. This was something else we learnt from the locals. When later on we had run out of medical supplies amongst other things, this was a method we had to adopt.

Chapter Twenty-Seven - Kyebogi Attacked

After being away from the camp for the best part of a week it was necessary to catch up on information and news from the Wilson camp. Not all was good. They had received another drop, this time from a fighter/bomber plane, probably a Spitfire or a Hurricane (these could, at times, drop a container instead of a bomb). Conversely, the Nips were also increasingly nosing about and making themselves a nuisance, with more patrols and the searching of local villages for the perpetrators of attacks on the roadway. The team was taking precautions against unexpected visits, although so far had experienced only several false alarms. All was very quiet and peaceful around the Boal camp, until about 10th June.

Early that morning the obvious sound of guns firing could be heard. Not just rifle fire, something larger, not too close, and echoing across the hills, making it difficult to be sure of the direction from which it was coming. It was repeated several times throughout the morning. Messengers were sent to the local villages seeking information but apart from confirming that the noise had been coming from the direction of Kyebogyi, the surrounding areas were quiet and no patrols seen. As the Boal camp was normally kept ready for any sudden emergency or unwanted surprise visits, a quick check around the camp was made and the afternoon passed without much more thought. We then retired to our hut to get out of the heavy rain. Late the following evening, alerted that someone was approaching the camp, Capt. Coomber and I went out to meet a small group which was staggering up the hill in the failing light; just a few Levies, who had with them Capt. Steele and Sgt Don Gibbs. All were on the point of collapsing with exhaustion and it was some time before they were able to recount their stories. Only after they had been refreshed with hot food and drink, their first and only meal that day, did they relax and relate the day's adventures.

Capt. Wilson had been away visiting Pop's HQ when the attack on Kyebogyi had started, with shells landing from a piece of light mountain artillery that the Japanese were known to possess. Already expecting an attack at anytime, Don was immediately sent with a small group which included Bill Beatson, who knew where the cache was, with the radio and other important equipment. He went back during a lull in the shelling to retrieve more equipment but had to withdraw again when troops resumed the attack. Meanwhile Beatson had done his disappearing act and taken off into the bush! Not knowing exactly where to find the cache, Don spent well over an hour searching before finding it with another levy. The attack continued and another of his men told him that the Japanese had surrounded the whole area including where the cached equipment was hidden. Unable to get back into their camp area, they took to the bush and followed a stream, heading for Dawta-ma. On route they were joined by Capt. Steele and another Burmese who had managed to get away, but all were very concerned about the fate of the morphine addicted Capt. Lockett. He had last been seen in the thick of the fighting, stark naked, having jumped up from his bed, grabbing his gun and joining the affray without bothering to get dressed! At the last sighting of him he was surrounded by Japs who were not shooting back at him. Whether or not they wanted to capture him alive was uncertain. The sight of this bearded, long haired, naked man must have had them perplexed and mystified, causing them to momentarily hold their fire.

As it was, the lone Capt. Lockett arrived at Boal's camp the next day, looking scratched, dirty and trembling a little, with the cold probably (?) as he was still barefoot and naked, apart from a long narrow length of black material. This was draped over one shoulder across his upper torso to the opposite side of his body, tucked in and held in place by his gun elt His carbine slung over his shoulder completed his outfit, his nakedness not at all hidden by the black piece of cloth. Certainly not a pleasant sight, enough to scare the daylights out of anyone! He had made his escape when, spotting a gap between the Japanese, he had dashed forward, firing as he went, and jumped over a precipice, which fortunately was not too high, into the surrounding bush and kept running for quite a long time. A very brave and lucky man!

After being fitted out again with clothes that others could spare, he was lodged in the village for a few days to recover. Don, too, was glad of some respite, but Lockett was soon back and asking him to return to Kyebogyi to try and recover the wireless equipment. This Don did, taking along some Levies. On their return they also brought with them Capt. Wilson, who had returned from the HQ camp with Capt. Troward, the HQ signals officer. He had found them already waiting at the cache with Maung Tin, who had stayed close to the cache site. They were unable to make the journey all the way back before dark and had to spend the night in the bush. Wilson, of course, was unaware of what had happened whilst he was away. He reported that the Japanese had left Kyebogyi after they had destroyed most of the houses and all the huts. One man, too old to escape, was found crucified on the wall of a house.

HQ was informed of this incident, by grace of Don's radio that he and I had managed to get working with the help of a car battery that had just about enough juice left in it, and a good directional aerial and compass. Pop's reply suggested that all should make their way back to HQ camp and, because of the increasing rumours and reports of Jap pressure over the whole WALRUS area, they may have to re-locate the teams. The four captains, Wilson, Steele, Troward, and Lockett moved out the following day. Capt. Wilson, who had informed Pop of Lockett's drug problem, needed to get him there for treatment or evacuation. Major Boal and our team meanwhile chose to stay because we wanted to finish building the landing strip and disbelieved the rumours of enemy patrols; so far, locally, they had always been proved false. Don and his radio stayed, as did Maung Tin who had taken a liking to both Don and myself and rarely left our sides. Maung Tin was originally part of Lockett's 'E' group. Two other tribesmen, who had attached themselves to Maung Tin, also remained with this small group, this latter pair were unarmed and were more Chinese-looking than the Karens but could have been from one of the more northerly tribes. They never spoke to anyone other than Maung Tin, only smiling politely back if they were addressed, probably not understanding the Europeans in the group any more than we could understand them. Nevertheless, all got on very well together, using mostly sign language for communication.

Chapter Twenty-Eight - Surprise Supplies

A morning or two later a break in the weather presented the team with clear skies and the welcome sound of an aircraft in the distance. We dashed out to the cleared dropping zone and each searched the sky in every direction hoping to be the first to spot it. 'Over there!' someone shouted, pointing towards the north east, the area of the now-abandoned Wilson's camp at Kyebogyi. Sure enough, in the distance, above the ridges of several ranges of high hills, a small plane could be seen circling, about eight to ten miles away. I dashed back to my kit in the shelter and returned carrying a heliograph, an item of equipment that had as yet only ever served as an unbreakable mirror, but which may prove useful one day. Quickly sighting it by using the triangle between myself, the sun, and the aeroplane, I focused it on the targeted plane, holding it in view as steady as possible. Almost immediately the aircraft veered off and headed towards my flashing signal. Reaching our prepared dropping zone a few minutes later and now clearly identified as a Dakota, it circled with its side doors opened wide and the dispatchers waving vigorously. Approaching the DZ slowly and very low, they pushed out sacks of rice in a free drop (no parachutes). These bounced high and several times along the ground before coming to rest. As they were wrapped in a double sacking, the inner sack often burst on impact but the contents were retained by the looser outer covering. We had been joined by several local villagers out of curiosity on hearing the aircraft, but the amazing sight of being unexpectedly 'bombed' in this manner resulted in men fleeing in all directions dodging the missiles. The Dakota circled twice more, dropping other supplies by parachute, before waving its wings in farewell and flying away.

The locals assisted the team's Levies to carry off most of the supplies of rice to their own storehouse, in return for the food and assistance they had rendered to the team. The remainder of the food, which was mostly eight man/day packs, was stacked in the team's own storage hut, which had to be rapidly enlarged. There were no boots or clothing, the lack of which was becoming a problem. What we had was well worn, torn and badly needed replacing. However, a container with much needed ammunition and explosives was well received. We were overjoyed with the food in the numerous tins of 'compo'. There must have been enough to last us several months! An orgy of eating was about to commence! First though, as there were no indications as to what was in the tins, only code numbers and letters being marked on the outside, we had no idea whether the contents were sweet or savoury. Fortunately, small tin openers found in the Australian emergency ration packets came in very useful. Taking note of the various codes and checking the contents of the various tins took quite some time. Delays occurred when something choice and long missed, such as a tin of pineapple, or whatever took one's fancy, had to be opened and sampled immediately. No other food had to be scraped together as an apology for a meal that day!

Breakfast the next morning was a choice of corn flakes or porridge followed by ham, baked beans in tomato sauce and scrambled egg. Albeit, the eggs were reconstituted powdered ones, as was the milk, but who cared! The only available earth-coloured rain water added a little 'tan' to the milk, but this was unnoticeable in the tea which, for a change, had both milk and sugar. Lunch time passed by with hard-tack biscuits which were made more tolerable when consumed with more cheese than biscuit. The evening meal needed a lot more thought, though. My oven which had suffered through a recent lack of use was rusty and needed to be rebuilt. A larger model was planned and reconstruction was well under way. With all these extra 'compo' tins there was plenty of material. A lack of tools was not allowed to hinder the construction process, most of which were replaced by machetes for cutting and back to the 'Stone Age' for hammers. A double-sized 'compo tin' oven with removable double door (flattened compo tin) replaced the old one, complete with chimneys made from smaller round meat and fruit tins. Larger tins were flattened and served as a stove and an oven over the fire that burnt underneath. My culinary masterpiece was completed by a covering of mud and earth and my next task was to provide my hungry companions with an edible meal!

With a large choice of various tinned meats and vegetables, the tin opener was put to some serious work. An offer of tinned sardines as a starter was declined because there was no toast! All eyes and noses were on the main course which was a mixture of stewed steak, corned beef and carrots, a very passable hot pot. New potatoes, green peas with a few freshly gathered bamboo shoots for added local colour, were served separately.

For dessert, there was a choice of tinned fruit, sliced peaches or prunes (the latter declined for obvious reasons; nourishment, not punishment was needed!), followed by cheddar cheese and coffee thanks to K rations. We were joined by the Sawbwa of Kantarawadi, who was lodging in a nearby village and who brought with him some of the locally brewed rice wine and a few cheroots. A very good evening was had by all! At least until our previously neglected and shrunken stomachs began to object to the unaccustomed richness of the food. There were not so many sore heads the next day, as sore tails!

The persistent rumours of Jap patrols searching the area in large and small groups continued although as yet nothing had been confirmed locally. With this knowledge and with Pop's suggestion that it would be safer if we all returned to his main camp for resettling elsewhere, Major Boal decided to at least despatch a large portion of the recently received supplies off to him. Capt. Coomber organised a convoy of elephants and porters and took with him the Sawbwa and everyone else except myself, Don, Maung Tin and the two Burmese who were with us. About a dozen local Levies also remained at the camp and Major Boal sent a message to Pop saying that, as he was not convinced of the veracity of the rumours, he wanted at that moment to continue with the development of the airstrip which could, when finished, be large enough to accommodate Dakotas.

Chapter Twenty-Nine - Unpleasant Retreat

Before leaving, Capt. Coomber helped prepare the camp for a quick departure, which proved to be a wise move because a day or two later another report arrived of approaching enemy patrols of thirty to forty men only two miles away and about three hundred men in all, heading towards the team's area. The items remaining in the camp store had been pre-wired with explosives, detonators and fuses. This time the report was confirmed by a runner from another village and we had to move fast! The first part of our getaway route was around the edge of the DZ screened by jungle, or across a fairly large stretch of open ground to a small hidden path through thicker bush, which led to our main escape route. When about to leave, Major Boal, who was ready to set the explosives off, called me back because the fuses were too short! We would not be far enough away before an explosion would bring the Japanese running towards the camp site. After taking off my Bergen rucksack I gave it to the Levies, who were acting as porters and, as it was too heavy for one of them to carry, they put it on a bamboo pole and carried it between two of them, and I gave them an extra silver rupee each for their trouble. (Porters normally carried about forty pounds whereas my rucksack was nearer ninety).

This small group of Levies and porters were then sent off ahead of us with the guide. Don, Maung Tin and the two other Burmese went around the open ground to a spot where the Major and I would have to make a dash over the open ground to reach it. From there they would also be able to see anyone approaching on the pathway from the village. Whilst the Major changed and lengthened the fuses, I arranged a series of booby traps with hand grenades and instantaneous fuse wire around the area. When ready to leave, I signalled to Don and Maung Tin, got thumbs up, and made the hundred yards or so dash across the clearing. Just in time, for as I was getting ready to signal the all clear for the Major to cross over the open ground, movement was spotted the far side of the DZ. Hidden from view on the shaded side of a tree, I stood up and held my left hand up palm outward, like a policeman holding up traffic, the right hand pointing towards the problem. When the coast was clear, I beckoned the Major over whilst keeping watch, carbine ready to cover him. We slipped away into the bush, glancing back in time to see more Japs approaching but not stopping long enough to get our breath back, we then moved off to catch up with Don and Maung Tin.

Our small party of six were at least half a mile away when we heard the first explosion as the remaining stores blew up with a '*whomph*' that echoed across the hills. We were probably too far away to hear any of the smaller bangs as we were keen to get a good distance between us and our antagonists. We could only imagine the mess and melange left behind, a mixture of condensed milk, jam, baked beans, and tinned fruit, tea, sugar, flour, egg powder, and sardines. At least the local insects and livestock would have a party!

Having made good progress and a fair distance away from the camp, our group had reached a wider pathway that allowed us to walk side by side in pairs, as opposed to the majority of the narrower tracks that forced a single file. We were all quite happy, descending a hillside led by Maung Tin and me, then the two Burmese with Major Boal and Don Gibbs covering the rear. By now we were several miles away and feeling more relaxed. We had not yet caught up with the advance party of porters, only expecting to do so that evening. Occasional footprints had been seen in damp soft ground in the less stony spots and not all were made by bare feet. As it was not unknown for the Levies to adopt salvaged footwear, not too much notice had been taken of this at first. Pausing to take a closer look at the next set of prints, Maung Tin and I noticed that one print was of a shoe with a divided big toe. These were known to be worn by the Japanese and thought to be an aid for climbing trees. As these were not so comfortable for the locals to wear this made us, the leading pair, rather more cautious, although having expected to see recent footprints of our advance party we were not too concerned. It was well over an hour since our departure from the camp and we had made rapid progress in that time. Ahead of us the downward path, which turned to the right around the hillside to avoid a steep drop on the left hand side, disappeared from view around the bend. We reached this bend, which had some large boulders to the left of it and thick jungle up the steep side of the hill on its right and, as we turned the corner, there in the centre of this wide track, just six to seven yards ahead of us, was my Bergen rucksack! It looked unreal, too neat and tidy to have been just dropped there. It had been carefully placed with the shoulder straps neatly placed across the front frame. Small stones had been placed around the base to keep it upright. Not a single footprint could be seen anywhere near to it, only brush marks on the ground where it had been swept clean.

Maung Tin, his carbine at the ready, approached the rucksack, his eyes searching the foreground ahead. With my Infantry training coming to the fore, I shouted orders to all the others and called Maung Tin back, saying, 'Wait, don't go past it. It looks as though it's been placed as a marker,' and again to the others, who had closed in on us, 'Take cover, in the boulders on the left!' Then again, 'Don't pass in front of the rucksack or touch it. It may be a marker or booby trapped!' I then took cover myself behind a rock on the left side of the path; the Major took up a position behind another boulder just in front and slightly to the left of me, with Don and the other two Burmese behind us. Maung Tin was still standing in the centre of the path in front of all of us and only a yard from the rucksack.

The following happened almost at one and the same time. Maung Tin had seen movement ahead and to the left of the pathway and raised his carbine shouting 'Japs' and taking aim. The Major and I also raised our carbines as we, too, had spotted the Japs darting one at a time across the path ahead, who were probably repositioning themselves to get a better angle on us. Maung Tin started to jump up and down, cursing and slapping his carbine because it had misfired. He was still in the centre of the pathway a few feet behind the rucksack. The Major then stood up doing something similar; his carbine had also failed him! I had a Jap in my sights and squeezed the trigger at the same time as the back of the Major's right shoulder presented itself right in front of my carbine! I closed my eyes expecting the worst to happen. Nothing! My carbine, too, had failed to fire! By some amazing coincidence all three rifles had failed to respond.

Note: *It must be explained here that, although these American semi-automatic rifles, as used by the Jeds, were ideal for their type of operations, there was one drawback. The safety catch and the magazine release buttons were very close together, one being a round button, the other square, both within easy reach of the trigger finger, making it too easy to press the wrong button. Pressing the magazine release meant that it would drop a fraction and had to be pressed a second time to enable it to be taken out or exchanged. Press it in error once, the magazine dropped a little but remained in place, the firearm looking normal, but it could not fire until the magazine was pushed back into place again. Slapping the base of the magazine to make sure it was always ready became a frequent habit from then on).*

With the Japanese gradually edging closer, I turned to Don and the Major and told them to get over the edge and down the side of the hill quickly before the Japs could encircle us, whilst I covered them... It was rocky, wet and slippery. The Major then helped Don over the side to lead the way, followed by the two Burmese, then the reluctant Maung Tin, who had wanted to stay with me and have a go at the Japs, and the Major followed him, but only after I, who was still well placed to watch their backs and keep an eye on the enemy, had produced a phosphorus hand grenade from my ammunition pouch, saying that I had got something that would make them keep their heads down whilst we all got clear. I'd follow as soon as this message is sent! I felt quite comfortable and at ease, after all not a single shot had been fired so far by either side.

Note: *(Phosphorus grenades make less noise, explode on impact and shower a large area with burning phosphorus, unlike the other type that breaks up into small pieces of shrapnel).*

The nearest Japs were still over thirty yards away and staying close to the edge of either side of the path and slowly approaching, too far away to reach with the grenade that would explode on impact. Overhanging branches would have hindered any long throw, so it had to be pitched as far and as low as possible to get the desired effect. As a practice shot and also perhaps to make them curious, I picked up a dark grenade-sized stone, stood up and threw it as hard as I could towards the Japanese position, aiming for the centre of the pathway. Expecting a grenade, they ducked down and awaited an explosion that never came. First one, then the others, came forward to inspect the missile, and satisfied that it was only a stone, started to move closer still in the centre of the path. Now, unscrewing the safety cap, I stood up again and threw the real grenade at them.

Without waiting to see the result, I ducked behind the rocks that had been protecting me, and slipped over the side of the hill before discovering I had made a very bad choice of rock in my escape. The boulder chosen was wet, green, slippery and egg-shaped! As my feet touched down my legs parted and slid down one each side of it. On touching bottom as it were, I let out a cry that brought the Major running back wondering what had happened. I slid the rest of the way down on my backside, carbine in one hand and my bruised pride in the other! 'Have you been hit?' the Major enquired, as the Japs had started firing. 'Are you OK?' 'Yes, keep going, I'll catch you up' I replied in a strained tone as our pace was quickened by bullets whistling by, too close for comfort. We reached the thick cover of the bush safely, the Major running, me hobbling along behind, doing a good impression of the hunch-back of Notre Dame!

It took some time to catch up with the others, who had made good progress. We all then kept going as fast as possible through thick jungle until, after crossing a small stream at the bottom of the hill, we found ourselves a good way up towards the top of the next ridge. We had been driven much further south by the ambush, and were now unsure of our exact position. Whilst stopping for a rest, we decided to carry on westward until we reached the main road, trying to avoid any pathways, trusting that after crossing the road there would be a better chance of finding out the direction of Pop's HQ. It was by then getting late and would soon be dark. The Major was all for pressing on, but it would have been too difficult at night. It was raining again and the two Burmese were reluctant, pointing to their bare feet and shaking their heads. We shared some of the rations and water we had with us, smoked a rare and valuable cigarette and then settled down for the night, with nothing to sleep in or on but the wet jungle debris; not a pleasant prospect. Insects of all shapes and sizes wasted no time in tackling an evening meal and, despite exhaustion, sleep only came for brief moments, protected as we were by only the clothes that we were wearing.

Tortured by the thoughts of all my worldly goods abandoned to the enemy, I wondered what use they had made of my lost kit, my change of underwear, spare socks, shirt, as well as personal papers, letters, and photographs. Worst of all, grace of the recent air drop of supplies, I had packed some extra tit-bits, and now as my belly rumbled, I thought of the food and extra rations no longer mine. Fortunately we had, at least, eaten well since its arrival. All that any of us had now was what we were wearing when evacuating the camp. The three Europeans only had well-worn boots and uniforms that were already torn and the bare essentials for immediate action attached to webbing belts. Mine, for example, read on my left side, hand gun and ammunition pouch with two extra loaded .45 magazines, and a water bottle. On the right, compass, ammunition pouch containing two loaded extra .300 carbine magazines and my fighting knife. Attached to the belt were also two shoulder straps, at the front of which were two large pouches. In these I carried spare K-rations, cash in the form of old Indian Rupees, and any other odds and ends that might come in useful, including ammo such as the grenade I had used at the ambush. We must have been an odd sight to the enemy. Tatty clothes, usually hatless because they made you perspire too much, bearded, with a sweat band of parachute material around the neck, my now longer hair tied back in a pig-tail with a piece of parachute cord! Of the three Burmese, only Maung Tin was armed with a carbine and they had very little else apart from one machete.

After a miserable night we were glad to be up and moving again at first light. It had stopped raining and it was soon, as usual, very hot and humid. On reaching the top of the ridge, we took a compass bearing and headed westward down the other side. We were soon completely out of water and food, even though we had drunk and eaten sparingly that morning. Thirst was now our main concern and we were hoping to find water on reaching the valley below. Disappointingly, the only gullies we passed were dry and thirst became a serious problem. Maung Tin and the other two Burmese came into their own and kept a lookout for jungle alternatives. Using a thin hollow cane as a straw, they demonstrated how water, held in the base of some plants where the leaves joined the stems, could be sucked up. This, of course, included the odd insect or two and goodness knows what else. Thirst, however, soon overtook prudence. Just close the eyes and spit out any solids! The locals may have been immune but weren't we Europeans? However there was enough moisture to wet the throat but not fully satisfy the need. In turn, I shared my own method of keeping the saliva going, by sucking a pebble and NOT swallowing it. All right up to a point but it did cause the stomach to expect food and give you wind, making one belch and feel even hungrier.

Finding food was even more difficult in the dense jungle. We would have to wait until we were nearer to a village or cultivated areas. Maung Tin did find a small group of wild banana trees and there were some fruits still on them. The bananas were black and we were all warned not to eat them as they would most certainly give you a nasty dose of dysentery (the continuous diarrhoea with which the Europeans had to contend was enough to be going on with at the moment). However, Maung Tin sliced off the top part of the tree with the machete leaving only about two foot in height still standing. He then cut the remaining stem off, a few inches above the ground. The piece he had collected was then stripped of its outside layers until only the centre core, which was white pith, remained. To look at it resembled a stick of sea-side rock. When eaten it was crisp and had a strong and sweet banana flavour. Not very filling, but it was most welcome and probably very nourishing. Having covered a fair distance by night fall and cleared another ridge, we then began another downward trek. Yet another night had to be spent in the bush on the ground. As it had not rained all day, it was at least relatively dry, not like the previous night. Exhaustion took over and, ignoring the ever present large ants and other beasties, we all dozed off into an ever disturbed slumber.

As soon as it was daylight we were up and away as there was nothing else to do; nothing to eat or drink anyway. At every clearing, eyes searched for a village until well down the hill and then we came to a pathway, narrow at first then widening out as we followed it. Yes! In the very near distance, habitation, at last! Yet, as the Major, Maung Tin and I approached, something made us hesitate, something was not quite normal, something was missing. The ground leading into the village looked well used; cattle footprints were noticed, probably water buffalo, all pointing outward from the not too distant huts. Then it struck us. There was no sound coming from the village. It was abnormally quiet - no chickens, no pigs, nor barking dogs. Almost at the entrance to the village we stopped and changed direction, having decided to skirt around to the left, keeping some trees between us and the houses. Peering through these trees we could not see very much, however the village appeared to be deserted, but then it was also still very early in the morning.

Selecting a tall tree, I handed my carbine to the Major and whispered to him that I would climb up and take a better look. Then, when I had just got nicely placed and settled among the foliage and branches with a good clear view of the central area, out of a house directly in front of me and about forty yards away, a door opened and out strode a Japanese officer, dressed in what looked like riding boots and jodhpurs, with a white open necked shirt. He stood in the morning sun, legs apart, with arms upstretched, and yawned. Looking down at the Major just below me, I held a finger to my lips and without making a sound, mouthed 'Shush! Quick, pass me my carbine,' as I pointed to what I could see. Boal took a quick look through the bushes and also saw the Jap. He signalled back to me, 'No, too risky, come down!' Not too pleased at this missed opportunity, I slipped quietly down. The Major then insisted we leave, adding that as we were not equipped or strong enough and having no idea how many more Japanese there were in the village, it would be far too dangerous. The others had, in turn, all peeped through the gap in the surrounding hedges to watch this solitary Jap doing his morning exercises on the porch of the house. I was not happy. I had not forgotten my lost kit and wanted revenge. Such an easy shot; I could have placed a single bullet anywhere I chose, preferably between the eyes. But I had to admit later that the Major was right. Without disturbing a possible hornet's nest we crept away and continued our journey.

With the jungle thinning out, no rain or clouds, the sun feeling hotter than ever, we felt even thirstier and the search for water was now urgent and intense as we wearily walked on, expecting the main road to be just over the next brow. It was not to be until that afternoon, as we descended yet another hill, a sudden rain storm brought us to a halt; rain pouring down formed rivulets on the ground around us. At first we grabbed hold of the nearest large leaf to drink as the water poured down off it directly into our mouths, then realised that some of this precious rain must be saved, so we tried to collect it in our water bottles. Directly off the broad leaves, and by scraping the earth to form a small dam, a pond formed from which we hoped to fill our bottles. Then as suddenly as the rain had started, it stopped!

We pressed on until nightfall, almost silently, saving what energy we had left for the wearisome journey and settling down yet again for a night under the stars; so tired, that we hardly noticed the disturbing bites from insects seeking an evening meal. Relief came with the early morning sun, when we could once more resume our trek, having lost count of the number of closely packed hills that had been climbed, and now faced with yet another, walked on. Up and over the apex to a steep descent that was so slippery that we had to hold on to trees and bushes for support. Lower down, the ground levelling out, was bare and strewn with rocks before rising slightly again. Then we saw it - 'The Road'. It was just in front of us, with only open ground between us and it! Suddenly realising how exposed and vulnerable we were to any passing traffic we threw ourselves down and were soon lying flat on the ground. We then contemplated the choice of whether to go on or wait until nightfall. If we stayed where we were, or went back, we may be seen. If we went on, there was a risk of being spotted by sentries posted at intervals along the road. The sentries were a long way off, placed at bends in the road and just about able to see each other.

On the other side of the road there was a very steep cliff, densely covered by undergrowth. At each side of the road there were the deep, wide storm drainage ditches. The desire to cross the road won. If we took our time and kept a careful watch, we could make the crossing one at a time. Aided by yet another downpour of rain, which helped to obscure us, we all made the crossing. Not though, without getting soaked, and not just by the rain. The ditches were too wide to jump over, making it necessary to slide in and climb out of them again. The water flowing in the ditches and the steep sides did nothing to help either. A short run for the cover of bush and trees soon brought us to the base of an almost vertical incline that had to be negotiated before we reached the top of the hill. We were forced to climb, using hands, feet and knees at times, frequently slipping backward, helping each other up over the more difficult sections, fortunately unseen from the road below because of the dense growth of trees and bushes. These also served us well as hand holds. Long before reaching the summit, lack of provisions had taken its toll in weakening us all, and on arrival we collapsed safe but exhausted!

The three Burmese were the first to recover and scout around the area, seeking a shelter. They returned in a very short time and led the rest of us to a cave they had found not too far away. Although it was still afternoon when we installed ourselves in it, finding it dry and with its own supply of water, we took the rest of the day off. This gave us time to make some running repairs to what was left of our clothes and to fill our water bottles with the good clear water, which was dripping from the roof in several places. Our clothes, tattered and torn, were repaired where possible, without the aid of needles or cotton. This meant mostly cutting or tearing off the useless parts. For example, my trouser legs were ripped so much, mostly from the knees down, that I transformed them into a rather natty pair of shorts. Then using strips of the saved material, I wrapped them round my feet, thus replacing my jungle boots which were by now worn out with loose flapping soles and, therefore, extremely uncomfortable. The long boot laces, however, came in very handy for this task! I was not alone in this attempt at *haute couture* as the other Europeans were now also reduced to going barefoot, with shirts and trousers torn and badly needing replacement. After getting a fire of dry brushwood going, which we found in the cave, and feeling more comfortable than on the previous few nights, we settled down thankfully to a well earned restful night.

Yet another day dawned and, refreshed by plenty of the good clean water which had been collected overnight, we set off once more. A long deep and wide valley lay ahead of us. We would have to walk zigzagging along and down paths before rising up once more to clear the next hill that could be seen in the distance. The direction we followed was as before, the one in which we expected to find Pop's HQ camp. We still kept a sharp lookout for Jap patrols, although we felt more relaxed now that we were away from the main road. Then about midday someone spotted a village part way up the other side of the valley, but still a good distance away. It was impossible to guess how far we'd travelled as we were backwards and forwards down to the bottom of the valley, then a similar climb up again to the village on the other side. Progress was slow as we hopefully trudged upward after reaching the lowest part of the valley. We were by now feeling very weak and tired and it was getting late in the day. Each of us was now walking at his own pace with the leaders well in advance of the rest of the group. Maung Tin and the other two Burmese, no strangers to the hills of course, were in the lead. The Major was following, but only just managing to keep them in sight, his pace well below his normal stride. Poor Don was very weak and struggling to keep going. I had dropped back and stayed with him, not that I was feeling that much fitter. As dusk approached, Maung Tin started to call out to the village, his voice echoing along the valley. He repeated his calls several times before receiving an answer. He shouted back again, then, a little later, it being by now quite dark, several torches of burning faggots could be seen bobbing towards us.

Relief was in sight, so we sat down to wait for our rescuers, and very welcome they were too. A small group of village men not only lit the pathway with their flaming torches, they also tried their best to assist the weakened men on the final part of the journey, which was not an easy task for Karens, being of a smaller stature than the Europeans. Once arrived in the village we were warmly welcomed and billeted in different huts, to be cared for with refreshing drinks of the local brew, sucked through a hollow cane in the ever present pot, which stood on the balcony. We were given bowls of rice and a few vegetables from a cooking pot over the fire in the centre of the hut and mats on the floor to sleep on with brightly coloured rugs to cover us. Maybe not a first class hotel, but certainly all that was needed and most welcome. In the morning we learnt that Pop's camp at Hpu Hkya Hku was only a few miles away and that we had, fortunately, been heading in the right direction!

Well rested and with fuller bellies, we regretfully departed the next morning; not too early for a change, as the final stage in our trek was not very far away. The journey, though not that far as the crow flies, took longer than expected, for although we were following a path along a valley, it was constantly uphill. The Major was showing signs of being unwell, certainly less enthusiastic about walking than he normally would be, and remarked on how he had perspired a great deal the previous night. When we finally staggered into the HQ's camp, we were welcomed with great surprise as it had been presumed that the Japanese had got us. Capt. Coomber had arrived safely with his 'caravan' of porters and supplies, but had also brought news of increasing enemy patrols throughout the area. The camp itself was in a good position high on a hill, encircled by a valley, giving a good clear view in all directions. It could be defended if necessary, but as the Japs seemed to be making a concerted effort against the whole group, Pop had decided to concentrate them all further north in Major Denning's area, around Dawrahku. Plans were already in place for yet another move. First the new arrivals had to be fed and re-clothed from the available supplies. Don and I joined Neville Wood, the HQ Wireless Operator, who was glad of the opportunity to get away from the HQ signals officer, Capt. Troward, whom he found to be too effeminate for his liking. The doctor had given some quinine to Major Boal to ease his fever and then he and Capt. Coomber joined the other officers and the Burmese sappers, who were out down in the valley setting up booby traps on all the paths approaching the camp. This was because there had been sightings of Japs in the surrounding areas. Stores that couldn't be immediately carried away were hidden or buried. During the day, Pop left for Dawrahku with an advance party and some supplies loaded on elephants. All remaining personnel returned to the camp for the night, except Major Boal, Capt. Coomber and another Burmese with a Bren gun, who chose to act as guards; a precautionary measure after further news arrived saying that two Japs were still in the village below. It was not usual for the Japs to attack at night, (at least locally), so no-one was too worried, but kit was packed and ready for a quick getaway if necessary.

Chapter Thirty - Pop's HQ's Turn for Evacuation

After breakfast the next morning Neville was sending a message to base on the radio, whilst I stood watching and Don was still resting, when suddenly distant bursts of Bren gun fire could be heard. The local Levies had opened fire on approaching Japanese patrols. Neville stopped sending his messages, saying 'Sod this for a lark. I'm off!' 'What about finishing the message first?' I asked. 'Troward can do that! I'm going!' he replied. 'Well, what's going to happen to the radio set then?' I enquired. I, who up till now had been starved of any radio work since arriving in Burma, decided to take over and finished sending the rest of the message before joining Neville and Don, who were by now well on their way out of the camp and halfway down the hill before I caught them up. After we had crossed the valley and were making our way up the other side, without having seen any Japanese or hearing any more firing, we stopped for a breather. While resting, the Sawbwa of Kantarwadi caught up with us, wearing a Japanese hat, as he often did, hoping that we wouldn't fire on him. Nevertheless, one day he may get an unpleasant surprise, if he is not immediately recognised! Our small group then carried on to the village of Ti-Ku-Le, which had been previously used as a DZ. There in the village we found Capt. Lockett, who was very ill, lying on the balcony of a hut, still waiting to be flown out. He occasionally called out for more Kaung-ye, the local booze, which helped to calm him down. We settled down for the night in a school hut which had the usual worthless Japanese paper money pinned to the walls for decoration. Other men from the camp rolled up during the evening as gradually the old HQ camp was abandoned. It was assumed that only a small group of about thirty or so Japanese had attacked the camp but it was almost certain they would return, as this was the third camp they had managed to trace up until now.

Most of the officers of Don's and my teams departed early the next morning, leaving the signals section, which now included Don and myself, to contact Pop by radio, mainly to let him know what had happened since he left the camp at Hpu Hkya Hku, and to let him know that the two teams were making their way to the new site at Dawrahku. After several unsuccessful attempts to contact him, we also packed up and followed the others, walking on again for the rest of the day to the next village where we finally caught up with the officers, who had already made themselves comfortable, with plenty of food and Kaung-ye already laid on. The evening ended with a sing song, much to the amusement of the locals who also joined in. The next day the villagers produced a couple of elephants to carry most of the team's kit and more importantly, to carry Major Boal, who was now seriously ill. We three sergeants, who had gone on ahead as the elephants' pace was slower, were well in front of the rest when it started to rain once more. Finding a cave en route we sheltered there until the elephants caught up. When Major Boal arrived he was made as comfortable as possible in the cave, where he wanted to stay at least until the rain stopped. He was so ill it was difficult to know what to do for the best, but he implored us to go on and leave him. So we pressed on to the next village and arrived about lunch time, when the villagers insisted on feeding us. The meal took a long time to prepare and by the time we were ready to eat, the elephants, and the Major, who had sufficiently recovered to continue on the journey and was walking again, had caught up with us! After enjoying a good feed, we pushed on and by the evening we had reached an abandoned village in which there were a couple of wooden huts, probably an ex-missionary hut and school, and these served us well for the night.

The next day's journey was to be surprise after surprise. Don, Neville and I were the first to set off, heading for Dawrahku, which was not that far away. It was still early in the morning, a dry, bright and sunny day. As we left the hut, we were greeted by a smiling young man armed with a cross-bow! He had been squatting outside the hut waiting for us as we prepared to leave. He beckoned to us, indicating that we should follow him. Well, he looked friendly enough, so we took a chance and did. He stayed several yards ahead of us, occasionally calling out to unseen persons as we journeyed on, giving the three of us the rather uncomfortable impression that we were being watched. There was something else that was different about this region we were now travelling through, but we could not quite make out what it was. The dress of this tribesman was similar to that of other Karens we had met, bare foot and wearing only a pair of shorts. The exception was the cross-bow, plus a rather longer and slimmer machete than seen before, attached to his side. The pathway became wider as we progressed, with fewer trees and more cultivated areas on the hillsides. It appeared to be more open countryside, neater and tidier. Women could be seen working in the small fields cut into the slopes. Too far away at first to see them clearly, when at last we could make them out we noticed that instead of the black twine the Karenni women had wound around their knees, these ladies appeared to have many yellow metal rings on their lower limbs and forearms. Later on, when we arrived at a clearing with a few huts each side of the pathway, we were struck by the neat appearance of it all. The huts were more like small single storey houses on stilts, with a fenced off garden around each one.

On seeing some young tribeswomen close up, the bands of yellow, which looked like brass and about half an inch thick, went from their ankles up to their knees, from their wrists to their elbows and also around their necks, from their shoulders until just under their chins. Those rings around the neck started wide enough to rest upon the collar bone and narrowed as they progressed up the neck where they gave the impression of forcing the chin up so that it was level with the base of the skull at the back of the head. They had to look down their noses to see anything in front of them and turn the whole body to see anything from the sides. With up to twenty of these bands of metal around the neck, it was stretched to an unimaginable length. Apart from making them look taller it also made their heads look smaller in comparison to the length of their necks. As if the weight of this metal was not enough, the women also wore long rows of beads around their necks. These consisted of very old silver coins attached to silver necklaces. We had arrived in the land of the Long Necked Karens, the Padaungs and their giraffe-necked women. Not all of the women wore the full set of course, only the older ones whose husbands were rich enough!

This naturally gave us plenty to talk about as we carried on without stopping, through this small group of detached homes, until a long way off, in the distance, a splash of green colour, lighter than that of the surrounding forest, intriguingly caught our eye. It was an unusual shade of green and just did not fit into the picture we were used to seeing anywhere else in the jungle or bush. Just a small dot of colour at first, it began to dominate our view, growing larger as we got nearer. Very puzzled by now, we came into another village, much larger than the last, but with the same neat rows of houses with individual fenced gardens around them. Tidy wide roads led us to the centre of this settlement, which resembled more that of a small town than a village. Then as soon as we turned the corner, there it was, the mystery was solved. Almost the last thing you would expect to see in the jungle; a very beautiful and large hardwood built church! The green colour we had seen from afar was its corrugated iron roof. That was not the only surprise either; as we approached the building in wonderment we were greeted by an Italian Roman Catholic priest! We found out that the church, which they were rightly so proud of, had taken fourteen years to build. The nearest town being about fifty miles away, all the materials, if not found locally, had to be transported there by elephant, along similar narrow 'elephant' paths that their present day visitors had become accustomed to travel on elsewhere.

Don and his two officers were to remain here and assist in preparing a new HQ camp and for the moment we were billeted in an older church building. There were two Italian Fathers living in this village, who are mostly remembered for introducing their new visitors to a very refreshing drink, which consisted of a little honey and a good measure of rum in a large glass, topped up with sweet lime juice. The meals they prepared for us were certainly better than those that we had been surviving on recently. There was the usual rice, to which they added some vegetables, such as spiced cabbage and the odd potato, and some chicken. They also served a pretty good coffee. We also noticed that there were not only Padaungs and Karens living in this village, but other Burmese, probably from the lowlands. Many of the women were quite attractive and smartly dressed compared to the hill tribes. But just the one night at Dawrahku didn't give us (or should I say, me, who was suffering from the lack of female company) much time to explore further!

By the grace of the Italian Fathers, a mountain pony was made available for Major Boal, who was still obviously feverish, to assist him in continuing the journey with Capt. Coomber, Neville and myself. Neville was at a loose end and glad to be away from the HQ camp and Capt. Troward for a spell. We were now on the last leg of our current journey to Hwariku, which was the camp of Major Denning, Capt. Cockle, and Sgt Norman Smith. Hwariku was about 10 to 12 miles further northward, with the usual ups and downs and winding paths that had to be followed, more than doubling the actual mileage covered. It took a full day's march to reach there. I would often wonder why these Karenni 'Hills' were so called; they were more like bloody mountains to a townie like me! Not surprising really, when you look at an ordnance survey map. These 'hills' were packed closely together in most places and varied in height from valley depths of between 1000 to 2000 ft above sea level, to peaks and ridges from 3000 to over 5000 ft No wonder they didn't have many bikes around here!

Chapter Thirty-One - Interlude in 'Padaung' Country

Still greater surprises greeted all of Boal's team and Neville at Hwariku. Apart from another even grander church, there was a 'Nunnery', a mother superior and several nuns! Although most of these were also Italian, there were also several novices made up from the native Burmese population. After a welcoming meal with Denning's team, in their rather comfortable westernised hardwood accommodation (probably an ex-school house or forestry commission rest house), we were taken on a quick visit to the village and its church. On the nuns' insistence, they immediately took charge of the sick Major Boal, put him to bed in their own sick bay and nursed him until he recovered from his fever. The following day Norman took Neville and me on a tour of the area. There was a very good aircraft landing strip capable of receiving light planes. These arrived as often as weather permitted, bringing a few supplies, mail, and usually gifts from their own mess; products of a whip round before leaving, including cigarettes, bottles of spirits and occasionally demijohns of rum. We spent most of the day, between mealtimes, making sure that the hard packed dirt runway was ready to receive a plane, expected shortly, to collect the sick Capt. Lockett. He was to be flown out for treatment and was due to arrive in Hwariku the next day; the plane and weather permitting.

By the end of June we had been also introduced to several locals, a few of them able to understand some simple English as taught by missionaries. One of these, an employee of the Sawbwa, whose main residence was in Loi-Kaw, the largest town in the region, was living in a hut close to the Denning's house and was responsible for our well being. He and a younger woman looked after the team's house and cooked for us. This was unbelievable comfort after our recent adventures. Even the nuns were soon making shirts for us, in return for the steady supply of parachute material they had received. On the first Sunday after arrival in Hwariku, which, if remembered correctly, was the 1st of July, Norman, a practising Roman Catholic, offered to take me along to the church with him, promising an experience that I would never forget. It certainly was! The church was full of people, no doubt from surrounding areas, Burmese, Karens, Shans, the majority being Padaungs. As well as those inside the church, there were also many more outside, although there were fewer men than women. The ladies, however, were all dressed in their finery, the most spectacular being the Padaungs, their many brass rings highly polished and glinting in the sunlight. When inside the church and the hymn singing began, a strange, extraordinary sound greeted its visitors. The voices of the Padaung ladies were pitched so very high, still tuneful but almost screeching, due to the stretching of their vocal cords as well as their necks! It was still a wonderful, though unusual, sound to hear. It's a great pity that we did not have the means to record the amazing singing.

Major Denning's camp was set on the outskirts of the village, which was almost a small town. It was on high ground clear of any trees giving, from several points, a good clear view of the surrounding area. Whilst telling us tales about the Padaung tribesmen, Norman took me around, showing us where to stand and which distant spots to watch if we heard any gongs sounding. These tribesmen claimed that no Japs entered their circle of villages and survived! Apparently each settlement had a gong on which they would sound a warning whenever their enemies approached. Men from all nearby villages or working areas would then converge onto the signal. They could be seen coming in from various surrounding areas jogging along at a steady pace, guns or bamboo spears in hand to deal with the invaders before returning to their daily tasks. The bamboo spears, green when cut and sharpened, were black and had been hardened by smoking them, suspended over the cooking fires of their huts.

If the alarm was given in more than one place at the same time, they had some (unknown to us) means of informing each other of the number of intruders at each place. Apparently the main object was to capture as much loot as possible as well as despatch the enemy. It was not unknown for them to break off an engagement, leaving a small group behind, to deal with a larger one first; returning of course to finish off the smaller band later. They were very confident in their ability to do so. They took great care of their weapons, having in addition to their long sword-like machete, spears, crossbows or rifles. Some of their rifles were very old models, even muzzle loading ones. Others, even if damaged when received, were repaired or adapted to be of service. It was not unusual to see a shortened barrel on a rifle if it had been damaged, or the butt replaced with a self carved one. They were very good skilled engineers, but the production of food from their jungle clearings was left, of course, to their womenfolk!

A couple of other after dinner yarns related to the new arrivals at Major Denning's camp about the Padaungs are also worth mentioning. One, concerning the use made of their slim machetes, with which they could behead a water buffalo with one stroke, was that they had been known to bang on the window shutters of a Japanese occupied house and when, or if, a curious head appeared, it was promptly lopped off!

Another, which had been witnessed first hand, involved both the men and their ladies. It went thus: a meeting had been called of some of the tribal leaders with the Sawbwa's employee, who spoke very little English, as interpreter. The problem to be discussed was the wastage of ammunition and their ever increasing demand for more supplies. Apart from using it for their own hunting purposes, apparently whenever the tribesmen fired on the enemy, be it one or dozens of them, they all kept on shooting until nothing moved. It was put to them that, in future, they would only receive, one hundred rounds per head of Japanese killed. Having nodded their agreement all was well, until at the arrival of the next aeroplane. Shortly after landing and unloading its supplies, a large group of the local women arrived on the landing strip, all bearing the usual cone-shaped baskets on their backs suspended by a head-strap. At first they were thought to be there to assist in the carrying of goods away to the stores. But the baskets were already full! Taking them off their backs, they proceeded to empty the contents onto the ground by the side of the aeroplane. Out of each basket rolled several, at least five or six, Japanese heads, for which they expected to be paid as agreed, at 'one hundred rounds of ammunition per head'! Not only did they get their reward (it would have been unwise not to do so), it had to be explained to them that in future it would not be necessary to bring proof, their word would suffice. When they departed they looked not only puzzled, it was thought, but also a little disappointed!

Feeling fitter after a few days' rest at Hwariku, I had very little to do apart from assist Norman with his radio work and pay a visit to the nuns during the day to check on the progress of Major Boal, whose fever was going to keep him out of action for at least another week. I also had my own leg ulcers treated by the nuns, these sores being the result of infected scratches as well as the lack of proper nutrition. They had to be left uncovered to dry but also attracted flies which left behind eggs that developed into maggots, which in turn were left to feed on any dead flesh. This process, we had already discovered, was the local manner in which the wounds were kept clean; although, if there were any available, sulpha tablets ground down to a powder were preferable! Infection by bites, scratches and leeches were a constant nuisance the whole time we were in Burma, but we accepted this as the norm. Even so the healing process was difficult and protracted.

In the evenings for light relief, both Neville and I started to take walks after supper. Not so much for the exercise, more in the hope of getting to know the only available female in the camp! This was after questioning Norman about the young lady who was helping to maintain the team's house for us. Having caught her eye several times I had noticed a timid smile or two! We had learnt from Norman that she was the widowed daughter-in-law of the Sawbwa's Burmese employee, and that her husband had been killed by the Japanese in the early part of the invasion. As her father-in-law was a widower himself, it was expected that she should take care of him. She cooked, cleaned and shopped for him, but was only allowed to sleep outside on the balcony of his house here, their own residences being in Loi-Kaw. They both dressed more like Indians or lowland Burmese, not at all resembling any of the hill tribes that we had encountered so far. Norman had said we were wasting our time and that her guardian seemed to keep a close and jealous watch over her! She was, however, quite pretty with a light brown complexion and a charming smile. A challenge indeed for two randy sergeants! On the second night of our stroll, as we stood on high ground overlooking the landing strip, watching the rapid fall of the sun setting over the distant hills, she joined us. She had quietly arrived without us noticing and was doing the same as we were, just a few yards away. All watching the sun finally disappear below the horizon. Then we two lads turned to walk towards the late arrival but she had already slipped away without a sound, making us even more intrigued!

Chapter Thirty-Two - The Temperature Rises

The hope of another interlude, another chance to get better acquainted, alas, it was not to be. The next day Capt. Coomber, Neville, and I received orders from the HQ camp to join others as soon as possible, at the new camp constructed at Dawrahku. Continued pressure had been applied by the Japs on and around the old HQ at Hpu Hkya Hku, which had finally been abandoned. The Japanese were making determined efforts to seek out their antagonists, having been attacked frequently on their supply routes to and from the southern front. From Japanese bases at Loi-Kaw and Hypru-So, patrols were sent in all directions, probably trying to eliminate them. So far they had only succeeded in driving the teams closer together into a smaller area. Their most recent patrols had been spotted both south and west of Dawrahku village and the nearby site of the new HQ camp. Frequent patrols were being sent out to trace the teams' bases but these were constantly attacked by the groups and their Levies. Some of the Japs must have escaped, however, because they were gradually getting nearer to the main group and HQ.

Recently received mail and supplies that had, at last, been brought in by the very small planes that landed at Hwariku, were loaded onto an elephant and taken with us when Capt. Coomber, Neville and I set off for Capt. Wilson's new area, now based in Dawrahku. These planes did not return empty handed. As well as mail and messages, the sick Capt. Lockett and later Sgt Gallear, both of E force, were evacuated by them from Hwariku, better weather having made the planes' visits more frequent. The skill of these pilots was amazing to those on the ground, who were always overjoyed to receive them and very grateful of their personal gifts to them. At the last moment, Major Denning decided to travel with the supplies and left the still-recovering Major Boal in charge at Hwariku. Their journey was uneventful and after spending a pleasant meal and a night's rest at the new Wilson camp, which was very comfortable despite being bothered by nearby Jap patrols, Capt. Coomber and the two sargeants, Wood and myself, continued our journey to Pop's HQ camp just a few miles away, close to another village. Once there, Neville went back to his post with the signals officer, Capt. Troward. Not too happily of course; he tended to avoid close contact with him whenever possible. Along with others, Capt. Coomber and I were shared out between small groups of men, made up of Karen Levies, some of whom were Padaungs, and a few of the Burmese sappers and miners. The pressure put on the whole group by the Japanese, had forced them to go onto the defensive rather than, as up until now, continuously attacking the Japanese supply routes. Pop had ordered that all paths surrounding a large area within easy reach of the new camp should be guarded, whether or not they led to the camp. The whole of the WALRUS personnel were now confined to a rather smaller area than they had previously operated in. If it were not for the ferocity of the Padaungs, who were guarding our backs, we may have had a great deal more to worry about.

'Pop' Tulloch, the diminutive figure to the left, meeting with the RAF

At about this time the Army had been advancing in three directions; from the north down between the western coast of Burma and the Irrawaddy River and were now pressing eastward towards the Sittang River approaching Toungoo; across northern Burma from west to east into China and now turning southward from Mandalay. The troops that had landed south around Rangoon, were also pressing northward up the Salween River towards the Mawchi mines and probably were as close as a hundred miles south of the Mawchi road. The only escape route now for the boxed in Japanese was eastward into Siam. Not surprisingly Force 136 was a thorn in their side!

Locally there were now distinct types of enemy patrols to be dealt with. One from the Japanese garrisons between Loi-Kaw and Hpru-So, who disliked the group's presence, was constantly seeking them out and had succeeded in herding the teams into a smaller operational area. These were well armed, and rather dangerous to one's well-being. Other patrols appeared to be rather ragged, poorly armed and short of supplies and ammunition. These were probably disillusioned troops trying to escape eastward into Siam, or deserters. Entering the loyal Karens' hills was their big mistake; very few, if any getting through. Most were dealt with by the locals; only for larger, better armed groups was any assistance needed from the teams. The Padaungs, of course, rarely needed any help; to them it was a local sport!

Attack being the best form of defence, Pop asked if I would like to go out with a group of sappers to cover one of the tracks between the new HQ and Hypru-So. From earlier conversations about my infantry training and my mission in France, his reasoning was that, now he'd heard from others how quickly I had assessed and dealt with the situation when recently ambushed, I might like the opportunity to get even with the Japs! As there was no wireless work for me to do at the moment, he felt that I had the experience and the training to be useful elsewhere. Having agreed as fast as the offer was made, I was then informed that Capt. Coomber had been allocated another task and I would be teamed up with the Burmese sappers and miners, Lt Rennie, two of the sappers and four or five Karen Levies. Pop then asked if this was to my liking or if there was anyone else I would prefer to have with me, so I inquired as to whether the Karen Maung Tin was available, as we got on very well together. He had also acted fast at the ambush and I told Pop that he was the type of person you could count on and would choose to cover your back. Having sung his praises, I included that he spoke very little English but spoke both Karenni and Burmese. Pop, mentioning that Maung Tin was not really one of his men, but of E force, continued by saying that, as his group had become defunct, he would approach him as he was now more often with the Burmese sappers.

That same afternoon Pop got us all together, Lt Rennie, me, two sappers, four Levies, and Maung Tin. Using maps, we selected a section of track about six miles away, more than two thirds of the distance between the camp and Hpru-So, past at least three or more junctions, so that if we failed to stop any of the Japanese or some got away, they could not easily trace where the group had originated from. These could also serve as escape routes for the team if necessary. Taking with us supplies for several days, we set off at daybreak the next day. Pop would arrange a relief to reach us in three or four days if nothing had brought us back earlier, messages being passed to and fro by locals as runners. By lunch time we had reached and chosen a site for our ambush and set about laying traps. This was the tried and tested method of stringing hand grenades on instantaneous fuse, lining one side of the track only with these, hidden by the bush. One man could easily cover over fifty yards each side of himself with two separate strings of grenades and a Sten gun to easily finish off anyone still standing, before they recovered from the surprise attack. Two men would be placed further down the track, a sapper and Lt Rennie, who would fire the first shot to signal that the patrol had entered the ambush. In the centre, the other sapper would control the firing of the grenades. Maung Tin and I would cover the front and leading edge of the Jap patrol, and pick off any who got past the grenaded section. The four Karen Levies would spread themselves along the opposite side of the track, staying well hidden until after the explosion of the grenades, then use Sten guns on any escapees. Once we were in position and the proposed ambush was ready, there was nothing else to do but wait.

This is perhaps the hardest part, when there was nothing else to do but go over and over in our minds the endless questions - had everything been set properly, would it work, would anyone come past this spot or elsewhere, what if the patrol was too big for us to tackle, and so on. It was not necessary to remain still or hidden all the time, as we knew there would be advance warning of any Japs approaching the area. The local Karens had a well organised system of runners to protect their villages. As soon as the enemy left the main road we, as well as the nearest village, would be warned and the inhabitants would take to the cover of the bush that they knew as well as Europeans know their own backyards. The Japanese were unwilling to leave the pathways, as they had learnt it was too dangerous to go far off the tracks without ‘disappearing’. The villages were often destroyed but mostly the inhabitants survived and quickly rebuilt their fragile huts. It was also known that the Japanese rarely, if ever, went off the main roads into the bush at night. True, as I had found out not so long ago when fleeing from our camp, it was exceptionally dark under the trees at night; without flares it was almost impossible to move. So, as evening drew near, the group closed up near the centre of our prepared site and settled down for the night. Able to eat and sleep close enough together to support each other was certainly better than passing the night alone. After a night-cap of the local brew the Levies had brought with them, we retired for the night.

It felt cold after the hot and humid daytime and those who had sleeping bags or hammocks used them. I wrapped myself up in parachute cloth and a local raffia-type bed mat, which I now used as a bed roll, having lost most of my own personal equipment earlier. Since then I had been re-equipping with whatever became available, so far a pair of jungle boots, trousers and a shirt from the HQ stores. The Sisters had made pyjamas and a shirt for me, and I had purchased a longyi back at the Wilson's camp, but not much else. My last thoughts that night were that I had not been too keen on the Japs beforehand; now I hated and had no respect for them at all. The time had come, I hoped, for them to suffer. Sleep came, brought on by fatigue more than comfort, only to be disturbed whenever the insect bites became extra vicious and no longer tolerable.

We were all awake at first light, packed up and out of the bush and off to check out our prearranged positions, staying there until midday when a runner from HQ arrived to check that all was well. With no news from the nearby villages, after an emergency ration lunch, we returned to our posts, undisturbed until the evening. We then repeated the previous night's rendezvous for a meal and another uncomfortable night, wondering of course, how long this would go on, and not sure if we should be pleased the Japanese had not appeared, or sorry we had not had the opportunity to stop them.

The next day started much the same, boringly quiet and undisturbed until a runner passed by Maung Tin and myself without stopping. Shortly after, Lt Rennie arrived to inform us that he had received a report of an approaching patrol of between fifteen to twenty Japanese, heading this way. He had decided to use only one string of the grenades if they were close enough together inside the prepared ambush site. It was necessary to be economical because of the general shortage of supplies held at HQ. The monsoon rains, although easing, had been preventing regular drops for some time and stocks were very low. He and his other sapper would open fire on the tail end to signal the firing of the grenades as pre-arranged, which was to be the signal for Maung Tin and myself to take care of any advance scouts, and the Levies were to open fire with their Stens, only if required, in the centre section. Over an hour passed before anything happened, it seemed like a lifetime. Hungry, mouths dry, bellies rumbling, busting for a pee and not daring even to break wind, we all remained silent and motionless. Maung Tin and I had arranged for each to cover opposite sides of the track, the one on the right to cover the left and the one on the left side to cover the right. This would give us a better sighting across the pathway as the leaders were expected to be on opposite sides of it. After taking up our positions, one each side of the pathway, we laid in wait alone. Then voices were heard; at first some way off, then louder. Whoever it was, they were not being very careful in their approach.

As expected, the two leaders paused as they came round a bend to observe the straighter stretch of pathway in front of them. After only a brief and rather casual inspection of the way ahead, they turned to beckon to those behind to follow them having, no doubt, decided there was no danger to their advance; certainly not as efficient as was expected of well trained troops, which gave additional confidence to those lying in wait to surprise them. The leaders waited until the rest of the patrol had reached them before continuing on their way, and then followed them, just a few yards behind. They were not paying much attention to anything around them and were chatting to each other. Towards the rear there was one man, rather better dressed, in riding breeches and boots with a sword at his side, obviously the officer in charge, followed by two or three more men. The rest was a group of about a dozen ambling along in pairs.

When they reached Lt Rennie's marker, he and his companion shot the two rear guards, which signalled the trap to be set. Almost immediately the string of grenades was fired instantaneously, catching most of the centre group. The two leaders, who were thrown forward by the blast, were brought down, as they tried to get up. Maung Tin and I had kept them both in our sights and hit them with double shots from our carbines. At the same time, the Levies rose from their cover and came forward, spraying anything that moved with short bursts from their Stens. It was all over in a matter of seconds. The enemy troops had had no time to fire a single shot in retaliation. Lt Rennie and I walked towards each other, inspecting the bodies. Three had to be finished off with our .45 semi-automatics because some movement was detected, although it could have been only the bodies' uncontrolled nerve reaction; experience had taught them not to take chances. Then the task of tidying up came. The bodies were moved off the path and into the bush after they had been searched for anything useful, maps, papers etc. Identity tags were also removed for handing in. These would be translated and radioed back to SF HQ. The Levies, assisted by some local tribesmen who had arrived, buried the bodies deeper in the bush. With machetes and brush-wood, the group then got to work removing all signs of what had taken place, covering blood stains, removing or hiding from view as much as possible, any damaged wood or bushes and sweeping the pathway with the damaged branches. A runner had been sent back to the HQ camp with all the details by Lt Rennie. By this time it was getting too late to move off to another site and, instead of changing their position, the team decided to stay put, at least until morning.

Sleep of course, did not come easily. The day's events repeatedly came to mind, impossible to judge how long it had taken or how quick the final attack had been. Over and over, again and again, and why did it all seem to happen in slow motion? As these thoughts ran through my head, I recalled other times when this dreamlike slowing up of everything around me had happened. Yes, that's it! It had happened before, in France, more than once, - yes, when, - and the other time when, - then again, when we were ambushed not long ago. Is it normal? Does it always happen or was my mind playing tricks on me? Better not to mention it to anyone, they may think I'm going nuts! I must have finally fallen asleep, because I awoke with a jerk and the sound of firing in my ears. I suddenly sat upright, only to find that the others nearby were still asleep. Bloody fool, I thought, must have been dreaming again! Too dark to see the time, I lay there wide awake; closing the eyes brought back images that I preferred not to recall. Unable to sleep, I awaited a dawn that seemed reluctant to arrive. Wondering how long it would be before…? Surely the overdue Japanese patrol would be reported missing. How long before they came looking? Would they know where to look? Had we been successful in removing all the traces from the track? A drop of rain would have been useful. But no, for once it hadn't rained; at least we'd all had a dry night!

A messenger arrived from HQ the next morning, bringing instructions to return, as apparently another group had been set up nearby, a little closer to the camp. Glad to be relieved, we all made a quick retreat, eager to get a decent meal and perhaps even a wash and brush up. If we were expecting any congratulations we were unlucky! There had been other incidents in other areas around the HQ camp. The Japanese were keeping up the pressure and supplies were getting very low. There had been a misdirected drop of supplies meant for the HQ, received at Hwariku, Major Denning's area, also a report of Japs being to the north of there. No doubt the Padaungs would soon see them off. Must have done, because the supplies of food and clothing, but no ammunition, arrived shortly afterwards transported by elephants! Then there was a sudden rush to defend the nearby village at Dawrahku. A fairly large raiding and foraging party of Japs from Hpru-so had arrived there and were rounding up cattle and pigs.

They, too, must have been getting very low on supplies. All the spare bodies in the camp were rounded up and sent off to assist in chasing them away. The enemy were far too close to the HQ camp for comfort! Our rest period being short lived, Lt Rennie grabbed hold of me and Maung Tin, and we were off with others to join the affray.

It did not take long to reach the area and in just over an hour we were taking pot shots at the intruders, with the intention of driving them away rather than anything else, because of the shortage of ammo. It lasted for the rest of the day, just picking off single sure targets whenever possible, making every bullet count. The Japs set fire to some of the houses before leaving and drove away some water buffalo, either for food or possibly transport. There were continuous almost daily spats with the Japs over the next ten days or so, but clearer skies and less rain had allowed a decent drop of supplies from two Dakotas, and a Lysander which had brought in some much welcomed mail. The Japs had also been back to Dawrahku and burnt the rest of the village, revenge no doubt, but it would not help them in getting supplies, only encourage the locals to retaliate. The Japanese must have known by then that the locals were receiving assistance and had noticed the air activities. Bombing them at Loi-Kaw and at Hpru-so had been considered but as they had spread themselves thinly amongst the local people, it was deemed not worth the risk of injuring those we were hoping to free from the Japanese.

Chapter Thirty-Three - Retaliation

Colonel Pop Tulloch had gone off on a mule, taking a few of the officers and men with him, to try and contact the army, which was now thought to be only a little more than 100 miles to the west of the WALRUS group. He was not expected back for at least ten days. The HQ wireless section was well catered for by the signals officer, Capt. Troward, and Sgts Neville Wood and Don Gibbs. Norman Smith was, of course, still with Major Denning's team at Hwariku, the Padaungs' main centre and the only team now outside the HQ's camp. Major Boal was also still there, recovering from his fever. Capt. Coomber was helping out at the HQ camp. This left me still spare and, as my team had split up, I became even more attached to the Burmese sappers and miners and Capt. Campbell. This suited me well as Maung Tin, whose E group had departed, was now also with the sappers. We had been brought together by chance, managed to communicate without much knowledge of each other's language, and knew that we worked well together and could be relied on to watch each other's backs.

On the weekend of 21/22nd July there was a report of a large party of Japanese, probably out of Hypru-So and/or from Loi-Kaw, sighted as being near Hto-du-ku, about 8-10 miles to the south east of the camp; also a few more in a small patrol, only a couple of miles away. Was it just a movement of troops to or from the front or something else? Every one was on standby; this looked serious. Had they made up their minds to try and eliminate the whole group of WALRUS, remove the thorn in their side for good? They had already forced the whole group into a very small area. Normal daily tasks were carried out as usual, if with a little apprehension; eyes and ears perhaps a little more alert than at other times. It was late afternoon before a sudden explosion had everyone diving for cover. A shell or mortar bomb had landed and exploded on the hill where the HQ camp was sited. A short burst from a Bren gun was fired almost immediately in reply, aiming at the puff of smoke that could be seen rising from the hillside on the other side of the shallow valley separating the two hills; then nothing more, which was very puzzling.

Guards were increased and, because of shortage of ammunition, urgent messages requesting supplies were radioed back to base. Apart from the odd rifle shot if someone managed to spot a target, it remained quiet until nightfall. Talk was mainly about why only a single shell had been fired at the camp; was it accidental or a warning? Did they think it would be enough to scare us away, or were they waiting for a counter attack? The answer came in the very early hours of the next day. Someone had said a bugle call had been heard a couple of hours earlier, but it was about five o'clock that Sunday morning, at dawn, when the Japs opened fire with what appeared to be a light mountain artillery piece. That woke me and my entourage, who were in position a short way down the hill, facing the area from where the previous day's shot had come from. Most of the shells fell short and were infrequent. Even those that landed on the camp's hill did very little damage or seemed to cause any injuries. The HQ camp site had the advantage of being on a higher hill than the one from which the Japs were attacking. This made it possible to spot the enemy between their cover, as their troops descended towards the valley between the opposing sides when trying to launch their main attack.

Having been warned not to waste any ammo because of the shortage, Lt Rennie, Maung Tin and I, who were together again with some sappers and a few Levies, spent the morning picking off any sure target that presented itself, and there were plenty! As we finally ran out of ammunition for our semi-automatic American Carbines, which were, after all, better for closer combat, we switched to using the longer ranged Lee Enfield rifles that had been supplied to the sappers and to the Levies. Although slower to use in comparison, it gave us the advantage of being able to accurately reach the enemy even higher up their hillside. If we were being fired on ourselves, we hardly noticed it; just the odd zing or thud as something missed. Thankfully the Japs were lousy shots! Around lunch time more Levies arrived at the camp and advanced down the hill, driving the Japanese back up their hillside, before returning with requests for more ammo. There was very little to spare and the situation was getting desperate.

We were taking a break in the firing from both sides and eagerly tucking in to some pre-cooked rice and K rations, but still in our positions, when we first heard it. Yes, at last, an aircraft. In it came, a Dakota. It circled just once above the camp and came in fairly low, and out came parachutes and containers. The first and second chutes landed on the camp and the rest followed one after another down the side of the hill. Flabbergasted, everyone in camp watched them float further and further away down the hillside, the last ones into the valley between us and the enemy! Cries of 'Oh no!' didn't help, only added to the disappointment! Lt Rennie was already on his feet calling to his men to follow him. He took Maung Tin with him and asked me to organise covering fire with some Levies if necessary. He was off without any hesitation, followed by Maung Tin, running towards the descending chutes and was at the first before the last hit the ground. Leaving the container to a couple of his men to attend to, he led the rest of his men on to the next, and then again to the next.

The Japanese, either taken by surprise or short of ammunition themselves, were very slow to react to the situation. I had taken over a Bren gun left behind by the sappers and, when the Japs started to fire on them, I fired back with short bursts over their heads. Rennie went on alone to the last package and was continuously fired on by the enemy. Recovering from the initial surprise, some of the enemy troops were racing down their hill hoping, no doubt, to beat him to the prize. I had by now been joined by another sapper with a Bren gun and between us we kept up a steady spray of short bursts, hoping at least to delay them. Meanwhile Lt Rennie had been dragging the container back up the hill alone. Maung Tin who had been helping to carry another container, turned back to assist him and together they brought it all the way back into the camp. No time to celebrate yet, the first of the containers was emptied and the ammo shared out. Unfortunately it was not enough to last us very long, as not all the containers contained ammunition. Some were of a standard packaging with a mixture of food, clothing, and equipment. Useful, but not exactly what we were looking for at that precise moment!

Spasmodic firing continued throughout the rest of the day and into the following night, with very little rest or sleep, the latter only achieved in short spells when men from higher up the hill made their way down from the HQ with supplies of food and ammo. By morning we heard that more Japanese had been reported heading our way, and that urgent messages had been sent requesting additional supplies of ammunition. I can remember that I had taken (along with others, no doubt), from my emergency pack of pills, a half of one of the Benzedrine tablets.. They were meant to keep you alert and awake, but they were also making me very thirsty, and I was in dire need of a long drink of tea. Nothing else could quench a thirst like that except tea! With the new day, we resumed picking off any target that presented itself and returned any fire that came our way, bearing in mind all the time that every round must be made to count.

Mid-morning, at last, the sound of aeroplanes reached our ears again. First a twin engine Beaufighter with a container slung beneath it, where it would normally carry a bomb. It dropped the single container squarely on the DZ, continued onwards and fired on the Jap positions before it rapidly disappeared, even faster than it had arrived. It must have been talked in by S phone as the result was perfect. (The S phone system enabled someone on the ground to speak directly to the pilot of the aeroplane.) The container landed on the DZ and the machine gunning of the Japanese position on the opposite hill was well on target. This was followed shortly after by two Lysanders. A radio message had been received earlier, asking for the DZ to be kept clear for them as they were going to try a free drop of ammunition and requested a reply as to whether or not it had been successful as it had not been tried before. So the signals section had been busy and was doing a good job!

The two planes, arriving in tandem, were impressive to see. First one, then the other came in as low and as slow as possible, and dropped box after box of ammunition, no chutes, just a little padding that could be cut off, boxes opened and ammo ready to be used immediately! They bounced along the ground; some broke open but most arrived in reasonable condition. The shorter rounds as used in the Stens and hand guns were mostly fine, although some of the longer, .303 rounds, as used in Bren guns and rifles, were bent or damaged. Even so, some of this ammunition was being shared out and in use whilst the two Lysanders were circling for another approach and further drops. Certainly, it had arrived in good time as other information reaching us on this day was that more Japanese were heading our way.

Now the slightest movement observed was hit by a burst of Bren and rifle fire. Then another surprise for the defenders! Not one this time, but two Dakotas arrived and dropped both containers on chutes, and more free drops of ammo. There were also other supplies, compo rations and even mail! All this left everyone in good heart and must have disillusioned the enemy who were forced to watch the arrival of supplies and support, something that they always seemed to be very short of. By the end of that day the enemy were being fired on by bursts from even more Bren guns and single well aimed shots from rifles at the slightest sign of movement. The defenders were also relieved after night fall when more Levies arrived from surrounding areas, having infiltrated through from the other side of the hill as soon as it got dark. This meant that the HQ could at last catch up on our lack of sleep over the last three nights.

The Levies also brought news of many Japanese between Hpru-so and the village of Ho-hso, a couple of miles west of there. A good eight to ten miles away, but a little too close for comfort as it was estimated there were around three thousand of them. Radio messages were transmitted about this with a request for an air strike.

As the Japanese were usually fairly quiet during the nights, Maung Tin and I went back up the hill for food and rest when we heard this latest news. We were, at the least, relieved to know that these other Japs were a good day's march away! We returned refreshed, with the others, to our posts shortly after day-break in case of an early morning attack. Once back in position we found the enemy still firing spasmodically and were only too pleased to reply rapidly at any convenient target. The whole day passed like this, exchanging occasional shots at each other, whilst listening intently for aeroplanes, but even though we saw what may have been fighter bombers flying over distant hills we did not hear any bombing. Perhaps it was too far away for us to hear anything, or the hills between them and us acted as baffles. This left us wondering if these extra troops were going to be reinforcements meant for our opponents. Another night approached and the day had passed with a lot less activity than the previous day. When the night watch took over and we were relieved to rest and eat, we retired early, not knowing what the next day would bring, to a rather more uneasy sleep.

On the sixth day, when returning once more to the defence positions, it seemed strangely quiet. No random shots to greet any movements, nothing! The hill opposite was scanned with binoculars, but it seemed deserted. It did not strike us immediately as being possible. Lt Rennie took a patrol of sappers and Levies down across the shallow valley on a recce, whilst the Bren guns covered them. A runner was back in under an hour with the news that the Japanese had withdrawn! Not only had they disappeared overnight, they had left behind many dead and wounded. They had not even bothered to bury their dead or take even a part of a casualty's body away for burial. It appeared that it was the custom to take at least a finger in order that the family or relatives could give the deceased a proper burial. This concept was new to the defenders and difficult to understand and just added to our surprise at the sudden disappearance of the Japs. Levies and sappers spent most of the rest of the day burying the dead and the locals took over 'looking after' the wounded, which were those who were too badly injured to finish themselves off, as appeared to be yet another custom of the Japanese. The totals were reported to be about 150 dead and 100 wounded, although it was impossible to tell if this was anything like a true figure, whereas none of the WALRUS group were killed and only a very few minor injuries were suffered. This left everyone rather puzzled as to why the enemy troops had withdrawn or what had happened to the presumed reinforcements. Had they exhausted their supplies, lost too many men, or received new orders? A great deal of discussion went on until late that evening and the following day.

Chapter Thirty-Four - Hwariku, the Good and the Bad!

Pop had now returned (most likely by air to Hwariku) after visiting a 14th Army base. It was apparent that no one was too sure of exactly how many, if any, Japanese there were between the group and the troops, who were approximately 100 miles to the west and a similar distance to the north. The 8th Army, which was of course still pressing northward in central and eastern Burma, was approximately the same distance to the south. The estimates of enemy troops in this box, bordered on the east by Siam, varied from 20,000 to 35,000 and it was also uncertain if they intended to make a stand somewhere along the Salween River or withdraw into Siam. The Karens and Padaungs, who hated the Japanese and were very loyal to the British, were now well armed and had given the Japs a sharp lesson on jungle craft every time they met up. Now it appeared the Japanese were becoming very reluctant to take them on. With these things in mind, Pop decided to send out patrols and seek out a little more truth about the enemy's present strength and positions within his area.

The HQ group and the Burmese sappers under Capt. Campbell were to remain in the area south-east of Dawrahku and keep up the pressure on the road between Bawlake and Hpru-So. Major Denning's team was to stay with the Padaungs covering the road from there to Loi-kaw. Capt. Wilson's team were to travel north towards the army and Major Boal's team westward to reconnoitre the area between the HQ camp and the Sittang River, over forty miles away as the crow flies; following tracks, up and down hills could easily double the distance. As Major Boal was still at Hwariku, I travelled there with Don and his team when they set off from Dawrahku on their way to journey northward on or about 28th July.

Back at Hwariku was like being at a rest camp with reasonable food under the tender care of the R C Sisters and protected by the Padaungs! Major Boal, now in better health, and Capt. Coomber set about organising the journey, assembling a convoy of elephants to carry equipment and supplies, and a few Levies as guides and protection. I had very little to do, apart from inspecting some radio equipment that I had, at last, taken possession of to use on the trip, so I spent time helping Norman with odd jobs around his camp.

On one occasion in the early morning, a couple of Padaung tribesmen whom Norman seemed to know quite well, begged him to go with them. That they had something to show him, was all that could be made out. Leading the way they took Norman and me to a hut on the edge of the town. We were greeted by another Padaung who knew Norman and could speak a little English. He informed Norman that they had captured a Japanese soldier who had been the leader of a party that had raided one of their villages and they wanted to give Norman the honour of executing him! On being ushered into the hut, we were greeted by about half a dozen other tribesmen and this one poor soul, who was squatting on the floor, barefoot and wearing only a pair of shorts. This was already very unusual as the Padaungs had no use for captives and did not keep slaves. Men built the houses and defended the villages and the women tended any livestock and worked the fields. On seeing the two Europeans, their prisoner crawled towards us. Hands together as if in prayer, he kept kow-towing and then tried to cling on to our legs, muttering something that, of course, no-one could understand. Then he motioned to us as though he wanted to write something down. Norman found some paper and gave him a pencil and with some difficulty the Jap managed to write something in his own script, which once again could not be understood.

Meanwhile, Norman was explaining to me that he dare not upset the tribesmen. If they felt that he was insulting them by not accepting the honour they were offering him, they may easily turn on us instead. After accepting the Jap's letter and after a great deal of discussion, Norman managed to persuade them that as he had not captured the man, the 'honour' must be theirs, although they could not agree on which of them it should be. He then went on to explain to them that they could all do it at the same time if the man was shot by a firing squad; they could all fire at once on a signal from him. They took a lot of persuading, not quite understanding the reasoning, but finally agreed, still not looking too happy about it. It was as though they did not trust each other to all fire at the same time! The victim was then ushered out of the hut between the tribesmen and marched along a pathway, up an incline until close to a cliff edge. They stood him a few yards away from the edge and then as they backed away from him, he began following them. This happened several times as he tried to stay close and in amongst his antagonists. It must have been obvious what was going to happen, and perhaps he thought he would be safer surrounded by the tribesmen. When finally their prisoner was far enough away, on the word of their leader, they all started firing with their rifles from the hip, not bothering to aim. The tribesmen were still in a semi-circle around the Jap as they continued to fire round after round in the general direction of the victim who was only about three yards away. How they managed not to hit each other instead was in the lap of their gods.

When the very first bullets struck their victim, the force lifted him off his feet and spun him around like a top. As the body fell to the ground they were still firing and Norman was yelling at them to stop. He then walked forward and fired a shot from his .45 semi-automatic into the back of the Jap's head. The body was still twitching but it is certain that he was already dead. The tribesmen were pushing the body over the edge of the cliff with their feet as Norman and I left them to finish what they had chosen to do. Walking back in complete silence, feeling rather inadequate, we were fully aware that, had we been on the receiving end and captured by the Japanese, our treatment would have certainly been far worse. Norman reported the events of that morning and handed over the written words and the identification disc of the late Japanese to his team leaders. It was discussed again at the evening meal but without any recriminations, the general feeling being that nothing else could have been done in that situation, by them or anyone else.

One of the Sisters was unwell, so the following day Norman took me with him to pay her a visit at the convent. Norman, himself being a practising Roman Catholic, had built a close relationship with the Mother Superior, who was always pleased to greet visitors from the team's camp. She even allowed us both to visit the sick Italian Sister, who was confined to bed in her own room. The patient thoroughly enjoyed the visit and repeatedly laughed at the thought of being alone with not only one, but two men in her bedroom. It had never happened before, she assured her visitors, and this alone seemed to cheer her up no end! On leaving, the Mother Superior presented us with another shirt each which had been made by the Sisters out of parachute material; a stark contrast to the previous day of aggression, hatred and death. Today was a day of caring love and friendship, which ended as we two sergeants watched the sun set behind the western hills that evening from the same spot where we had so often stood before. As on another previous occasion we were joined by the young woman housekeeper whom I had seen before. She stood only a few feet away but we only acknowledged each other with a casual glance and a nod. But I also smiled in her direction and was quite certain that I had detected one in return. I tried to find out more about her from Norman who, apart from telling me that she spoke very little English and was not available, seemed uninterested and so I learnt very little more than I already knew; except that this time I did manage to find out her name. Norman said that he always addressed her as 'May', although, he added, it was actually something that sounded more like Ma-yea, or Ma ye-er. As all three walked back together and parted at our respective billets, I noticed another shy smile on her lips and her eyes were shining as we bade each other good-night. She really was very attractive and that twinkle in her eye was very intriguing.

Boal's team was aiming to leave on the first of August on our trek westwards, which kept us busy during the day organising supplies and transport and in the evenings studying possible routes out and back. Before leaving, I was occupied mainly in using Norman's steam driven charger and trying to recharge a couple of car batteries. These were selected out of several that had been salvaged from damaged Japanese vehicles. Although I now had a radio transmitter and a small receiver, there was no means of recharging the batteries that we could take with us. Whether or not the batteries would hold their power for long was unknown and the only hydrometer available was a barely workable Japanese one! However, two batteries would be less difficult to transport than a petrol or steam driven battery charger and the fuel it would need to run it. Ah well, we had all been constantly so short of supplies that we were becoming expert at making do with anything to hand. Why, for example, could we not be supplied with the type of hand generator that had been used in France? It was small, light, and could be used without any fuel other than one person turning a handle. But then, cursing the unknown powers that were responsible was also very therapeutic!

The team would be ready to leave a little later than planned the next morning. Just one more thing I wanted to do before leaving and this was to take a walk up the hill to watch the sun setting. This time I went alone. The evening air was warm, so calm and peaceful that it was hard to imagine the turmoil that had been caused by the Japanese invasion of such a beautiful country. For what reason, what use was it to them? I was of course hoping that 'someone' might join me, but not too sure that she would. However, I did not have to wait too long before she approached. I had been leaning with my back against a large boulder, shielding my eyes from the descending sun, taking a frequent glance sideways in the direction that I hoped a lone visitor would appear. When I did first spot her coming my way, I just kept looking in the opposite direction, waiting to see how close she was going to come before stopping, a little scared that she may be frightened away or change her mind if I moved too soon. Suddenly there she was in front of me and smiling, her hand held out, offering a piece of paper. A little puzzled, I accepted the note, unfolded it and began to read. It was a short letter that she had persuaded someone to write for her in rather strange primitive English. It went something like this: 'Me your sister, you my brother. I like very much. Tomorrow you go away. I also go away Loi-kaw, buy things for house and longyes for me. I wish that we meet again. I wish that you return in good health.' Confused at first, until I remembered that the local teachers were RC religious ones, and realised that their teachings probably included that all humans were 'Brothers and Sisters'! Holding both hands out towards her, I beckoned her to come closer. As she did so, I bent forward and kissed her on the cheek (something I had learnt in France?). She neither resisted nor drew back. Taking her hand, I urged her closer until we stood side by side watching the sun sinking over the hills, still hand in hand. There was no need for words, as we both shared a universal language. As darkness fell in too short a time, we walked back to our respective houses, not knowing if or when we would ever meet again. Did we kiss again? Well yes, just a quick peck, but on the lips this time. After all, the men folk in this region were known to be very possessive. Although not a Padaung, prudence was called for!

Chapter Thirty-Five - The August Tour!

Major Boal and his entire group set off immediately after breakfast, only a day later than originally planned. It had taken extra time to get enough elephants together for the convoy. There were four in all, one, a large cow and three smaller, younger ones. One of these was a rather frisky male. The large female took charge and insisted that she lead the youngsters by trumpeting and lashing out with her trunk if ever any one of them tried to pass in front of her. They were well loaded, as the intended journey would take at least two weeks, possibly three or more. It would depend on what we found and reported back to the HQ camp. Boal, Coomber, and I took it in turns to lead or cover the rear. The whole group was comprised of two guides, five Levies and us; all ten were, of course, well armed. Our kit and stores were shared out on the elephants, leaving very little room for anyone hoping for a free ride. We would be able to support ourselves if necessary, but were also expected to pick up other willing, possibly armed, volunteers on the way. Our first overnight stop was a good 10 to 15 miles away south-west from Hwariku to Kwetolak, where there was a river to cross. Hopefully it was through valleys most of the way, between hills from 2000 to 3000 ft high. It was expected to be an interesting excursion. The weather had been drier of late and there was plenty of shade in heavily wooded country. 'In other circumstances, a holiday safari!' quipped Norman, as we departed. Always a bit of a comedian, he often referred to himself as being only a 'tourist', but this was usually believed to ease his own anxieties.

The day's journey had been pleasant enough, no sign of the enemy, but then we were still in Padaung country, sighting only the occasional cultivated clearing tended by women and, wherever there was water, a few cattle, usually water-buffalo, and paddy fields. There must have been plenty of wildlife, but of course it was rarely seen, the creatures having sensed our presence first; the exception being those that wished to sting, bite or suck blood, which were only spotted after they had been felt! Unpleasantness was alleviated by the rarer appearance of beautiful butterflies and occasional birds. In other circumstances it would have been a very picturesque country to be visiting, Tourists? Perhaps Norman was not so wrong after all! This thought was endorsed by our arrival at the river adjacent to the village where we were to spend our first night. The elephants, trunks raised to sniff the air and detecting the approaching stream, had quickened their pace and had to be restrained by the mahouts. They had some difficulty in halting the animals before they rushed into the water, but quickly managed to bring them to their knees to unload them. Like children on a seaside visit, the young ones dashed into the river, splashing everything and everyone nearby. The older and more sedate female took her time and selected her own spot in the shallows away from the juniors, taking her time to suck up a trunk full of water and spray it over her head and back, including her mahout who was still sitting there! He slid off and rubbed her down with a brush made of young twigs and green branches. The juniors amused themselves spraying each other as well as their own backs, their drivers keeping well out of the way. There was no doubt that all were enjoying themselves as were all the humans, not just watching but doing likewise, a little further up stream!

In this fairly large village we were warmly welcomed by one of the elders who offered us plenty of the local rice wine. The three Brits were escorted to a well built wooden hut that would be ours that night. It was probably the old school-house and food was brought to us by some of the womenfolk. Our two guides, who spoke reasonable English, and a small group of older men joined us for the meal. The others on this expedition were shared out amongst the locals in their huts. Having eaten and drunk plenty of the local brew, there was much music and singing going on in the village for quite a while that evening. As for what was sung, that has long been forgotten in a drunken fog! There were many thick heads and a late and reluctant departure for us all the next day.

Fortunately there was a small village only 8 to 10 miles away called Tha Auk, which we expected to reach before nightfall. Thus it was, in a lazy hazy day, that the convoy made an almost silent journey. On arrival we were quickly returned to reality, and our reasons for being there. The village was deserted and almost completely destroyed. Only a few huts, although damaged, remained standing. A cautious approach showed only too clearly what had happened. Nothing living remained, only traces of dead chickens, pigs and dogs. The stores of rice had been raided, and that which had not been taken away was strewn on the ground and left to rot.

It must have had happened quite recently as it had hardly been disturbed since. The next village was too far away to reach that night, so after a quick temporary repair job on some of the less damaged buildings we decided to spend the night there, first making sure there would be a double guard and a constant watch throughout the night. The senseless waste of shelter and food was incomprehensible. Whoever they were, they gave no thought at all to others, even of their own kind who may be following them, for they too could be just as needy as us. In the early morning, a visiting tribesman of the local area put the team in the picture and gave us the direction in which the departing patrol of about twenty Japanese had gone, just two days earlier. This information was radioed back to HQ later that day, when I found some higher ground during our lunch break. This was on our way westward again, to Maungpalaw, a village only about eight miles away, but because of the numerous hills between, we were unsure of how long it would take us. The village after that, Kyekadaw, was larger but would mean a further six miles' travelling; making it doubtful we could reach it before nightfall.

It was also now thought wiser to have our own small patrol a half mile or so ahead of the elephants, just in case we bumped into any opposition on the way, which proved to be the right decision. It was late afternoon by the time we all arrived in Maungpalaw; some of the hills had been rather steep and this had slowed up the elephants a great deal. Again we were well received by the inhabitants and given a simple meal of rice and vegetables accompanied by the usual rice wine to drink and a Burmese cheroot to smoke. Not such a riotous evening as our first overnight stop, but certainly better than the last.

Continuing the journey towards the Sittang River, we headed towards Kyekadaw the next morning. The route would take us down a gradual descent from over 3500 ft to around 2000 ft through dense forest, much of it bamboo and difficult to penetrate; forcing our way along the elephant pathways, through winding valleys and following streams most of the way. This was fine for the elephants, who enjoyed playing in the water whenever they were allowed to, but the panoramic views were obscured most of the time by the vegetation. Most of the walking was done in the shade of the trees which completely overhung the paths. Constantly wading through the stream as it criss-crossed its way down hill, brought the misery of blood sucking leeches, wet feet and clothes that steamed as body heat attempted to dry them. 'So that's why the locals are barefoot and wear only shorts,' I remarked as I picked off another batch of newly arrived leeches!

In Kyekadaw that evening we were greeted by a large crowd of adults and children who, thanks to the rather efficient Karen 'bush' telegraph, had been well informed of our impending visit. The village itself was the largest we had seen so far on this excursion, and accommodation in the local schoolhouse was already prepared for us. The local tribal leader joined us for the evening meal which was brought to us all, ready cooked, by several of the women. Although it was the usual simple fare of mainly rice, eggs and a few vegetables, it was, of course, very welcome to empty stomachs. During the meal, with the assistance of our guide/interpreter, the headman informed us that he had invited other headmen from the surrounding area to come and meet us the next day, as they were concerned about the increasing number of Japanese going through their areas. The team were a little sceptical at first, thinking that the crafty old devil was just after extra arms for his men, who had already received a reasonable supply through Pop's HQ. However, having little choice in the matter and needing a break from the amount of walking we had done over the past few days, we agreed to meet and talk with them. We also agreed amongst ourselves not to drink too much of the local brew for once and keep clear heads for the morrow!

A good night's sleep for all was enjoyed, knowing that the locals would warn us well in advance of any unwanted visitors. After a breakfast of tea made with sweetened condensed milk, and hardtack biscuits, we amused ourselves making utensils out of the green bamboo we had collected on route, using different sizes for such items as mugs, dishes or even spoons and scoops, with one of the favourites being pipes for smoking our mixture of carefully saved cigarette ends, used tea leaves and, of course, the butt-ends of the Burmese cheroots. This noxious mixture was made even better by the addition of a drop or two of rum whenever available, as it improved the flavour and counteracted the stink! These were the days when nearly everyone smoked tobacco. It kept us sane in times of stress and eased hunger pains as well as giving pleasure, sadly though, in short supply here. In France, I recall, I could buy cigarette papers to roll my own recycled dog-ends, at least until American cigarettes arrived on the black market. In the jungle though, neither were available. A green bamboo bowl and a hollow cane for a stem made a pipe that would last until it became too dry and the wood started to burn, when the bowl had to be exchanged for a fresh green one.

Note: *(One of these pipes can be seen amongst other Jed artefacts at the Carpet Baggers Museum at Harrington)*

The headmen with whom we were waiting to confer, arrived in dribs and drabs throughout the day, coming in from the surrounding villages, some a fair distance away. Gradually our team was able to build up a picture and find out more about the Japanese movements. News of the British Army's progress in Burma had been sadly lacking, and only by listening in to the BBC news bulletins on the radio receiver did we work out that those descending down the Arakan on the west coast, had linked up with others who had landed south around Rangoon. The latter had advanced northward up as far the Mawchi road, running westward towards Toungoo. North of there in the Pegu Yomas, somewhat south of Meiktila, between the Irrawaddy and Sittang rivers, there were the remnants of defeated Japanese troops, hungry and ill-supplied, hoping to cross into the Karen Hills and escape eastward to Siam. According to the information received from the local headmen, there were large, whole company sized groups, and smaller groups of soldiers of 10 to 20 men. Some of the smaller groups they referred to as 'bandits' and were thought to be deserters. The Karens made no attempt to hide their contempt of Japanese and the team could have easily raised another army with the men who offered to help track them down. Some were already armed but the team had no arms to spare for the others.

Once more, it was noticeable that they were very pro-British. Some who had been missionary taught, could manage to converse in English and spoke well of the Forestry Commission. Although we tried to avoid politics, the locals gave us the impression they were not too enamoured with being under the control of lowland Burmese, and hoped that the British would one day allow them to run their own affairs. Unfinished business and the late arrival of even more headmen meant that another two nights had to be spent in Kyekadaw before we could continue our journey. During this period I passed on several messages to HQ relating to items we had learned so far, keeping it short because of the limited amount of battery power we had with us.

Conserving batteries meant that only on rare occasions (or when bored) could I listen to the BBC news programmes. There had been much talk about a new bomb that had been dropped in Japan. The Americans had been bombing the Japanese mainland for some time but this was something different. A single bomb had been dropped on 6th August which had destroyed a large area, a whole city! There was talk of a demand sent to the Japanese to surrender or another of the same type of bomb would be used again, perhaps even on Tokyo itself. Having passed this news on to my two officers that evening, 8th August, we decided to stay where we were for a little longer and see if there was to be any further development. This would be no hardship for us as, so far, we had been made very comfortable and had obtained a great deal of useful information about local Japanese movements. The following day the news was that the enemy had not surrendered and another of this new type of bomb had been dropped on the mainland of Japan. (These, as we later learned, were the first atomic bombs ever used in warfare; the first on 6th August '45 on Hiroshima and the second on 9th August on Nagasaki.)

Information on what was going on in the world about us was sparse. If it wasn't for the bush telegraph, which was more or less better informed, we were ignorant of what or where anything was happening locally. However, whether the Japanese in this area knew or not about happenings in their homeland, they did not appear ready to give up fighting. Further news arriving by runners, reported frequent Japanese troop movements. Between Yeni and Myonla they were crossing the Sittang River singly and in small groups, and apparently reforming near Yegon in the lowlands, then heading eastward and south-eastward presumably heading towards Leiktho, which was about 12 to 15 miles south of the team still at Kyekadaw. Leiktho was only 25 to 30 miles from Toungoo, which was already in British hands. The impression was that they were on the run from the British army in the west and poorly armed. It was decided to try and drive them south into the army's hands and stop them escaping east into Siam.

Gathering together as many of the already armed Karens in the surrounding area, our team set off on the most northerly route towards the Sittang lowlands via small villages heading for Mi-i, which was about half way between our present base and the Sittang. From there we hoped to harass the Japanese enough to send them southward towards Malaukchaung, out of the hills as much as possible and further south towards the British army. Taking only arms and ammunition, the team travelled fast and light on small paths through the bamboo forests and, as did the local Levies, relied on the villages for food and lodging. By 11th August, patrols were out on a regular basis, comprised of one or two of the team's original party and additional local Karen Levies, on the lookout for any stray Japs. Up until 15th August, this pattern continued with frequent success, the Karens proving to be far better at jungle craft than the enemy. The Japanese, it must be said, were in a sorry state, looking bedraggled and half-starved, most only travelling in small groups which varied from twos and threes to rarely more than half a dozen at a time. When fired on, they tried to escape into the bush, where they were quickly brought down by the Karens. As some failed to retaliate, it was assumed that they either had no arms or very little ammunition left. They must have had a rough time fleeing through the Pegu Yoma, where other groups of Special Force 136 were operating.

On 15th August 1945, all three of our team were on a recce and making our way down out of the hills to a lower ground level, where there were more cultivated areas of cleared jungle and paddy fields. Taking a break at midday, we chose to rest in the shade for a while, in a hut on low stilts that we had spotted in the middle of one of these cultivated fields. This gave a clear view all the way around the area up to the surrounding jungle, giving us the added advantage of seeing anyone approaching, before we ourselves could be seen. As I had with me a small radio receiver that was powered by a dry battery, and news bulletins were broadcast usually on the hour, I tuned in to the BBC in the hope of hearing the latest news. (The same set incidentally on which I had first heard in July that, following a general election, Winston Churchill had been replaced by Clement Attlee as Prime Minister! By the way, no-one had bothered to ask us if we wanted to vote!) The big surprise this time was that Japan had surrendered! The Emperor Hirohito had himself apparently broadcast a message to his people telling them of the surrender.

Having passed on to Major Boal and Capt. Coomber what I had just heard, they decided we should stay where we were and wait for the next news bulletin on the following hour, just to be certain of what was happening. Of course nothing ever goes exactly to plan. Sure enough, in less than half an hour a few Japanese were seen walking along the path between the edge of the field and the surrounding trees. We had spotted only four or five were carrying rifles and one had a sword. At approximately 60 yards away they were any easy target. I was all for picking them off, pretty certain that they would do the same to us, given the chance. The Major, though, had said 'No, we can't do that, because if the ceasefire order has been given, it would be illegal!' So, we kept quiet and watched them walk off into the trees. After what seemed a never ending wait, holding one earphone each, the Major and I listened to the next broadcast. Yes, apparently the war was over, although it was not too clear as to whether or not there had been an order to 'Cease Fire', which left us in a quandary and very uncertain as to what to do next. Rather than go after and contact the enemy, it was thought to be more prudent to return to the village and contact Pop at the HQ camp by radio that evening.

Retracing our steps up the hills, through the mainly bamboo forest, two hours later and roughly halfway home came yet another surprise that day. In single file on the narrow track I was in the lead, the position I preferred so that I could set the pace, rather than have to keep catching up with the long legged others. My carbine was slung on my left shoulder because of the closeness of surrounding trees and my .45 semi-automatic cocked and ready in my right hand. Then in a flash, jumping out from behind a large tree, a Jap with his sword held high above his head in both hands stood a few yards in front of me! This man was coming straight for me. Then, as if in slow motion, a double shot from my .45 hit the Jap in the body as he lunged forward. As he fell slowly to the ground at my feet, the sword continued coming down towards me and I had to lean backward to avoid being struck on the chest. My companions had opened fire behind me but I had hardly heard the shots. Then, as suddenly as it had started, it was all over. One of my team members, I do not remember who, shouted, 'Are you all right?' then, 'You're bleeding, there's blood on you!' I had felt nothing but looked down at my shirt front and saw that I had escaped serious injury with only a torn shirt and a six inch scratch down my breast-bone where a thin red line of blood oozed slowly. Was it the same group we had seen and let go earlier? Impossible to say, but an everlasting thought!

Back at Mi-i village, after a night's rest, the local people who had heard the latest news were gathering together to celebrate. Being close to the lowlands, many Burmese who had fled to the safety of the hills were also appearing, these being easily recognised by their different mode of dress. It was a pleasant change to see ladies in long colourful clothes, similar to that of the Indian and Ceylonese women, after seeing only the black short skirt and robe worn by the Karens for so long. So much so that all the team members decided to have a wash and brush up for a change! Difficult, as we had not had a change of clothing or a shave since our arrival in Burma. A scrub up in the nearby stream was the best we could do under the present circumstances! Wearing longyis, which we normally wore instead of torn trousers to sleep or relax in, and with long hair tied back with parachute cord, we looked almost respectable.

Tables, and even a few chairs, were arranged in the shade between the huts and laden with a variety of foods, rice, chicken, pork, spices, potatoes and other vegetables and fruits. Although there was very little meat, of vegetables there was a plentiful variety; more food ready to eat than we three Brits had seen presented at one sitting all the time we had been here. Not forgetting the obligatory rice wine and even a stronger unknown distilled spirit! Not even the children were allowed to touch any of the food until, as honoured guests, we had been invited to start. As we hesitated, not knowing which of the tasty morsels to try first, one of the ladies, followed by the others, stepped forward to serve us. There appeared to be no rush to finish the meal, as between the different dishes there was entertainment of singing and dancing, mostly done by the children with some of the ladies joining in. Some of the tunes and words were those they had been taught by missionaries, others in their own language and music. After the wine had flowed for a while, the Levies were brave enough to sing something unrecognisable to us Brits, but very amusing to the locals judging by the reception and applause they received. Not to be outdone, our trio of Brits had to keep face by giving a rendering of 'On Ilkley Moor ba tat'! Again! Even these pathetic efforts did not bring the day's frivolity to a close, which went on well after nightfall.

Radio contact had been made the previous evening and the team had been advised to return to Pop's HQ at Dawrahku. As it would be a good 15 mile hilly trek from Mi-i back to Kyekadaw and would take a full day's march, a very early start would have to be made. On arrival back in the village it had been too late to contact the Mahouts and we were glad to retire early in the old school house that we had used before. It would take most of the next day to round up the elephants and prepare for our departure, but even after the night's partying, the head man had other plans. His was the largest village around and, not unlike our arrival the first time, he was not going to let us leave without marking the occasion! This time he had the excuse of having heard the latest news about the war and was eager to celebrate.

Whilst preparations were being made for more festivities later in the day, we spent our time in Kyekadaw resting and wandering around the village. More women and children were about than there had been on our previous visit, perhaps taking the day off from working in the cultivated areas. The children were amusing themselves, as they would do in any country, with their own particular children's games, except that here they also had a young elephant to play with! It seemed a little older than the one that had accompanied me on my arrival in Burma, but then again, it may have been the same one, it was difficult to tell! The first youngster came up to my knees and this one was hip high, but that was three and a half months ago and I don't know how fast an elephant grows in that time. It did, however, have a knowing look in its eye as it gambolled up towards me, stopping briefly as it brushed its shoulder along my thigh as it passed, allowing me to pat its head in return. It was as though we were acknowledging each other, in a kind of greeting. Other times it approached, not unlike a mischievous child, looking sideways out of the corner of its twinkling eye pretending not to be there, an 'If I don't look at you, you cannot see me!' type of look! Coming up slowly, trunk curled inward, head down, until it gently pressed against my thigh and hipbone with its forehead. It then pressed a little until it felt some resistance, then standing firm, all four legs kept stiff and straight, would lean forward a little by just shifting its weight and without moving its feet or legs, pushed harder. The more resistance it felt, the more it leant forward. This developed into a game of push and shove between us, me bracing myself to push back as hard as I could, the baby elephant just leaning forward, eyes obviously laughing by now! It was not going to be beaten!

Its next trick was to uncurl its trunk and quietly and gently try to hook it around my lower legs, then pull, in an effort to trip me up. Side stepping to get out of reach of the searching trunk meant relaxing the pressure between my thigh and the youngster's head, which it instantly sensed as victory and pushed a little harder. This continued until I had to break away to avoid being trodden on. My playmate just trotted away, trunk held high, turning in a semi-circle to approach once more from behind when it thought it could do so without being noticed! If I gave up first and climbed the ladder back up to the hut, it would wait a short while underneath before giving up and going off to find some children to run around with. After a short siesta, an invitation arrived to join the headman and his other friends for another celebratory party, which started in the late afternoon and continued until late that evening. It was very much like the previous one, but without the team having to render a return musical performance, making it a little more sedate.

After passing another night in the village the team headed back the way we came, towards Dawrahku. In no particular hurry, we had time to enjoy other celebrations in each village we passed or spent the night in, as news of the end of the war spread. It was noticeable that the villagers were much more relaxed when unknown visitors arrived, allowing the children and womenfolk to mix and greet us more freely. The men were keen to inform us of their most recent encounters with any stray Japs that they had quickly 'despatched'. Although there were now far fewer Japanese wandering through the hills, we still had to keep on the alert for any stray groups trying to escape via Siam. This part of our journey was quite uneventful apart from one more elephant tale.

The returning convoy consisted of the same four elephants as on the outward journey, one large female and three younger ones, one of which was a male. Having less to carry than on the outward journey, there was enough room for one or two persons at a time to hitch a ride. An enjoyable journey up and down hills through fairly thick jungle, sometimes nervously crossing gorges faster by what looked like very fragile vine-bound bamboo bridges, giving us extra time to rest or admire the view whilst the heavy beasts of burden descended the valleys to wade across the streams. The young male was noticeably 'friskier' this time, his mahout having difficulty at times to keep him under control and maintain his position in the convoy.

On the second or third day of our journey the young male kept annoying one of the young females by dropping behind her and trying to touch her with his trunk. He was getting more and more excited and she was not amused! At last she'd had enough of the randy bull and made a dash off the pathway and headed for the thicker cover of the bush. The mahouts, doing their best to pull them back, were brushed off their animals, one after the other, by overhanging branches. The team were treated to the sight of irate drivers picking themselves up and running after their animals, waving their drivers' sticks in the air as they disappeared into the jungle. Helpless with laughter, there was nothing we could do but take a break by the side of the track until order was restored, some two hours later, when the very hot and flustered mahouts returned with their disobedient charges. The panniers that had been ripped off their backs by the dense bush had been collected by the other two mahouts and their elephants. When at last we resumed our journey, young 'Randy' was kept well back in the procession and, for his pains, had his back legs anchored by a drag chain which was normally only fitted at night.

By the time the team had arrived back at the Dawrahku HQ we were exhausted and Major Boal was suffering from another bout of fever. We managed to scrounge a couple of M and B tablets to grind down into powder to treat our infected scratches, sores and leg ulcers. These were still a constant nuisance and part of our daily lives, refusing to completely heal and, no doubt, not helped by our meagre and poor diet. Doc (Capt. Harrison) had moved on somewhere else, so after a few days' rest, Capt. Coomber joined the other officers taking out patrols to try and contact remaining garrisons or large groups of Japanese, still present and using the Loi-Kaw/Hpru-So/Bawlake road. Major Boal, who had once more been lent a mountain pony by the Roman Catholic Fathers, was despatched to Major Denning's camp for further treatment under the care of the Sisters at the convent in Hwariku. I had been given the task of accompanying him, which pleased me no end, for reasons I kept to myself! Would 'she' be pleased to see me back again I wondered? Setting off with a guide and the pony carrying the Major fairly early in the morning, we hoped to reach our destination the same day. The Major though, had to be assisted frequently and this slowed us up no end. His fever caused him to perspire one moment and shiver as if very cold the next. I had to walk alongside him to prevent him falling off as he was slumped over the animal more often than sitting up to ride it correctly. As it grew later and darker we sought out a small cave in which to rest for the night. Once settled inside, the invalid was made as comfortable as possible under the circumstances. I made a fire to keep him warm and boiled some water to drink, and shared what little food we had brought with us, just some boiled rice to supplement a 'K' ration each, originally intended for the midday break. Resuming the journey the next morning we finally arrived in the early afternoon, safely back in Denning's camp at Hwariku.

It was by now the end of August and we had been away since the 2nd on an extraordinary journey, over hills and around hills, up and down valleys, through dense bamboo forests and over mountain streams, covering an uncountable number of miles and with many different experiences - and the war was over! Or was it?

Chapter Thirty-Six - Loi-Kaw Reclaimed

Safe at the Convent, Major Boal was placed in the hands of the Mother Superior, Mother Harriet and the Sisters. Norman, who had accompanied me, learnt that the young Sister Bernadette was still ill with malaria and, on inquiring about her well-being, we were invited to pay her a return visit, in bed, alone, in her own room. Usually bright and sometimes a little cheeky, Sister Bernadette remarked on seeing us that she was not really sick, just enjoying the chance of entertaining the two of us in her room once more. She was obviously getting better and recovering from her fever!

On our return journey to the camp I inquired after the only other person I was eager to meet again in Hwariku, 'May' or 'Ma-yea', as I had not yet seen her around the camp. Norman replied that the last he had heard was that she and her father-in-law had been preparing to return to their home in Loi-Kaw, and he was not sure if they had gone yet. His team, too, was preparing to move into Loi-Kaw, as there were now believed to be only a very few Japanese administration staff still in occupation there. Most had already fled into Siam. I was left with very little to do whilst waiting for new orders and the recovery of the Major Boal; there was only very little radio work to be done and this was dealt with by Norman. Apart from hearing that Don Gibbs and the Wilson team had safely reached the 14th Army in the North and that they would not be returning because of the ceasefire, there was no other news. With no light planes arriving recently, all news reports scarce and supplies very low, it seemed as though now the war was officially over we had been forgotten! The British troops, as far as we knew, had stopped where they were at the ceasefire to date, not venturing north, south, or eastward to clear the area of Japanese boxed up between them and the Siamese borders. The Japanese, too, were equally ill informed, not at all convinced about the cessation of hostilities and did not believe the leaflets that had been dropped by air on their remaining troops, telling them of their country's surrender. They appeared to be out of touch with their commanding officers and determined to continue to retreat into Siam, obeying only the last verbal orders that they had received.

Until the Major was well enough, which was expected to be about a week to ten days later, I returned to Pop's HQ in Dawrahku. There I joined the other officers and Burmese sappers in their regular patrols, following up any reports coming in of Japanese movements northward, along the main road between Loi-Kaw and Bawlake. Roadblocks had been set up just north of Hpru-So, where there was still a small Japanese garrison which appeared to be directing any new arrivals eastward towards the Siamese border. This suited all of us in Pop's WALRUS group of Special Force 136, as we had neither the food nor facilities to enable us to take prisoners. Neither did we desire to argue with them, or be obliged to open fire on them. At the roadblocks, made of broken down and abandoned vehicles and farm carts, the encounters were of a familiar nature. White flags were flying and armed men posted each side of the road under cover. Any Jap groups, large or small, which had not turned eastward at Hpru-So, were called on to halt and one or two of their group called forward to parley under the white flag. They were met by one of the team's officers and an interpreter. Fortunately more than one of the Burmese sappers could speak a little Japanese. They were told that they could not be allowed to travel further north with their arms. If they gave them up they would be taken as prisoners of war and escorted by the local tribesmen to Loi-Kaw and handed over to the local (non-existent) Burmese troops who were in command. This they, as was expected, refused to do without receiving direct new orders from their commanding officers. Knowing that they were very wary of the local tribesmen, they were then informed that they could only retain their arms, for their personal protection, if they were to turn eastward immediately and travel through the tribal lands to Siam.

As the Japanese had only one desire, which was to get back to Japan even if they had to walk all the way, this option was usually accepted by them. There were, though, several occasions when they were belligerent or at first a little reluctant to accept the terms offered. Whenever this seemed a likely response, a show of force was made by the armed men lining the road. They would be ordered to show themselves briefly, holding their firearms in the air, then to take cover again with their arms pointed at the Japanese. With men on both sides of the road and ahead of them, this usually encouraged a quick departure, any reluctance and a few shots over their heads helped to reinforce the order. There were also occasions when the Japanese fired first. This was always quickly dealt with by a short burst of fire. As they, being poorly armed and probably very short of ammunition, realised they were surrounded and facing some fearsome well-armed opponents, they hurried away even faster!

When I returned to Dawrahku after a couple of weeks' tour of duty with the sappers at the roadblocks on the main road to Loi-Kaw, the HQ was preparing to move into the town as it was now fairly certain it had been abandoned by the Japanese. I was informed that Major Boal was now well enough to travel and I was sent on to Hwariku to rejoin him, with instructions to prepare to proceed with him on the journey and to meet up with others, who by then would be installed in Loi-Kaw at the Sawbwa's large house (mansion or palace, no-one seemed to know what to call it). It was, apparently, the largest building and not far from the river that flowed around the northern side of the town. Resting only the one night after a full day's march back to the HQ, I set off for another 15 mile march, this time with only a porter/guide to accompany me. The journey was uneventful and I was able to travel up and down the hills at my own pace, stopping to rest whenever I felt the need or to enjoy the scenery. On arrival in Hwariku I found Major Boal was the last of the British remaining there. All of Major Denning's team and Capt. Coomber had departed for Loi-Kaw two days earlier. Major Boal, who was keen to follow them as soon as possible, had the mountain pony packed and ready to depart. So, once again after just one night's rest, I was on the road again, this time to Loi-Kaw, a good 20 miles away. The Major was now free of his fever, although he was not quite as fit as he would have liked to have been and rode on the pony most of the way. It certainly came in very useful for the first part of the journey, which took us up and down hill after never-ending hill, this time with me holding onto the pony's tail when climbing uphill for additional support! Having started our journey in the early morning, by afternoon we were experiencing seemingly more downhill than upward slopes, as we were levelling out to far flatter land. Pathways were getting wider, making it easier to walk and it was now possible to see a greater distance in front and round about. Not only that, the jungle had gradually melted away. Having been in the 'bush' for so long we had gone native!

It had been over four months since we had last seen so much level ground. There was though, among the last few hills before reaching the outskirts of the town as evening approached, just one last hillock standing almost alone. Looking up to it we could clearly see a small cave, lit by the rays of the setting sun. Stopping to rest a while, a clearly marked pathway leading up to the cave could be seen. It seemed to be inviting us to pay a visit. It was a steep but easy climb up the winding track, to the sunlit entrance and the rays of light that shone into its depths. The opening was large enough for one person at a time to walk in without bending and wide enough inside for two or three persons to walk side by side. On entering we saw, at the far end about 12-15 ft away, a flat stone not unlike a small table, with shallow stone dishes containing water and grain placed before a small statue of Buddha. We had blundered into a primitive temple. With a mixture of self-consciousness and embarrassment, we made our apologies and backed away. Returning to the still sun-lit entrance we both stood outside facing westward, looking towards the distant hills just as the sun was sinking behind them. The sky, the hills and the jungle between all changed colour as we watched the sun rapidly drop down behind the hills in a spectacular blaze of glory, a panorama to be long remembered. It was as though the hills that had protected and provided for us for so long were bidding us goodbye!

With the daylight rapidly failing, the last part of our journey into Loi-Kaw had to be a hurried one. Although almost complete nightfall before we arrived, the house we sought was easy to find as it was probably the largest as well as the only double-storied building in the town. Thankfully, after a decent mug of tea and a meal it was early to bed, further inspection being delayed for later the next day.

The remaining sergeants, Neville Wood, Norman Smith and I were accommodated on the first floor in a very large room. There was only one double bed, which the first two shared. Although big enough for all three to sleep on I chose to make my bed up on the floor, in a far corner of the room well away from their snores. Bedding was the usual salvaged parachutes, which served as both mattress and cover on the plaited bed mats that all were well accustomed to using by now. Food was still sparse and a repetitive mixture of local (mainly rice) and emergency American and Australian rations. Some of the Burmese sappers were repairing a small airfield the other side of the river at Loi-Kaw. The others and the Levies, with the officers in turn, still kept a close watch on the remaining Japanese, contained in a couple of large groups well out of reach of the town, who were still reluctant to return home, or even to believe the war was lost and over! There were also isolated small groups trying to flee Burma, thought to be deserters. All sides, if able, were still exchanging fire when getting frustrated with each other - available ammunition permitting! The Japanese final surrender had been signed a month ago, but no-one seemed to know or care about what was going on away from the old front lines since the ceasefire. If it wasn't for the BBC's news programmes we would have been completely isolated.

All three of us occupied ourselves by setting up a radio room on the new site with a decent aerial on the roof, but messages received were rare and answers to ours even rarer, until at last we were informed that two Japanese officers would be arriving on the next plane, the first passengers to arrive at the Loi-Kaw airstrip. They were going to assist in making contact with the renegade enemy troops that were still making a nuisance of themselves and causing the team, as well as the local population, a great deal of worry and distress. The need of supplies meant they were raiding nearby Karenni and Padaung villages, which had been very loyal to the British throughout the war. These gallant warriors had deserved better treatment and all the help that could be obtained for them. Alas, the WALRUS team, limited in number and supplies as we were, could not give them all the help that they needed. When, if ever, were our own armed forces going to arrive, was a frequently asked question!

The morning after this latest news, in our spare time, of which we had plenty, we were cleaning our carbines in the hope of some decisive action in the near future. We were in the back garden which looked out over the countryside when we spotted a flock of birds circling high in the sky some distance away from the outskirts of the town. All were fascinated watching them as they came closer and closer towards us. Such sights of any high flying birds had been rare up till now, as the thick canopy of trees in the bush had prevented anything but brief glimpses of patches of sky. As the flock moved nearer they were easily identified as vultures, about a dozen of them. Several of the officers, who were called out to watch, joined the small crowd now gathering in the garden. Amidst comments about the ugly beasts, that they were probably seeking dead bodies, one of the officers called out to us, 'One shot each, double rations at the next meal, to the first one of you who can bag one!' First Neville, then Norman fired and missed. I waited until I had fixed my sights on one bird, keeping it in my sights as it circled, holding my aim on it and waiting until it appeared to be flying towards or away from me, rather than across my vision. I had to allow for the target's movement, remembering skills I had learnt poaching in Beccles and anti-aircraft defence in the KRRC. My tactic worked perfectly. A single shot had hit it in the breast, and it fell out of the sky like a stone, a good two hundred yards away. A cheer went up and couple of young Karen lads ran off to bring in the trophy. On their return one of the officers produced a camera and took a photograph of me holding up the rather unfortunate ugly beast. It was enormous, over six feet from head to tail and a wingspan about a foot longer, the breast as big as a man's. Certainly bigger than its adversary, and only with its head hanging down on its chest, could you see who was holding it up!

For other distractions to while away the time, I chose to go for a ride on Major Boal's mountain pony around the town, or wander down to the river just a short walk away from the house. There was a beach area there, giving easy access from which one could bathe or wash clothes. Whilst out riding, it was noticeable that the local people were still very nervous of strangers. Sitting in the saddle made it possible to see a little further ahead than when walking. This gave the advantage of being able to see the odd person who was still on the outside of their house, first. Then I would see them slip back into their homes, doors and shutters on windows being closed at the first sound of anyone approaching. There were large numbers of small wooden huts on low stilts which had been damaged and not all were yet repaired. The Japanese had left their mark on the people as well as the town during their long occupation. It was sad to observe the terror and the horror it must have caused for civilians obliged to live in such circumstances. Soldiers could fight back; not so the innocent, who had no alternative but to suffer. It was unanimously agreed not to walk around the town unless absolutely necessary, until the population got used to having more friendly visitors.

Chapter Thirty-Seven - Entertaining Japanese Visitors

The day the two Japanese officers arrived, Major Boal must have been the only senior officer available, Pop having flown out on the same small aeroplane that brought them in. It was known he was seeking assistance for his men, as well as the locals, and wanted a meeting with others back at the base, now thought to be in Rangoon instead of Calcutta. No-one was sure where exactly orders came from; these things were not discussed nor usually worried about. Trained to deal with anything thrown at us was normal and being left to our own discretion was fine and to be expected, but such shortage of supplies and information from the base was getting tiresome. If it had not been for the loyalty of the local population the whole group would have died off long ago.

The arrival of the two smartly dressed Japanese officers put every one to shame, and this had the effect of a sudden dash back to our rooms for us and several of the officers, who were also dressed in the same casual manner. We must have made a peculiar sight for the visitors, dressed as we were in a mixture of colourful longyis, khaki shirts made out of ex-parachute materials and most barefooted, wearing around the waist a webbing belt on which hung our .45 semi automatic, fighting knife, ammo pouches, compass and water bottle as well as any other 'maybe useful item'! Most of us had beards and long hair tied back with parachute cord, and must have looked more like local bandits than military men. We sergeants begged, borrowed and swapped bits and pieces from each other, mainly from Norman, of Denning's team, which had been operating the only decent airstrip and were well protected by the Padaungs as well as the Roman Catholic Sisters. Had they been having first pick of any goodies received? Mirrors were a thing of the past but I still had my polished steel heliograph mirror, which all wanted to use at once, checking ourselves to see if we were looking clean and tidy, if not shaven. Combs, too, were in short supply, so fingers run through our hair had to suffice.

When at last we presented ourselves (in borrowed boots in some cases) we looked a little more like soldiers. Heaven knows what impression we made on these two Japanese, who themselves were immaculately dressed in spotless uniforms that looked brand new! They were also very young and must either have just left an officers' training establishment, or perhaps come straight from a school's officer cadet force. Kow-towing a great deal and a little apprehensive at first, they were soon strutting around in a very arrogant manner, one hand steadying the swords swinging by their sides. They were not viewed as being welcome but it was thought that they may be able to assist in convincing the last remaining Japanese ground troops that the war was definitely over.

They could not speak any English or seem to know anything about the British way of life or customs. The team did have an interpreter among the Burmese sappers and he had to be sent for before any conversation was possible. Meanwhile, Major Boal, as acting senior officer in charge, decided to arrange a special meal that evening in an effort to 'civilise' them a little, as all agreed the new arrivals needed bringing down a peg or two. At great sacrifice and expense, by using up a great deal of our precious food reserves, this was organised. The dining room was laid out as formally as possible, with old damaged furniture draped in silk, (ex-parachutes that had been serving as bedding) cutlery polished (rubbed in sand), plates obtained (scrounged) from somewhere unknown, possibly from the Sawbwa's secret stores via one of his servants who had been attending to our needs since arriving at the palace. All in all, it did not look too bad, or too good for that matter. Even the 'glasses' for the rice wine looked reasonable, being as they were made from bamboo! Overall, every one in camp that day did their little bit towards making it a success. Using a sign language we had all used frequently with some of the locals since our arrival in Burma, such as motioning to eat and drink and pointing to a watch, the guests seemed to get the correct message.

We were all were standing to attention, ready behind our chairs and trying hard not to laugh, when the guests arrived on time. They were shown to their places next to the Major's chair and shown by example to remain standing until he arrived to take his place at table. When seated, he turned towards the Japanese inviting them to do the same and the rest followed suit. The Major, addressing his mob of depraved conspirators, whispered, 'I think this is a good time to give the Loyal Toast.' At which point he rose and raised his 'glass'. When all were upstanding, including the guests, we sang the British National Anthem then drank to the health of His Majesty the King, inviting our guests to do likewise. The meal then commenced. There were though, no chopsticks - not much use for the first course anyway, as it was soup! Having raided the last of the 'compo' tins for as much tinned meat and vegetables, definitely no rice, as we could find, we followed this with a dessert of tinned mixed fruits, then cheese and coffee extracted from the life-saving American 'K' rations. Much to our amusement and half hidden smirks, the Japs struggled to copy us by using knives, forks and spoons, probably for the first time in their lives. It must be said that their obvious embarrassment was a pleasure to watch. Considering the cruelty the Japanese had been observed dealing out to others, they got off very lightly indeed. It had been agreed before the meal, that drinking would be kept to a minimum and that there should be no singing afterwards. No-one wished the evening to be considered a celebration of any kind. At the end of the meal the Major was the first to rise from the table; he then went outside to the garden before lighting his first cigarette of the evening. The rest of the British group did the same, ignoring the two Japs, leaving them standing, not knowing what to do next. Having finished our last smoke of the day, we then retired to our rooms after bidding our guests goodnight. The poor, 'wet behind the ears', stiff and arrogant visitors must have still been hungry as they had been seen picking scraps of leftover food off the table with their fingers. They had had great difficulty managing to eat using cutlery instead of chopsticks, in trying to copy us Brits.

Next morning the two Japanese were going to be taken to their first encounter with the renegade Japanese, entrenched 15 miles down the Loi-Kaw/Bawlake road, near Hpru-So. Dressed and ready to leave after breakfast, I went down to the large hallway to await the arrival of the others of my team, who were escorting them and looking forward to travelling in style for once instead of walking. The journey was going to be made in one of the salvaged Japanese trucks on which the Burmese sappers had been working. The two ex-enemy officers were not only already there, they were practising their drills with swords drawn and prancing around slashing at invisible adversaries. As I approached, one of them turned towards me and kow-towed, as they frequently had the habit of doing. The other turned and keeping his sword high above his head, his feet one in front of the other, took slow but deliberate steps towards me. I was furious. He had fixed his gaze on my eyes, and his sword was being brought up and down in a chopping motion whilst moving gradually towards me.

As we stared at each other, my hand went for my .45 semi-automatic hand gun, as my mind flashed back to the last time something like this had happened to me. I cocked the gun and pointed it at the Jap's head in a very steady double handed grip, shouting at him at the same time with a lot of abuse. One more step and he would have his head blown off. The Jap dropped his sword down to his side and started to kow-tow repeatedly. Still not satisfied, I shouted again and again indicating that I wanted him flat on the ground at my feet. I had every intention to put my foot on the man's neck and disarm him. I was so angry I wanted to break the sword in two. One of the officers from among a gathering crowd which had heard the uproar stepped in quickly and made the Jap put his sword back into its scabbard, while I demanded to know why the Japanese were allowed to keep them? It was explained to me that if improperly dressed, and that included their swords, their compatriots would not respect their authority over them. My response was to the effect that as there were no other Japanese thereabouts in Loi-Kaw, there was no reason for them to wear their swords here, and I insisted they be ordered to be unarmed at all times whilst in the house, or, I added, next time I might fire first and ask questions later. Others agreed with me and it was translated to the two Jap officers. The incident had annoyed me a great deal and I referred to them as 'being overgrown schoolboys playing at soldiers' and I had no difficulty in convincing all the onlookers. An hour later Boal's team and the two Japanese were boarding the vehicle that was to take us all towards the roadblocks, and the swords were returned their owners.

The journey along the unmade dirt road was a slow, bumpy and uncomfortable experience, not helped by the frequent roughly repaired pot holes, caused by the explosives used when the group had attacked previous enemy convoys. Many damaged carts, trucks and other debris littered the roadside and blocked the deep drainage gullies each side of the track in places, evidence of the past activities of the WALRUS band of merry men. Even this though, I thought, was better than walking, which is not my favourite occupation. Major Boal sat next to the driver, Capt. Coomber and me in the back of the lorry keeping an eye on the two young Japanese officers, making sure they did not change their minds and disembark before encountering the renegades they were due to meet. Greeted on arrival by the Burmese sappers and local Levies on their tour of duty guarding the roadblock, no time was wasted. Immediate contact with the entrenched garrison was made and they were called forward under a white flag.

Less confident now and rather nervously, the two young Japanese joined the two British officers, who had moved forward to speak to the garrison miscreants who had emerged to parley with them. The sight of the two young smartly dressed Japanese alongside the British was an obvious shock to their war weary half-starved compatriots. They made their disbelief clear to all, in words that were not yet understood but the tone and actions spoke volumes. When translated later, they had accused the new arrivals of being traitors, and of being forced to speak to them. They were still unable to accept that their country had capitulated. One drew his hand gun and would have shot them there and then, had not the Levies, who were keeping watch, stood up immediately and levelled their rifles at them. Doing a quick about turn, they withdrew to their cover without bothering to bow out in their usual manner. This first effort was over in a very few minutes and it was decided to try again later, when it was hoped that things may be a little calmer.

After a break for a meal of rice and bamboo shoots, and a lot of 'Kaung-ye', the local rice wine, the two Japanese were brave enough to try again. They took this time something they had been writing down during the break. This was checked by the interpreter first, just in case they were informing their countrymen of the British team's own strength or weaknesses. As before, a meeting was called for under the white flag and, after a brief delay, two different Japanese came out to join the British officers who accompanied the two visiting Japs. It started very formally with the usual kow-towing, a few words, and the reading of the written message. Then the talking began, calm at first, but gradually growing more excitable, then threatening, until the two young Japanese officers turned on their heels and ran back towards the Levies. They dived for cover behind the roadside barricade. Needless to say, the Brits were doing likewise not far behind them. Whether by design or accident, the entrenched renegades did at least wait until all were under cover before opening fire. Their first half-a-dozen bullets were answered by a volley of rapid fire from the Burmese sappers, Levies and British, then followed spasmodic firing from both sides at any movement or possible target for the next hour before the Japanese broke off the engagement. After a pause, when things had returned to a semblance of relative calm, with a constant watch only being maintained by both sides, I was sent back alone to Loi-Kaw in the lorry, taking with me a full report to the HQ. My two officers were staying as additional support, at least until a fresh relief arrived.

Back in the more peaceful surroundings of Loi-Kaw, it was already late in the evening and after informing the duty officer of the day's misadventures, I quickly retired, exhausted. Sleep though did not come easily, repeated images of the days happenings flashed back again and again. Why were we still being shot at? Wasn't the war supposed to be over? Fortunately, there had only been a few very minor injuries on our side; it could have been worse. Luckily the Japs were poor shots as usual. Not so lucky for them though, as I had seen several of them fall. One particular image kept repeating itself of a Jap falling from a tree, about a hundred yards away. I had spotted him climbing, rifle slung over his shoulder, up a tree, probably trying to get a better angle for his sights. I could only see part of his body as he climbed but took a chance and fired, aiming at the chest beneath an upturned arm seeking a higher grip. He fell backward twenty or thirty foot disappearing into the bushes below. Over and over again it flashed before my eyes, and in my mind the thought, how much longer must this go on? In a war that was supposed to be over. It was by now the first week of October! Having survived this long, who wants to get bumped off now?

Chapter Thirty-Eight - A Pleasant Reunion

After a restless night, I had nothing important to do. The other two NCOs, Neville and Norman, were occupied along with the signals officer, coding and recharging batteries at the new radio station they had been organising, in a building close to the landing field on the edge of the town. Having first cleaned my trusty American carbine, which I neglected to do the night before, feeling hot and still a little weary I decided to walk down to the river to wash myself and a few clothes, or even go for a swim. Casually dressed, wearing only a shirt (grace of the nuns) and a longyi, and bare foot, looking more like a local than anything else, except perhaps for my webbing belt on which, among other items, I always carried my .45, I set off. Halfway down the path to the river, a ten minute stroll away from the Sawbwa's palace, I passed a small damaged house on the edge of a plot of cultivated land with another larger house at far end of it, which was all part of the Sawbwa's estate. This I had noted, but as yet it meant nothing more than another piece of evidence of Japanese vandalism.

Once down by the river I found a gentle sloping beach with a few large boulders of the type which women would choose to do their washing, not unlike sites I had seen before, both in India and Ceylon. As this was an isolated spot I undressed, down to just the loincloth I was in the habit of wearing. The river was running fairly fast and while contemplating whether or not it was safe to swim in it, my mind was made up for me by what I saw! First one, then another, with only their heads just above the water, passing in front of me, were two very large snakes, their long wriggling bodies stretching out behind them. Keeping a sharp lookout for any other interlopers I bathed myself by the water's edge. I then washed what few clothes I did have, the Indian way, without any soap and bashing the wet clothing on the boulders, then drying them and myself in the hot sun.

Only half awake in a dreamlike way, something, perhaps a movement from behind, made me stand and turn around. Yes, there was someone, a slim figure, a young woman, and then came the realisation that it was someone I knew. She was smiling at me; me, almost naked apart from the wet and near transparent loincloth! It was as though the impossible had happened. It was May. We had found each other again! Snatching up my longyi to cover my embarrassment and running towards each other, we embraced like long lost lovers. There were words spoken to each other and although the languages were not understood the meanings were not in doubt. We were overjoyed at meeting once more, just standing, laughing, and happily holding each other tightly in our arms, with frequent kisses on cheeks and lips. She happily helped me to dress, showing me the correct way to hitch up my longyi, having laughed at my clumsy efforts. Then she covered my webbing belt that I had added to my outfit, by pulling out my tucked in shirt so that it covered and hid my fighting knife and .45 sidearm. Then we reluctantly left our spot by the riverside hand in hand, walking slowly back towards the Sawbwa's house. By communicating by signs as well as words in our own languages, for example, pointing to her and saying the word for 'you' or pointing to myself and saying 'me'. This same method also worked easily with objects, as we gradually increased our own new vocabulary. A hand on the heart and pointing to one another with eyes shining and laughter happened frequently and it was easy to interpret the warmth of the feelings that were flowing between us.

Upon reaching the small damaged house built on stilts that I had passed by earlier, May indicated that we should enter. Hesitating at first until she explained that it was hers, we climbed the ladder and squatted down in the centre of the main room. The damage was minor and only affected the roof and one corner of the house. Whilst trying to chat and putting together what I had been told by Norman when I first met 'May', I understood that this was where she had lived until her husband had been killed by the Japanese about two years ago. Her widower father-in-law, to whom she was subservient, lived in the larger house at the other end of the plot of land. It was there that she resided now, with her own room, to take care of him. Breaking off after many preliminary hugs and kisses she indicated that she was going to the other house to collect something and would return.

After what seemed like an eternity but was probably only a half hour or so, she came back carrying a large bundle. There were sleeping mats, a meal of rice and bamboo shoots and mangoes, rice wine to drink and also something to clean and dress the ever present open sores on my legs. The latter were dealt with first, using the local potions we had got used to whenever visiting a hillside village. After which we enjoyed our first meal together. She made it known to me that I could stay and live there in her house with her by linking the third finger of her left hand to mine. Did this mean we were 'engaged' or 'married' I thought! At that moment I felt so happy and content I really didn't care. She had undone her hair that had been neatly tied back and shaken it loose. It now hung down to her almost bare shoulders, black, shiny and silky against her light milk chocolate coloured skin. A very beautiful lady, sitting there in her brief colourful loose-fitting blouse and sari; it was not long before we were locked in another kind of embrace, which was not of the kind that one would do in public. Sometime later, we fell asleep, naked in each other's arms.

Accepting the change of residence was not a difficult choice to make. I returned to the HQ in the Sawbwa's palace, simply informed the other two sergeants that I had found somewhere else to sleep instead of sharing with them, conveniently forgetting to mention that it was not in the same house. Probably pleased at the thought of having more space to themselves, they never questioned my move. They had their radio work organised between them, and the officers, in shifts, were engaged elsewhere, some occupied with the Japanese at the roadblock, others with sappers repairing lorries and building rafts on which it was hoped that, in due course, all could leave en route by river and road for Rangoon. Not that I was in any hurry to depart at that precise moment!

My team officers had informed me there was very little action now at the road block and there was no need to take extra risks. The two young Japanese officers were shot at whenever they showed themselves and were useless. It had been decided to sit it out with the remaining renegades, in the hope that lack of supplies would in the end drive them away and over the border into Siam. They would have to leave before they ran out of ammunition if they were going to protect themselves from the local Karens, and no doubt others, on the last leg of their journey home. WALRUS group's own supplies being rather depleted prevented us from taking more direct action. It was not even certain that we could legally do so unless it was to defend ourselves. All this left me (happily) with very little to do at the moment, except to be seen occasionally, in case I was wanted. I collected together what very few possessions I had left and a couple of redundant parachutes for bedding and relocated myself in May's house down the road.

Very comfortably ensconced, May and I spent as much time together as we possibly could, without being discovered. We ventured out separately only to meet again down by the river to bathe, splashing about in the shallows, washing each other and reliving our recent reunion with hugs and kisses before returning once more to our love nest. We dined on a mixture of my rations and what May produced, communicating, of course, by touching and signing and living a life akin to newly weds, sleeping off our excesses by day as well as by night.

This was all very well, but! Preparations for the departure from Loi-kaw were well advanced. The abandoned lorries had proved easy to repair as they appeared to be Japanese copies of Ford trucks and several were now ready for the journey. It was now the end of the third week of October and Pop, on receiving the news that the last remaining Japanese had dispersed over night, decided it was time to go. Major Boal's team, he said, was the only team to stay behind as they were the last team to be dropped in. All the others would depart the next day. As we were also leaving the Sawbwa's house, Boal's team (Maj. Boal, Capt. Coomber, and myself), was to relocate at the DZ, Airstrip and Radio Station. Pleased at last to have my own real job back as a wireless operator, I was certainly not so happy at having to leave my present but temporary home life. As always, army life with frequent moves had never been anything but cruel to relationships. This one, if it had been possible, I would have been content to remain in; I had not been so happy for a long, long time. It was going to be hard to say farewell; even harder without the language to do so with any proper understanding. After what was to be our last night together I gathered up my few personal possessions, leaving the parachutes and anything else we had shared. She gave me a small clay model of Buddha to keep me safe as we sadly kissed goodbye for the last time.

Chapter Thirty-Nine - Adieu Force 136

The whole group moved off early in the morning, heading for the river at the other side of the town where the rafts had been built and were now anchored to the bank next to a newly built ramp. Only two lorries were starting off from the river, others were going by road and meeting up later, somewhere further south in the Mawchi mines road area. It was a slow and delicate process loading 2-ton trucks onto the rafts but, with willing hands, it was accomplished and, after some careful balancing, they looked reasonably safe. When the front wheels were driven on board the raft had been in danger of tipping up so men, and some of the cargo, had to be placed at the opposite end to counterbalance the whole affair. Shallow water at the riverbank's edge saved the day as the raft touched ground amid shouts of alarm and roars of laughter at that particular anxious but comic moment. The river was running fairly fast and, as expected, when the loaded rafts were at last released they were rapidly swept away. When the pressure of the water on one side tipped the raft down so much that it looked dangerously close to capsizing, the men on board had to rapidly throw themselves down at the opposite side as counterweights. Even so the whole process and progress looked far from being 100 percent safe! Those already on board had said their farewells and cheers, then singing, burst out from those remaining ashore - 'I want to go home, I want to go home, me oh my, I don't want to die, I want to go home!'

The second party then took off by road, feeling no doubt, even with a bumpier ride, far safer if less adventurous! This left just Boal's team of three, who were for the moment remaining at Loi-kaw. We paid for and took a small ferryboat, steered by one man across the river. Spanning the river, attached to each bank, was a long cable, with another looped over it and hooked onto his boat. By steering into the river's fast current at a 45 degree angle, the river itself supplied the power to push the boat over to the other side. We made our way from there on foot for about a mile or so before arriving at our new billet, which was a reasonably large teak-built house at the side of the airstrip. I duly installed myself in the already prepared radio room, feeling important at last, with my own radio station and office. I was unhappy, though, because it was too far from my current love interest to be able to make even a brief visit. Such is the loneliness of war; frequent disruption of relationships, responsible for the breaking of many hearts, the need for comforting, warm and willing arms, resulting in infidelity to one or other of the parties, if not both. Remembering the promise given when volunteering for the Far East - that when the job was done we would return home - I began to wonder when that would be!

Any spare moment, at this time, I spent hunting something for the pot to spice up our meagre diet. This particular area, being flatter and more cultivated, attracted flocks of birds and other wildlife. Catching it was the problem. There was no point in setting snares for rabbits as I had not seen a trace of one in Burma, probably because there weren't any! In any case, a snare would most likely catch some other unknown wild beast, a little more dangerous to extricate. Waiting for barking deer to come down to drink at night would mean sitting in the dark or waiting for a moonlit night. Even then, with so much water in the area, finding the right spot was too difficult to determine. There were though, great flocks of very large birds on the paddy fields who were obviously feeding on something. They would all take to the air at the slightest movement or when any one approached, having no doubt been hunted frequently by their previous visitors. Nevertheless, the flocks were so large that just one shot into the white cloud of birds could hardly miss. I successfully tried this method but having to retrieve the trophy from knee deep muddy water was not very pleasant and the rather scraggy birds were not all that appreciated. Fishing was tried next. After all, the birds must have been eating as well as resting on the waters. A fishing line proved useless as the fish were far too small, and having nothing that could be turned into a net meant that the hunting expeditions were not very successful. It did, though, help to pass the many idle hours while waiting to be evacuated.

At last the long awaited message arrived. A plane had been detailed to pick up the team and we could be at least in Rangoon by 31st October. We were watching the sky anxiously on the day, expecting one or two of the usually very small spotter-type supply planes, and wondering how we would all fit into it, complete with baggage, when we saw a single but larger aircraft circling and, as it approached, recognised it as being a 'Lizzie', the affectionate name for the well admired Lysander, which was successfully adapted and used throughout Europe for agent pick-ups. A beautiful sight to see at anytime, it could land almost anywhere reasonably flat and only needed about a five hundred yards long runway.

The plane landed, the pilot staying on board while his navigator helped to load the passengers and their baggage. The rear compartment only had two seats and the baggage had to be packed into the rear of the cockpit, in the place meant for the passengers' feet under the pilot's seating. Fortunately there were only two surviving rucksacks and a small bundle of odds and ends, including several ex-Japanese swords labelled with their new owners' names. The two officers sat side-by-side on the rear seating; I squeezed between them and sat on the floor. Because of the baggage, I couldn't stretch out my legs and kept my knees tucked up to my chest. Only half of my head was visible above the height of the surrounding metalwork, not exactly very comfortable. By the way, the officers were, of course, not pulling rank. I was 'volunteered' as being the smallest, but who cared anyway; we were on the first leg of our way home!

The flight would take about an hour and a half. The view from our seating, through the clear dome that covered the cockpit, was fantastic. The plane flew along valleys between the higher hills and over the smaller ones; it was not unlike flying through a maze as the plane banked to port and starboard around the hills. It was also a little disturbing to see trees at times higher than the aeroplane, on both the left and right of it at the same time. The pilot had another surprise for us about a half an hour after take off. He took the plane higher and told his passengers to hold on tight. He cleared a hill then dived down into a valley and, from a view of nothing but sky, we were treated to the sight of the ground coming up fast towards us! As the plane got lower and pulled up again, we could see a group of men waving and running to pick up small packages on tiny parachutes the pilot had dropped for them, probably mail. The aeroplane climbed away higher now for the final stretch towards Rangoon. Then, as we circled for landing, the large town's splendid sights came into view. The river, taller buildings, and the most prominent features of all, brilliant in the sunlight, the magnificent Golden Temples shone in all their glory.

The sudden and very distinct change of scenery and sounds from the jungle to a large bustling town had us turning our heads and pointing out the very different and strange things we were now experiencing whilst being driven to our first destination. Would there be a welcome committee, perhaps, or a final debriefing? Oh, no! We found out, on arrival, that the first stop was to be at the local hospital! Split up, of course, no time for goodbyes; officers one way, other ranks another and that was the last we saw of each other! I was allowed to shower and given a dressing gown to wear but, as there was no barber, I retained my beard and long hair which was still tied back in a pigtail by parachute cord. The big surprise was that the MO was a lady doctor. Very unusual! Not only were female doctors a rare sight in those days, but I cannot recall having seen one at all before that particular time. After being weighed and told that I had lost nearly two stones, she gave me a very brief examination, told an orderly to treat my festering sores and gave me a rather large injection of penicillin in my rear end. Finally, after checking my teeth, she said 'You have not been cleaning your teeth lately, have you, young man?' 'Been a bit short of many things, ma'am,' I'd replied. Before I left I was given a supply of multivitamin capsules to take, and that was it. What a welcome! After I had been given a new uniform, underwear, socks, and boots, I was driven to a small hotel which was being used as a rest-house whilst waiting for repatriation to Calcutta. My two officers, having no doubt had similar experiences, were despatched to another, meant for officers only. We were never to meet again.

The accommodation was certainly very comfortable; a single room or a small dormitory if preferred, and the food excellent. There were a just a few other NCOs there from different groups but none from WALRUS. I did not know at that time if they had been and departed again, or if they had not yet arrived. Greeted and shown around by a very charming young Burmese lady, more in hope than expectation, I chose one of the single rooms. This was heaven, my own room with washing facilities, a real bed with sheets and mosquito net! There was a small group of other well spoken and very polite young Burmese ladies whose job appeared to be the welfare of the visitors. They all spoke in almost perfect, understandable English and were well educated. They also cooked and cleaned or took time to chat to their guests and offered to escort them if they wished to visit the town's sights and scenery. BUT, yes, there is always a big but when things are going too well, they were not 'available' by night, or day for that matter. They all had regular boy friends already, mainly from amongst the more permanent officers, who probably helped them to get these comfortable posts. I found this out as we sat chatting, watching the world pass by, when I was taken by one of the young ladies down to the very large river that flowed through the town. Well, I had to at least try, didn't I? Disappointed, yes, but the company was very pleasant anyway. This near paradise did not last long. At the end of the following week I was on my way by plane, back to Calcutta. Not too soon either, the strain and temptation of being among all these pretty young maidens was getting dangerously unbearable.

On arrival back in Calcutta I was driven directly to an army holding barracks on the edge of town. This was certainly a big come down from my last digs! There I found a good many other Special Force 136 men, including a number of SF Jedburghs. My kit-bag and suitcase containing my army and personal effects, which had been left behind in 'safe' storage at Ceylon, had been forwarded on and were handed back. These I had to sign for before they were handed over, much to my regret, because I later found that they had been rifled through and many items were missing. When complaining about this, the excuse given was that this was how it was received and any complaints would have to be made when I got back to the camp at Horana in Ceylon. Of course, later, when I did return to Horana camp a similar story was told, and that it was all correct on leaving there. Some of the most important missing items were from my last birthday at home, my 19th chronologically, or my 21st, my army age. I'd received many special presents including a Parker fountain pen, a hand-made cigarette lighter, a leather wallet, and my wristwatch that I had used in France. These, among letters and photos and other personal items, had been done up in a separate parcel to be sent home to my parents should I not survive my current mission. Not at all the kind of treatment one would expect or endear to a life in the regular peacetime army, or one that I have ever forgotten. The sooner I was returned home, as promised when volunteering for this last mission, the better, I had thought.

Disillusionment was to come when I learnt in the Calcutta camp something which partly explained the lack of support at the very end of our mission in the Karenni hills. Apparently there had been a new supreme commander in the Far East, who had ordered that all what he termed as 'private armies', should be disbanded and their members be returned to their regiments or other regular army units in the Far East, to complete their full three year foreign service, as all regular units were supposed to do, cancelling all previous promises made by the now almost defunct SOE. Although this probably originated from the old fashioned thinking of regular army staff officers at high command, who were known to be jealous of the successes of small numbers of men in what they termed as un-military operations, the blame was placed firmly on the back of Louis Mountbatten, who was despised for it. As we all know now, these types of British-developed operations are, at this time of writing, copied throughout the western world, even using the name of 'SPECIAL FORCE'. Our own staff officers though, were wiser and more honourable. They spent a great deal of time seeking out units due to return home shortly, before sending as many of their colleagues to them as possible.

While waiting for my new posting, freshly equipped and wearing some new footwear I was looking a little smarter, almost soldier like, except for the beard and very long hair. A visit to the best hair dresser I could find in the high street and main road of Calcutta was called for, before having a night on the town. Neville Wood and Norman Smith, who had already arrived ahead of me, said they knew of a very good one and a Chinese restaurant where we could all adjourn afterwards. My long hair and beard must have puzzled the Red Caps, because I noticed that they looked the other way rather than question me whenever I passed by them. Perhaps they thought I was a newly released POW. Although eating better meals now, I did still look rather skinny and my clothes a little too big for me. First call was to the barber for the full treatment, shave, hot towels and *eau de cologne*, followed by a haircut and head and neck massage.

The next stop was to the photographer for a photo of the new man. Foolishly, I had forgotten to have one taken before the treatment; a before and after picture is sadly missing! The Chinese meal was a moderate success, considering we were not too sure of what we were ordering and even less sure of what we were eating. Meanwhile, there were letters to be read and answered, the arrival of which had been very sparse over the past few months and impossible to answer earlier. Surprisingly, there were several from Lucette, the girl I had left behind in France. Mme Bignoneau, the Scottish woman, had written to my mother to get my address for her. There was also a parcel of cigarettes from the Boys Brigade of Goodmayes Methodist Church, who had very kindly thought of me. After a short stay of less than a week in the Calcutta camp we were travelling again, this time on the long train journey from Calcutta to Madras, followed by a one day break, then on again from Madras to Colombo.

Whether it was the journeys or all the sudden changes to my system, but soon after arrival at the Horana camp, I had my first attack of malaria, despite being back on Mepacrine, the preventative tablets that had been sadly missing for months. A fever first, then a complete collapse and I was rushed to the hospital in Colombo. At least I was in the correct place and received the appropriate treatment. Within ten days I was back in the Horana camp and ready for my new posting. Of the WALRUS Jedburgh NCOs, Norman Smith had been found a place and a nice cushy job at the transit camp in Colombo, along with another ex Jed Ron Chatten. Don Gibbs, who had been in the services longer than most of the other Jeds, was awaiting his return home at the RAC depot in Poona, for demobilisation. Neville Wood and I were informed that we were to be transferred to a West African regiment which was due to return home shortly.

Other Jeds were still spread out throughout the Far East war zone in places such as Australia, Borneo, Malaya, New Guinea, Sarawak, and Sumatra. Some of whom were, some time later, involved in counter Communistic uprisings, anti-colonial and nationalistic forays. Those due for early release, remaining in Indian transit camps such as Deolali, found jobs on the staff to keep them occupied until their ‘number came up’. One’s number was dependant on the date one joined the Military Services; whether you were conscripted or volunteered, made no difference. This was done to ease the steady release of personnel onto the civilian labour market. My number was 46 and Neville’s nearer 40, which meant that it would be some months yet before it was our turn for demobilisation. I had joined in March ’42 so all those who had been serving since ’39 were being released first. This was probably the fairest way of demobilising large numbers of troops, but I was not too pleased that no consideration had been made for those who had signed on for the ‘Duration of the War’ now that the war was supposed to be over! Some bad experiences of ‘Regulars’ had left me with no desire to stay on in a peacetime Regular Army, even though letters I was now receiving from home suggested that, as I was already a sergeant and doing so well, I might be better off doing so. This, they hinted, would be rather better than to risk the type of unemployment and slump that had existed after the previous great world war.

Chapter Forty - African Safari

By the beginning of December '45 both Neville and I were on our way once more, this time back to India by train and ferryboat from Colombo to Madras, then by lorry to the West African 5th Gold Coast Regiment, which was camped under canvas well away from any large town, in hot, dusty countryside with only a small village nearby. There were no facilities whatsoever, except for the usual Sergeants' Mess. We were allocated posts in separate companies, replacing two other sergeants who had been demobilised. The European NCOs, (sergeants, staff sergeants and company sergeant major) had nothing very much to do, other than to sit in the mess and drink. The African NCOs looked after the men, and the Europeans just kept an eye on them (well back out of the way!) whilst they did their job most efficiently.

The officers were rarely seen and had their own facilities. All the Europeans were allocated a 'boy' who acted as batman for them and kept the accommodation and equipment clean for them. The Africans themselves were charming and pleasant to talk to, and had apparently acquitted themselves excellently against the Japanese in Burma, proving to be much better than the Japs at jungle warfare, although liable to fire first at anyone in front of them and look to see who it was afterwards! Most were 'bush men', that is to say uneducated and very childlike in their actions and humour. All conversations were in pidgin-English, even those who were missionary educated. The latter, strangely enough, were usually less trustworthy, knowing more of the bad than the good in so-called civilised behaviour. They would wash themselves by standing in a bowl of water, naked, with their manhood tucked between their legs, so that it couldn't be seen from the front. The fact that they could not see themselves from the rear apparently did not concern them! They received free supplies of soap, razor blades, condoms and talcum powder. Many of them shaved their heads leaving only a small pimple of hair on the crown of the head, and mocked the Brits by flicking back an imaginary forelock from their bald head saying 'Me European'! They also smothered themselves in talcum powder, which they liked for drying the skin and its perfume, then saying 'Me white man', always laughingly but in a complimentary manner.

Childlike and playful, they were full of fun when off duty and also very musical. They made their own instruments; one was a type of xylophone, the sound box consisting of a scooped out triangular hole in the ground, the outside edge lined with narrowing slats of wood, the wooden keys in diminishing lengths laid across the slats producing notes when struck with a wooden hammer. They also had other instruments, some not unlike one or two string banjos, and another type consisting of several short metal prongs of different lengths which were twanged to produce rhythmic tones, a kind of thumb piano. I was advised by the other European sergeants not to wander amongst the men alone but, after my first visit on duty, inspecting their tents with an African NCO, they spotted that I was wearing parachutists' wings. The Africans, who had travelled (and hated it!) and been supplied by air, questioned their sergeant about them. After learning what I had been doing in Burma and France, they renamed me 'Sergeant Bird Man' and from then on, when off duty, I often walked alone among them in their part of the camp. They always welcomed me and gathered round to talk and teach me rude words in their own language. Some I found could also speak French. Why the other Europeans remained aloof from them I couldn't understand; I found them just as cheeky and full of fun as any other group of youngsters. I treated them with the same respect as I would any other soldier and found them very co-operative in return.

My own 'boy', Kwami, had been given the job simply because he was small; he was also bright and well educated. He was not too pleased at being given the task but did it without complaining. After a very short time we got to know each other and settled into a good relationship and I found him very trustworthy. But it was not so with some of the Europeans. A great deal of our spare time was taken up by some very heavy drinking. I had accumulated a great deal of back pay and was in the habit of carrying a large sum of money around with me, usually paying more than my fair share towards the bar bill. If, after the usual night's heavy drinking, my boy helped me to retire; Kwami would, when changing my clothes, always hand back to me my roll of Indian Rupees that he had guarded for me overnight. One particular evening the man who was running the bar, whether through jealousy or bravado, kept challenging and pushing me to drink more, to see who could drink the most. He may have even mixed the drinks, which resulted in my being carried off to bed! The next morning of course, Kwami, who was very worried, informed me that all of my money was missing. When first questioned he would not say what had happened. Only after a great deal of persuasion and the promise that he would not be in any trouble did he admit that he knew who had taken it. Initially he would only say that it was a European, but then later, that I should speak to the barman as it was he who had brought me back to my tent. Of course, when questioned, the barman denied any knowledge, or that it was he who had put me to bed. Rather than argue or take the matter further, I decided then and there to never set foot in the bar again. Overall this proved to be a blessing in disguise as it broke what had become a very bad, as well as a very boring, habit of constant heavy drinking.

Having plenty of time to catch up on my mail both to and from home and France, I also wrote to the old SOE address in Calcutta regarding my lost Japanese sword. The answers I received indicated that one had been seen there with my name on it but its whereabouts were now unknown. I received a very sympathetic and personal reply from the popular Jed, Major 'Dick' Rubinstein, better known as 'Ruby', regretting that it could not be traced, even offering me one of his own if all else failed. Following this, as I not had any official leave since arriving in the Far East, I decided to take 14 days' leave and travel back up to Calcutta. Unfortunately by the time this happened I could no longer trace anyone there who could help, as all the old members of SOE, Force 136, and the Jedburghs had been dispersed. As it took over half of my leave-time travelling there and back again, I had insufficient time to look further into the matter so, with regret, gave up hope of ever seeing it again.

Gold Coast Regiment February 1946. Here I am wearing my medal ribons and jump wings

Gold Coast 1946

An unremarkable Christmas came and went as the regiment awaited repatriation back to the Gold Coast. However not all my spare time had been wasted; I had witnessed a very beautiful, sad young lady saying goodbye to one of the regiment's officers who was off home for demobilisation. The Africans were cheering as she hung a garland of flowers around his neck and embraced him before he departed from the camp. A word or two with Kwami was all that was needed and I soon found out who she was and where she was living in the local village. Her name was Lachmi and I asked Kwami to let her know that I would like to talk to her and, if she agreed, to arrange a meeting.

Meanwhile, I had learnt from the other NCOs that it was apparently a custom followed by most, if not all, of the Europeans on the Gold Coast to employ a young woman as a housewife, as well as having a boy to take care of their needs. In India, many of the troops carried on the tradition. For a small payment of about one pound to thirty shillings a month, they would be responsible for seeing that the boy did his work properly, while she looked after the decor, flowers and fruit, comforts of the home by day and her 'master' at night! The young girls in Africa, I was told, did this to pay for their further education, and were usually very young. The Indian girls were different in that they hoped for something more permanent.

Early one evening a week or so later, Kwami brought Lachmi to my tent, where I spent time alone, reading or writing now that I was not staying in the bar drinking after dinner. She was even more attractive up close than I had noticed before, well dressed and wearing a very colourful sari, and she spoke near perfect English with a slight Indian accent. We were soon happily chatting away after she had told me of her sadness of losing her 'man', who had made promises that he had not kept. I told her that I would be getting married when I returned home and that I could not offer anything more than friendship, but would welcome her company if she wished to visit me, adding that I was often lonely there in the camp and not on very good terms with some of the other European men. Kwami came back to escort her safely off the camp and to her home some three hours later. The following Sunday afternoon, when it was normal for all still in the camp to retire to their beds after lunch for a siesta, she returned. This time she brought with her some fruit, mangoes and sweet limes, and I sent Kwami to the canteen to buy some fruit juice and chocolate bars, for them and myself, before going off duty.

Very quickly, over the next few weeks, Lachmi and I became at ease with each other, talking about what and where else we had lived and done, later reading to each other from books and novels that just happened to be there. On one occasion we were doing this, sitting close together, leaning at times on each other's shoulders, laughing at the mispronunciation of some of the words that we were reading, in a book which just happened to be the 'Kama Sutra'. This book had been doing the rounds in the Sergeants' Mess, and by strange coincidence, had found its way into my tent! She had picked up the book, glanced at it and thrown it down, with a 'Bah! This is not good! Practice is better than theory. I will show you how we make real love in India!' With only one chair, a table and a single camp-bed for furniture, we were sitting or squatting on the carpet covered duck-board flooring, using my pillows and bedding for added comfort. This had brought us closer together than when one sat on the bed, with the other on the chair. Thus, in Lachmi, I had found myself another very charming companion and teacher. From then on, alternate weekend meetings were held either in the same place or at Lachmi's house in the nearby village, where we were less likely to be disturbed, in a comfortable carpeted room strewn with large soft cushions. I admit to being her very willing pupil!

With no consideration for my newly-established home comforts, the New Year brought forth the news that the regiment would soon be leaving India and preparations were being made for its departure. First it would move by troop train to Goa, a Portuguese colony in south-east India, thence by troopship to Takoradi on the Gold Coast. The only compensation was promotion to Acting Company Sergeant Major until arrival in Takoradi, replacing the original man who had departed for demobilisation. Not that these preparations made a great deal of difference to the workload of the Europeans; just checking work and lists of names already completed by the African NCOs. For some reason it was assumed that some of the Africans would not wish to return home, and they were confined to barracks. One of the stories circulating was of one man who, because he had lost part of one of his ears, bitten off in a fight with another tribesman, would not be accepted back in his tribe! Despite much scarring already covering his face and body from tribal markings, he was certain that it made him look ugly, or at least unacceptable to any prospective wife! Others, too, were uncertain of being accepted back in their tribes because of various misdemeanours contrary to their own tribal customs. Nevertheless, despite patrols of regimental police, the last few nights in the local village were very lively, packed with men having their last fling with music and dancing until the early hours. This was witnessed, of course, by me, who was dutifully saying goodbye to Lachmi, having been escorted in and out of the village by a couple of my own section of African men whom I had befriended. Having taken to their 'Bird Man' sergeant, they had been insisting for some time that they should protect me whenever I was off camp which made me, at times, feel very privileged. They had their own routes in and out of the 'out of bounds' village, thus dodging the unsuspecting Redcaps.

It was another long tedious journey by lorry to Madras, then by train to Goa. There we were placed in a transit camp barracks for a few days to await the military transporter ship which was to take us back to Africa. We had all been warned from the start that everyone was restricted to only two pieces of luggage, comprising just one kitbag and one medium sized suitcase. This had been the rule throughout, both going to and returning from the Far East. The transit camps for homeward bound men seemed to have a wonderful racket going on, very carefully checking that no one exceeded their entitlement. Souvenirs, bulging out or not, were refused acceptance and confiscated at the slightest excuse, no doubt easily disposed of back to local traders waiting to resell them to other unsuspecting customers. One particular item that I desperately wanted to keep from my Burma mission was a Padaung crossbow, but even taken apart it was too large to hide in either my kitbag or suitcase and it had to be abandoned.

Goa itself, though cleaner and less crowded than Calcutta, was very much like other places in India, but then with only a couple of days there it was difficult to judge. Something that did stand out as unusual was the frequent sighting of people with very large bloated lower limbs. It was referred to as 'elephantiasis'. The afflicted were wheeled about with the enlarged leg or legs stretched out on a wooden support on what frequently resembled a wheelbarrow. As the disease could also infect the scrotum the comedians in the area would boast of having seen the man with a wheelbarrow carrying his manhood before him. Let's hope that they never have to suffer themselves. However, judging by the number of prostitutes that seemed to be doing a roaring trade prior to the ship's departure, they were most likely the types to be taking with them more than they had paid for!

I had met up with Neville Wood again whilst travelling on the train to Goa. Neville had been working with a different company in the same regiment. Since joining the train the Europeans and Africans had been separated into different sections of the train and different transit camps, although all would be sailing on the same ship. No reasons were given other than the information that others supplied who had sailed out with the regiment, that the Africans hated travelling on board a ship even more than by air. The Europeans would occupy the three upper decks and the Africans the two lower decks. It was also forbidden, or at least unwise, for any European to go down to the lower decks, supposedly because of the stench there would be from the sickness and general conditions they would encounter there. The reality was that, once on board, the officers, who were all Europeans, had exclusive use of A deck, the European NCOs shared part of B deck with the officers for recreation and slept on C deck. On the lower decks the African troops had a little open deck space, but most of their accommodation was probably below the water line. Very few of them ventured up to their deck space, choosing apparently to lie in their beds for most of the journey, many refusing to eat.

By contrast, the sea voyage from Goa up through the Suez Canal into the Mediterranean was like a pleasure cruise for the Europeans, with entertainment laid on and good food but, of course, like all troop ships, no alcohol was allowed. It was noticeably much colder than when I had last sailed through the Mediterranean in February. Although the temperature must have been similar, I was more acclimatised to hotter weather than when coming outward from the UK. The ship did stop to take on supplies mid Suez and in Dakar but anchored well off shore, in the hope that none of the Africans would disembark. After all, who could blame them; no European would have tolerated such conditions on these 'Empire' Lines troop ships, although I am told that some had to in an almost similar manner. After arriving at the Gold Coast, the ship was unloaded in the port of Takoradi and the troops separated into transit camps in Sekondi, the nearby town. By a strange coincidence, for me, the name of the village in France, next to where I once camped in the forest of L'Absie, bore the similar sounding name of Secondigny!

Once ensconced in the transit camp, there was no further contact with the 5th Gold Coast Regiment, no thanks or goodbyes. I was informed that I would be staying on the 'Coast' for about six months because I was not yet due for demobilisation, whereas Neville, who had a lower demob number, would be on the next ship due to sail for the UK. The heat on the Gold Coast, even close to the sea, was very different to that of India or Burma, being very humid and depressingly heavy compared to the previous drier heat, even during the monsoons, to which I had become accustomed. Within the first week after arrival I was back in hospital with a reoccurring attack of malaria, brought on perhaps by the changes in temperature. By the time I came out and back to the transit camp ten days later, Neville had gone and was on his way back to the UK. He had called in and left a note for me at the hospital, but I was in no fit condition at the time to remember his visit. That was the last contact with any of the Jedburghs I was to have for many years to come.

It was, by now, the beginning of March '46 and about another 9 months before I could hope to be released from my supposedly voluntary contract for the 'Duration of the War'. Waiting to hear about when and where my next duties would be left me in limbo. No interview, no memo or news, nothing. Most of the other men in the transit camp were new arrivals from the UK and they looked very young and inexperienced, probably conscripts and not too sure why they were there. The accommodation was sparse, just a space about 12 to 15 ft square on an open walled balcony which ran all the way round on the second floor of a block of old barracks. This contained a mosquito-netted bed, a bedside table and one chair for each person, but was far from being fully occupied. On a piece of rough ground, separating another block where there were a few Africans, stood a smaller, rarely used drill hall which was used as a sports centre. I tried it out only once, when I found and joined in with a couple of Africans sparring in the boxing ring. It didn't work very well as they were hesitant about boxing with a European, so I ended up just spending a little time coaching them.

Very few things broke the monotony of this dreary hole, one of which was when the occupants were woken early one morning. The noise coming from a hubbub had everyone racing down to the ground between the two buildings. There strung up on a tree was the body of an African soldier who had hung himself during the night. The Africans who had found him had run away, refusing to cut him down. The cadaver was already bloated to almost twice its normal size by the constant heat. The military police were sent for and the task was left to them. It was reported back later that it had been one of the Africans who did not want or was afraid to return home. Another incident concerned a newly arrived European. The change of climate was apparently having a disastrous effect. He would get out of bed frequently throughout the day and night, and start running around the balcony at top speed. It was impossible to stop him. He would barge anyone trying out of his way, his bulging eyes staring into the distance. He was taken away by the medics who had the task of finding out if it was a genuine breakdown or if it was an attempt to get his 'ticket'!

Fortunately there were other more agreeable distractions in and around Sekondi. For example, in the town there was a very busy and colourful market. The shops were mostly managed by Indians, many of them Sikhs who seemed to be the main businessmen in Africa. Incidentally, I purchased an excellent Swiss wristwatch from one such establishment, replacing as closely as possible the one which had been stolen from my supposedly safe kit, whilst away in Burma. The receipt, which I still have, gives the date 29/4/46 and the place as Kumasi, so it must have been purchased a little later after moving on from Sekondi. The price was eight pounds ten shillings, a good two weeks' pay for most adults at that time. The guarantee for ten years did far better than that; it is still in working order and was in daily use until I received a replacement for 35 years service with British Rail in April 1983!

The stalls selling mostly fruit and vegetables in Sekondi were managed by very large African ladies dressed in long colourful robes and headdresses, very loud, full of fun and jollity. They were always referred to as the market 'Mammies' and their produce looked as welcoming and as colourful as they were! There was also another group of 'Mammies' who could be found down on the beach. This was a long stretch of sandy shoreline a little further along the coast. These were also very large and colourfully dressed ladies whose duties appeared to be that of looking after very young children. They would walk slowly up and down the beach carrying a child on one hip or on one of their arms. On closer inspection though, the babies were mainly boys, and the free hand would be caressing the child's genitals! Holding the boys' penises, they stroked and proceeded to pull and squeeze on it in the manner of a milkmaid milking a cow. Whether this was to improve the size of the young boy's manhood or to advertise another occupation of theirs was open to question. Anyone taking the risk of accepting a night of love with one of these huge ladies would probably not be in danger of falling off, but at great risk of suffocating in the abundant rolls of flesh!

In due course news arrived of my next posting. I was being sent to a training establishment for new African entrants into the Gold Coast Regiments, at a camp further north, inland at Kintampo. Firstly though, to reach there I would have to go to the large town of Kumasi by train, and then wait for road transportation to be arranged for the last part of the journey; naturally, not without a couple of incidents.

At Kumasi I was directed to a building used as a stopover point for people in transit, where I was to reside until receiving notification of the date on which the transport would be available. A rest centre and dining room were in another part of the town about 15 minutes' walk away. Not too much of a problem, just a nice stroll through the shopping area. Only a handful of other men were using the facilities, most, like myself, chose to wear lighter civilian clothes whilst staying there. On my first evening, though, I had worn my uniform and, it being a hot and steamy night, had forgotten to pick up my bush hat on leaving. A nuisance, but not a problem, for the next morning after breakfast, dressed in civilian style clothes, I walked back to my digs carrying the retrieved hat in my hand. Waiting to cross a roadway, a very large chauffeur driven limousine carrying a single passenger pulled up in front of me. The occupant, a rather overweight rotund man dressed in all white tennis gear, beckoned me over. Thinking that it was one of the European gold miners known to be in the district, I readied myself to decline any offer of a free ride because I had not far to go, so just greeted him with a 'Good morning, sir'. I was cut short with a curt, 'What's your name, young man?' Taken aback, I replied, 'Well, my friends call me 'Harry'. What's yours?' 'Do you know who I am?' was barked back. 'Sorry, I've no idea. I'm new around here.' 'I am Major Xxxxx (a forgotten name) and I want you in my office at ten o'clock tomorrow morning,' he said, giving his address. I simply shrugged my shoulders, turned and walked off. Making inquiries when back in the lodgings, I found out that the supposed civilian I'd been accosted by was in fact, the Provost Marshal. Having never heard of such a person before, I was also made aware that it meant he was the chief of the military police in the area. So what, I thought. I still had no idea why I had been stopped in the first place.

I had recently received long delayed and forwarded letters from India, amongst which was one with the notification that I had been awarded a Mention in Despatches in August 1945, and it also contained an Oak Leaf emblem to add to my campaign medals. The next morning I arrived early, smartly dressed in my full uniform this time, showing my rank and wearing my medal ribbons, including the Oak Leaf, as well as the Parachute Wings and Special Force badge. On arrival at the office, I found out I was going to be charged as being improperly dressed, i.e. not wearing army issue shirt, shorts, boots, socks and puttees, also with carrying my hat instead of wearing it and, in addition, refusing to show my ID papers and being insubordinate to boot. Unhappy as I was at being in Africa in the first place, I was now feeling angry and in no mood to be intimidated by any bully boy, officer or not.

Dead on ten o'clock, I knocked on the door and without waiting for an answer; marched in without any escort. 'You wanted to see me at ten o'clock, sir,' I said in a loud voice and saluting. It must have surprised the major a little because he stared at me and said nothing while looking at my campaign medal ribbons, none of which he himself was wearing. He stood up, put on his cap and saluted back. He had probably expected a rookie and a new arrival on the coast to impress, but I had no intention of being intimidated by him. Then my antagonist went on to say that he was going to charge me with being improperly dressed etc. 'Are you willing to accept my punishment?' he added. 'Certainly not,' I replied. 'I shall be denying it and do not accept that you can be both accuser and judge. I will be reporting this matter myself to my CO on arrival at my destination and am seriously considering a counter charge of an official vehicle and staff being used for non-service activities.' 'Very well, you may go,' the Major answered. 'I will be writing to your CO myself.' I saluted him, but he turned his back without acknowledging it, and walked out via a side door, mumbling something about a Court Martial. Doing a smart about turn, I marched out, ignoring puzzled Red Caps in the outer office who had without doubt heard most, if not all, of the raised voices. Well, that's settled it for now, I thought, wondering whether or not he would carry his threat further.

In the very few days I was in Kumasi, there was one other strange happening. An older African woman with a young girl in tow called in to see me one afternoon. She introduced herself as being the mother of the child, who had just finished her state schooling and was now seeking employment to pay for her further education. The girl looked very young, although the woman said that she was mature and would make a good house keeper. Bearing in mind the tales I had heard previously in India about employing and paying monthly for such services, I had to decide quickly on how to decline the offer. To me she looked like a child, although pretty by African standards, with pert firm little breasts that were certainly not yet fully formed, pushing proudly out of her half open shirt front. She could have been about 14 years old, as I had been told, but certainly appeared to be more likely only twelve. My answer to the woman was that I was not staying in the area, and where I was going would be too far for the girl to travel home. Despite this, the woman tried to persuade me that it would be all right as she could live in! She even offered to reduce her first pay request from one pound ten shillings a month to one pound only. Her insistence made me wonder if it was really her daughter or if she was some kind of agent working on commission. Only a blank refusal in the end made the woman leave with the child, and she was not very happy at having to do so!

The day before I was due to leave Kumasi there had been a report that a local chieftain had died. Because of this it was recommended that no one should venture out that night in case of trouble in the town. On previous occasions there had been riots and further deaths 'to accompany the chief on his final journey' and everyone staying in the building decided that prudence was better than valour and stayed in, drinking Lagos Lager, the favourite drink on the Coast. In the morning no news had reached us of any trouble and my transport arrived on time. An early start with a seat in the front cab of a 15 cwt personnel carrier for me as I was the only European, the other passengers were new African recruits with some of their wives or followers. The journey of nearly a hundred miles was through forests all the way and a rather agreeable uneventful four to five hour trip, with occasional sightings of ape-like wildlife, and all the passengers arrived in time for lunch.

After lunch was siesta time and an appointment with my new CO had been made for four o'clock. Shown to my own round thatched roof hut, I made myself comfortable and settled down for the customary afternoon nap enjoyed throughout the tropical climes. The accommodation was comfortable, over 15 feet in diameter with two windows and ample room for a full sized, mosquito netted bed, two chairs, and a table. I quickly decided to cut up a couple of my old longyis to make curtains for the windows and, with the aid of some spare ex-parachute cord, made the whole place look rather homely, or as near as I would be getting for some time yet. A 'boy' had been assigned to me, who brought a mug of tea at three o'clock so that I could shower in the block not far from the hut, before going to the CO's office for interview.

In the orderly room I was shown into the CO's office where I was greeted cordially by my new boss who asked me to take a seat, adding that he liked to get to know any new staff before finding them a suitable post. He went on to say that I had been highly recommended by my previous units and that he could see that I had seen action in Europe as well as the Far East. After he had asked for more detail about my earlier exploits, I had to tell him that I had signed the Official Secrets Act that forbade me from giving precise details for 30 years, but told him briefly that I had been working for SOE and the Special Forces in covert operations and about the specialised training that went into the job. This had been far different of course, from the training given for normal army use; faster Morse, different coding and wireless communication procedures, handling of enemy arms and materials, guerrilla warfare, the use of explosives for demolition and booby traps. In addition, I was accustomed to working as part of a team of three which included two Allied officers, all three being capable of replacing each other if necessary, and that we could expect to be regarded as patriots or terrorists depending upon which side of the fence one was standing. The CO congratulated me adding, 'It sounds as though you have well earned your Mention in Despatches,' to which I replied hat I had also recently received a letter telling me the French Army Corps had awarded me the French Croix de Guerre and showed him the citation. As I had not yet received the medal, I could either have it sent out by post or wait until I got home and have it presented at the French Embassy in London. The CO then offered me the chance of having it presented there, when the next batch of Africans had their passing out parade. Feeling rather self-conscious after being informed that the local chieftain would put on a really good show for such an occasion, I declined the offer, saying that I preferred to wait until I got home when my parents could be present. At the end of this very pleasant meeting during which we had shared afternoon tea, the CO then said, 'Now there is another matter I must discuss with you, about a letter I have received from the Provost Marshal!' 'Oh dear, now there will be a change of tune!' I thought.

I was asked to give my own account of what had happened, as now that the CO had read the letter, he wanted to know the full story from both sides before making any decision. Feeling in a better mood at that moment, rather than angry as I had been at the time of the incident, I went on to explain my side of the story, giving my own account in a more humorous frame of mind, including, 'When first stopped and shouted at by what I had thought was a rather ridiculous overweight civilian in white tennis gear, I was angry and had shouted back. Unfortunately it turned out to be someone different! Perhaps I should apologise to him,' I offered. The CO was by now finding it difficult not to laugh, and said 'I'm going to enjoy relating this in the mess tonight. Leave it to me, I will reply to his letter and let him know that I am certain that you have a better case against him, and will suggest that he drop the matter. I do rather out-rank him!' He added that I should forget all about it as he was certain I would hear no more about the matter. 'Now, more importantly, what am I going to do with you? There are no posts here that I can let you loose on, and I think that you have earned a respite from army routine whilst waiting for your repatriation to the UK. How do you feel about supervising the Sergeants' Mess for the rest of your stay?' I thanked him, we then both shook hands and I was dismissed with smiles all round.

Settling down into my new environment proved to be a simple exercise. The Europeans lodged well apart from the African quarters which

I had no reason to visit. There were only about a dozen or so NCOs to be catered for, and the mess room I was to keep an eye on was staffed by an African sergeant who controlled his other ranks, who did all the work. Similar to the manner employed when I was with them in India, the European NCOs' main occupation was to check that their African counterparts kept everything running smoothly. Daily timetable was: early morning tea and biscuits served in our individual rooms at 6 a.m. so that we would be ready for the first parades at 6.30, returning for breakfast at 9 a.m. At ten it was back to work until lunch between 1 and 2 p.m. We were then off duty until afternoon tea between 4 and 5 o'clock in the afternoon, followed by recreation, sports etc., there being just enough of us for a five-a-side football match, and a couple for tennis, with dinner at 7 p.m. Evenings, if there was no cinema or lecture which was very rare, were spent in the mess drinking, playing snooker, cards or any other reasonably quiet game. 10 p.m.lights out! Not what you would call a hard day's work, plenty of spare time and very little toil, and what there was, was done in the coolest parts of the day! The only task that I had to do daily, apart from keeping the billiard table cleared of dying insects once the lights were on, was to accompany the African sergeant on his rounds to the cookhouse every morning. All the food for the camp was prepared at the same place, a hive of activity with great cauldrons of a stew-like mixture and yams always being prepared, which was the African troops' staple diet. The European food was only just palatable, not much variety, fresh as well as tinned meats and a mixture of fresh and tinned vegetables; with one important exception. It was impossible to get any potatoes! In their place were served either sweet potatoes or yams. And I hated both of them! There were though, ample supplies of tinned Cheddar cheese, which became a main part of my daily diet. I could be seen at almost any time of the day munching on a large chunk of cheese, whilst of course doing nothing much else.

A few weeks after settling in, my boy arrived one afternoon during siesta time with a young woman from the nearby village, whom he introduced as being in search of employment as a housewife. Not surprised, as I knew of the custom and all the other men were known to have one of their own, I agreed but insisted that she return home each evening. I was not that much interested in the 'wife' side of the deal and didn't fancy having her hanging around at night. Not only, dear reader, for the reasons you may be thinking! I was frequently getting severe headaches by nightfall and thought it might be because of the rather heavy and at times, depressing climate. I had seen the MO about these headaches and been given aspirin tablets but they gave only partial relief. But they certainly came in very handy once though. That was the evening that, when I went to take a shower before retiring for the night, and in the half dark with no light, I trod on a scorpion! Wearing only a pair of flip-flop sandals at the time, I felt a sharp pain in my right instep. I only found the half squashed insect when I went back with a torch to find out what had stung me. Fortunately it was a young and quite small one and I went to bed with a sore foot, after giving the tiny wound a squeeze to clear anything in it. An hour later I was awake in agony, the whole foot had started to swell and it was turning a darker red as it spread from the bite mark, to almost black in places. Not able to walk on the foot, or put it down on the floor because of the pain, I took a razor blade and cross cut the bite area. Then I squeezed out anything still in there until the blood ran freely. I tied up the wound with a strip of cloth and a handkerchief, took some aspirins and tried to go back to sleep.

After spending a restless night, when my boy arrived in the morning the foot and leg were swollen almost up to my knee and looked a very funny colour. By then in a great deal of pain, I sent him off to get someone from the medical room. On seeing the injury, the doctor who had come out to see me gave me an injection, dressed the wound and said that, as I had done the right thing and already got rid of most of the poison, it would get no worse if I kept my leg up high, and that it should abate by the afternoon; which it did, but only after a very uncomfortable day. I definitely would not be going out again at night with no shoes on! The consolation was having my housewife there, taking care of me as well as watching her chase my boy around, keeping him busy and inspecting his work. She had sent out for fruit and made sure I had plenty to drink, bathed me and made me comfortable. By the end of the day I was seeing her as an asset and in quite a different light. She also insisted that she should stay with me for the rest of the night. In no mood to argue I agreed, and continued to do so frequently from then on. I am saying no more, other than to admit that she was extremely athletic!

My very easy and relaxed style of living progressed reasonably comfortably, except for the persistent headaches. The MO, after several visits, recommended a hospital appointment for X-rays to check out the cause. This entailed a trip back to Kumasi, the nearest place with the appropriate facilities. In due course I was seen by a doctor in the hospital there. After examination and X-rays I was diagnosed as having sinusitis, and treatment was to be given whilst I was there to avoid another long journey. This entailed being seated in a steel dentist-like chair, having a couple of orderlies hold me still while a steel tube was put up my nose. Another long steel spiked rod was then inserted into the tube and hammered past an obstruction, to enlarge the natural drainage system which was then flushed out! Painful? Yes! Tightly gripping the chair arms, I had bent them inward enough to prevent rising from the chair when they were finished, and the two assistants had to prise the chair arms apart before I could get out of it! Resting on a bed in the ward afterwards, I began to regret having mentioned another problem that I had been experiencing!

During the preliminary examination the doctor had asked if there were any other problems that I would like to have attended to while I was there. Perhaps they were short of patients. Well yes, I had said, there was one that interfered with my love life, making intercourse sometimes uncomfortable. My foreskin seemed to be too tight and when pulled back, it obstructed the blood flow which caused swelling at the tip of the penis. After inspecting the offending object, the doctor said he could easily correct it with a circumcision. Not too sure of what that meant, I agreed to have it done. The following day I was relieved to find that, at least, this time the action would take place in a proper operating theatre, complete with anaesthetic, an item that had been sadly absent the previous day. All went well, knowing nothing about it until I awoke ,tucked up in bed in the hospital ward. On the doctor's rounds later in the day and after a routine inspection of his handiwork, the doctor suggested that I would need an ether spray to cool my ardour, which could otherwise, because of the extra swelling, cause the stitches to tear apart. There were about eight of them holding the cut edges round the wound together.

The ward was a long one with beds on either side; the far end, which was curtained off from the rest of the ward where the various illnesses were treated, contained men practically in isolation because they were being treated for venereal diseases. The nurses were all religious nursing Sisters and after the first night in the main ward they shifted me into the curtained off area, where the infected men were treated only by the African orderlies. The Sisters refused to have any dealings with them. I voiced my objection to this to the doctor and also complained that although I had requested the ether spray several times, nothing had been forthcoming. Even though the doctor spoke to the Matron about it still nothing became of it. Every night, and sometimes during the day, my stitches were getting torn, the wound was bleeding and where healing had started, a much wider scar began to form. Most of the time I had to take care of myself by changing my own dressing and going to the washroom to spray my unruly member with cold water. A week or so later, when the doctor came to remove the stitches there were only two remaining, the others, having burst from continuous internal pressure, had removed themselves! Soon after this tortuous adventure I was on my way back to the training depot. Were things getting better? Well no, not quite!

Bored with being driven for the third time on the long four hour journey with the same driver, this time with a full cargo of new recruits and their women folk and baggage in the back of the lorry, I persuaded the very good driver to let me drive for part of the way about an hour or so before we were due to arrive back in camp. Not a good idea! Reluctant at first, the driver finally agreed. It had been raining a little during the journey but was now fine and the sun shining, with a partial steamy mist rising from the surrounding jungle. There was a bend to the right in the dirt road ahead as we approached on a downward slope. As I started to enter the bend I braked to slacken the speed and hit a stretch of darker coloured earth that turned out to be soaked in a layer of water that had trickled across the road. The lorry skidded and then, in apparent slow motion, began to roll over onto its left side with a final bump! The driver was unhurt and quickly disconnected the battery to avoid a fire from spilt fuel. Climbing out, I went around the back to see what could be done for the passengers, some of whom were by now screaming. Two had broken forearms, others had various bumps and bruises, but not as bad as it could have been. I had a bump on the side of my head and the little finger of my right hand had been dislocated.

While I gave first aid and pacified the passengers, the driver ran off with another man to get help from the camp. When he returned it was with another vehicle, the quartermaster sergeant and a troop of men. Another larger group of men, who were following them at the double, arrived a short while afterwards. The new vehicle was loaded with the injured and the women folk and just before it departed with me and the new driver, I saw the amazing sight of the upturned lorry being righted. This was done purely with manpower, no mechanical aid at all. The African troops had swarmed all the way around the fallen truck. A drum was being beaten to a set rhythm that got them all chanting at the same time. Working as one, on the loudest beat they all pushed or pulled together and gradually the lorry was tipped back into an upright position. As it bounced back onto its own wheels again they all whooped with joy and danced a victory dance around it! Amazing! It really was, no one in Europe could ever have imagined such a feat, let alone accomplished it.

Back at the camp the MO had those who required it checked out and attended to. While I was required to make a report to the Captain Quartermaster, (a post usually earned after many years as a quartermaster or regimental sergeant major). I told the truth about driving the vehicle myself and asked the captain not to blame the driver in anyway at all, because he was a brilliant driver and only gave in to my request to drive under pressure and at my insistence. I had, of course, driven such vehicles before in the RAC, as well as many other types, including tanks. Having convinced him, the QM said to leave it to him, and he would put it through as an unavoidable mishap, thus saving a lot of unnecessary paperwork. So, some old soldiers do know better after all! The MO, who had arrived in the office while this was going on, took a look at my dislocated finger, told me to look out of the window while he gave the finger a sharp pull and repositioned the joint, strapped it up and told me to return to the hospital again with the lorry the next day to get it X-rayed! Oh no, not that journey again! I argued, but he insisted.

'What, you again?' I was greeted with back at the hospital. This time I was placed in a bed along a long corridor of single-bedded rooms, well away from the other ward. The X-ray dealt with, I had to wait there for a few days before the lorry was due to make its next journey back to the camp and even the nursing sisters were more civil towards me this time. I had time to spend a few pleasant days watching colourful tiny birds feeding on the nectar from flowers outside the bedroom window, and enjoying visits from some of the patients whom I had spent time with a few days earlier.

One night there was a terrible tropical storm. It was very hot and I lay in bed under the mosquito net which I had not tucked in to get more of a breeze, listening to the noise outside. The noise got louder and appeared to be coming from the corridor. The noise became a racket, an African orderly burst in, banging at something on the floor. Curiosity aroused, I was going to get up out of bed but was told to stay there and tuck the netting in. When things had quietened down I was told that the orderly had spotted a black mamba snake in the corridor which had come in out of the rain, and was making its way into my bedroom. The orderly had hit the thing with a lump of wood so hard that he had dislocated his shoulder! When I did get out of bed to see the snake it was stretched out and pinned down at full length under the feet of and between two armchairs! It was reckoned to be over ten foot long and very poisonous. Someone really does not like me at the moment, I was beginning to feel! A feeling that was confirmed in my mind two days later when I suffered another relapse of malaria! This entailed another 10 days' treatment at the hospital; or was it luck to be already in dock when it happened?

Once back in the training camp, it was back to the old boring routine of doing nothing important, other than keep an eye on the smooth running of the NCOs' mess. The depressing headaches getting no better, I decided to say no more about them other than to blame it on the heavy atmosphere of this apparently God-forsaken country. On the bright side was the parcel that I had been informed was being held for me at the local village post office. Puzzled as to why it had not been delivered, I took a stroll down to the road to find out what was causing the delay. The African postmaster informed me that there was a Customs demand for payment to be made before it was handed over. 'How do I know if it's worth the charge you are asking for if I don't know what it contains?' I complained, refusing to immediately comply with the request. 'I cannot release the package until the duty is paid,' was the reply.

The argument went back and forth for some time before the postman finally reluctantly agreed to let me see the contents. It was ten packets of twenty cigarettes sent to me by The Boys Brigade, which had followed me across the world via India and were looking a little the worse for wear after their long journey. 'What will happen if I don't pay?' I asked and was told that they would be confiscated. Certain that the fellow would claim them for himself, I finally paid up an amount larger than that I would have had to pay for cigarettes bought in the camp, relieved at least by the thought that no-one else would have got them for nothing. Still, it was generous of the lads in the Brigade to think of me and I wrote a letter of thanks, not mentioning of course the minor dispute that had arisen.

Letters were now arriving a little more frequently as I too caught up with correspondence after many months in Burma being unable to do so. There were regular letters from France, mostly from Lucette who was still as faithful as ever and writing even when I was unable to reply. Marriage on return to England was definitely on the cards. Another person to write and say she was waiting impatiently for me to return was from May, the girl who lived opposite my home in Chadwell Heath. This time it was my turn to reply with a 'Dear John' letter, telling her that I was engaged already to the girl I had met in France. Pity really, because I was very fond of her!

Unmemorable days followed, relieved only by warm bedded nights until the day arrived for my departure. The only other relief was the day the recent batch of recruits had their passing out parade; a great occasion locally when the local Chieftain, as guest of honour, arrived with his entourage consisting of dozens of servants, one group supporting a huge parasol that was held above his head as he was carried in towards his place at the parade ground. When seated, ready to take the salute as the troops marched past, the parasol was bounced up and down above his head to cause a down draught of cooler air for his comfort whilst everyone else was sweating buckets.

The whole show, complete with many drummers, was very colourful, clothes, head-dresses and parasol all very elaborate. As I had not been involved with any of the training I had a seat in the shade on the side-lines and was grateful at not having to parade with the rest of the Europeans, who were suffering in the heat of the day. Most times I wondered if they cared whether I was there in the camp or not; they certainly wouldn't miss me when I'd gone!

Chapter Forty-One - Homeward Bound

So insignificant was my departure in August ’46, that I only have vague memories of saying a few goodbyes, the drive back to Kumasi, a train journey back to the port, joining those boarding the ship and others already on board from other ports. I knew no-one and was just grateful that this ‘Empire’ Troop Ship was, at last, taking me back to the UK. The three week ‘cruise’ stopped only once in Dakar, where we watched again young boys diving off small canoes to catch coins thrown into the sea before they sank too deeply, placing them in their mouths and coming to the surface, signalling for more to be thrown down. Then the ship was on its way again, next stop, Southampton! It was getting colder, winter was approaching. It wasn’t long after leaving Africa before the passengers were changing back into the warmer serge uniforms and packing away their tropical wear. At Southampton a restrained welcome awaited us; after all they had seen it happen many times before. A small military band played and flags were flying on other ships as well as on ours. Ships were sounding off their sirens and a small crowd of local people waved us in, some obviously in the know, senior officers no doubt, or wives of crew members perhaps. The officers were among the first to disembark, the rest were called forward in alphabetical order; the Vs for Verlander, of course, well down the list.

There were many warnings that the Customs men in Southampton were very thorough, also plenty of whispered offers from crew members to take things ashore for a small tip. I did wonder how many idiots were trapped by this old double trick; they would certainly never see the perpetrators or their possessions again ever. True to form, the customs were a real pain asking and searching all baggage and there were piles of odds and ends stacked up behind them. You could not blame the many adverse comments flying around as to how much would actually reach the customs stores, and to whose benefit went the proceeds!

Another long wait at the railway station, the first trains already full and departed, long before the later releases from the end of the alphabet had arrived; cheered only by the thought of the 10 days' disembarkation leave pass and a free railway ticket home made it all just about acceptable. Then came the welcome home, with the usual 'Where have you been? How long are you here for, and when are you going back?' Catching up on the many changes there had been back home though, was a priority. My young brother David, now well over four years old, was not in the best of health. Spending all his early years sleeping in the air-raid shelter in the front garden had left the young lad with bronchial problems. Baby sister Valerie all grown up, soon to be seven, was doing well at school, middle sister Lily, who had been evacuated for long periods during the war, was now home again but still at school, due to finish at fourteen the following year. Iris, my eldest sister who was married during the war, was now living locally with her husband who had already been demobilised from the army.

This had left my mother alone at home to look after the younger children because our father had left her again! Dad had been redirected to do war work down in Devon after leaving the job as an air-raid warden. When he returned at the end of hostilities he had started up a building firm, repairing bomb damaged property. This took off and was working very well. Several of the Verlander brothers came in with my father Sidney, amongst whom were my uncles Edwin, Frederick, and Joseph. They relaunched their family business name, established in 1867 by G G Joseph and Sons of Bromley-by-Bow, and were doing extremely well, with my sister Iris, who had given up her job in London, doing the books. The pay roll was running at between thirty and forty persons per week and my mother was helping to run the office. That is, until the new Labour government placed restrictions on building works because of the shortage of supplies, authorising only essential or urgent repairs. The business then declined rapidly, assisted by the not infrequent visits to the greyhound racetrack in Romford by the men folk! Disillusioned, Sidney was then on his bike again, no doubt returning, as he had done frequently, to his long term mistress!

Worse thoughts were in my mind though. My orders and railway ticket for the return to duty were back to that blot on the landscape in Yorkshire, Catterick Camp. I had been returned to where I had volunteered to escape from, transferred back into the Royal Armoured Corps. 'Perhaps it will not be too bad after all, it will soon be September, and I'm due to be released in early December,' I had mused. Until then, there was the Ilford Palais de Dance to visit, where it was at least possible to find a dancing partner, even easier now that there were fewer troops around. The very popular variety theatre, the Ilford Hippodrome though, was no longer. It had been destroyed by a V2 rocket late in the war and all that remained was a pile of rubble. Luckily there were very few casualties even though it was situated in the centre of the town. There were many other such sites all around the areas of Ilford, Barking, Romford and Dagenham, some beginning to be tidied up, others just boarded or closed off waiting for rebuilding. In places whole streets had suffered damage, from V 1s and V 2s right up until the end of the war in Europe. The 10 days' disembarkation leave soon passed with relatives to visit and all wanting to know what I had been doing, and why I could not write for long periods. Unable to tell them too much because of the secrecy papers I'd signed, I just said I had been working as a wireless operator on top secret work that I was not allowed to talk about, and while doing so was not allowed to communicate with anyone else. It was easy enough to get away with, the war had been over for some time by then, and everyone had been involved in one way or another. Most wanted to forget it, even though there was still rationing and coupons required for many things before you could purchase them, if available.

Reporting back at the RAC depot in Catterick was as bad as expected, a massive remote place outside Richmond. It may have been September but it already seemed like mid-winter. Fortunately, after reporting in and receiving instructions relating to demobilisation and having a medical to report any existing maladies which had to be dealt with before leaving, I was issued with a few clothing coupons to purchase some civilian clothes in addition to those that would eventually be issued. It was noted that there was a great deal of annual leave to my credit which they said should be used up before I was released, so I was immediately given 14 days' annual leave, issued a pass and sent home again to get rid of some of it after spending just one night there! There was also a very large sum of money dormant in my pay book, built up during my missions in France and Burma; while there, of course, I could not, or even had need to draw on my own money. Operational and escape money was just signed for and handed over. Even after leaving Burma, when all parachute pay and danger money had ceased, I had reasonable pay as a sergeant which I rarely had to take full advantage of in the remote parts where I had been stationed. The danger money did not even show in my pay book. That was always paid by SOE into a separate post office savings account. Thus I returned home again, this time after drawing a larger sum than usual.

On this leave I decided to buy a new civilian suit, shirts and shoes, feeling the need to be like many others, back in 'civvies'. My old clothes, what remained of them, no longer fitted me. One of my first calls was to

Burton's, whose 50 shilling suits now cost 115 shillings (plus 26 coupons) and a long waiting list. That was on 7th September '46, according to the deposit of 10 coupons and twenty shillings and a retained receipt. Incidentally, the suit was collected on 4th July '47, but only on production of the additional 16 coupons as well as the balance of payment. However it was a very good suit. It was another suit entirely, that was to cause me some embarrassment. After meeting an attractive young lady at the Ilford Palais the previous evening while wearing my uniform, I had successfully arranged a second date, always a good and promising next step. I decided to wear civilian clothes when escorting her to the pictures that evening, always another good opportunity to get closer in the dark. We had arranged to meet outside the cinema at Gants Hill. Only on arriving there did I realise that on changing clothes I had forgotten to put my wallet in my pocket!

Now these were the days when a man would never dream of not paying for his partner, it was simply not done. I was seriously contemplating disappearing, but too late, she arrived on time. Rather than going to see the film, I suggested, 'Would you mind going for a walk instead?' But no, she preferred the cinema. Then I had to confess that I'd forgotten my wallet and hadn't enough money. 'It doesn't matter, it's all right, and I can pay for the tickets,' she answered, and into the cinema we went. So ashamed at this development, I sat quietly right through the programme, not daring to even hold her hand; which would normally have been the next step towards a kiss and a cuddle in the dark. Even though I had promised to reimburse the young lady, we both parted disappointedly without making a further date, so that was the end of what may have developed into something a little deeper. The only other enjoyable day out recalled from this leave was my sister, Iris, taking me up to town to see a very good variety show in which a new comedian by the name of Ken Dodd was appearing.

In due course, back at the Catterick barracks, there was another occasion that simply had to happen and that was crossing paths with the Regimental Sergeant Major. Or rather crossing the parade ground on my way out for the evening, instead of going around it! Parade grounds were something forgotten about since my departure from Catterick over three years ago. Dressed in my finery, complete with an Australian style bush hat on my head to impress the local talent, (I hated wearing the black beret of the RAC), I was on my way out for the evening. A very loud bawl came across the parade ground, 'Come here, Sergeant! You do not use 'my' parade ground as a short cut!' And as I approached the voice, 'Where do you think you're going dressed like that?' Yes, it was him, the RSM, a real old bully boy of the regular army who had, without doubt, spent the whole of the war residing in the family quarters with his family. No use arguing with this one I thought, he is only used to dealing with raw recruits. 'Sorry, sir,' I said trying to make a jovial reply 'Not been any parade grounds where I've been for the last three years.' Pointing to my own medal ribbons at the same time probably was not a good idea, as the RSM was not wearing more than a long service medal ribbon. 'Come with me, Sergeant! You're no longer in the West African Frontier Force. We are going to the Quartermaster's store and you can get yourself properly dressed before leaving here!'

So that is how I lost my treasured 'Bush Hat'. It could have been worse though. The RSM had also questioned my right to be still wearing 'Parachute Wings' above my medal ribbons, but I did manage to convince him that like pilots, the Wings could be worn after doing operational jumps. All the Jeds had been doing so since their operations in France, although it was uncertain if this was correct and the RSM, unable to prove otherwise, let it pass. After another lecture about the rights and wrongs of crossing the parade ground when not using it for official parades, I was allowed to proceed out of the camp, but ill-at-ease with the new badly fitting black beret bonnet on my head; a very poor exchange! Defiant to the end though, the RAC badge was removed when out of the camp and exchanged for my beloved KRRC badge! Whenever away from Catterick, the black beret was swapped for the green one that I had adopted back in Peterborough, and my sergeant's stripes on my best uniform were the red and black ones of my original choice of regiment.

Within a month of this episode, whether it was by accident or design, I was marked down for a tour of duty as guard commander at the Catterick Military Hospital. There were several POWs being treated there and a full twenty-four hour guard had to be maintained on them which was changed at 7 a.m each morning. Although not feeling too well, with my habitual headaches, I didn't report sick or try to dodge it, deciding instead that it would at least relieve the monotony of the usual boring inactivity of the day and the cold and miserable October weather outside. The guard duty itself turned out to be easy enough, the eight troopers detailed for the guard being agreeable and friendly. Like me, they too were just passing time, whilst awaiting their demobilisation. There were only eight prisoners, all German, to watch over, only two of them fit enough to be allowed out of bed. Not that any of them would want to escape, they were probably better off in Britain than back home in Germany at the moment anyway. Hospital food was better, both for them and the men guarding them.

All went well during the day, the off duty men resting, playing cards or huddled around the central stove in the guard room yarning about past exploits. I was still not feeling too well, and as the day wore on, my headaches seemed to be worse than usual. I was also shivering at times but put this down as an effect of the weather because it was very cold outside. I'd mentioned the fact to the Orderly Officer when he came on his daily rounds, whose only reply had been 'Well, you're in the right place, plenty of doctors and nurses around here, ask one of them for an aspirin,' obviously not wishing to give himself any additional work in arranging a relief. If I felt the same way after the guard duty was over I intended to go and see the MO back in the camp, but for now, I carried on with duties as normal.

One of these was to enter the POWs' ward at each meal time to ask if they had any complaints about food or treatment. There never were any but one of the prisoners who was up and partially dressed did keep staring at me in a puzzling way. Then, after the evening meal he at last addressed me in reasonable English, saying something about a feeling he had that we had met before somewhere! After being asked by me where he had been during the war, he reached for his cap, and showing it, said, 'I was an officer in the German Navy so I have been in many places.' 'France?' I inquired. 'Yes, the Mediterranean ports of France and Spain, and the western ports of France also.' 'Did you ever visit La Rochelle?' Was my next question, adding with a faint smile of recognition, 'Do you remember the Frenchmen you spoke to in English and Spanish because you did not understand French? At a bar in La Rochelle in September 1944, one of them could not understand English!' By then we were both certain, and I admitted that it was me and gave him a packet of cigarettes adding, 'I owe you these. I think you will find them better than those Spanish ones you gave me the last time we met!' Agreeing it was an amazing coincidence that we should meet again, we wished each other good luck in the future and warmly shook hands before parting.

Later that same night, back in the guard room my health got rapidly worse. Holding my head in my hands, I sat close to the coke burning stove, alternately shivering and perspiring. Even with my blanket around my shoulders, I couldn't get comfortable. The corporal had to take over changing the guard and offered to send for assistance but I insisted that I should and would be able to finish the Guard duty and go sick the next day. Apparently it was from this place in front of the fire that I finally collapsed into unconsciousness and I have only a faint recollection of events after that for the next 10 days, some of which was of being in a bed, hands touching and turning me over when only partially awake, someone saying you have soaked the bed again, for a full 7 days. From then on the realisation dawned on me that I was still in the hospital, that I'd had suffered a serious relapse of malaria, and the hands I'd felt when disturbed were those of nurses bathing me and changing the bedding that had been soaked with perspiration. I was kept in the hospital until the end of October, and letters that had been sent to my home address, thence to the camp at Catterick, from there to the hospital and back again to the camp, I eventually received on the 30th of that month. The last memories I have of the Catterick Military Hospital were my uniform, correctly hung and displayed at the head of the bed, and lying to attention in bed when the Matron did her rounds every morning; I only did that once! From then on, I was, or more likely appeared to be, on my side rather than on my back, feigning sleep!

More sick leave days were allowed following this illness and on return I was transferred from Catterick to Westwick Camp at Barnard Castle. At least there were fewer troops there and the small town only a mile and a half away. Still under the care of doctors at the military hospital in Catterick meant several regular visits back there via Darlington and Richmond. This always gave me an opportunity to stretch out the time I was away from the camp's routine and to break my journey en route in either of the towns, by booking into a bed and breakfast boarding house or hotel for a night or two. Still having plenty of spare cash to my credit in my pay book gave me the means to do so, and it was definitely better than staying in barrack rooms. It also gave greater opportunity to stay out later and perhaps, if lucky, entertain a lady and be able to walk her home instead of dashing off back to camp.

The medical visits back at the hospital were to follow up my complaints of frequent headaches, which I had brought up at the time of the malaria attack. The doctors had arranged a series of tests and X-rays in an effort to find the cause. Sinus problems had been mentioned and an operation on my nose to repair some damage recommended. More importantly all these medical queries had to be attended to before I could be discharged from the army. That date was now getting very close, already into November and my release date early in December. I was placed on the sick roster and, until I was fit for duty again, could not be demobilised. Worse was still to come. The operation could not be done until the weather improved. The weather? Oh yes, it was now snowing! There had been very heavy snowfalls with much drifting causing havoc all over Yorkshire.

Accommodation at Westwick Camp was just about adequate, at least in normal conditions. The long wooden hut that I and about twenty other men were to share was heated by a single central coke burning stove. The windows along each side were a good five foot higher than the internal floor and about eight foot higher on the outside; standing on tiptoe enabled one to look out, but not inward from the outside. This was because there were three wooden steps to mount before reaching the door, the floor being clear of the outside grounds. In the beginning the snow was kept clear of the surrounding pathways to the mess-room and even more importantly the WVS canteen. This canteen was staffed by a team of mature women and one younger lady, who flattered their customers with such delicate morsels as mock banana sandwiches! Delicious they were too, even though they were made from turnip or some other root vegetable and flavoured with banana essence. Not that anyone could remember what a real banana tasted like as they had not been available since the beginning of the war.

After several heavy falls of windswept snow, it was not long before it reached the height of the front door. As time passed, and a great deal more snow fell, the build up continued until it became necessary to cut steps into the packed snow upwards to get out of the front door. The snow reached the lower levels of the outside windows long before Christmas. Beds were re-arranged nearer to the stove, those closest to it becoming benches for the internees huddled under blankets even by day. Normal activities at the camp became almost non-existent - but not quite. This was still the ARMY and volunteers were called for – 'You, You and You!' - to clear snow drifts. Squads of men were mustered to dig out buried trains and buses trapped in cuttings by deep drifts of snow. Thankfully, the benefit of being on the sick roster saved me from being detailed for such arduous duties.

Being 'excused boots', as it was colloquially called, had its uses. One day, while others were out shovelling snow and a small group of the men remaining in the hut were huddled around the red hot cast iron stove, I had a bright idea. I still had two Fairbairn fighting knives, one of which had a broken tip. This had happened when someone had thought they would make good throwing knives, but of course they are not intended to be used as such. The handles were heavier than the blades and, unless perfectly straight when sticking into anything hard, the weight on the handle was carried through until the very sharply pointed tip, unable to bend, was snapped off. My brain-wave was to poke the knife into the glowing embers of the stove, to soften the hardened blade enough to enable me to use a metal file on it, to reshape the tip and renew the point. Unfortunately, what actually happened was that the end of the blade, after a very short time of being poked into the fire, began to melt. As it was withdrawn from the stove, liquid metal dripped back into the fire! Well, as I mentioned earlier, the stove *was* very hot, often glowing a bright red, perfect for toasting bread and the odd rasher of bacon!

For Christmas '46, and what would have been my true age of 21 on the 27th of that month, I was granted leave. I intended to leave on an early morning train from Barnard Castle on Saturday. The difficult part was getting from the camp to the station but this was solved by the WVS supply truck, which had struggled through the packed snow-covered road into town. Travelling down on the Friday evening, I was accompanied by the 18 year old girl who worked for the WVS. We knew each other quite well from our frequent chats in the canteen. I also knew that she was interested in me but I had told her I would be getting married as soon as I got my discharge from the army. She wanted to go to the dance in town that evening, and I had planned to spend the night in the local inn before catching the train the next morning. With nothing else to do that evening, I decided to accompany her.

It had stopped snowing but it was a slow and difficult ride into town, but we did arrive safely and in time for the dance. All went well and we had a pleasant evening together until it was time for the young maiden to go back to the camp. It snowed again while we were enjoying the dancing and, now with the fresh new soft snow and un-cleared roads blocking the way, it was impossible to get any transport back to camp for her. Plus, the inn was full and the only room they had spare was a double at the very top of the house, where water was dripping constantly through the roof! With no other choice, I persuaded the inn keeper to let us have the room, even though he had said we may be disturbed during the night because he had to regularly empty buckets catching the melting snow dripping from the ceiling! It was so cold that we shared the bed with most of our clothes on and did manage to curl up close enough to keep each other warm. A goodnight kiss was as far as it went, the weather managing to cool our ardour. We continued our respective journeys the next day, the young lady back to camp and me off home for the festivities.

Two things happened on my return to the camp. Firstly, I learnt that the young girl had been dismissed from her job at the WVS for staying out all night, which was rather unfair as she had no other choice, there being no available transport. Secondly, in the New Year a telegram arrived from my mother telling me that Lucette, who had secured one of the first holiday visas issued to foreign nationals following the war, had arrived from France on the first day of its validity the 1st January '47. Hardly able to speak more than a few words of English and travelling alone, she had managed to reach London by train, cross the city from Victoria to Liverpool Street station, go on from there to Chadwell Heath railway station, and arrive at my home. All on the strength of a piece of paper with the postal address on it! The problem on arrival was, however, that she and my family were having difficulties in communicating with each other. On presenting the problem to the CO, I received an additional 7 days' compensatory leave and was able to return home after being back in camp for only a few days. There was no real break in the wintry weather of 1946/47 and, although slightly milder in the south, it was still very cold and the snow was widespread. The chances of my being called forward for the pending operation remained remote, making the CO's decision a little easier.

Together again for the first time since November '44, the first week was spent at home with my mother and the three younger members of my family. As it was only a two-bedroomed cottage, even using the down stairs front room as an additional bedroom made it rather over crowded. Additionally, with Lucette's visit being longer than originally expected, coupled with my leave due to expire, we decided to both travel back to Darlington and spend the last few days of our time together there. On arrival back in Darlington, Lucette was booked into a boarding house and I reported back at the camp; we then spent the rest of our holiday together by commuting between the camp and the town. The introduction to the rules and regulations of Bed and Breakfast lodgings in those days was a real eye opener! Notices were pinned up on the walls everywhere, expressing the dos and don'ts of the establishment! No visitors after 8 p.m! Breakfast between 8 and 9 a.m. only! All rooms to be vacated between 10 a.m. and 4.30 p.m!

There was even more explicit information about the use or abuse of the toilet and bathroom, including when and where to empty the chamber pots! When Lucette finally returned to France, I took her to the railway station at Darlington and she bravely faced the long journey home alone, facing the same arduous ordeal she'd encountered on the way out. In her letters sent after her return home she did remark that everyone had been extremely helpful to her. I had tried to get another leave to be able to travel with her, in conjunction with an appointment I had at the French Institute in London on Wednesday 15th January, but I was only granted a 48 hr pass and Lucette had, unfortunately, to be back home at work on Monday 13th, forcing her to leave the weekend beforehand. The short 48 hr pass begrudgingly allowed me was so that I could attend an Investiture and receive my award of the French Croix de Guerre from the French Ambassador. With the long journey by night train each way, this gave me barely enough time to get home, return to London, collect my award, and start the journey back to camp!

So it was, once more, a return to the old routine at Barnard Castle, bored and idle with nothing to do, awaiting the date for my hospital appointment and a break in the continuously cold and snowy weather. Time dragged on, February passed, and on 1st March I even voluntarily did a guard duty just to break the monotony! It was a night duty at the camp's detention centre with just three guards and a trumpeter, where a dozen men were confined. That I should actually choose to cover the post because of the shortage of NCOs (others were occupied on snow clearing duties) is a fair indication of my chronic boredom. After all, I was still on the sick list, excused all duties, and should have been released months ago. The only bright spot was that the young lady who had worked for the WVS had called back to the camp to renew our friendship and we had been going to the local dances together. She had secured another post nearby and had made some new friends there. Meanwhile, the weather was getting milder at last and the deep snow drifts that had covered the whole countryside for months were gradually diminishing, giving at least some hope that the long waiting period would soon be terminated. Weekends were spent mostly in Darlington where there was always the Nuffield Centre where troops could pass their time during the day, with cheap canteen meals, free entertainment, darts and a billiard table, and dances in the evenings. It was a relief to get away from the unending white snow-covered fields of the countryside into the town, which was at least swept clear of snow, even though the weather was still cold and miserable. Rather than returning to the camp, nights were spent in one of the plentiful B&B establishments.

It was not until Easter approached that I was warned I could be called forward at any time and that operations had restarted at York, where I was due to go for my treatment. There had been a flurry of snow again on Easter Sunday, 6th April '47, which caused a brief doubt in my mind, but immediately after the bank holiday I was at last on my way to York General Hospital. The rest of the Easter week was spent being examined by different doctors, new X-rays and pre-operative procedures. The civilian hospital itself was noticeably far more relaxed and comfortable than the military hospital at Catterick, and the nurses charming. A far cry from the lying to attention for the Matron's inspection every morning at Catterick! It was explained to me what they were going to do and they assured me that, although I would not be completely anaesthetised, I would not feel anything because the nose and the area around it would be numbed with a local anaesthetic. All this was very reassuring at the time but in practice, when the time came the following week, I found there were a few surprises that they had not mentioned, not least of which was no food or drink for 24 hours beforehand, apart from a few sips of plain water.

Early that morning, after a bed bath, I was given a capsule that was to induce a state of calm and relaxation, followed a little later by the arrival of a nurse and a doctor with a large bowl full of wet narrow finger bandages. These were soaking in a concoction that was intended to deaden any feeling in the areas where they were to operate. Flat on my back, head back, with gloved hands and tweezers, the long lengths of wet bandage were induced into the nostrils, yard after yard, up each side, as far as they could go, packed tight, making the nose feel many times larger than normal. Coldness and numbness gradually spread out from the nose to the whole facial area. The relaxant drug taken earlier was now taking effect, making the procedure endurable if a little uncomfortable at the start. I was then left in the care of a nurse, to remain quiet and not to touch anything, until the full effect took place. A doctor came back, did a few tests, asking if this or that could be felt, as he poked or jabbed at surrounding areas, then gave the signal to wheel his patient away to the theatre. I was picked up and plonked onto what felt like a bed of cold steel, with hands from all sides immediately clamping down my legs and arms so that I could not move, and my head was clamped between padded buffers to hold it steady. Feeling uncomfortable at the shoulders and thighs, I tried to readjust my position slightly to be more at ease. The response was instantaneous and even more pressure was applied on my arms and legs, making the discomfort worse rather than better. Bright lights came on and a cloth was placed over my eyes.

Now I could neither see nor feel anything, but I could hear everything, even though the protagonists were whispering. The bandages were withdrawn and instruments inserted into my nose. There was no feeling, no pain, only the discomfort of my back and limbs. Then the sound of chiselling, drilling and sawing reverberated in my head! Every movement could be heard if not felt! It was like a medieval torture chamber without the pain, only the discomfort. How long did it last? Probably not as long as it seemed, but it was certainly a great relief to be back in the ward when the time came. Then I was kept in bed for a few days until the packing and plugs were removed, the swelling had subsided and I was breathing freely through my nose again. The following weekend there was a surprise visit from my most recent young lady companion, who toured the ward cheering up the rest of the inmates. She seemed to be in a very happy mood and informed me that she was now dating another sergeant. Knowing that I would soon be leaving the army and intended to return to France and get married, she had come to say goodbye to me.

On my discharge from the York hospital I returned to Barnard Castle and remained under the care and observation of the camp MO for another month. Then on Friday, 23rd May, the MO finally signed a chit authorising that I was fit for release. By this time I was ready to agree I was fit for anything! I could have been suffering from anything under the sun but certainly would not have admitted it. The sole thought in my mind was to get out of the Forces as soon as possible; the delays had gone on far too long already. Night sweats I put down to being a hangover from frequent bouts of malaria, pains from old injuries I had already learnt to live with, I could breathe easier through the nose, and the headaches that had plagued me, yes, they did still return at odd times. In fact, it wasn't until the 1980s that I discovered that they were mainly caused by an allergy to cheese! No wonder I'd had such a problem on the Gold Coast; it was the only decent food that I'd enjoyed whilst there!

The process of demobilisation kicked into gear immediately after the weekend. There was the fitting out with a supply of civilian clothes, which included a suit, a choice of blue, brown or grey, and a Raglan overcoat. No shoes, socks or underwear which could be retained along with boots and best uniform. A supply of clothing coupons was issued to assist in the replacement of army kit where necessary, and arrangements made for war gratuities to be placed in a post office savings account. An interview and application form for training in a new civilian occupation proved to be a complete farce. There was a fairly long list of trades in which one could request retraining. I applied for one as a plumber, as the Verlander family were all in the building trade and was ever hopeful the business may start up again. This was also the one job my father had admitted that he was not good at. The reply I got back was that this and all the others were already fully subscribed, except one, and that was to do with laying tarmac! Not wishing to become a navvy, I chose to wait until I returned home and seek something else myself.

My last interview on the 27th was with a Captain Thomas, whom I had never met before, with my AB 64, which recorded only brief details such as dates of changes in rank, pay and courses passed in the RAC. The Captain had to ask me what I had been doing in the services before he could write out his testimonial. He had never heard of SOE, let alone Jedburghs and Force 136. Restricted by the Official Secrets Act, I gave him a brief description about assisting guerrilla forces behind enemy lines and trusted that he believed me. Having very little space allocated for the testimonial, he did manage to make a reasonable five line report by keeping his writing very small. Not that there was anything in it that would assist civilian employment. The last rites were accomplished the next day, 28th May 1947, with my departure by night train from Darlington to Kings Cross for the last time, with enough paid leave to last until 15th August, after which I was transferred to the army reserve. I finally arrived home the next morning, Friday 29th May, ready for my first weekend as a free man! Celebrations? There were none, really, apart from with immediate family and a drink in the local pub. The war had been over for a long time now and everyone had been involved one way or another. Most people preferred not to mention the war any more - they had more than enough memories of their own. Perhaps that is why it has taken me so long to relate and share some of my own.

Operation Character Burma 1945 SEAC

Walrus Personnel

HQ Personnel

Lt.-Col.Cromarty Tulloch (Pop)		Force 136
Sgt.Neville Wood	W/T Op.	Jedburgh
Mjr. Lewis		Force 136
Sgt. Clift	Burmese W/T Op.	Force 136
Capt. Campbell	Intelligence Officer	ditto
Capt. Troward	Signals Officer	ditto
Mjr. Warren		ditto
Capt.Harrison	Medical Officer (Doc.)	ditto

Burmese Sappers and Miners (attached to Force 136)

Sgt.Carroll
Khan Chauk
Lt. Rennie
Mjr. Charlesworth

Field Operatives working to HQ

Mjr. John Denning		Jedburgh
Capt. Cockle		Force 136
Sgt. Norman Smith	W/T Op.	Jedburgh
Capt. Wilson		Force 136
Capt. Steele		ditto
Sgt. Donald Gibbs	W/T Op.	Jedburgh
Mjr.Alexander Boal (Sandy)		Jedburgh
Capt. Coomber		ditto
Sgt. Harry Verlander		ditto
Bill Beatson	(Anglo- Indian)	Force 136

E Force

Capt. Lockett
Sgt. Gallear
Maung Tin Interpreter to E Force later attached to Boal's Group mainly working with Harry.
Paul Chi Swe

POST WAR

In 1994 I visited France and the pictures which following were taken. They at least give the reader a visual aspect of some of the places which are mentioned in Part One.

The field outside La Plaineliere where I landed

Above, the extension at the rear of the bakery in La Plaineliere which the missing pannier crashed through. Below the baker (left) and his gardener (right) who actually carried my broken rucksack for me

Outside La Place du Roulage by the doors that were double locked (see page 138). I then went around to the back to try to climb into my room (see opposite).

At the rear of Place du Roulage where my nocturnal adventure nearly came to a tragic end (see page 138). My room was at the top left and my radio aerial was strung across to the tree.

EPILOGUE

By Elizabeth Verlander

Of course that is not the end of Harry's story.

After he was demobbed in 1947, he returned to France and in December of that year, married Lucette, the girl he had met in Niort in 1944. Because of the Communist uprisings and general unrest at that time they decided to return to England where Harry joined British Railways Continental Services, based at Victoria Station in London, in April 1948. He became Senior Clerical Officer in the Car Ferry Department where his fluent French proved to be a great asset.

Following his divorce from Lucette he married another French girl, Dominique. Sadly she died in 1987 and then, in 1993, he married his present wife, me.

In 1984, on the 40th Anniversary of the Liberation of France, at the invitation of the Mayor of Paris, the Jedburghs held their first reunion and it was there that Harry met his old comrade and friend Pierre Jolliet, who had been with him in France in 1944. As you may imagine, it was an emotional occasion, particularly as Harry believed Pierre had died. Further reunions were held in 1988 in Washington, USA, where they were invited to a reception at the White House as guests of President Ronald Reagan. An American Jedburgh, William Colby, was Head of the CIA at the time and took them on a tour of the Headquarters. In 1991, a further reunion was held at Milton Hall, Peterborough, where a plaque commemorating the Jeds was unveiled (see over).

In between times, the Jedburghs have held more informal gatherings but now time and infirmity have taken their toll, and those who are left keep in touch by phone or email.

In 1994, the 50th Anniversary of the Liberation, the Jeds all met again in St.Malo, Normandy, as guests of the Americans for the International Service of Commemoration Omaha on the 6th June. A truly memorable occasion. Later that year, Harry returned to Deux-Sevres, where he was made a *Chevalier d'Honneur* of the town of Niort and given the Freedom of the City. He was interviewed for French radio and the local press and generally fated. He was also invited to unveil a memorial plaque in L'Absie, the area in which Team HAROLD operated in 1944.

Harry's connections with the Jedburghs have featured in the Imperial War Museum's prestigious project 'Their Past Your Future.' He was able to return to Niort in 2004, through 'Heroes' Return' when he had the honour of laying a wreath on the Memorial there, to *'les soldats sans uniformes'* (soldiers without uniforms). He has been interviewed and filmed on various occasions, last year for instance, by the BBC for the 65th Anniversary of D-Day and also at The British Film Theatre, together with Virginia McKenna, when the film 'Carve her Name with Pride' about the agent Violette Szabo, had a 60th anniversary showing.

The highly emotive monument to the 'les soldats sans uniformes,' in modern day Niort.

For several years now, Harry has also been involved in giving talks to children and young people about some of his experiences, mostly about being evacuated to Suffolk. He also gives talks in greater depth, about his training and missions on Special Events Weekends, originally run by Stakis, then Hilton Hotels and now by Travel Editions. These weekends include visits to Milton Hall and Harrington Aviation Museum, Northampton where all Harry's military artefacts are now displayed together with other Jedburgh and Special Force memorabilia. The guests who attend these weekends are always very complimentary and appreciative and Harry has met many who were themselves involved in various areas in WW2, for example, people who worked at Bletchley Park, decoding messages sent and intercepted from the Occupied Countries.

This book has been a long time in the writing, over ten years in fact, but I believe it is well worth the wait.Harry owes a deep debt of gratitude to all those who encouraged, badgered and nagged him to put his experiences on paper and then into print.

Harry with Mme Michonneau, widow of Capt Michonneau, who was involved with team HAROLD in Niort in 1944. These 'Site de la Resistance' signboards are becoming more common throughout France, aiding visitors to find the key sites

Acknowledgements

In no particular order –

Clive Bassett – Harry's archivist, co-founder of the Harrington Aviation Museum and good friend to all the Jeds; as well as Mary, Clive's wife.
Nigel West – renowned author and expert on Covert Operations who has contributed such a marvellous foreword to Harry's story.
Steve Lovell – Harry's guide in getting to grips with modern technology.
Colin Burbidge – organiser and host of the first Secret War Weekends and nephew of Captain Victor Gough, who designed the Special Force Wings worn by the Jedburghs.
Members of St.George's Church Congregation, Beckenham, in particular, Jenny Froude, who has written two remarkable articles about Harry for the magazine.
Peter and Carol Osborne - publisher - Independent Books, Keston, Kent.
Karen Stringer of Millennium Mums - she first got Harry writing on the computer.
Members of the Special Forces Club.
The Volunteer Helpers at Harrington Aviation Museum and Shoreham Aviation Museum, Kent.
The Guests on the Secret War Weekends – desperate to read 'The Book.'
Family and Friends too numerous to mention individually – Thank you all for your support and encouragement. He got there in the end!

Memorable quotes collected by Glyn Loosmore
Jedburgh Team ANDY

'The Jedburghs were perhaps the most amazing conglomeration of unusual people ever pulled together in one military unit.'

John Malony.

'I believe that the Jedburgh operation was the most decorated of the Second World War.'

Lt Colonel J.D. Sainsbury, Medals Section, Ministry of Defence

'They were, I believe, the best guerrilla fighters in the world.'

Colonel Frank Mills.

'When I go to France, I am feted and wept over and honoured, just because I am my father's son.'

The son of a Jedburgh.

'They were a lot of comedians.'

Anon.

INDEX

NOTES

NOTES

NOTES